WINCHELSEA

A PORT OF STRANDED PRIDE

principally telling

the story of the Ancient Town during

the Nineteenth and Twentieth

Centuries

Malcolm Pratt

by

MALCOLM PRATT

with a Foreword by Lord Briggs of Lewes (Asa Briggs)

This book is for
BRIDGET
with much love

Published by Malcolm Pratt, 16 Downlands Avenue,
Bexhill-on-Sea, East Sussex, TN39 3PL.

ISBN 0 9532411 0 6

Typesetting, design, printing and project liaison
Authors' Publishing Guild
Hadlow Down, East Sussex, TN22 4ET.
Tel: 01825 830319

Dustjacket photography (David Brown)
Front: Strand Gate from Strand Hill
Back: Friars Road, west side

Endpapers (Source: Winchelsea Museum)
Front: High Street, early twentieth century
Back: The New Inn and German Street, early twentieth century

CONTENTS

APPENDICES

(1) Winchelsea Corporation gathers before the mayoring, Easter Monday 1997.
(left to right) Bernard Dibble (town chamberlain), Rev. Keith Wood (mayor's chaplain), Robert Beecroft (mayor elect),
Major Peter Hoskins (jurat), Squadron Leader David Bourne (deputy mayor), Guy Hughes (jurat),
Lt. Col. Henry Dormer (mayor), Donald Cameron-Clarke (jurat), Malcolm Pratt (town clerk), Anthony Sandeman,
Peter Stevens, Knightley Chetwood, John Dunk, Anthony Moore, Roger Neaves, Anthony Tremeer (jurats),
Neil Clephane-Cameron (sergeant-at-mace).

LIST OF ILLUSTRATIONS

(and acknowledgement of sources)

I gratefully acknowledge the supply of illustrations by the following:
Melvyn Pett 1, Winchelsea Museum 2 3 7 9 11 12 14(RH) 15 17-20 22 24 30-32 35-38 44 48(RH) 52 56 59 67-69 73-78
Winchelsea Museum/British Museum 27
East Sussex Record Office/Winchelsea Corporation (all RH) 4-6 13 16
East Sussex Record Office (all RH) 23 29 39 50
East Sussex Record Office/Helen Goldie (all RH) 10 43 51
Robert Collins 25, Knightley Chetwood 41 42, Sheila Bristow (all RH) 45 47 49 55 62 65, Phil Barling 40 53 71, Helen Goldie 46(RH), Antony Sandeman 54(RH), Winchelsea Corporation 56, Ron Turner/Peter Turner 64, Cecil Barden 66 70, Peter Stevens 72(RH)
The following are my own: 8 21 26 28 33 34 58 60 61 63 65
It was not possible to retain many illustrations and photographs for the printer. Copies were therefore needed and this work was undertaken by my friend Reg Hawkins, photographer, of Bexhill to whom my warm thanks are due. Those reproduced by him are marked RH in the above list.

FOREWORD

For anyone interested in the history of Sussex this is an indispensable and distinctive book. It is based on careful research from scattered sources, but it also draws deeply on memory and experience. Malcolm Pratt's own concerns as Town Clerk of Winchelsea since 1984 lead him across what to him is familiar historical territory. Just as important, he has collected reminiscences, oral as well as written, which add to historical knowledge and stimulate historical interpretation.

As an historian who has been deeply interested in local history, medieval and modern, I was honoured, therefore, when I was asked to contribute a foreword to a book on Winchelsea, a place which figures in all local histories, recognising that Malcolm Pratt's book stands in its own right and needs none. As a former householder in Winchelsea for fourteen years I was delighted to write it. I grew to love a place which was rich in history and got to know much about it from talking to some of the people to whom Malcolm Pratt has talked, among them the Turners. I was also deeply attached to the ancient church which in my judgement has some of the most beautiful modern windows in the world. The house where I lived with Malcolm Saville as a neighbour, and where I wrote more than one book, had been partially destroyed during the Second World War. Its name, Boundary House, related directly to Winchelsea's medieval topography.

I have learnt much about medieval deserted villages and new towns from Maurice Beresford, a contemporary of mine at Cambridge, who realised when we were both young how important it was for a historian to possess a pair of sturdy boots. R.H. Tawney said the same. I am glad that Daphne Lovegrove is still living in the house which she and Captain Lovegrove, who was four times Mayor of Winchelsea, acquired from my family. I feel that there is continuity there.

I was interested in reading Malcolm Pratt's book, the first full length history of Winchelsea to be published for more than a century, to turn to his Chapter 19 on the Freeman succession, about which I know very little. I did not know, for example, that G.M. Freeman, Mayor of Winchelsea, became a Baron of the Cinque Ports in 1911 and in that capacity attended the Coronation Service of King George V and even wrote a leaflet about his experiences. I did know, however, that the Freemans gave the land to Winchelsea for the construction of the New Hall in 1924. Anthony Freeman was Mayor in 1962, two years before we arrived.

The Freeman I have always known best as an historian is E.A. Freeman, the great nineteenth-century historian, who edited a series on *Historic Towns,* the first of which appeared in 1887. According to W.G. Hoskins, the outstanding twentieth-century historian of local history – and of local landscapes – he mistakenly treated local history as only national history writ small. Whatever it is, it is not that, as Malcolm Pratt's book demonstrates. It has rhythms of its own.

It has always been my own hope that a new and richer version of national history will be produced as a result of the multiplication of local studies. As Hoskins appreciated, many past local studies were designed to illustrate national history from local sources. The outline of national history was taken for granted. Now at last we are prepared to revise our interpretations of national history in the light of both comparative national histories and of local histories based on detailed research. We are building national history from below. We also bring our histories up-to-date. As Malcolm Pratt notes, in 1942 William Maclean Homan ended his unpublished history of Winchelsea, from 1292 to 1800, with the words 'It would be of comparatively little interest to pursue the local history of the Town during the last century and these notes therefore will not deal with it'. He was even more mistaken than Hoskins suggests that Freeman was. After all, the Victorian revival had already begun.

Local history has been transformed since 1942 – in content, in methodology (camera, tape recorder, computer) and above all, in appeal. The numbers of people interested in it are still growing. They sometimes work singly, often in groups, and they sometimes work alongside professional historians, sometimes on their own. They relate what they discover about their family history, another thriving subject, to what they discover about community history. They also cross centuries. They never say, as too many professional historians say, 'this is not my period'.

Malcolm Pratt's book reflects the kind of local history that now attracts a readership outside the particular community being studied; and since Winchelsea is a place that people visit – for its associations as well as for its buildings – there will be an intermediate readership among the visitors also. Some of them both from home and abroad will add memorable postscripts of their own. Winchelsea is on a world map.

ASA BRIGGS

(Lord Briggs of Lewes)

INTRODUCTION

It is more than a hundred years since a full-length book about Winchelsea was published and almost two hundred since the end of the period when the town's history has been covered in any detail. As these pages will show, many records and documents unavailable to earlier writers have been discovered during that time and this, coupled with the events of those years as they have affected a unique community, have long made it my ambition to bring the story up to date. In view of the writings of Cooper and Inderwick (see bibliography) and the extensive references to Winchelsea's early history in such formidable volumes as the *Victoria County History of Sussex* I have covered that ground only in five introductory chapters before expanding my tale to recount the development of a tiny town during the two centuries which have seen it change beyond all recognition save for certain unchanging landmarks.

A study of this kind touches upon and opens up endless opportunity for the exploration of more general historical topics. In Winchelsea's case these include various aspects of social, parliamentary, local government, military, legal, naval, family and ecclesiastical history. Although considerable opportunities are available to me for future research into such areas, much which is touched on by this story remains for the time being unresearched for fear that the word 'endless' might take on too great a significance. When I began work in late 1992 I set myself a target of attempting to publish within five years. At the time of writing I hope to achieve this in only one year more than that. It must therefore be accepted that there are many leads not followed to a conclusion and many statutes affecting Winchelsea of which my knowledge is limited. I hope one day to carry out a detailed study of life in the town during the seventeenth and eighteenth centuries; unfortunately my own inadequacy in understanding the original documents is likely to prevent such work on earlier periods. Other stones have been left unturned. I am sure there are more people to whom I should have talked about their memories of Winchelsea. It would give me great pleasure to hear from them and from those readers who spot the mistakes I fear I have made.

It has been my exceptionally good fortune to be connected with and to observe the ancient town, although initially intermittently, during fifty years, a quarter of my principal period. After many convoluted attempts at referring to 'the author' and 'the present writer' I have reverted when recounting my personal experience to the more relaxed use of the first person. On the other hand, where my present official duties touch the story, 'the town clerk' remains.

The actual writing of the text, as opposed to the research, took place between March 1995 and November 1996 with some later updating. All references such as 'now', 'currently' and 'at the present time' must therefore be taken in that context.

No comparisons are made between our present currency and that of pre-decimal times. Pounds, shillings and pence are used as though readily understandable to all readers which clearly they are not. It must suffice to explain here that before 1971 the pound was divided into twenty shillings and the shilling into twelve pence, the pound therefore containing 240 pence instead of the present one hundred. Of other terms used, a guinea was one pound one shilling (£1.05) and half a crown was two shillings and sixpence (12½p). Relative money-values over the nineteenth and twentieth centuries are difficult to establish precisely. Such research as I have been able to carry out suggests that one pound in 1900 is equivalent to £96 now. The inflationary tendencies of the twentieth century had a much reduced influence in the nineteenth and the difference between 1800 and 1900 would be very small by comparison. If these assumptions are correct, changed values can be placed more in context by saying that in our terms Edwin Freshfield (pp.87-88) paid £33,600 for the Court Hall which he presented to the corporation and an additional £6,500 for the roof repairs. Similarly, among the many contributors, the schoolchildren (p.60) collected seven pounds eighty in gratitude to Thomas Dawes for his gift of the Town Well, John Carey's fine for destroying property and stealing poles (p.68) was, as recorded in the court book, just over £31 and bail for Thomas Street (p.70) was in the sum of about £2000.

In 1942, at the end of his unpublished *History of Winchelsea 1292 - 1800* William Maclean Homan wrote. 'It would be of comparatively little interest to pursue the local history of the Town during the last century and these notes will therefore not deal with it.' I do not share that opinion but I am grateful that he held it for he has left the field open for me. Should my readers obtain from the book a fraction of the pleasure the research and writing have given me, it will have been a worthwhile project indeed.

Finally, there are two people into whose hands I dearly wish I could have placed a copy of this book. My mother first took me to Winchelsea half a century ago and always enjoyed the recollection of our times together there. Charles Croggon, who served the town with such distinction, first suggested to me that I should bring Winchelsea's history up to date. Sadly neither lived to see the work completed.

Malcolm Pratt

16, Downlands Avenue,
Bexhill-on-Sea.

June 1998

ACKNOWLEDGEMENTS

I must record first my warm appreciation of those former Winchelsea residents whose written reminiscences, whether published or unpublished, have added to my story so much colour which would otherwise have been lost for ever: John Carey, Alexander Finch, Katharina Forbes-Dunlop, George Mallows Freeman, Margaret Muggridge, Maud Peel, Ernest Skinner, and Richard Stileman. Their willingness to record such material should be a lesson to us all.

My grateful thanks are due to many others:

To those who have talked to me about their Winchelsea memories and about particular aspects of the life of the town and the area: Petronilla Barclay, Cecil Barden, Philip Barling, David Bourne, Margaret Bowen, Sheila Bristow, Marcia Bruce, Peta Cameron-Clarke, Jessie Carter, Ken Chetwood, Mary Chetwood, Ben Chishick, Bob Collins, Alan Cooke, the late Anne Croggon, John Dunk, Helen Goldie, Guy Hughes, the late John Lucas, Basil O'Ferrall, Len Polhill, Lord Ritchie of Dundee, Michael Saville, Peter Stevens, Ted Streeton, the late Douglas Turner and Ron Turner.

To Winchelsea Corporation for permission to use the town seal which is definitely its copyright and any other material which might be adjudged to have that status.

To those who have so kindly assisted by reading the working draft of my text and advising in many ways: David Bourne, Roger Davey, Helen Goldie, Alan Judd, Brion Purdey, Anthony Tremeer, Ron Turner, and Christopher Whittick. Despite this help, responsibility for any errors remains entirely mine.

To the following for permission to use material both published and unpublished: Sheila Bristow, The British Museum, John Caffyn, Dr. B. N. Floyd, Helen Goldie, David Higham Associates (work of Ford Madox Ford), Richard Merricks, Anthony Neville, Frank Palmer, Len Polhill, Hugh Rowlings (Editor: *Sussex Express*), Cecily Skinner, Melvyn Pett and Anthony Thomas. I regret that it has not been possible to trace the present copyright holder of *Thirty Years with G.B.S.* by Blanche Patch, published by Victor Gollancz.

To Mrs. Hilary Moore, Headteacher of St. Thomas's C. of E. School, Winchelsea for permitting me to examine school log books still closed to public view.

To the staff of the East Sussex Record Office where the Winchelsea Records are kept along with a mass of other invaluable material for a study such as mine. I used their excellent facilities for the vast majority of my research and for almost all the actual writing of the book. I am particularly indebted to the county archivist, Roger Davey; to Philip Bye and Pauline Colwell for their constant willingness to advise and to support my work in many ways throughout the time I have spent on the project and to Christopher Whittick who not only made a detailed and exceptionally helpful study of my first draft, but also, while working on the Winchelsea archives, transformed our knowledge of how Queen Elizabeth I came to grant land in Winchelsea to the corporation, enabling me to replace my incorrect assumptions with facts.

To Steve Benz, Colin Brent, Roy Hunnisett, Linda Steward and Peter Wilkinson for most helpful support and advice.

To the Megit family – Anne and Robert who started the word processing of the book and, when I realised what a daunting task this was to ask of others, however willing, Bob (my friend and former colleague Dr. R.M. Megit) who generously and enthusiastically set me off down the path to word processing literacy, a path I never expected to tread.

To Lord Briggs of Lewes for so kindly writing a most generous foreword.

To David Brown and Peter Gillies of the Authors' Publishing Guild without whose skill, enthusiasm and dedication it would not have been possible for me to provide for my readers a volume of this kind.

To those whose help is acknowledged in the text and to all others, particularly my family, who have supported the project in many ways.

(2) Aerial view of Winchelsea – August 1962

PROLOGUE

I will go out against the sun
Where the rolled scarp retires,
And the Long Man of Wilmington
Looks naked towards the shires;
And east till doubling Rother crawls
To find the fickle tide,
By dry and sea-forgotten walls,
Our ports of stranded pride.

A casual traveller, driving through the little Sussex town of Winchelsea two or three minutes before eleven o'clock on any Easter Monday morning, might well be surprised at having to stop to permit a short civic procession to walk into the road from the ground floor of the medieval Court Hall and wend its way to climb the stone steps to the upper floor. This procession, consisting mainly of elderly gentlemen in blue gowns and cocked hats, but preceded by two resplendently uniformed macebearers and including the scarlet-robed mayor, his chaplain and the town clerk in legal dress, might seem a considerable anachronism in the fast-moving, electronic, computerised world of the late twentieth century. If he parked his car and, curiosity roused, climbed another set of outside steps at the opposite end of the building, our traveller would witness a ceremony which, at its core, has remained unchanged for many centuries. That core is the election of Winchelsea's mayor.

It is not only the ceremony but the setting which demands attention. When Rudyard Kipling, whose poem *Sussex* is quoted above, moved to live in the county he said that he could feel history there 'twelve men deep.'[1] Here are those 'twelve' men, sitting facing a packed audience of invited guests, with members of the public standing at the back, all in an ancient room adorned with the memorabilia of past ages, lined with boards listing those who have held the office of mayor since 1295 and dominated by a fifteenth-century kingpost roof of stunning strength and craftsmanship.

In this atmosphere, redolent of all the drama of the trials, elections and disputes which the room has seen, the ancient ceremony proceeds through the welcoming of guests, calling the roll of the freemen of Winchelsea, the proclamation of the 'Hundred Court here assembled', and a report by the retiring mayor on his year of office, until it reaches its climax, the announcement of the name of the new mayor.

The Mayor of Winchelsea has been elected on Easter Monday for more than seven hundred years, without interference from legislation either local or national and this unique record supports the town's proud claim to have the only unreformed corporation in the country. Since 1615 all Winchelsea's other civic appointments have been made at the same ceremony.[2] Those still surviving are the offices of deputy mayor, jurats, town or common clerk, chamberlain and sergeant-at-mace. Each swears an ancient oath, read by the town clerk. All 'shall faith and truth bear to our sovereign lady the queen's majesty, her heirs and successors' while individually the mayor 'to rich and poor shall ever do right', the jurats 'to the mayor's counsel shall readily come', the town clerk 'the counsel of the said mayor and jurats shall secret keep', the chamberlain 'shall true accounts keep without any concealment' and the sergeant-at-mace 'shall be ready at the mayor's commandment'.

Finally, with the ancient maces carried before him, the new mayor leads the corporation between the ranks of guests, leaving the remaining regalia displayed on the table and the ceremony at an end for another year.

To set the scene for the story of this tradition's remarkable survival we must travel far further back than the two centuries which are the main scope of this book, only to find that Winchelsea is not even in the same place!

1. DEVELOPMENT AND CONFEDERATION

At some time in the Dark Ages settlement began on the tip of a shingle promontory extending from Fairlight Head across what we now call Rye Bay. This position controlled the entrance to the enormous natural harbour which then occupied the low-lying areas of the Brede and Tillingham valleys. A community of sturdy fishermen, not averse to piracy when the opportunity arose, prospered and grew. Such a substantial bank of shingle no doubt made its inhabitants feel as secure as do those living in the twentieth-century bungalow development on the shingle which has turned the mouth of the River Adur at Shoreham Beach.

Before proceeding with an account of how that confidence proved misplaced, albeit over a very long period, it is worth considering two subjects which have consistently puzzled scholars; exactly where was 'Old' Winchelsea and what is the origin of its name?

Regarding its position, one learned and intensely interesting treatise is charmingly dedicated by Professor B. N. Floyd to his parents 'whose delight in Winchelsea initiated this study.' The professor identifies no fewer than thirteen possible sites suggested in maps and records.[1] Many other writers have entered the controversy. A detailed study of their conjectures leaves the balance of probability that Old Winchelsea lay a short distance seaward of the present mouth of the River Rother.

The most recent attempt to discover archaeological evidence took place in August 1959 by the Underwater Searchers' Club of London who launched into their project with high hopes armed with advice from the Department of Antiquities, the Department of Medieval History, the Map Department of the British Museum and the then mayor, Captain Herbert Lovegrove, R.N., who was the acknowledged local expert. They found that the bottom was hard sand, there were powerful currents, visibility was poor, there were sea-urchins there, 'one of our members put his hand on one', but like all their predecessors they found absolutely nothing else.[2] The forces of nature have totally obliterated all evidence of Old Winchelsea's existence.

The waters of conjecture about the origins of the town's name are also muddied. Elements of Old English, Anglo-Saxon and Latin have been spotted by various authorities who render it into modern English as 'water in an angle of land', 'the island on the corner', 'Wincel's river', 'a corner or projection by the sea', 'founded by Wincheling, son of Cissa' (the first king of the South Saxons), and 'shingle isle on the level'. In this last probably lies the key for the Anglo-Saxon word for shingle was 'chesil' and, considering Winchelsea's original site, that word must surely be at the heart of the name. The most imaginative but regrettably unlikely version was suggested by Samuel Jeake, writing in the late seventeenth century, who included in a Latin list of the Cinque Ports the name 'Frigemareventus', the translation of which he gave as 'wind chills sea'![3]

Whatever may have been the origin of its name, there are no confirmed documentary references to Winchelsea before the eleventh century. Its existence as a borough in the tenth century used to be claimed on the evidence of a coin bearing the legend 'Wencles' having been struck there in times when only a borough would have been permitted a mint.[4] However, that name has now been authoritatively attributed, not to Winchelsea but to Winchcombe in Gloucestershire. Coins discovered in the late nineteenth century may well have shown that the town had a mint later but before 1031 we are left with nothing but uncertainty.

In that year King Canute granted to the Norman Abbey of Fecamp the manor of Rameslie which included Hastings, Old Winchelsea and Rye. The grant was made partly in fulfilment of a promise made by Ethelred the Unready when the abbey gave him refuge in exile and partly to propitiate the Pope whom Canute had deeply offended. The abbey's possession of this land, later confirmed by Edward the Confessor, was to have a powerful effect on the course of English history for it gave the Dukes of Normandy, patrons of the abbey, a foothold and influence on the English coast and laid foundations for the success of the Norman Conquest.

The only recorded direct association Winchelsea has with the conquest is that on 7 December 1067 William landed there on his return from a visit to Normandy and by his sudden arrival prevented the success of plans agreed by the English to overthrow him. This use of Winchelsea illustrates its convenience as a channel port for travellers and we must assume that its growth towards a population of seven hundred households (four to five thousand people – a considerable size for a town in those days) was well under way together with the development of thriving industries in fishing, shipbuilding and salt manufacture. Its importance as a port lay not only in the fine natural harbour and proximity to the continent but also in the ready availability from the dense forests of the Weald of enormous quantities of timber which formed the basis of extensive trade, particularly with France.

Such success and the resulting wealth could well have led to friction between the English crown, traditional beneficiary of harbour dues, and the Abbot of Fecamp who was receiving them. In fact an agreement was reached in 1130 that such dues should be shared.[5]

By the end of the twelfth century, as a further result of this prosperity which was largely shared with Rye, the two towns were added to the Confederation of the Cinque Ports as 'members' of Hastings, a port badly needing assistance for it was the first sufferer from the eastward drift of the shingle eventually destined to destroy every natural harbour on this part of the channel coast.

Here we should pause briefly to consider the origins of the Confederation of the Cinque Ports. In pre-conquest times of peace the English Channel was a thoroughfare to be crossed and recrossed; in times of war a frontier to be vigorously defended. In either case the little ships of the ports of the south-east corner of England were a vital resource much coveted by the crown. Available for both transport and warfare, with removable embattled fore- and sterncastles, these vessels proved vital to the welfare of the country. The monarchs of the time, unable to afford a permanent navy, granted special privileges to the five principal ports able to assist in return for fifteen days a year free 'ship-service'. These ports were Hastings, Romney, Hythe, Dover and Sandwich. A number of ships required was allocated to each of the five and every vessel was manned by a crew of twenty men and a boy.

It is not the purpose of this book to provide at any stage a history of the Cinque (pronounced 'sink') Ports although many developments of that unique organisation, which is at the root of the survival of the ancient ceremony with which we began, will be touched on. It must suffice to say here that when the first of Hastings' several harbours was blocked by the elements, the town could not provide its quota of ships without help and that help came from Rye and Winchelsea which were initially subordinate to their 'head port.'

2. A CENTURY OF STORMS

When the thirteenth century opened Winchelsea's membership of the confederation, with its accompanying privileges, was firmly established and the men of the town were enjoying considerable prosperity. Their circumstances, though, were destined soon to change. In 1204 the loss of Normandy, through King John's disastrous rule, turned the opposite shore of the channel from a friendly port of the same kingdom into the base of an active and persistent enemy; an event with far-reaching consequences.

First came the years of war during which King John's great army moved from Dover to Winchelsea to take up defensive positions against the threat of Philip of France's troops assembled at Rouen; later Winchelsea's ships served gallantly with Hubert de Burgh. Second there developed the sporadic clashes which led, justifiably, to Winchelsea's reputation for piracy. Before the middle of the century a third result was the resumption of the Manor of Rameslie, which we have already seen included Winchelsea, to the English crown from the Abbey of Fecamp in exchange for lands in Gloucestershire and elsewhere. This was done on the grounds both that it was too dangerous for a Norman abbey to have a foothold on the English shore, and that Henry III wanted greater control of the developing piratical activities of the men of the area.

Well before this time, though, it was clear that the elements were to have an even more wide reaching influence on Old Winchelsea. In 1233 thunder and lightning are said to have been incessant for fifteen days accompanied by hurricanes of wind and rain.[1] Such conditions rapidly supplemented the eastward drift and the erosion of Fairlight Head in weakening Winchelsea's formerly sound position. By 1236 the town earnestly petitioned the king for help as the shingle spit on which it stood was being carried away. Murage grants for sea defence were made but improved the situation little and in mid-century the first devastating blows were struck.

Holinshed describes how on the first day of October 1250 'a great tempest of wind' such as had hardly been known or heard of in living memory caused the sea to flow twice without ebbing and created such a roaring as struck fear into the hearts of those dwelling far from the shore. Ships at anchor were totally lost. 'At Winchelsea, besides other hurts that was done, in bridges, milles, breakes, and banks, there were 300 houses and some churches drowned with the high rising of the watercourse'.[2]

In 1252 another massive storm broke which, as Matthew Paris reported, 'drove ships from their anchorages, raised roofs of houses many of which were thrown down, uprooted completely the largest trees, deprived churches of their spires, made the lead to move, and did other great damage by land, and still greater by sea, and especially at the port of Winchelsea which is of such use to England and above all to the inhabitants of London'.[3]

From this time on it was clear that in the long term nothing could be done to save Old Winchelsea, so vital to the economy, communications and defence of the country, but it was a human conflict, the Barons' War, which triggered the eventual solution to its plight. The men of the Cinque Ports enthusiastically took the side of Simon de Montfort against the king and fought successfully with him at the Battle of Lewes, a victory which led the citizens of Winchelsea to feel that all control had been removed from them and to resort to the worst excesses of piratical activity of which they had always been accused. William Durrant Cooper refers to:

> 'these lawless habits which made them, as marauders on the seas, the terror of foreign mariners and the dread even of English vessels... they... carried out to the fullest extent the practices which have left a deep stain on their name.' He adds in a footnote,

'To this day [1850] when the boats of Winchelsea or Hastings enter some of our western ports, a hatchet is held up to them as a sign of their ancestors' conduct.'[4]

Hardly an enviable reputation.

Retribution, though, was at hand. Following the death of de Montfort and the restoration of Henry III's authority, Prince Edward visited the Cinque Ports, punishing the guilty and demanding obedience, loyalty and subservience. Only Winchelsea was brave enough to resist, with a force of character which the prince, as Edward I, was not to forget. At the time this resistance was fiercely put down, the town's leaders being mercilessly slaughtered but the ordinary people spared. An order was issued that they should 'abstain from piracies which they had before greatly used.'[5]

King Edward had memorable personal experience of this 'piracy' at the tender age of fifteen when he was about to set sail for Gascony with his mother and brother. The prince's ship had been supplied for him by Yarmouth, intense rival of the Cinque Ports. When the men of Winchelsea saw that it was bigger and better than the ships they were preparing for the queen they attacked it, killing many of the crew.[6]

It is convenient here to point out that any abstention which followed the king's order was far from long-lasting. Even under the cloak of respectability which attached itself to New Winchelsea with its royal patronage, the violence was never far beneath the surface. In the early years of the fourteenth century when an English ship named *Mary of Bayonne* was wrecked on the Gascony coast it was immediately plundered by sailors from Winchelsea, Rye and Romney who stole its valuable cargo. Seeking to control and reduce this type of outrage the Lord Warden of the Confederation of the Cinque Ports, in the spirit of Prince Edward's order, set up a judicial inquiry to be held in Winchelsea. The men of the three towns 'by force and violence prevented the investigation from taking place.'[7] Similarly, about twenty years later, one of the king's ships lying at anchor at Winchelsea was boarded and stripped of all her tackle and gear. The *Victoria County History of Sussex* comments: 'If they had sufficient audacity to do that with a king's ship lying in harbour, what fate awaited strangers at sea!'[8]

However, while this violence lay in the future, the violence of the elements in attacking Old Winchelsea continued unabated. By 1271 part of the church of St. Thomas had been washed away and the accession of Prince Edward as King Edward I the following year brought renewed appeals for help. Fortunately the calibre of the men of Winchelsea during and after the Barons' War had made a deep impression on him and this, combined with national concern at the potential loss of so valuable a trading centre and link with Gascony led to his paying a personal visit in 1276. The need for drastic action was clear. Eventually a commission was set up under Sir John de Kirkeby, Bishop of Ely and Treasurer of England, one of the country's most senior and influential officials. An easily defended new 150 acre site was chosen on the hill of Iham, where Winchelsea now stands. Here the town would be free from the ravages of the sea, could have its harbour on the then mighty River Brede at the foot of the hill, and its anchorage for the fleet at the camber from which the present village of Camber takes its name. When land had been acquired from the manor of Iham and the parish of Icklesham, levelling work began.

The town was to be laid out in the regular gridiron pattern fashionable in the construction of the French bastides, with thirty-nine 'quarters' which actually look like squares and are best described by Geoffrey Bagley's admirably coined adjective 'squareish'![9] This pattern, valuable for reducing the threat of widespread fire among closely-packed wooden buildings and unusual in having its streets named first, second, third etc. as in future American style, allowed the allocation of appropriate plots for residential, business and public use. A focal point was specifically reserved for the construction of what was to be the massive replacement for Old Winchelsea's Church of St. Thomas the Martyr. By November 1281 an order was issued that sites were to be allocated to individual residents of Old Winchelsea and in October 1283 instructions were given for building to commence.[10] The construction of the new town was therefore well under way when Old Winchelsea was dealt a final devastating blow. On 4 February 1287 a storm of unprecedented ferocity struck southern England making 'pitiful waste of people, cattel and of houses in every place.' The largely abandoned town was totally destroyed not only by gigantic waves and hurricane-force winds but also by the scouring away of what remained of the shingle foundations on which it was built. It is easy to imagine the people of the partly constructed replacement town as crouching, petrified witnesses from the comparative safety of their hill. For them, though, security had been provided by the foresight of their monarch. No such arrangements existed for the people of Broomhill and Romney. Broomhill, a little town associated with Old Winchelsea within the Confederation of the Cinque Ports and situated on the opposite side of the harbour, vanished overnight. Romney never recovered. The coming of daylight revealed to her few remaining citizens that shingle, mud and silt had been hurled into the town with such force that even today you have to descend five steps from street-level to reach the floor of the parish church nave. Far worse, this inundation had totally blocked the mouth of the River Rother, causing it to change course to reach the sea at Rye and leaving Romney deprived of her harbour, the very reason for her existence.[11]

For about five years Old Winchelsea's site was partly visible at low tide but eventually the sea completed its work and all remaining evidence of the existence of a once thriving community finally disappeared.[12]

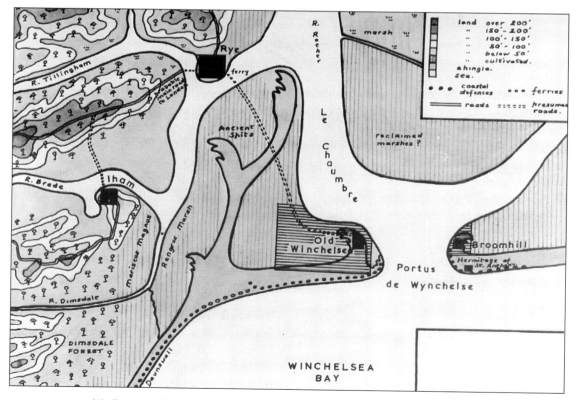

(3) Conjectural map showing the most likely site of Old Winchelsea (B.N. Floyd)

3. PROSPERITY

This sad demise coincided with the pinnacle of Winchelsea's power and influence achieved at its new and flourishing site with the added distinction of being, within the Confederation of the Cinque Ports, no longer a limb of Hastings but a head port in its own right.

In 1288, the year after the fatal storm, Edward I formally granted to the barons of Winchelsea the freehold of the newly laid-out town, keeping for himself a considerable area near St. Leonard's Church, more recently the site of the windmill so dramatically destroyed in the seven-hundredth anniversary storm of 1987. In making this grant the king confirmed all the rights and privileges conferred by his ancestors and arranged payment of a tithe of £10 per annum to the Vicar of Icklesham to compensate him for the land acquired from his parish. This tithe was paid until at least the middle of the nineteenth century. An elaborate handing-over ceremony was held in the presence of Sir John de Kirkeby, 'the Sheriff of Sussex and other nobles as well as knights and many others of the said county'[1] and a further arrangement was made that the citizens should enjoy the land rent-free for seven years.

Building continued apace, principally, of course, of timber-framed houses. There was almost certainly a stone structure on the present site of the Court Hall but the surviving gates, or their predecessors, are likely to have been added rather later when the threat of attack became greater and reinforcement of the original defences was urgent. The chapel of the Greyfriars, who moved to the new town from Old Winchelsea, the gable end of the Hospital of St. John, and many of the cellars are likely to have been contemporary with this period of development but by far the most important structure of which part survives was the Church of St. Thomas. If it was ever completed the building was of cathedral size, reflecting the national importance which Winchelsea then enjoyed.

The climax of this intense activity came in 1292 when a rent roll was compiled listing the names of all the residents to whom plots had been allocated. Two copies of this invaluable document, in medieval Latin, are preserved at the Public Record Office and William Durrant Cooper renders many of the names delightfully and evocatively into English. They are listed according to the street and quarter in which their plots were situated and include Sander de Brokeye long, Walter Spytewymbel, Stephen Blaunchpain, John Squathard, Wymarch Piggesteil and William Halfhering. The attractiveness of Winchelsea as a place to settle is reflected in the inclusion of Stephen of Canterbury, John of Dover, Andrew of Folkestone, Stephen of Portesmouth, John of Sandwych and many others. Most noticeable is the repetition of the names of distinguished Winchelsea families, particularly Alard, of whom more later, and Cogger, a family whose descendants lived in the town until the end of the nineteenth century.[2] Apart from the names, the areas and rentals of the plots are also listed. The rentals when payable after the permitted seven years, would total fourteen pounds eleven shillings and fivepence three farthings on land covering almost 150 acres.

It was the detailed and precise inclusion of the areas, so accurate as to be still measurable, which enabled William Maclean Homan, a resident of the town who was its most dedicated and learned twentieth-century historian, to calculate that the names were listed beginning with those in the south-east corner of each square or quarter and thus construct a detailed plan of the town as it was originally laid out.

The rent-roll also gives us a major clue about Winchelsea's civic development at this time. In the late 1280s the barons of Winchelsea had submitted to King Edward I a petition seeking the right to elect their own mayor rather than being governed by a King's bailiff. The reply was terse and decisive, 'Let them have a bailiff as they are accustomed.'[3] However, the importance of Winchelsea with its exceptional trading capacity was so great that somehow the king was persuaded to change his mind and the twenty-seventh quarter reserves land for the 'Mayor of Winchelsea for the time being.' Probably this was the site of the original court hall.

The right of the freemen to elect their own first citizen was a very important concession. The bailiff or mayor had extensive powers including being chief magistrate, with authority to appoint the other magistrates or jurats, the right to sentence erring citizens to death and to ensure that the sentence was carried out. The mayor was also the coroner, a position of enormous influence, and controlled a wide range of legislation including weights and measures. Should such power fall into the wrong hands the remedy was now with the townsmen who could vote an unwanted incumbent out of office at the Easter Monday hundred court.

The influence which enabled Winchelsea to lobby successfully to be granted a mayor is further illustrated by the town's position relative to its fellow members of the Confederation of the Cinque Ports. When King Edward I required the ports to undertake their ship service for an expedition to Gascony led by his brother Edmund in 1294, Winchelsea provided 13 ships, Sandwich 12, Rye 7, Dover 7, Romney 5, Hythe 3 and Hastings 3.[4] It was seldom in subsequent years that Winchelsea provided a number of ships greater than any of her fellow head-ports but her enormous maritime strength led Professor Montagu Burrows to write in the late nineteenth century:

> 'Winchelsea on the whole figures as the representative port. There is a public spirit and dashing enterprise about its barons which, though sometimes wrongly directed [a scarcely veiled reference to piracy!] is of the same character as that which made, some centuries later, the seamen of Holland the saviours of Europe and those of England the founders of her empire.'[5]

That may well be a somewhat fanciful assessment but Professor Burrows was a learned and impartial observer and his comments reflect a town and people of great character.

It was at Winchelsea, when King Edward I was visiting the mighty fleet which it led, that an incident occurred which has entered both history and legend. He is said to have been approaching the low parapet which served as a defence at the top of a steep cliff when his horse was frightened by the noise of a nearby windmill and refused to go any further. 'Vigorously urged on by the king' the animal suddenly and unpredictably leapt the obstruction and disappeared from sight with the king still in the saddle. All present feared he must be dead but despite the considerable drop the road beneath was deep with mud, enabling the beast to keep its feet and the king to keep his seat with the assistance of the 'longshanks' by which he was known.[6] He rode back into the town amid great rejoicing but with anger in his heart for a beast so easily frightened and clearly unsuitable for battle. Later the horse was somewhat impetuously sold for half its actual value.[7] Topography and the available evidence suggest that this incident took place near the Pipewell Gate rather than at the cliff beyond the house in North Street now known as King's Leap.

Another royal visit drew Winchelsea once more onto the national stage for it was in 1297 that a scene took place there which has been said to have 'exalted Winchelsea into a second Runnymede'.[8] Edward I, a headstrong, independent monarch, had tended to ignore the rights of the barons established eighty years previously by Magna Carta. It was complained that he had raised revenue and imposed taxes to support his wars without the required consultation and agreement. Much important principle was at stake. When the king and his entourage reached Winchelsea they were met by a deputation of barons demanding redress before any further money would be granted and before they would accompany him on his proposed expedition to France. The king's natural instinct was to refuse but fortunately he acceded with the words, 'Send the deed after me.' The royal seal was later attached, outside the walls of Ghent, to a reaffirmation of the principles agreed by King John, and a further conflict was avoided.

Thus we come to the period during which Winchelsea's leadership as a town was epitomised by the wider leadership of one of its citizens, Gervase Alard. His family had been leading members of the Winchelsea community for centuries, their name being derived from the Saxon Aethelwald. The 1292 rent-roll shows land allocated to a large number of family members, the site of the present Court Hall being, for example, the home of Reginald Alard. They were rich, successful and influential, not only in Winchelsea. Another family member, Thomas, was summoned by King Edward I in 1297 to a conference at Harwich so that he could use his experience of the planning of New Winchelsea to advise on preparations for the reconstruction of Berwick.[9] The Alards were traders, vintners and goldsmiths, not averse, like many of their fellow citizens, to some profitable piracy when the opportunity arose. In 1295 Gervase Alard, junior, (there were three of the same name during the late thirteenth and early fourteenth centuries) became the first Mayor of Winchelsea whose name is known to us through its inclusion in a British Museum document. Even more influentially, five years later he was appointed by the king to lead the Cinque Ports fleet with his command eventually including the whole fleet of the southern shore as far as Cornwall. His reward for this considerable responsibility was the princely sum of two shillings a day and the rather misleading reputation of having been the first admiral of the fleet. In 1308, following the completion of these duties, Gervase Alard became once more Mayor of Winchelsea shortly before his death.

(4) The Strand Gate – eighteenth century

4. DECLINE

While much remained to be achieved, the death of Gervase Alard can be taken as symbolic that Winchelsea's influence had passed its peak and that many years of trouble and decline lay ahead. Man's influence on the process had been insidiously under way since Roman times when the construction of the Rhee Wall enclosed large areas of Romney Marsh and kept out the sea. This process was enthusiastically continued by the landowning churches and other agricultural interests, constantly, if not always deliberately, to the detriment of the seafarers. Reclamation of marshland over the centuries reduced the scour of the tides, encouraged silting, made harbours shallower and rivers narrower. The effect on the River Brede where Winchelsea's quay was situated was particularly noticeable for during the fourteenth century a bridge was built across it to provide a land-route to Rye via Udimore where previously only a ferry journey had been possible. By 1336 only ships carrying as little as twenty tuns of wine could reach Winchelsea town although the anchorage at the camber was still a considerable facility for the fleet. Ironically the sea frequently reversed the process, breaking through badly maintained embankments and making life more difficult for the inhabitants in a different way by ruining the reclaimed land used for growing food.[1]

Far more obviously indicative of Winchelsea's decline were the raids carried out by the French during the comparatively frequent periods in the Hundred Years' War when England lost maritime control of the channel. The first major raid affecting Winchelsea may well have been as early as 1326 for the King's Bailiff's accounts show that a large number of houses had been completely destroyed.[2] The cause of this destruction is not stated but there is reliable evidence that eleven years later a major attack occurred in which the French fleet, having been deterred further along the coast by the strong defence of Sandwich, fell upon Rye and Winchelsea and destroyed almost a hundred houses in Winchelsea and about half that number in Rye.[3]

In considering the cross-channel warfare of this extended conflict we must remember that towns such as Winchelsea were not only the victims. It is clear that there were times when inadequate defences, poor resources in terms of defenders, and in at least one case negligent or treasonable watch-keeping contributed to these disasters but the character of the Winchelsea men, their skill at sea and their inclination to violence led them to mount revenge attacks which created similar destruction in towns of the French shore.

Against the third factor influencing Winchelsea's decline there was, however, no defence and no revenge. Between 1348 and 1350 the Black Death raged across the kingdom and is said to have claimed the lives of almost half the population engaged in agriculture. We do not know the extent of the effect on Winchelsea but the townspeople would certainly have been susceptible because they were weakened by suffering from privation caused during the war. One piece of direct evidence is that in 1355 the Hospital of St. Bartholomew within the town was excused ten years' rental because 'since the pestilence [it] is depressed in many ways in its facilities'.[4]

However, in 1350 Winchelsea was not badly enough affected to prevent Edward III from mounting a major naval action there. Contradictory motives have been suggested for the Battle of Winchelsea, also known as the battle of L'espagnol sur Mer. John Cammidge in his detailed account, while acknowledging that the attack was upon a Spanish fleet generously endowed with valuable cargo, suggests that the principal reason was revenge for numerous attacks made on the English shore during the annual Spanish trading visit to Flemish ports.[5] Homan, on the other hand, is far less charitable, suggesting that, motivated by greed and a weak financial position, the king ambushed an innocent trading fleet whose ships had sailed together as some form of protection against just such a piratical attack, and with whose country England was not at war.[6]

Whatever may be the truth of this Winchelsea was still strong enough to play a full part both in the naval action and as a base. The king's own ship was the cog Thomas of Winchelsea with its captain, Richard Large, and three other Winchelsea ships, one of them captained by Stephen Alard, took part. The fighting, which took place off-shore from Winchelsea and was distantly visible from the town, was violent and intense. The smaller English ships grappled the considerably larger Spanish carracks and the king led one of these attacks in person. All on board the enemy vessel were slaughtered and the ship captured. Prince Edward, the Black Prince, whose ship was the cog Edward of Greenwich, was less fortunate and was saved only by the intervention of others in the fight to board a Spanish vessel as his ship sank beneath him. They day ended with a glorious victory, or so it was certainly perceived. More than half the Spanish ships had been profitably captured, many others sunk, and the remainder scattered in confusion.

On landing the king and the prince, with their retinue, travelled to Udimore where the queen was staying and there was much rejoicing. Next day St. Thomas's Church witnessed a solemn service of thanksgiving and at the Court Hall the king's faithful subjects were thanked and dismissed at the end of their summons to arms.

Such scenes would have been far from the minds of Winchelsea's residents a decade later during the most devastating of the French attacks when, on 15 March 1360, three thousand Frenchmen subjected the town to a most terrible assault. They fired the houses and burst into the church where the terrified citizenry had sought sanctuary, murdering and raping indiscriminately. This awful scene is likely to have taken place at St. Giles's Church for an extension of the churchyard was needed to permit burial of so large a number. The adjoining lane retains Deadman's Lane as one of its names to this day.

In 1366 the number of Winchelsea houses listed as 'waste, burned and uninhabited' had risen to 385.[7] This situation would not have been greatly aggravated by the next major raid in 1377, launched within days of the death of King Edward III, for on that occasion, while Rye suffered appallingly, Winchelsea's defence was organised by the Abbot of Battle, a skilled soldier, and was so spirited that the attackers went elsewhere, destroying, among other targets, St. Clement's Church at Hastings. In the early stages of this raid Rye was subjected to the great indignity of having its church bells stolen. A combined retaliatory assault the following year on the coast of Normandy, mounted by a well-supported force from Rye and Winchelsea, slaughtered those they met, held to ransom any they thought might be valuable in that way, destroyed houses and churches and recovered property taken the previous year, most significantly Rye's church bells.[8]

At this time the fickle sea was again causing problems for a commission was set up as the result of a complaint from Winchelsea that the roads leading to Battle and Hastings had been destroyed by inroads of the sea thus isolating the town from help in the event of an attack.[9]

If any action was taken it was ineffectual for in 1380 even preparations made by the Abbot of Battle for Winchelsea's defence were insufficient to prevent the town being crushed into terminal decline by a final major attack led by France's Spanish allies.[10] Tradition has it that this was the occasion when the enemy were treacherously admitted at dawn through the New Gate. Again the town was burnt. The Pipewell Gate and St. Thomas's Church were severely damaged. The former was rebuilt in 1404 but the latter has never fully recovered. Homan suggests that the town's principal church may have been the subject of direct assault, not because it was being used as a place of defence and refuge as was St. Giles's in 1360, but because at the time the English and French were recognising different papal authorities and the church thus became a specific target for religious reasons.[11]

Subsequent national concern was insufficient to achieve Winchelsea's restoration to a position anywhere near its former strength. In 1384 the House of Commons petitioned King Richard II to take steps to defend Rye and Winchelsea because 'if these towns were taken, which God forbid, the whole country would be destroyed.'[12] The residential areas of the town lay so desolate that it was scarcely possible to distinguish one man's plot from another. Rather than take direct action the king told the owners that unless they repaired their houses so that they could live in them or let them, their land would be confiscated. The town accounts for 1388 suggest that this had some effect for considerable re-occupation had taken place.[13]

The final principal reason for Winchelsea's decline and the growing inadequacy of its harbour was the subject of a directive issued in the first year of the reign of King Henry IV (1400). The inning of the marshes has already been cited as a cause of silting but seamen's even more direct action in jettisoning vast quantities of ballast in the River Brede accelerated the process rapidly. The king was told that mariners both native and foreign were filling up and obstructing 'the channel of said port from a place called Camber as far as Bodiam with stones, sand and other ballast' thus making its profitable use by trading ships much more difficult. He ordered that convenient sites were to be selected where ballast could be unladen without affecting navigation. Officers were instructed to provide strict supervision to ensure compliance.[14]

It was too late.

(5) Pipewell Gate – eighteenth century

5. FOUR CENTURIES OF IMPOVERISHMENT

The continuation of this process not only through inning and ballast-dumping, but also through relentless accumulation of the shingle was the principal geological development affecting Winchelsea during the four centuries which passed before the period on which this book will concentrate. During those centuries the marsh land consolidated, the eastward drift protecting it with vast shingle banks, and the sea steadily withdrew from the town it had once sustained and succoured. King Henry VIII built Camber Castle to protect the entrance to the harbour as it then was. Now it stands alone among the fields. By the late eighteenth century the ground which currently supports the villages of Rye Harbour and Winchelsea Beach was largely established although not settled. One last attempt to provide a replacement harbour took place at that time, but the shingle won again. However, that new harbour, constructed with such high hopes, was intended for Rye not Winchelsea and its story belongs to the history of the Harbour of Rye[1] or the village of Winchelsea Beach. It was not until the 1920s and early 1930s that the whole process was once more reversed. The sea smashed its way through inadequate defences at Winchelsea Beach and threatened to destroy the bungalows and shacks which had been built there. By then the area was no longer under Winchelsea's jurisdiction and Winchelsea Corporation wisely declined to become involved in the resulting controversy which led eventually to the construction of the sea wall.[2]

What, then, of Winchelsea during those four hundred years? We have time only to catch glimpses of its usually impoverished state largely through the recollections of visitors who have left their impressions of its plight.

Unfortunately there are no personal accounts of this type dating from the fifteenth century but we can gain from other sources some revealing insights into the style and nature of life in the town at that time and the impression is that, even if Winchelsea was not thriving, it was certainly lively.

A series of ordinances or byelaws was issued by the corporation in 1427 for the regulation of life in the town. There seems to have been particular concern about the presence and influence of strangers who had to trade only in the market place and might only buy from and sell to inhabitants of Winchelsea, on no account with other strangers. If they were vintners the permission of the mayor was needed to conduct any trade at all. They also required permission to stay for more than a very short time. Any person running an inn or lodging house was liable for punishment if he permitted a 'suspected person, vagabond or stranger' a bed for a second night without telling the mayor the circumstances. It was probably the potential malicious influence of strangers which also led to strict control of the porters whose job it was to carry goods from the quay up to the town. They had to swear an oath that they would certify to the mayor and the common clerk how much wine, oil, honey, wax or any other merchandise they carried up whether it is 'tonned, pyped, barelled or bayled' and would declare from whom it came.

The authorities were also anxious to control butchers who were ordered not to throw 'gore and filth' beside the walls. A requirement that they should sell only wholesome meat to 'the king's liege people' was logically followed by one that they should not keep bad meat on their stalls. The disposal of carcasses was the worst problem. Butchers were firmly told that they must not dump them in the streets or 'cast them over the cliff' which we must assume was a common practice.

The streets were the subject of the largest number of regulations. 'Common women' might not live there but only 'in the utmost part'; they must be hooded and must not be found walking in the town after curfew. Anyone allowing pigs to run in the streets should expect that their pigs would be killed but sheep received slightly less harsh treatment for while they were required to be kept 'in close pasture' the punishment if they were found loose was a fine. Dunghills in the streets or in front of houses were expressly forbidden, reflecting the fact that the highways provided the only sewers.

Further human activity in those same streets is reflected in the document by a ban on carrying a sword or any other unlawful weapon, and on the playing of illegal games. This extended to the town green and the games banned included tennis, dice, cards, quoits and bowls. The fine was one shilling for each person every time he played. If that byelaw is still in force Winchelsea Bowls Club must owe the corporation a great deal of money, but no doubt its members will plead that in the twentieth century they play neither in the streets nor on the town green.

1427 is one of the very few years since 1295 for which we do not know the name of Winchelsea's mayor. He must have been an incredibly busy man. Among his numerous other responsibilities were ensuring that nobody undermined the cliffs by taking sand from them, receiving evidence about citizens who had thrown anything into the harbour and regulating the weekly baking of fourth class or common bread which the ordinary people could afford. In the unlikely event that the *Oxford English Dictionary*'s definition of 'bolk' and 'bulke' applies to those words as they appear in this document the mayor's permission had to be sought to belch. Surely not!

There were, of course, perks available for these arduous duties. The corporation collected a levy of one penny on each 100 pounds of corn purchased in or outside the town. This weight was fixed because the roads were so bad that no horse could be expected to carry a greater amount. The mayor himself had to be offered the surplus of any goods sold above a value of one hundred shillings and when each 'fisher boat' from Picardy came into the harbour it was required to pay five shillings. On each subsequent visit the mayor received three mackerel 'if there are that many in the boat.'[3]

The comparatively active community reflected in those byelaws may well have owed such relative prosperity to the fifteenth century enthusiasm for pilgrimages, particularly to the shrine of St. James of Compostella for which Winchelsea was a principal point of departure. Cooper gives some details of this traffic, stating that in 1434 licences were issued for 2433 pilgrims to be taken from Winchelsea, as many as sixty at a time in small ships. The pilgrims had to give an undertaking that they would not carry money above their reasonable expenses and that they would reveal no national secrets to foreigners.[4] These were uncomfortable voyages. Caxton offered advice for pilgrims to the Holy Land which might well also have applied to those to St. James. They were urged to take a cage containing half a dozen hens or chickens, to take a little cauldron, a frying-pan, dishes, plates and cups of glass. They were also strongly advised, 'In a shyp or caryk choose a chamber as nigh the middes of the ship as ye may, for there is least rolling or tumbling, to keep your brain or stomach in temper.'[5]

Cooper refers obliquely to this when quoting the opening verse of what he calls 'the earliest English sea song', the latter part of which reads:

> 'For when they [the pilgrims] take the see
> At Sandwyche, or at Wynchelsee,
> At Brystow, or where that it bee,
>   Theyr herts begin to fayle.'[6]

He does not, however, go on to make clear what good reason their hearts had to fail. The second part of the final verse describes how:

> 'For when that we shall go to bedde,
> The pupe was nygh our bedd hede,

(6) New Gate – eighteenth century

> A man were as good to be dede,
>   As smell thereof the stynk!'[7]

Surely that needs no elucidation.

These pilgrims have left a permanent remembrance of their voyages. On the pillars of St. Thomas's Church can be seen to this day the crosses they carved when waiting for a favourable wind and no doubt praying fervently for calm seas and a safe passage.

It is not until quite late in the sixteenth century that we are afforded an insight into Winchelsea's condition as the result of a visit. In 1573 the visitor was no less a person than Queen Elizabeth I. Samuel Jeake records how, following persistent urgent appeals for money to provide a new harbour the people of Winchelsea received no help but were honoured by a royal visit when her majesty saw what a good position the town had. She probably already knew of its favourable reputation as a healthy place which had been used as a sanatorium for troops during the 1563 outbreak of the plague. 'The ancient buildings, grave bench of a mayor and twelve jurats in their scarlet gowns and the city-like deportment of the people among whom were several gentry' impressed the queen who is alleged to have referred to the town as 'Little London'. Surely she must have been joking for just two years later Lambard published his *Topographical Dictionary* in which he reports that there were in Winchelsea 'not then above sixty households standing and those for the most part poorly peopled: all which happened by reason of the sea having forsaken the town.'[8]

Another source suggests that urgent appeals for help were made directly to the queen during her visit.[9] Would the citizenry have dared? It was not until thirteen years later that land freed by the dissolution of the monasteries came officially into the possession of Winchelsea Corporation. To this subject we shall return later (see p.38) because after a lapse of two hundred and thirty years the document detailing the grant suddenly re-appeared to the considerable surprise of the then mayor and jurats who knew nothing of its existence.

Any resulting prosperity, though, was insufficient to enable Winchelsea to provide even one ship to fight the Armada.

John Norden, the famous map-maker, gives us, when reviewing the condition of Sussex towns in 1595, a fairly standard account of how Winchelsea was constructed by King Edward I, remarking particularly on the way the streets were 'artificially laid out' and 'lay all soe direct that view might be had in every one of them from the one end of the towne to the other.' That might appear to be true when looking at one of his maps but it seems unlikely to have been written from personal experience! He goes on to describe how the stones of the town seem to weep that 'so pleasing a plot and so well contrived should suddenly sustayne desolation' and to regret deeply that the vaults and cellars instead of containing 'pleasant vines and rich merchandise' should now 'yield harbour to the loathsome vermin.'[10]

And so with this unpleasant picture of Winchelsea's rat-infested cellars, many of which were at the time used as cesspits, we move to the seventeenth century during which four visitors have left us their impressions.

The earliest of these was a certain Lieutenant Hammond who made *A Short Survey of the Western Counties* commencing on the 4 August 1635. Quite how Winchelsea qualified as being in the western counties is not clear. The lieutenant was much impressed by Rye where he stayed at The Mermaid but commented that to march up and down her steep streets for two hours would be 'sufficient to founder a soldier.' The journey across the marsh to Winchelsea he found less impressive for he had to take two ferries, one out of Rye and another into Winchelsea; no doubt this added substantially to his expenses. Once in Winchelsea Hammond was struck by the regularity of the street pattern and by each square having the same two-acre area as the churchyard. The cellars he observed as being in use as stables and possibly for leather-craft for he says that in them 'the coulter cutts', a coulter being a knife. On the subject of the various ruins Lieutenant Hammond was much more vague, finding their purpose impossible to identify for 'worm eating time had so much extinguished all possibility of deciding whether they were castle walls, old churches, or the remains of some ancient monastery for hospitalitie.'

'Hospitalitie' seems to have been difficult to come by for where it was said there had once been 'fifty brave tavern signs' the lieutenant had a problem finding 'one signe for a cup of good beere.' His account of the church quotes the doubtful tradition that some of the tombs in St. Thomas's were brought there from Old Winchelsea at the time of its destruction – indeed, his account may be the source of that tradition. Whatever shortcomings the town may have had as he saw them, Lieutenant Hammond stayed much longer than he intended and he had to hurry off past Broomham Place, unable to reach his lodgings in Hastings until after nightfall.[11]

Seventeen years later, during the Interregnum, John Evelyn, the famous diarist, was kept waiting at Rye for his wife's return from France and took the opportunity to walk over 'to survey the ruines of Winchelsea, that ancient Cinq Port.' He deduced from the layout that this had been once a large city where were still to be seen 'vast caves and vaults, walls and towns, ruins and monasteries and a sumptuous church.' Of Winchelsea's condition at the time of his visit he commented that there was rubbish everywhere with only 'a few despicable hovells and cottages' standing. His astonishment that such a place should still have a mayor is perhaps understandable. On his return to

Rye John Evelyn discovered that his wife's ship had escaped the Dutch fleet during three days at sea but otherwise this was not a happy time for him because on his way back to London he was robbed by highwaymen of his diamond buckles and rings.[12]

The following year John Taylor, a London waterman who had been King's Waterman in the time of Charles I but had since, after becoming a publican, fallen on hard times, made a tour of Sussex which he described in verse. The verse is not of high quality:

> 'At Hastings I staid not, but hastily
> I ambled six miles into Winchelsea'

but there is an interesting observation that at that time Camber Castle was twice a day surrounded at high tide:

> 'And when the floods are ebbed into the main
> Three miles in sands 'tis compast round again.'

Of the ancient town as he saw it Taylor is dismissive:

> 'Of Winchelsea that now is I could ken
> Nothing worth observation of my pen.'[13]

After another third of a century we can glimpse Winchelsea through the eyes of commissioners who reported on St. Thomas's Church. Its condition at the time is reflected in their comments that the two aisles were seriously dilapidated, the roof leaked, all the bells had been sold except one, there was no linen cloth or napkin for communion, pigs were kept in the churchyard and the rectory had been pulled down for the profit that could be made by selling the building materials. Not impressive stewardship![14]

However, at least the last of these defects had been corrected by the time Celia Fiennes, who so graphically recorded her travels in the late seventeenth century, came to Winchelsea in 1697. She travelled from Rye via the Udimore ridge thus avoiding the ferries which had annoyed Lieutenant Hammond. Her first impression that it was not a large place was contradicted when she stood within the town and realized its original size for 'the remaines of pieces of walls in most places you see.' She rode up 'the middle street' and saw what was left of the churches and halls but otherwise she observed that 'grass grows now where Winchelsea was, as was once said of Troy.' Very few houses were to be seen, although she thought the mayor's house and the parsonage did the town credit, but the corporation was still in existence with the mayor and 'aldermen', thirteen in all, making up most of the inhabitants. It was Celia Fiennes who made the claim that Winchelsea's is, 'the ancientest corporation in England' stating that if the Lord Mayor of London meets the Mayor of Winchelsea the Mayor of Winchelsea must have precedence. She is also the first of our visitors to mention Winchelsea's continuing right to elect two members of parliament.[15]

Daniel Defoe, writing a quarter of a century later, was, however, outraged by this survival. He scathingly describes how the town, if it deserves such a name, has had cornfields made out of the streets and how the plough went over the foundations and even the first floors of the houses. It is to Defoe quite deplorable that more money was spent at elections than the total lands of the parish were worth. He had been told that on one occasion there was such rivalry between Sir John Banks and Col. Draper that the colonel spent £11,000 at one election and still lost. 'What the other spent who opposed him may only be guessed at, seeing that he who spent most was always sure to carry it in those days.'[16] To the fascinating subject of Winchelsea's development as a rotten borough we shall return.

Parson Gilpin, writing after his visit in 1774, ignores Winchelsea's corporate and parliamentary situation but reinforces the view that much more then remained to be seen of the ruins of Winchelsea's past glories. He states that while 'desolation is spread over the entire compass of the hill' and the residential area is 'shrunk into a few houses in the corner of its ancient site, a variety of Gothic remains are spread over the whole surface of the peninsula.' He cannot think of any example in history of 'so flourishing a town [being] reduced to such a state of entire insignificance.'[17] No doubt this situation had been accelerated by the entrepreneurial activities of the residents who sold stone from ruined buildings for such projects as the building of the New Harbour at about this time. That was certainly true of the then rector, the Rev. Drake Hollingbery, who had the surviving walls of St. Giles's Church taken down and sold for this purpose, subsequently rejoicing that he had acquired a beautiful flat garden.[18]

The propensity for such treatment of remains which in the twentieth century would be preserved with reverence is even better illustrated in the Hon. John Byng's account of his visit in 1788. On his second day in the town he came upon The Old Friary, now Greyfriars, although the house which Byng saw was the predecessor of the present one. He describes the shell of the chapel where the inner walls were weakened and disfigured by having fruit trees nailed to them, where the sight of an eagle chained in 'misery, dirt and clamour' caused him much distress, and where the tower was used as a lookout by officers of the customs. The 'noble arch' at the western end was heavily shaded by ash trees which the gardener favoured removing. Perhaps that would not have been too disastrous but that worthy was also recommending his master to pull down one side of the chapel and build a greenhouse against the other side. Byng comments resignedly, '[this] glorious advice will probably be followed as the general wish of all possessors of old buildings is to put them to some gardening or farming use, or else to pull down the material for the repairing of pig-styes or the roads.' Fortunately on this occasion Byng's fears were not justified.

This is a highly personal account. The writer, having taken rooms at the New Inn for himself and his friend whom he identifies only as I.D., went in search of a haircut, believing that the barber would be able to provide him with all the local gossip. Unfortunately the barber turned out to be stone deaf. During their stay John Byng and I.D. walked out to Henry VIII's Camber Castle, 'a specious safeguard to the nation he so plundered.' Despite this disapproving attitude the visitors, after finding a door open, made their way in and sat for half an hour on the battlements enjoying 'the views, the evening, the sea breeze and the sight of haymakers.' The prospect from what present residents call The Lookout, beside Strand Gate, also brought comment. The following morning the visitors sat 'enjoying by two borrowed telescopes the views over Romney Marsh and of the Kentish coast almost as far as Hythe.'

Leaving Winchelsea was not so agreeable. 'The removal of our baggage was a great plague to us.' But eventually a carrier was found. The weather was threatening but the New Inn's bill was felt to be not unreasonable despite the tough chicken they had been asked to eat. The landlord insisted that it was 'just killed to tempt us by its freshness.'[19]

And so we reach the last of the seventeenth and eighteenth-century visitors whose impressions have come down to us, John Wesley. Wesley's association with the town was much closer than any of the others. He had been visiting since at least 1771 when he preached in the 'new square'. In January 1778 he described his journey to Rye and Winchelsea as the worst he had ever had but such an intrepid traveller would not have allowed the appalling conditions of the roads to prevent his supporting the Wesleyan communities of Rye and Winchelsea which were the first in Sussex. In 1789 'I went over to Winchelsea… the new preaching house was well filled with decent, serious hearers who seemed to receive the truth in the love of it.'[20] We do not have the actual figure for membership of the Winchelsea class in 1789 but in the following year there were 13 on the roll. No doubt they, with friends from the town and from Rye, would have made this little building look 'well filled.'[21]

Despite Wesley's implacable opposition to 'that accursed thing smuggling' which was prevalent in the area at the time, he continued to visit and preach. His abhorrence of smuggling was reinforced by a family tragedy for his daughter's fiancé, Captain Henry Haddock, commander of a Rye revenue cutter, was shot by a smuggler during an engagement off Dungeness. Eventually Winchelsea entered Methodist history by being the site of Wesley's last open-air sermon. 'I went over to that poor skeleton of ancient Winchelsea. I stood under a large tree and called to most of the inhabitants of the town, "The kingdom of heaven is at hand, repent and believe the gospel." It seemed as if all that heard were, for the present, almost persuaded to be christians.'[22] That famous tree was blown down in 1927 but its scion, with a commemorative plaque, still flourishes in German Street.

Following Wesley's death the fortunes of the little Winchelsea chapel declined. By 1803 there were only nine registered members and by 1807 the group had disappeared from the records. However, in 1808 a revival was inspired by the presence of the military garrison. They appear under the heading 'Soldiers North Yorkshire Militia - Winchelsea Class.' Sixteen names are listed, only two of them being readily recognisable as those of Winchelsea residents.[23]

It is to the wars which brought those soldiers to Winchelsea that we must turn first in the story of the two centuries on which this book will concentrate.

(7) The original Wesley's tree, beneath which he preached his last open-air sermon, fell in 1927. The present one is a scion of the old.

6. THE NAPOLEONIC WARS

The nineteenth century began with Winchelsea a garrison town at war for the first of three occasions within 150 years. The impact of the garrison was as extensive as the impact of defensive preparations on the landscape. During the Napoleonic Wars the threat of invasion was heard vociferously and publicly from the emperor's own lips with the proximity and topography of the south-east coast of England making it the defensive focal point, and thus recalling the original reasons for the establishment of the Confederation of the Cinque Ports. At one time at Boulogne and smaller neighbouring harbours were gathered 120,000 troops and 2,000 small boats. It is unlikely that the threat they posed could ever have been successfully realised for Napoleon's officers foresaw that these little vessels, confronted by the British fleet close to the British shore would face disaster. Napoleon fancifully hoped for a dark night, a thick fog, or a diversion to draw the fleet of his enemy away from the scene. Of his navy he demanded twenty four hours' control of the channel – a demand it could not deliver. The emperor's arrogant confidence even led to the striking of a medal commemorating the fall of London.[1]

This awful prospect provoked frantic activity on the coast of Kent and Sussex and at this time it was not only national events but also a national figure who strode onto our small stage. William Pitt the younger was both prime minister and Lord Warden of the Confederation of the Cinque Ports. His responsibility, even when out of parliamentary office, was the successful defence of this vulnerable coast and no one can deny his single-minded pursuit of that aim. Pitt led by example, enlisting and drilling as a private soldier in the Cinque Ports Fencibles. He also led through his drive and personality; in 1803, at the height of the danger, arming almost all the fishing luggers within the area of the ports and their liberties with either a twelve or an eighteen-pound carronade. These boats saw a certain amount of service. Ford Madox Ford calls them the last fleet of the confederation and reports that Lady Hesther Stanhope, Pitt's redoubtable niece, who also lived at Walmer and commanded them in his absence, was very scathing about the French fishing boats they faced. One they captured was loaded with gin – to keep up the crew's spirits she presumed; another contained stale bread and a third a large chest of medicine, enough for the whole fleet.[2]

This comparatively minor defensive gambit was overshadowed by two major projects. While others recommended, designed and built the Royal Military Canal, it was to Pitt's further credit in his dual role that he enthusiastically obtained government sanction and personally persuaded the landowners to agree to the acquisition of the required land without the statutory procedures. To do this he perceptively used the canal's potential value to farmers in reducing flooding and as a source of irrigation for the marshlands rather than its intended defensive purpose of impeding the advancing hordes of Napoleon's army.[3] Whether such a feature, thirty yards wide, would have held up a force which had already successfully crossed the English Channel has always been in grave doubt but it certainly provided the means for quick and efficient transport of troops and equipment which the existing roads would have made impossible. For Winchelsea an added advantage was the adjoining road, built with removed spoil, the line of which today provides the main route to Rye.

The canal was constructed by a large combined civilian and military workforce using spades and wheelbarrows. It swept in a great arc below the cliffs of the old shoreline from Hythe to Iden Lock, used navigable sections of the Rother and the Brede and, under the stern gaze of the Strand Gate, began at Winchelsea its final section to Cliff End. There, though in true peace, it still lies.[4]

From Winchelsea visible evidence of the second great defensive construction project of that time has gone. It was William Pitt again who issued the instructions for building the Martello

Towers, an even greater and more expensive task. Each tower required half a million bricks and to look across the marsh towards the sea while they were being built must have been to look at a vast and apparently chaotic building site. Here the defensive potential was far more clearly appreciable and the massive impact on the view would have been readily acceptable as a wartime necessity. The towers provided enormously strong gun emplacements, only six hundred yards apart, from which an invading force could have been ferociously dealt with. Eight of them, numbers 31-38, stood between the mouth of the Rother and Pett Level; the sea and the Royal Engineers have disposed of them all. However, 'The Enchantress', tower No.28 at Rye Harbour, survives though sadly neglected.[5]

The irony of these enormous undertakings is that long before both were finished the invasion threat had gone and Napoleon, having lost his fleet at the Battle of Trafalgar, had turned his attentions elsewhere. It may have been prudent to continue construction after that time but the canal was never used in anger and neither were the Martello Towers except against smugglers.

Now we must turn our gaze into the town to see what was happening for a great upheaval was caused to the life of Winchelsea's citizens by the presence of the garrison and the prosecution of the war. The concentration of troops along the coast from Eastbourne to the Kent border is illustrated by the following table:

	Infantry	Cavalry
By Grand Redoubt, Seahouse	1500	800
Pevensey	800	
Bexhill	5000	100
Bo Peep	230	
Hastings	800	170
Winchelsea	500	
Nook Beach	100	
Rye No.1	800	168
Rye No.2	80	

Seahouse was Eastbourne. One of the batteries referred to in the article from which these figures are taken is said to have been at the New Harbour mouth at Winchelsea Beach.[6]

Winchelsea's population has remained remarkably constant since there are records to provide evidence. In 1801 it is estimated to have been 627, a figure almost doubled by the number of soldiers and even further increased by their families.

From these days have come down to us such names as Barrack Square, Cooks Green, Magazine House, and The Armoury. Tower Cottage had no less illustrious a visitor than the Duke of Wellington on a mission of inspection but it is perhaps most rewarding to examine the effect on the ordinary people of the town.

The earliest call on them, long before the invasion threat materialised, came when the government, deeply alarmed by the French revolution, demanded the proper reinforcement and updating of the navy to defend the country's shores. Sailors were needed. The enforcement of the resulting act of parliament was the responsibility of the magistrates of boroughs such as Winchelsea and a meeting of the petty sessions was duly held in the Court Hall on 26 May 1795. Henry Waterman, town clerk, was appointed to oversee the requirements and the town constables were summoned to appear before the court on 9 June to receive their instructions. They were told that they must seek out any men who were 'able bodied and idle.' These were to include anyone who could not show that he was conscientiously following a trade or employment, anyone who could not financially support himself, any 'rogues, vagabonds or disorderly persons,' and anyone who had recently offended against the law of the land, particularly those convicted of illegal landing and carrying prohibited goods; the smugglers at that time were a constant thorn in the government's side.

We do not know with what enthusiasm either the magistrates or the constables pursued this quest. Maybe word was passed round in advance to warn away any likely candidates in such a close-knit community because the constables returned on the same day to announce to the court that no such men were to be found within the town or the liberty. They returned again on 15 June and 23 June with the same result. When Captain Ballard of the Board of Admiralty arrived to collect Winchelsea's conscripts there were none to collect.[7]

The situation was not a great deal better after William Pitt set about compulsorily boosting the numbers of the soldiery for the defence of the coast. On 1 September 1803 he wrote from Walmer Castle in his capacity as Lord Warden calling 'A General Meeting' of the Cinque Port towns.[8] The Mayor of Winchelsea responded to this summons and attended at Dover Castle on 6 September with some of his 'brethren', and the representatives of the other ports. It was decided that a total of 400 men should be recruited for the Cinque Ports Militia and a specific number was allotted to each town:[9]

Hastings and its members	22
Sandwich and its members	67
Dover and its members	137
Romney	9
Hythe	14
Rye	16
Winchelsea	5
Faversham	24
Folkestone	13
Seaford	9
Lydd	8
Fordwich	2
Tenterden	25
Deal	43
Pevensey and its members	6
	400

The Privy Council subsequently thought it unlikely that so large a number could be raised and reduced the overall total to 280 of whom just three were required from Winchelsea. Recruitment was to be by the drawing of lots. The constables were called into action again to compile lists of those liable. In the first class were men aged between 17 and 30 who were unmarried and had no children under 10. They were followed by men aged 30-50 in similar circumstances. Those next in priority were from ages 17 to 30 who were married and had no more than two children under 10. Lastly came all remaining men between 17 and 55.[10] Lists were accordingly drawn up. One is headed 'Constable of Winchelsea's return of men liable to be balloted for in Winchelsea to serve in the Army of Reserve'. 97 names are included with occupations, infirmities and the grounds on which they claim exemption. Among the occupations there were large numbers of labourers, several excise officers, a surgeon,

(8) The Barrack Houses as they are today.

a schoolmaster and all the wide range of trades current at the time. George Dawes alone is listed as 'Gentleman'. Some candidates declare infirmities. Solomon Suter, a carrier, is a cripple; Thomas Seere is subject to fits and a cripple; William Adams, labourer, has lost an eye and a thumb; Stephen Lawrence junior, glazier, is lame and an apprentice. Of the exemption claims the vast majority are because a man has two or more children under 10 to support. Others include John Neeve, servant, who is excused on the grounds that he is under 5'2" tall; William Weller, footman, has a rupture; James Tutt, seaman, is serving in a revenue cutter; Joseph Weller has already been discharged from the militia as unfit for service. Once this weeding-out process was complete 50 of the men remained for the ballot, including George Dawes.[11] A remarkable survival among Winchelsea's records is a set of small pieces of paper, each showing clear signs of having once been folded smaller, and each inscribed with the name of a liable resident. We do not know into what receptacle the slips would have been placed but they provide clear evidence of how the ballot was actually conducted.[12]

It was, however, by no means certain that any man whose name was drawn would have to serve. His first way out was to pay a substantial fine. If he could not afford that there was a co-operative arrangement whereby all eligible contributed ten shillings and sixpence or one guinea, according to their means, into a central fund from which substitutes would be enrolled at a cost of £30 each. In Rye, for some reason, the contribution was double this amount.[13]

One annual return for Winchelsea shows that, of those whose names were drawn, William Sargeant was unavailable because he had been appointed Overseer of the Poor, William Humphreys had left Winchelsea before the ballot took place and another man, unnamed in the document, on hearing his name called immediately ran away. Only Edward Ticknor, who presumably could afford neither the fine nor the contribution towards a substitute, was chosen and enrolled.[14] At least Ticknor would have the consolation of not having to serve abroad. The oath of loyalty made the Militia an early form of Home Guard by requiring the recruit to declare '… I will faithfully serve in the Local Militia of the Cinque Ports, the two Ancient Towns and their Members within Great Britain for the defence of the same… so help me God.'[15] A later version is more specific, referring to: 'Great Britain and Ireland or in the island of Guernsey, Jersey or Alderney for the defence of the same.'[16]

Others who were balloted might well already have obtained exemption through a medical certificate which they carried for protection when needed. Abraham Claise had one of these. Henry Sutton, surgeon, certified that Claise was 'incapable of serving His Majesty as a soldier by reason of not being able to discern objects at a greater distance than twenty yards.' Fisher Clark, miller, was amusingly described by the same physician as being 'lame of the left arm' but the word lame may have had a wider meaning than currently.[17]

All these potential loopholes and evasions made this method of recruitment of extremely limited value. When the Lord Warden's committee met to consider the relative success of the various ports in raising their quota Winchelsea was found originally to have enrolled all three but one man had deserted, one was listed in the column headed 'Deficiency' and one, or his substitute, was actually serving. This one-third success rate was surprisingly good. Of Dover's requirement of 97 men only five were serving, of Deal's 30 none at all. One of Hythe's ten enrolled men was already dead, one had been discharged and six had deserted. Only Faversham beat Winchelsea by a fraction having six men serving out of a requirement of seventeen.[18]

When it came to volunteers rather than conscripts the situation was remarkably different. Winchelsea provided No.4 Company of the 3rd

(9) A Martello Tower at Winchelsea Beach submits to the sea.

Battalion, Cinque Ports Volunteers. Armed with 'brown bess' muzzle-loaders and bayonets they were dressed in scarlet coatee with yellow facings and silver cross-belts bearing the crest of the Cinque Ports.[19]

Winchelsea's 1803 list of volunteers to serve in the event of an invasion shows equal enthusiasm. It contains 174 names, many of them above and below the ages of eligibility for the ballot. The social mix is far greater. Among the volunteers are Rev. Drake Hollingberry aged 60, who offers to serve in any way useful. Edwin Dawes, gentleman, aged 54 who reports that he is already enrolled as a volunteer in the London ward of Broad Street but offers his four horses and his cart for the public service. Richard Stileman who was later to buy 'The Friars' and will soon become important in our story was listed as aged 15 and at school in Chelsea. Nevertheless he would serve if needed. There were many who volunteered as riflemen, among them Richard Maplesden aged 52, a shopkeeper who lived in German Street, offering this service if it was felt proper. Others felt they could be of use as pioneers (labourers) or as drivers of sheep and cattle and conductors of waggons, or offered to serve with their horses and carts. Thomas Easton, maltster, was more specific and suggested his usefulness as 'Conductor of Waggons with women and children.'[20]

These men's suggestions about their potential service arose from their prior knowledge of the original plans which had been drawn up in the event of Napoleon's invasion threat being successful. The policy was basically a scorched earth one; to impede the enemy by abandoning the area and removing wherever possible the means to sustain the invaders. All the civilian population were to leave. Women and girls over seven and boys between seven and fifteen were judged to be capable of removing themselves. Women with babies at the breast and children under seven would require help. The bakers agreed to keep at least a ton of biscuits available in reserve for the population. All corn-mills were to be rendered useless by breaking cogs, burying millstones and cutting off windmill wings. A complete census of cattle, sheep, oxen and horses was carried out so that they could be rounded up and taken inland. The aim was that all human civilians and all stock should be at least twenty miles from the coast.[21]

Later it was realised that such a policy would be almost impossible to put into practice and alternative instructions required the magistrates remaining in the area to sit daily after any invasion to take action and receive reports. All trustworthy 'housekeepers and others' were to be encouraged to enrol as special constables who would be required to quell disturbances, convey offenders to prison and supply escorts for military service. They would also conduct night patrols, supervise and control the use of public houses under the direction of the magistrates and bring before the bench all unknown persons who could not give a satisfactory account of themselves.[22]

This anxiety about aliens, obvious under invasion threat, persisted long after that threat had gone. It is best reflected in a document issued by the government on 1 January 1812. The complaint was that even though aliens had been clearly told that their residence for longer than 24 hours 'in this Kingdom' without obtaining a licence was illegal, many were failing to comply. The suspicion was that they were entering the country in an attempt to assist prisoners to escape. The letter draws attention to Section 30 of the Aliens Act which states that all householders receiving aliens to lodge or reside in their homes for more than 24 hours without complying with the provisions of the act were liable to a fine of £10. It would appear that the 1427 Ordinance issued by the Mayor and Corporation of Winchelsea (see p.14) now had a national successor.[23]

While the instructions for the civilian population were being carried out the duty of the military, regular, conscripted and volunteer was clear. Orders were issued that from the moment an enemy landing was attempted the most vigorous discipline had to be enforced. The troops must be assembled with maximum speed and the prime objective was to throw the enemy back into the sea while he was at his weakest. The British soldiers' fearsome reputation for bold use of the bayonet meant that there could be no doubt of their success. Nevertheless a morale-boosting qualifying clause was included to say that if they were overwhelmed by superior numbers and had to fall back they must be ready to turn and make a stand at the earliest opportunity. Flight was unthinkable.[24]

The volunteers had little chance of formal military training and the regulars would have been scornful of their value in such circumstances but at least one colonel realised that their existing skills might be extremely valuable and took the timely practical line of encouraging their training by gamekeepers and poachers rather than by drill-sergeants.[25]

But the invasion never came. Life in Winchelsea went on with the garrison in residence for a long time. Their presence caused numerous frictions and social problems. The billets for the men were in Barrack Square which thus acquired its present name; formerly it had been Bear Square and Factory Square. The houses facing east which can still be seen were supplemented by a similar and longer row in what is now known as Mill Road, making a substantial L shaped block. The Mill Road part fell into disrepair later in the nineteenth century although two remaining dwellings are discernibly part of the one-time barracks. The married men and their families lived on the ground and first floors. On the top floor, running the whole length of the block, was a large dormitory for the single men. The cellars were used for storage. Some officers requisitioned or built houses in the town, others lived at the Court Hall for which the corporation was paid the generous annual rental of £80 by the Barrack Master General.[26]

It must have been a turbulent and sometimes violent cheek-by-jowl existence. The Rev. Drake Hollingberry, he who volunteered his services at the age of 60 in any way needed, was responsible for this teeming parish. Miss Maud Peel, one time owner of The Armoury, researched in detail the background to Winchelsea's involvement in the Napoleonic Wars. She pays tribute to the rector's tireless work. He faced constant change with one regiment regularly succeeding another and all needing to be cared for. He would have observed constant activity on the drill square, the daily playing of the military band in Castle Street and the reviews held near Camber Castle.[27]

Mr. Hollingberry's perpetual involvement is reflected in the parish registers where are recorded 56 marriages of military personnel, the baptism of 212 children born to serving fathers and 72 soldiers buried in Winchelsea between 1794 and 1814.[28] The majority of the deaths would have been of those returning wounded from the Peninsular Wars with the squalid conditions in the barracks almost certainly a potent additional cause.

During this time the soldiery frequently annoyed the citizens as is shown in the records of the grand jury, a body which received and made complaints about abuses observed within the town. On 15 January 1805 they accused the barrack master general of failing to complete the building of the privy at 'the new huts.'[29] The following year when the privy had been completed the barrack master was in trouble again for allowing sewage from it to run into the street.[30] Later it was the commanding officer who incurred their wrath by allowing sentry boxes to stand in the public high roads.[31]

It is hardly surprising that considerable numbers of the births mentioned above were of illegitimate children whose fathers were soldiers and whose mothers were Winchelsea girls. The most notable of which details survive in the parish records was the case of a Major Winter. He was accused in a sworn statement by Jane Coppinger of being the father of her unborn child. The major, eager that this indiscretion should not come to light, refused to have a bastardy order made against him or to give an indemnity to the parish authorities accepting financial responsibility for the child during the time that it might be a charge on the parish. Instead he offered a cash sum of £120 to discharge his liability for all time. This was accepted and paid. The major thus managed to retain his anonymity and avoid scandal but the child was stillborn. He then took quite a different view of the matter and demanded his £120 back. The vestry meeting, presided over by Rev. Mr. Hollingberry, involved as always, resolved firmly that it would vigorously defend any action brought against it and seek to keep the money.[32] Many would feel that Major Winter received his come-uppance.

The parish authorities were harassed in numerous other ways during the garrison's occupation of the town. One fairly constant problem was the fraudulent claiming of benefits by soldiers' wives for non-existent children. The punishment here, though, was physical rather than financial. Convicted offenders were treated as vagrants and publicly whipped.[33]

Such claims sought to exploit a system which had struggled for a long time to cope with poverty within local communities and was, in Winchelsea, to be stretched to its limits by the strains which followed Wellington's glorious victory at Waterloo and the end of the Napoleonic Wars.

7. POVERTY AND THE WORKHOUSE

The returning soldiers' need of employment and the agricultural depression which plagued the country caused bitter resentment among the labouring classes of which Winchelsea's post-war population was almost exclusively comprised, and invoked no little sympathy from those whose position was financially more secure. 'The long awaited peace brought little to the victors but suffering and misery' parliament was told, 'thousands of people are living on twopence halfpenny a day.'[1] It may well have been many tens of thousands.

How, then, could a small community like Winchelsea cope with such a situation? For the administration of the poor laws the town still stood alone. The union of rural parishes with a view to greater financial resource and security came only when the Rye Union was formed after the Poor Law Amendment Act of 1834. Meanwhile the parish of St. Thomas's had to manage as best it could.

Of actual agitation resulting from this deprivation Winchelsea saw little. The fury fuelled by such injustice came to a head in 1830 with the 'Mobbing Winter' during which many magistrates were dragged from their beds to read the Riot Act. There was, however, an example of these problems at nearby Brede. In November of that year the rector met local farmers at the Red Lion. The farmers were anxious to achieve a major reduction in the poor rate so that they could pay the increased wages demanded by the angry mob outside. The rector, equally anxious to have enough money to meet the parish's commitments, refused any reduction. '[In] the uprising which followed, the parish overseer was run out of the village in a cart.'[2]

In Winchelsea, too, the rector was expected to lead and he was joined by prominent citizens who would naturally assume such public duties as the responsibility for poor relief. They were trying to administer a system with its roots in a statute of 1388 which took stern action against vagrancy and required beggars to remain where they were. This was refined in the seventeenth century to establish that poor relief should be provided only in or by the parish of a pauper's birth or legal settlement. 'An industrious worker for whom there was no work in his own parish was thus prevented by law from going in search of it unless he could fulfil conditions beyond his power.' These included renting a house valued at £10 per annum or obtaining a surety to cover any costs which might be incurred by his new parish.[3]

Not surprisingly this led to numerous disputes between parishes, actions to prove the place of a person's birth, service or employment and unseemly removal of paupers to the parish which was allegedly responsible for them. Sometimes they were as speedily returned. Later came the dreaded workhouse system to which so many were confined.

One safety-valve during the period we are considering was emigration. Despite hardships easily equivalent to those of the earlier pilgrims who had sailed from Winchelsea, many left the town and the area, particularly for Australia and America, attracted by stories of unrivalled possibilities and the availability of land. Later in the century this trickle became a flood. 'Letters sent home from Australia gave the impression that it was a land of opportunity and that settlers were needed. Queensland was a colony with some sixty thousand people and in a short time in early 1864 nearly fourteen hundred more English settlers arrived.'[4]

One of Winchelsea's best documented examples of the earlier departures is recorded in the minutes of the vestry meeting held on 20 February 1829 presided over by William Lipscomb, formerly private tutor and chaplain to the Duke of Cleveland, patron of Winchelsea's parliamentary seats. Lipscomb was later to become one of Winchelsea's shortest-serving mayors, twenty-one days being his total in office. The meeting was anxious to support Samuel Easton's wish to emigrate to

(10) Mariteau House as painted by Mary Jane Denne, the owner's daughter – early nineteenth century.

America with his wife and eight children. Despite the prospect of losing financial responsibility for ten people the committee members were cautious. The advance of a sum of £60 was agreed but in return Mrs. Easton had to sign away her £15 annuity to the parish for four years. A further £10 was to be provided so that the family could have clothing for the journey and the overseers of the poor were to seek legal advice as to whether such an advance could be made on a majority decision or whether a unanimous vote would be needed. The actual voting is not recorded.[5]

Such departures naturally lead to interesting returns. W.R. Easton was born to a later generation of the family at their home, 2, Friars Road, in November 1891. He lived there until he was twenty one when he, too, decided to emigrate. In the early 1970's William Easton paid a nostalgic visit to the town of his birth and was shown round his old home by Mr. Robert Goldie. In his letter of thanks, addressed from 4104 East Edgewater Place, Seattle, Washington, he wrote, 'My early school days were in the little school [in St. Thomas's Street] they have just pulled down. In later years I went to the school on Mermaid Street at Rye. In 1912 I came to U.S.A. and expect here I shall continue to reside. There will always be fond memories for England and especially dear little Winchelsea.'[6] Many residents of far-off lands would similarly remember the nineteenth-century Winchelsea which could not support them.

The responsibility for the administration related to both those emigrating and those remaining fell to the overseers and assistant overseers of the poor. To qualify to be an overseer you had to be 'a substantial householder' with the support of three magistrates. The job was certainly no sinecure. John Woods and Henry Barham were appointed overseers for the parish of St. Thomas, Winchelsea in 1822. Their job description headed, 'The Instructions and Directions for the Overseers above referred to' runs to some 2,250 words. They were required to meet the churchwardens every month and to deal with all matters related to paupers within the parish. These included 'setting to work' all children whose parents could not support them and all adults having no means to maintain themselves. Where appropriate children were to be found apprenticeships. The overseers had full authority to provide workhouse accommodation. They must keep books to show all payments which had been made and they must return to their parishes of origin all persons deemed rogues and vagabonds or who had been convicted of larceny and were unable to support themselves. Critically they must also supervise the collection of the poor rate which provided the funds for their work.[7] The overseers were supported by assistant overseers who must be 'substantial housekeepers.' Presumably the distinction was that the overseer must be an owner while his assistant could be a tenant. David Laurence was appointed assistant overseer in March 1828. His job description is even longer. The actual accounting and the day-to-day administration lay in his hands and he was a paid official who put into effect the decisions of the vestry meeting.[8]

We have seen that the gentry, the rector, the churchwardens, with the overseers and assistant overseers worked together, often under difficult circumstances to provide for the needs of less fortunate inhabitants. There must have been forms of corruption involved; equally clearly the provisions were often only tardily forthcoming and not to the liking of the recipients. Winchelsea, though, provides good evidence of the system at its best, particularly in levying the poor rate.

On 9 November 1800 a vestry meeting was specially summoned to consider 'the present state of taxation.' The large amount of money needed to make payments in cash and kind to paupers and to maintain the workhouse was causing great concern but so was the way in which that money was raised. Complaints had been received from 'a number of land occupiers' who had to pay the poor rate and these were considered to be 'neither vexatious nor unfounded.' There were real problems and something must be done about it. It was therefore resolved to make a survey of all the land and houses in the parish. A fair and equitable rate of taxation must be fixed according to their relative values in so far as it was possible to fix these precisely. A similar survey conducted in a neighbouring parish by 'two indifferent persons'(!) had been unsuccessful and in order to be scrupulously fair it was decided to set up two separate committees. One would be responsible for making the assessments. Its members were to be six carefully selected leading citizens with the help of Messrs. Blackman of Hooe and Griffiths of Bexhill, professional valuers. When the work was completed appeals would be heard by Messrs. Denne, Hollingberry and Marten as the second committee.

The assessment was due for completion by Sunday 14 December when it had to be affixed to the church door. Following publication, the committee of appeal would meet on 22 December. 'The Camber Lands', still Winchelsea's responsibility, were included and certain assessors were allocated to deal with the houses there. The committees met in private, 'that a serious and minute investigation of all circumstances may take place with the least interruption possible.' A member had to declare any interest he might have had in a property under consideration.

This timetable of work was strictly adhered to and, although Mr. Denne could not serve on the appeals committee because of other commitments, the remaining two members were deemed competent on their own as they could always call on advice from the professionals if needed. The very detailed record of this work concludes with a vote of thanks to those of both committees, 'for the faithful discharge of the duties imposed upon them and for the great care and attention they have manifested to obtain an equal and fair valuation of the land and houses of this parish.' All within two months. What a wonderful example of real local government at work![9]

The resulting rating assessment would still have been in use for the accounting year from

Easter 1815 to Easter 1816 for which I have carried out a detailed study. The first and most startling information which emerges is that during that period the parish of St. Thomas's, Winchelsea raised no less than £1035. 7s. 7¾d. to provide for the needs of its poor. Of this £914. 12s. 0d. came directly from the ratepayers. It hardly needs pointing out that that was an enormous sum of money in those days. Rates were collected three times during the year, once at four shillings in the pound rateable value and twice at two shillings. There were one hundred and ninety-two separately rated properties including houses, shops, stables, fields, gardens and land. The amount actually accruing from each collection was quite substantially reduced by the existence of six empty properties and house occupation by no fewer than thirty-six paupers who were not required to pay. The lists indicate that the main centre of poverty was 'the Square', now Barrack Square.

When the rate was set by the Vestry Meeting at two shillings in the pound the largest individual amount, £15. 2s. 0d., was paid by Samuel Southerden who lived at Camber and owned most of the land there. The highest amount paid for property without land was £2. 10s. 0d. for 'a house with garden, coach house and stables' (Mariteau) by Richard Denne. The smallest amount, sixpence each, was paid by William Martin and Thomas Osbourne who shared a garden. It is quite clear from the figures that the 1800 re-valuation had placed a very high premium on land rather than buildings. George Bray, for example, paid eighteen shillings for his house, garden, lodge and stable but, separately, £7. 18s. 0d. for a farmhouse, barn, lodge and several pieces of land including Pear Tree Marsh. This is further emphasised by the rating of five landowners who did not live in the parish and are listed as 'out-dwellers'. They paid between them, on nineteen pieces of land or marsh land, £63. 17s. 0d., a very high proportion of the total of £177. 7s. 0d. received from the second two shillings in the pound collection.

Of the payments made by the parish during the year by far the largest amount was spent on maintaining the workhouse and providing for its residents. Of this, (the figures are approximate) £117 was spent on bread and flour; £39 on meat; £45 on general and grocery supplies such as mops, brooms, tea, vinegar, matches, candles, sugar, soap, cheese, and butter – snuff and chamber pots are also included; £70 on clothing which included supplies of various types of material together with breeches, trousers, jackets, frocks, tailoring, alterations and washing; £21 on the provision and mending of boots and shoes and £20 on supplying and delivering coal. Additionally, bricklaying and carpentry work on the fabric of the workhouse cost £120 and Francis Bellingham, surgeon, was paid £24 for 'attending the sick and administering proper medicines excluding venereal and inoculation of the Small Pox and Cow Pox.' One considerably less expensive account was received from George Haisell who charged £2 for shaving paupers and cutting their hair. Haisell himself is listed in the rate book as poor but I have not found any record of payments made to him other than this.

Twenty-nine paupers who were the responsibility of the parish of St. Thomas's who did not live in the workhouse but had homes in Winchelsea or elsewhere, received regular weekly payments varying between one shilling paid to Master Tapp and six shillings paid to Mrs. Tilden of Dover and Mrs. Foster. A further twenty-six residents received casual relief when in difficulties including, most commonly, when 'out of employ' and when sick and also 'for a coat', 'when lame', 'at the time of her lying in' etc. Other less usual payments included £1 charged by Mr. Walker for 'a coffin for Mrs. Booth's child', four guineas paid to Mr. Griffiths of Bexhill for a detailed survey of the workhouse, ten shillings charged as expenses 'for taking Mrs. Breeds to Northiam with Order of Removal' and five shillings paid to an unnamed 'Poor Man whose Wife was left at the Poor House sick.' A touch of thoughtfulness is recorded by the entry 'The [workhouse] Children's Pence and Box Money – Eleven Shillings and Sixpence'.

Although much remains to be done, I hope eventually to make available my detailed transcription of these accounts which might be of interest to those wishing for information on either social or family history.[10]

One of the officers later responsible for these complex financial arrangements was Charles Arnett who served as assistant overseer in the 1820s and was succeeded by David Laurence. Unfortunately Arnett's career in Winchelsea ended in controversy. The minutes of the vestry held on 20 February 1829, the same meeting that helped the Eastons to emigrate, recorded, 'The chairman to write to Mr. Arnett, the late assistant overseer, to liquidate the balance of certain errors standing against him [in his accounts] and informing him that legal proceedings will otherwise be resorted to.'[11] It would appear that some resentment had been created by the way that Arnett had left to take up a similar position in Bexhill, and that this was a form of revenge. Anyway, the protests which the chairman's letter drew in response certainly ring true. Arnett wrote pointing out that the accounts he submitted while in Winchelsea were approved by the churchwardens, the vestry meeting and the magistrates. Now it was being alleged by those opposed to him that they had been inaccurate. That was wrong and he owed nothing. To add insult to injury, Mrs. Arnett had never had her leaving present![12]

Charles Arnett was appointed in August 1823. One of the conditions of his appointment was that he would live in and presumably supervise 'the poorhouse' of which his wife was to be matron. On payment of two shillings and sixpence per week their son was allowed to live there as well. Arnett's salary was £15 per annum. He was certainly highly thought of initially for William Hunter and William Woollett were each willing to provide a security bond of £50 for him.[13]

Looking back over a period of more than 170 years our gratitude to Charles Arnett has to be that he kept his files meticulously. Throughout his time in office he carefully retained all the letters he received from Winchelsea's paupers living outside the parish, sometimes asking politely, sometimes pleading and sometimes demanding payments for their support. To these have been added some letters passed to him by his predecessor and some which were received after his departure. The whole archive provides a wealth of human interest reflecting the most extreme hardship, occasionally tragedy, frequently distress and at times, unexpectedly, humour.[14]

There is obviously not room here to deal with all this in detail. We will therefore concentrate on the most poignant case which the correspondence reveals, that of John Eagles, a Winchelsea man by birth who had lived there until at least 1820.[15] He first wrote from Newgate prison on 2 March 1827. He regrets to report his unfortunate case. He is confined in Newgate under sentence of death. The parish of his most recent residence, St. Saviour's, Southwark, where he has been living at 22, Free School Street, has been supporting his wife and children aged two and four months but will no longer do so. His wife's brother who lives at Minster on the Isle of Sheppey would keep the family for one week but please will St. Thomas's, parish of his legal settlement, send money or after that week they will have to return to Winchelsea. Surely it will be cheaper to aid them while they are in London. Eagles eagerly asks for a reply by return.[16]

He wrote again on 16 March saying he had been visited by a man representing Mr. Dawes of Rye (a solicitor) who confirmed that Eagles belonged to Winchelsea. St. Saviour's would have nothing to do with him. He again pleads for help. If his wife is forced to come back to Winchelsea he will have no one 'to wash and do for me as I have no friends in London.' He thinks it will be a month before he knows whether he will die or be transported. If the latter he hopes friends will assist him in raising enough money to take his family with him.[17]

By 18 April things were getting desperate. His wife is seriously ill. She is going into decline and the doctor says she should go to Mr. Gooding, her brother. Please will Winchelsea allow sixpence a week for her and her two children. The parish officers on the Isle of Sheppey would pay on Winchelsea's account. 'I expect the report every hour so that I shall know my fate. If, please God, my life is spared of which I have hopes and I should go to bottany bay [sic] and [my] wife's health gets better, with my friends' help I will get her over to me as that is a good country and healthy.'[18]

Mr. Tonge of Sittingbourne wrote to Charles Arnett on 22 May, 'Feeling great interest for the family of poor Eagles now under sentence of death.' Mrs. Eagles is deeply distressed not only by her illness and lack of money but also by the constant fear of hearing that her husband is 'left for execution.' Surely in these circumstances Winchelsea could send her some relief, 'Eagles is racked with the idea of leaving his beloved wife and children unprovided for.' A letter offering hope would help him make his peace with God.[19]

It is indicative of the harshness of the times and the system that this story has no happy ending. On 29 May Charles Arnett replied. He had deliberately waited until sentence had been carried out on Eagles. It was expressly understood that the £3 already sent to Mrs. Eagles was to pay her expenses home to Winchelsea. The vestry had forbidden him to reply to any letter seeking weekly pay. Winchelsea workhouse particularly needed a woman like Mrs. Eagles and now that her husband was beyond help that was where she must go.[20]

It was a one pound note which cost Eagles his life. After leaving Winchelsea he took a job with the Post Office working at their sorting office in the parish of St. Mary Woolnoth in London. On 1 May 1826 three letters addressed to A.W. Roberts Esq., M.P. passed through that office for delivery; two contained money, only one of them was delivered. That afternoon Eagles paid a debt of two shillings and sevenpence halfpenny and purchased twopence worth of gin from William Evans, landlord of the Queen's Arms, Great Guildford Street, Southwark. Evans wrote Eagles' name on the back of the note he paid with before passing it to the brewery's clerk. The note's number had been recorded before despatch to Mr. Roberts. The detailed account of the evidence is followed by the stark legend 'GUILTY – DEATH Aged 35'.[21]

And so to the workhouse to which Mrs. Eagles was forced to return. In Winchelsea it stood at the foot of Strand Hill and is now known as Strand House. The poverty prevalent in the town was the cause of a major decision made on 4 May 1800. The workhouse as it then existed was far too small to contain 'the number of poor that the parish officers might find it convenient to place in it.' It was therefore proposed to buy an adjoining property for the sum of £40. The appalling condition of the original building and the cost of linking it with the new one meant that another £80 had to be spent. As the poor rates were substantial, 'because of the high cost of corn and other provisions' the churchwardens and overseers were empowered to borrow £125 over five years to help them over the difficulty.

Even the provision of this extra accommodation would not help an unfortunate man by the name of Ceinon. The minutes of the same meeting record that he was afflicted with a cancerous disorder which was too offensive for his residence in the poorhouse and the parish would therefore suspend the usual by-law and pay the rent for his home.[22]

The 1800 extension was only adequate for a quarter of a century. On 22 April 1825 even more space was needed for Winchelsea's poor and another adjoining house, occupied at the time by Thomas Wimble, was purchased for £80 from Mr. Chatterton who was mortgagee and was empowered to sell it.[23]

For a time during the period between these two enlargements Winchelsea's workhouse was the responsibility of a formidable woman by the name of Mercy Eastman. Her story was declared to

(11) The former Winchelsea Workhouse – late nineteenth century

the magistrates when at the age of '70 years and upwards' she wished to establish her claim to be the responsibility of the parish of St. Thomas's. Sadly this may well have been because she was about to end her days in the workhouse of which she formerly had charge. Mercy Eastman was born in the parish of All Saints, Hastings and worked as a servant, her last position being with Miss Sally Crouch of St. Clement's parish, who paid her three pounds a year. She later followed her trade of mantua maker (dressmaker) and married William Eastman, a hairdresser. They had one son, with whom at the time of her statement she had lost touch but she thought he was living in Peru. All she knew about her husband's place of settlement was that he had been apprenticed in London whither he had returned but she had refused to go with him. Instead she moved to Winchelsea with her son, William, and pursued her dressmaking trade. She was mistress of the workhouse for about seven years, receiving £4 per annum in wages plus board and lodging for herself and her son. When William left her pay went up to £12. After leaving this employment she continued as a dressmaker in the town and having never had any other place of legal settlement, claimed to be chargeable to the parish in her old age.[24]

Of the regime which Mercy Eastman ran, or that of Charles Arnett and his wife, we know nothing. We do, however, know that the workhouse brought considerable custom to local traders. A number of Poor House Books, listing their dealings, have survived. Messrs. Robert and George Jenkins supplied meat. Other accounts were for the provision of oats, flour, milk, yeast and beer, for shoemaking and mending. Income was received from employers of workhouse boys.[25]

During the time that active use of Winchelsea's workhouse was drawing to a close the overseers were asked to reply to official inquiries seeking information. These responses are not dated but were almost certainly written during 1835 when the government was struggling to implement the Poor Law Amendment Act of 1834 in the face of enormous variations of practice within parishes. A study of them shows that the overseers were asked to produce the rules and regulations governing the workhouse. There were none and they can be imagined attempting to compose as convincing an explanation as possible:

> 'The poor house is frequently visited and the verbal instructions from time to time given to the mistress being duly attended to and the inmates being few in number and no work of any kind being done in the House (except occasional outdoor work on the roads) it has not appeared necessary to have any written Rules. We can conscientiously state that the poor have not to our knowledge or belief any cause of complaint.'[26]

Replies to other questions show that until 1831 'indoor' paupers were maintained as a family in the House but at that time the practice of having a housekeeper was stopped and the inmates began to receive an amount each week for their maintenance. This proved a great advantage to the parish through a substantial reduction in the poor rate. The overseer's statement of the current situation is most revealing:

> 'There are four indoor paupers who are old and infirm and are allowed a weekly sum of four shillings each out of which they maintain themselves. There are also two lads who are allowed to earn enough to maintain themselves but are lodged in the House and there is a little child for whom two shillings a week is allowed. And besides these there is a family consisting of husband, wife and three children – the husband can only partially support his family and the wife is allowed four shillings per week to act as Mistress in superintending the Poor House and she has two shillings a week allowed in coals and candles and the three children are allowed to lodge in the House. Occasionally a sum is allowed to the indoor paupers for clothing. £20 per annum is allowed to a surgeon and apothecary for attendance on the Paupers of the Parish and medicine. The amount of money expended for the Relief of the Poor for the year ending Lady Day 1834 is £   .' [the amount has not been filled in].[27]

The document goes on to explain that able bodied men with three children may receive the price of half a gallon of flour per week with an increase if there are more children and that allowances are occasionally made for the purchase of clothing when children go into service. Casual relief is sometimes given to men out of work in winter, either as a cash payment or by allocating them work on the roads.

The transactions and arrangements which were common at that time are well represented by one example taken from the letters received by the overseers:

15, Nile Street, Brighton
27th November 1837

Gentlemen,

You have a lad named Henry Hoile in the Winchelsea Union Workhouse who was put there by a person of the name of Crouch at the Five Houses, Winchelsea. I beg leave to inform you, Gentlemen, that I am uncle to the boy and am living at Brighton, as above, and if you will send the lad to me I will take care of him. I am a basket maker by trade and shall be glad to have the boy and hope you will do me the favour to send him the first opportunity.

I am, Gentlemen, your obedient servant,

John Hoile

Someone else helped by writing the letter but he has countersigned it himself: 'I have sined my name John Hoile that I have received the Boy save.'[28]

When, after the Poor Law Amendment Act, Winchelsea no longer had to provide its own workhouse, this became the responsibility of the Rye Union of parishes. The buildings were situated at the top of Rye Hill. 'To the able bodied but unfortunate labourer it deals out a harsh and unmerited degree of severity and punishment.' This included 'separation of men and women, restrictions on leaving the premises, limited visiting and hard manual work. One man, shaved for the first time on the orders of the matron is said to have cried for days.'[29]

Many writers have spoken of the dread with which all the poor viewed the prospect of finishing their days in the workhouse. Ford Madox Ford graphically wrote of a workhouse near Lyminge as 'the house of them that failed. Of all the many hideous erections in the neighbourhood it is the most hideous, the most comfortless in appearance, the last home to which we've "all got to go" as the country people say. The saying is as true as it is sad. Those down near the earth slip inevitably into this atrocious place.'[30]

Margaret Muggridge recalled her feelings, as a child in Rye, about that unlovely institution and its residents:

'At the top of Rye Hill, what is now Hill House Hospital, was a workhouse and on Saturdays the inmates were allowed out. The men wore corduroy trousers and jackets and hats like Mr. Quaker Oats, and they had a little donkey cart in which they collected the bread. I well remember them about the town. We always felt ashamed of the workhouse, as if it was people's own fault being reduced to that, but I'm afraid it was the fate of many old people, unless they shared the home of some of their family who could ill afford to help them. Some people went to the workhouse for the winter months and worked on the land in the summer time.'[31]

With responsibilities thus handed over, the sale of Winchelsea's workhouse was eventually agreed as a fund raising measure at the request of the Guardians of the Poor of the Rye Union on 14 May 1840.[32] The building had served its purpose for a long time. It would be a forlorn hope to believe that it was anything but another example of the unyielding severity which the workhouse system represented over a wide span of this country's history.

8. SMUGGLING

As we have seen, the conclusion of the Napoleonic Wars inflicted upon Winchelsea an increasing burden of poverty. Many of the male populace, seeking ways of breaking out of this demeaning situation, turned to smuggling where comparatively large sums could be earned in return for considerable risks. They were living in the right place! At that time Winchelsea stood independent of the county of Sussex because of its status as a Cinque Port, a privilege granted centuries before in return for ship-service. Its liberty or area of jurisdiction stretched from Pett coastguard cottages to Jury's Gap including parts of the parishes of Pett and Icklesham and all of Camber. There could hardly have been a more opportune, remote and convenient stretch of coast for carrying on 'the trade.' The men of Winchelsea entered into it with enthusiasm.

The earliest personal recollection we have of the operations of the smugglers in Winchelsea was written by Richard Stileman recalling the days at the end of the eighteenth century before he purchased and rebuilt The Friars. He remembers that living in the same row of houses as his family were Widow Holt and his great friend, her son Dick. Dick's father had been a smuggler and must have been followed by his son for the widow was often to be seen 'weighing out the tea and tobacco with a sort of mysterious anxiety, desiring Dick to keep the door shut whilst she was thus engaged in the snug closet.' Her only condescension to the presence of the revenue officers who lived opposite was to place a cover over any bottle she might be using and to require her visitors to conceal parcels as they went in and out of the door. Those were the days of a cosy relationship between the excise and the smugglers, the former being so grossly understaffed as to be impotent. Co-operation therefore became the norm and a riding officer would receive his share of two or three tubs out of a hundred brought ashore. Thereafter 'for better appearance he was seized, his hands tied and laid on his back in a friendly way... the officers were neighbours and friends and wished to live and let live.'[1] Urgent requests for military reinforcements to be a real deterrent fell on deaf ears.

Richard Stileman and Dick Holt may have lived in Friars Road; representatives of the customs certainly did. Charles Stephens had lived at No.2 for a considerable time serving in that capacity and Mr. R.J. Davis, the owner of White Cottage on the corner of Friars Road and Back Lane recalled in 1937 how, when the property was being repaired and old wallpaper removed, early in the twentieth century, a preventive officer's diary was found painted on the wall. This showed where he had gone on different days to prevent smuggling. Friars Road would have been a particularly convenient place of residence because the customs watchtower was on the ruins of Greyfriars Chapel.[2]

The considerable presence of excise officers within the town may be part of the reason why the use of the thirteenth-century cellars for storing contraband, part of Winchelsea's folklore, is not supported by any documentary evidence known to me. Some would certainly have been suitable but many have such visible and obvious entrances in the streets that, at least while preventive work was being done conscientiously, to use them would have been folly. Much more discreet stores were needed.

The fear of discovery which increased as preventive measures were strengthened was matched by the ordinary resident's fear of defying the smuggler. E.W. Skinner, physician and mayor of Winchelsea, recalled being told stories of how smuggling was carried on in the early nineteenth century. He tells us that within Winchelsea's liberty it was a well organised traffic. Those who financed it were never seen – others took the risks. There were thought to be two active groups, the seamen who brought the contraband over from France and the landsmen who took charge of distribution to hides. For this purpose horses were frequently taken out of their stables at night and quietly returned next morning with a keg of spirits as an unsought recompense. The fear of violent reprisals kept mouths sealed.[3] One countryman, moving from outside Kent and Sussex to a farm on Romney Marsh, fell foul of a similar requirement. Soon after his arrival he received a note saying that his horses would be needed at a specific place on the coast the following night. Indignant and inexperienced, he failed to carry out this instruction. Retribution was swift. He was woken a few nights later when his garden gate was thrown through his bedroom window. On looking out he was 'greeted by a charge of small shot.' Next morning he discovered his horses ham-strung. In future he complied.[4]

Such incidents very seldom came before the courts but as enforcement improved Winchelsea's magistrates became busier. Documents dating from 1820 record that among the officers valiantly striving to carry out their duties to prevent smuggling was James

(12) The interior of Wesley's chapel where he would have preached powerfully against smuggling

Alexander McLeod, midshipman, who was in charge of a party stationed at Camber watchhouse. These men were from H.M.S. *Severn* and there was certainly no longer any suggestion of corrupt co-operation. Mr. Midshipman McLeod brought before Winchelsea's magistrates in the Court Hall on 14 March 1820 one Samuel Barber who had been seized between the hours of four and five that morning while carrying 'two kegs of spiritous liquors on his back.' Barber was fined £100, a vast sum, but this was remitted to £25 with the remainder payable should he re-offend within three years.[5] On 8 May McLeod had another success. The previous night he had arrested John Ockenden of Winchelsea who between ten and eleven o'clock had been 'attempting to work a certain boat near Camber Farm within the liberty of Winchelsea.' When taken he was actually lifting four tubs out of the boat. Ockenden was similarly fined but would not pay. He was then given the option of serving His Majesty in the navy. Wisely he turned the opportunity down. The magistrates were left with no alternative but to commit him to their prison, then in the lower rooms of the Court Hall, until the fine was paid.[6]

(13) The Roundel, used as a watchtower by officers of the excise, stood near the present site

Such committals caused the Winchelsea authorities considerable problems. In the same year Thomas Sylvester Keene complained bitterly to the mayor about 'the additional duties that are imposed on him as gaoler on account of the present commitment of smugglers.' His demand for more pay was referred to the magistrates.[7]

If it was granted it might well have been later reduced again for prisoners kept escaping. Later in 1822 poor Keene had to swear an oath before the magistrates declaring that Thomas Warden, convicted for revenue offences had unlawfully escaped on 8 April.[8] This would have caused the gaoler and the authorities particular anguish because two years earlier the escape of Pierre Joseph Masier, a Frenchman captured and convicted of smuggling, had led to an inquiry. Two solicitors from Rye examined the Winchelsea gaol in detail and found it to be insecure. The catches to the locks of the prison door were not of iron, the yard wall was in a dilapidated state and the 'buildings contiguous to the entrance to the prison do not form a sufficient barrier to the approach of persons from without.' The words 'from without' are firmly underlined.[9]

Later in the decade, whether or not still insecure, the gaol must have become extremely crowded. One gaol book, commencing in 1828, has 'Breech [sic] of Revenue' in the column headed 'crime' against the names of the first sixteen offenders. Other crimes incur a sentence specified in days but smugglers' committals are listed as 'During His Majesty's Pleasure' and last for up to two years. Like John Ockenden they probably could not pay their fines. Those confined included men from Ramsgate, Rye, Wittersham, Sedlescombe and Icklesham but only one from Winchelsea, George Buttenshaw, a member of a notorious smuggling family. In the absence of any notes about transfers elsewhere we must assume that before a major discharge on 23 January 1830 there were at least twelve men imprisoned in the cramped conditions of the gaol. Later that year two more were

'Removed on Board H.M. Ship.' Not an enviable end to their sentences.[10]

Throughout this period the trade continued virtually unabated and led to many violent confrontations. Typical was an incident in 1826 when 'a smuggling galley chased by a guard boat' was beached near Rye Harbour and proceeded to fire on its pursuers. When the men from Camber watchhouse hurried to the aid of their comrades and arrested one man, 'a body of not less than two hundred armed smugglers rushed from behind the sandhills and commenced to fire on the blockade, killing one and wounding another.' The smugglers were eventually driven off and their boat captured but they managed to save their wounded by carrying them with them.[11]

A similar earlier incident which led to what is known as the Battle of Brookland had also started when a large number of smugglers went to Camber beach at three in the morning, some detailed for carrying the contraband, others for fighting if necessary. When the alarm was raised a party of men led by three midshipmen attacked and pursued the smugglers inland to Brookland where there was a pitched battle leading to the deaths of one midshipman and four smugglers.[12] Of course not all major incidents ended in violence. Kenneth Clark records that in 1829 'seventy or eighty men, each carrying two tubs, went through Winchelsea about four in the morning.' No doubt the residents disturbed by this procession remained cautiously abed.[13]

The violence surrounding 'the trade' was further reflected in a report made by the commissioner investigating Winchelsea's affairs prior to the Municipal Corporations Act of 1835. He noted that the number of inquests conducted by the mayor as coroner was 'greater than might be expected.' One reason was that smugglers were occasionally shot by the coastguards, another that 'several instances also have occurred of persons employed by the Government in the blockade service having destroyed themselves.' Clearly the pressures were much greater than in the times of Stileman and Holt described above. The quality of the men was poor, their continued service compulsory, their punishments excessive and some took the only way out. The commissioner, writing in 1833 or 1834, noted smugly, 'The system seems to have undergone a thorough change in this respect.'[14]

Sadly violence did erupt during the run which has given Winchelsea its place in the annals of smuggling. Edwin Nathaniel Dawes then in office as town clerk, told William Durrant Cooper, historian of Sussex smuggling as well as of Winchelsea, that Thomas Monk, 'a poor fiddler' of Winchelsea, was the last man to be shot in an affray between smugglers and the coastguard.[15] Monk's family lived in German Street and he was related to the Buttenshaws. Whether he was involved through the financial reward, the excitement of danger, or threats of what would happen if he did not help we shall never know, but Thomas Monk's presence near the mouth of the Rother on Sunday 1 April 1838 cost him his life. At a quarter to three in the morning a boat landed a cargo of spirits. All but a few of the barrels were being taken from the scene when the vessel, for some reason unknown, ran aground near an officer from the Camber coastguard station who was on guard. He was Henry Hyde, a young man petrified by the prospect of violent confrontation. He walked to the end of his beat keeping the boat in sight but failed to raise the alarm. His colleagues 'observing a great number of smugglers and among them several armed men' hurried to the scene and firing commenced. At about the same time Hyde was joined by his superior, Mr. Wren, who according to the newspaper account was already wounded. They made their way across the shingle to easier walking on the sand. Hyde recalled when giving evidence to the inquest next day that he heard whistling and shouts before the men went by, saw three or four flashes and heard gunshots. When he approached the party of about fifteen smugglers he began firing his musket. The firing was intense. The smugglers, supremely confident in the face of their enemy, gave a good account of themselves. One cried, 'Load and fire away, if a hundred come we are their match.' Hyde's relief when the men made off across the beach and the firing ceased can well be imagined. Conscientiously persisting in his duty he went to the boat and pulled it ashore. There was just one tub left aboard. Then he noticed something floating in the water nearby – the body of Thomas Monk.

The gathering of a jury and holding an inquest on the following day seems commendably efficient. The impartial composition of the jury is, however, thrown in doubt by some remarks made during the proceedings, presided over by the mayor of Winchelsea as coroner. One juror commented, 'He had no firearms; he wasn't dead when I left him.' Another interjected, 'They were carrying and firing at the same time.' The jury having heard [and given!] evidence, viewed the body. After a short consultation they returned the verdict that 'Thomas Monk was on 1st April found lying on the seashore and having received a gunshot wound there languished and died but how or by whom such shot was fired the jury have no evidence to show.' Possibly not such a biased verdict as it might have been in the circumstances. Thomas Monk was laid to rest in St. Thomas's churchyard on 9 April.[16]

After this time the incidence of smuggling in the area began to decline. There were, however, interesting smuggling implications at a later inquest in 1842. This was conducted by the same Richard Stileman whose childhood friend had been the smuggler Dick Holt. The investigation was into the death of Charles Crompton whose drowned body was found near the mouth of the Rother. Crompton, butler to a Mr. Dawkins, had been seen with other servants of the same household to enter a boat at St. Leonards and make towards some French fishing boats. Witness William Shaw declared that he was watching through his spy-glass but 'I did not perceive that they had anything from them.' About a quarter past seven in the morning the same witness 'saw the boat upset.' At the time it was about a mile and a half from the French boats and the same distance from the shore. With intriguing understatement Shaw added, 'There appeared to be a little gust of wind at the time.' The jury, full of sound Winchelsea men, returned a verdict that Charles Crompton had been 'precipitated into the sea and accidentally drowned.'[17]

E.W. Skinner recalled being told as a boy by a man called Fellowes, grinder at Icklesham mill, how he used to lie awake when his brother was out with the smugglers listening to the shots. On one of those nights men were drowned trying to cross the Royal Military Canal when being pursued. Skinner also states that the last man who served a sentence in Winchelsea gaol for smuggling was called Field. He was stupid enough to be caught in broad daylight walking up Strand Hill with a sack over his shoulder carried in such a way that anyone could see the shape of the keg inside![18]

Winchelsea gaol book's last entry about a convicted smuggler was on 8 September 1868 when Captain Parker aged 40 of Winchelsea was fined eleven pounds thirteen shillings but not committed to prison.[19] It would have been only a little later than this that Anthony Eldridge of Winchelsea Beach, as a boy of only nine, drove a wagon from Pett Level to Battle – 'The load, ostensibly hay, concealed casks of contraband.'[20] The easing of the customs laws and the improvement of policing had reduced smuggling from a major wealth-generating industry for the people of the area to a comparatively petty criminal activity.

9. PARLIAMENTARY REPRESENTATION

Since the middle of the fourteenth century Winchelsea had in many ways been supported and sustained by the importance accruing from its election of two members to parliament. The decade which saw the death of Thomas Monk saw also the removal of this important right through the long overdue Reform Bill of 1832. Winchelsea's parliamentary representation had begun all those centuries before as a proud privilege; it ended in farce.

King Edward III initially recognised the importance of the Cinque Ports in the nation's counsels by granting each of them two seats in the House of Commons. Until that time Winchelsea's representatives attended only by invitation. The vital importance of the confederation and the powerful independence granted to the ports made their inclusion understandable and necessary. During three centuries Winchelsea properly elected its leading citizens who could speak on the concerns of the town related to those of the country. A glance at the lists of mayors and members for parts of this period shows as examples:

Robert Londeneys	Mayor 1364; Member 1369, 1373
Robert Badding	Mayor 1363, 1376; Member 1372
Robert Arnold	Mayor 1358, 1359; Member 1377
Thomas Silton	Mayor 1456; Member 1452
Robert Basele	Mayor 1476; Member 1473
Richard Davy	Mayor 1467, 1473, 1474; Member 1473
William Eglestone	Mayor 1554, 1559, 1560; Member 1554
Goddard Whyte	Mayor 1558, 1565, 1566, 1579; Member 1558
Adam Moyle	Mayor 1586-1588; Member 1586, 1588[1]

As the centuries passed and the importance of the town declined these duties were viewed as an increasing imposition by the corporation who felt that the effort and expense could not be justified. This feeling increased because Winchelsea was not involved in any financial debates, frequently the most important ones. Like the other Cinque Ports its privileges included complete fiscal independence.

The Lord Wardens of the confederation lost little time in taking advantage of this declining interest. Their office was a powerful one and its sixteenth- and seventeenth-century holders exerted increasing pressure on the ports to elect the nominees of the Lord Warden of the day. In some cases both seats came under his control, in others only one. The Lord Warden's position was strengthened because the official notice of forthcoming elections was sent to the ports through him. He passed the documents on with the names of his candidates. Winchelsea compliantly conceded the nomination of one of its members to the Lord Warden on 7 October 1597[2] but so far as we can tell never conceded both.

Since only the freemen had the vote, the key to the whole process of parliamentary elections lay in determining who were the eligible freemen, a decision depending on whether they were resident and paying taxes within the town.

The mayors had this responsibility for they were ex-officio returning officers and sometimes made controversial decisions which affected results. One of the best known cases of this kind was that of Paul Wymond, mayor in 1623. Wishing to be as secretive as possible Wymond issued the notice of a forthcoming election only during the night before it was to take place. Additionally he

deliberately failed to inform two freemen called Tilden.
When the corporation gathered next morning the
Tildens had heard about the summons and they
turned up, whereupon the mayor disqualified
them from voting on the grounds that they had
not been resident, one for five months and the
other for six, claiming the passing of a byelaw
in support of his ruling. After a considerable
rumpus the disqualified voters left,
announcing that they would have voted for
Sir Alexander Temple. The ballot then took
place. Wymond and seven colleagues voted
for John Finch, eight others for Temple. To
settle the tie the mayor gave a casting vote
for Finch and declared him elected. Uproar!

Understandably Temple protested and
the matter came before parliament. The
debate went extremely badly for the mayor. He
was declared to have given inadequate notice of
the election, to have disqualified two genuine
voters and to have exercised a casting vote to
which he was not entitled. Paul Wymond was
imprisoned by the sergeant-at-arms until Mr.
Speaker ordered that he should kneel at the bar of
the house and make acknowledgement of his fault.
He then had to do the same at Winchelsea in the
presence of the jurats and freemen before calling a

(14) Henry Brougham
M.P. for Winchelsea 1815-1830

new election. Wymond certainly did not lack courage and acted with absolute consistency. The
candidates were the same, potential supporters of Sir Alexander were once more disqualified and he
again declared Finch elected. Despite a further protest and inquiry, parliament, no doubt to
Wymond's intense relief, eventually confirmed the election and accepted Finch as the rightful
member.[3]

Such controversies constantly stained Winchelsea's record in election matters in those days.
Inderwick tells us:

> 'The Borough was twice disfranchised, once by Charles I on account, I think, of the
> quarrels of the corporation with the citizens and the officers of Camber Castle in the
> course of which episodes the mayor shot the member's dog and sent his principal
> supporter to prison; again under the Commonwealth, when Cromwell took away its
> two members and gave them to the large midland towns which were then
> unrepresented.'[4]

The Lord Protector was well ahead of his time. England had to wait another 180 years before
the electoral injustices which he recognised were put right. On the restoration of Charles II his
reforms were reversed and Winchelsea's seats restored.

Buoyed by the return of their votes, Winchelsea's freemen on one occasion broke their agreement with the Lord Warden and defied his nomination, an incident which outraged Samuel Pepys. The Lord Warden was no less a person than the Duke of York, later to become King James II. He required that Baptist May, Keeper of the Privy Purse to King Charles II should be elected for the seat he controlled. Unlike the vast majority of candidates in parliamentary elections May took the trouble to travel 'in great state' to Winchelsea to be present at the proceedings, a journey he must have regretted for instead of respectful subservience he was subjected to taunts and insults. The electors 'cried out that they would have no court pimp to be their burgess,' and refused to vote for him.

This, too, led to a parliamentary inquiry. The investigating committee, no doubt wishing to please, recommended that the election be declared invalid on the technicality that the mayor 'had not within the one year next before his election taken the Sacrament of the Lord's Supper according to the rites of the Church of England.'[5] The House of Commons, though, was more robust, refusing by a large majority to ratify this decision and declaring the other candidate, John Austin, duly elected. Pepys felt that the country must be going to the dogs. 'These are things,' he commented, 'which bode very ill.'[6]

After 'the glorious revolution' the Lord Warden's influence over Cinque Ports elections was ended as corrupt and both Winchelsea's seats fell under the control of the Treasury which operated a system whereby they were held by supporters of the government of the day. The Treasury's own candidates, frequently customs officers employed in the area, were appointed as freemen and exercised a decisive majority of votes. Before this influence was clearly established another mayor, Edward Marten (1700), natural successor to Paul Wymond, was imprisoned by parliament because he was 'guilty of threats and indirect practices in order to procure an election of members in this present parliament for this town.' Despite strong support from the Treasury whose instructions he was carrying out, the unfortunate Marten was also ordered to be dismissed 'out of all employments in His Majesty's Customs.'[7]

One story of corruption dating from about this period must surely be apocryphal but is too good to leave out. Published in the *Sussex County Magazine* as a reader's letter over the pseudonym 'Busy B' it records how towards the end of the seventeenth century Winchelsea's freemen, fearing that a forthcoming uncontested election would yield less profit than usual, sent a deputation of eight to Sir Edward Frewen of Brickwall, Northiam. These worthies assured Sir Edward that, if duly rewarded, they would all vote for him were he to become a candidate. Thinking eight to be a good majority in a constituency with only thirteen voters Sir Edward agreed. The delegation members kept their word, voted for Frewen and divided their second votes four each between the other two candidates. The remaining five voters, in no way committed, cast their votes for both the others. Result: the two former members nine votes each, Sir Edward Frewen eight. 'Thus he lost his seat and his money and was laughed at all round the neighbourhood.'[8]

One of Winchelsea's least prepossessing members represented the town, presumably with the blessing of the Treasury, soon after Marten's time. He was George Bubb Dodington who later became chief adviser to Frederick, Prince of Wales, in the time of George II; after the prince's death transferring his attentions and influence to his son, the future George III. The 'gross and ugly' Dodington who fawned and ingratiated himself in court circles, was particularly sought after by the new heir's mother who thought he could help her find ways of improving her son's education. Dodington appeared willing and capable to give such advice but the principal motive for his involvement was the acquisition of a peerage to go with his great wealth. This ambition he later achieved as Lord Melcombe.[9]

The Treasury's influence in Winchelsea which had been challenged in the days of Edward Marten was eventually ended through the activities of Arnold Nesbitt who, while acting as the Treasury's agent, acquired so much land in Winchelsea and the surrounding area that his personal nominees to the freedom were able to outvote any other interest and Nesbitt took control. Arnold Nesbitt's career and influence produced a series of disputes and actions known as the Winchelsea Causes which make the problems of Paul Wymond and Edward Marten look comparatively small beer. The cases hinged on which of the current voters had been legally installed at the time of their appointment as freemen or had achieved such entitlement since. Sadly it is not possible to detail them here.[10] Despite persistent but eventually unsuccessful opposition by Edwin Wardroper, a Rye attorney who was the Treasury's Winchelsea agent, Nesbitt initiated the firm grip which the patrons held on the borough from this time until 1832. After his death his interest was purchased by Richard Barwell, an Indian nabob of dubious reputation who returned to this country at the age of 38 an exceptionally rich man and purchased Stansted House and Park near Chichester in West Sussex. Barwell had supported Warren Hastings on the Supreme Council of Bengal, thus 'enabling him to carry out the policy which contributed much to the building up of British India'. An opponent on the council described him as 'cruel, cunning, rapacious, tyrannical and profligate',[11] a reputation to which he later lived up, among other things as the begetter of illegitimate children in Stansted's parish of Westbourne.[12]

Barwell's partner, who joined him as M.P. for Winchelsea, later buying his share and assuming total control was William Harry Vane, third Earl of Darlington, later first Duke of Cleveland. His title when a member was Viscount Barnard but he was no great parliamentarian, more of a country gentleman, sportsman and huntsman. His opposition to the construction of the Stockton - Darlington railway was based on its potential destruction of a favourite covert. Racing was another great enthusiasm, his horse Chorister winning the St. Leger in 1831.[13] He was of local importance as the owner of Battle Abbey and his name remains current in Winchelsea through Cleveland House, Cleveland Cottage and Cleveland Place. Vane's influential patronage at Winchelsea and elsewhere – he controlled six parliamentary seats in the years leading up to the Reform Bill – was of vital importance considering his enthusiastic support for the reforming Whigs.

As we have seen the patron could control quite ruthlessly the number and identity of the freemen eligible to vote. Under this system the medieval qualification of a year and a day's residence, the payment of scot and lot and engaging in a lawful trade were abandoned. The mayor, who acted on the patron's instructions, simply vetoed any undesirable nomination or application. When the appointment of William Lipscomb, formerly the noble lord's tutor, was proposed the mayor wrote to the deputy mayor who was acting for him with the simple explanation, 'It is Lord Darlington's wish he should be elected.'[14] As reform approached agitation to extended the franchise increased. In 1830 Mr. Daniel Dawes appeared before the mayor and jurats who were the magistrates. A member of one of Winchelsea's most influential families he said that he had been born in Winchelsea and was the eldest son of a freeman. His credentials were indeed impeccable but Col. Barwell Browne, a supporter of the patron's interests, when pressed to give a reason for the refusal of the application, responded feebly, 'It is not convenient to admit Mr. Dawes.' To add insult to injury Dawes's relative, John Haddock Lardner, the town clerk, was refused permission even to enter the application in the official record.[15]

On 10 October 1774 the first personal patron, Arnold Nesbitt, was himself elected as M.P. for Winchelsea for the second time, in harness with one of the town's most interesting members, Charles Wolfran Cornwall, who rose to be Speaker of the House. Cornwall's appointment as

Speaker in 1780 brought favourable comment about his voice, figure and deportment but conceded that his family connections were much more important: Lord Liverpool was his brother-in-law. Cornwall's reputation as holder of his office is, however, dubious. He is said to have 'relieved the boredom of debates by fortifying himself with porter' and to have frustrated Pitt's far-seeing wish to arm the dockyards by giving his casting vote against the government. After Cornwall's death in 1789 it was spitefully written of him: 'Never was any man in a public situation less regretted or sooner forgotten.'[16]

William Pitt the younger, with equal foresight, also proposed parliamentary reform but was, as were a number of subsequent attempts, thwarted sometimes by the Commons and always by the Lords. When addressing the House of Commons on 7 May 1782 Pitt, while being generally cautious in attacking the rotten boroughs, drew attention to the pernicious influence of men like Barwell, mentioning particularly 'the newly rich such as the Indian nabob'. The division at the end of that debate which was lost by 161 votes to 141 was the closest to achieving reform until the eventual success of 1832.[17]

But the injustice of the large representation of the rotten boroughs as compared with the non-representation of the ever-growing towns and cities could not last for ever. Neither could the tenuous connection between the members and the places they represented. On one well known occasion William Wilberforce, a worthy member if ever there was one, is reported to have asked when travelling through Sussex for the name of the place he had just passed. On being told he remarked, 'Oh, Bramber. Why, that's the place I'm member for.'[18] Many Winchelsea representatives

*(15) Winchelsea Court Hall when in use as a prison and as it was when
the last of the town's parliamentary elections took place in the upper room*

must have had a similarly vague idea of the town which elected them.

A great step forward was taken in 1832 with the passing of one of the most important pieces of legislation ever enacted, not only for what it achieved in itself but also in paving the way for further progress. Winchelsea lost both its seats, coming initially within the Rye division, for her sister ancient town retained one member. Reaction in the area was varied. Hastings, which had retained both seats, celebrated noisily the extension of the vote to many more of its citizens. The church bells were rung, guns fired on Castle Hill and no fewer than six thousand people sat down to a banquet in Priory Meadows.[19]

In Rye there were also celebrations. Mr. Isaac Parsons was reported by the *Hastings and St. Leonards Observer* in 1898 as recalling that Col. de Lacy Evans, a supporter of reform, visited Rye and as he passed through Landgate Tower 'chains which broke as they fell were thrown at the gentleman's feet.' The crowd chanted 'Col. Evans came amongst us, broke our chains and set us free.'[20] The chains were those of the old Rye Corporation which had exercised tight control of the vote. Its last patron was Rev. George Augustus Lamb D.D. from a family with enormous influence in the borough.

In Winchelsea the excesses which had oppressed the people in parliamentary matters had been even worse. Horsfield describes election day in the years leading up to 1832. He records, as we have seen, that the members 'seldom had any communications with their constituents or with the town itself.' Those with the vote did not know until election day for whom they were to vote. On that morning a letter would be received by the mayor from the Duke of Cleveland's agent giving the names of those to be returned. When this was known the freemen were summoned to the Court Hall and 'the mummery of a nomination having been gone through' the worthies were declared unanimously elected. Since they were invariably not present two Winchelsea men employed by the corporation took their places and led a celebratory procession round the town. At each corner of the churchyard a salute of three guns was fired which Horsfield suggests as being symbolic of the burial of the town's freedom. The company then adjourned to a local inn for a celebratory election dinner, this in turn being followed by 'a dance for the wives and daughters of the respectable inhabitants.' Next day his worship would write to the members informing them of their election. He would invariably receive a gracious reply.[21]

Instead of expressing delight that this pantomime was ended the men of Winchelsea petitioned for the right to retain their parliamentary seats. This appeal came not from the mayor and the jurats but from the ordinary residents who had been methodically prevented from exercising that right for so long. Led by Richard Stileman fifty citizens of the town sent a petition to 'The Right Honourable Lord John Russell and the Right Honourable Lord Althorpe and others the Lords of His Majesty's most Honourable Privy Council.' They claimed retention of the right to share in the return of representatives to 'the Commons House of Parliament which was given them by Royal Charters in the Reign of King Edward I.' The dubious historical accuracy of this claim (the grant was by Edward III) in no way detracts from their totally justifiable complaint that they had been prevented from exercising their rights through 'the undue influence exercised by others who were strangers' over their corporation. This they felt to be deeply undesirable. While acknowledging that reform was overdue they urged the government to permit Winchelsea's continued representation. Supporting evidence states that the town's 'liberty' covered a wide area, cites the ship-service duty which led to the town's enfranchisement all those centuries before and points out the expense (£150 per annum) of sustaining the duties conferred on them by membership of the Confederation of the Cinque Ports.[22] Understandably, while ingeniously thought out, all this was to no avail.

Even if Winchelsea benefited little except by the interest its parliamentary seats generated, we are entitled to ask whether the country was so very badly served by such a system persisting for so long. In many cases the result must have been pernicious and corrupt but it is difficult not to conclude that, at least during the last quarter of a century before reform finally came, great benefits accrued from the service of those who were elected at Winchelsea at the whim of the Duke of Cleveland. He operated a meritocracy on the basis of his strong support for the Whig cause and the progress which he thus espoused.

The career of Stephen Lushington, a barrister who supported the abolition of slavery, petitioned on behalf of 'people of colour in the West Indies' and urged that they should be given the full protection of the law, promoted parliamentary reform and later supported the abolition of capital punishment, briefly touched Winchelsea when, vitally important to the Whigs, he was elected there after failing to secure a seat at Reading in 1830. True to his beliefs he went on to become the first member for Tower Hamlets and finished his career as Judge of the Admiralty Court.[23]

I cannot resist including here a coincidence of family history. Stephen Lushington's mother was Hesther, daughter of John Boldero of Aspenden Hall, Hertfordshire. Boldero was my wife's maiden name and she is descended from a branch of the same family.

A far better known national figure than Lushington was Henry Brougham who represented Winchelsea for no less than fifteen years. He most famously gave his name to the one-horse carriage popular in his day. Brougham was another leader of the Whig party, a constant supporter of reform and a personal friend of the patron. As an advocate he came to the public's notice through his robust defence of Queen Caroline at her trial in 1820. Here was a man of real if somewhat eccentric distinction, freed by the patronage of the duke, who provided his Winchelsea parliamentary seat, to serve his country in many ways. In 1830 he moved to represent the county of Yorkshire and in 1831 was elevated to the peerage, taking the post of lord chancellor.[24]

As agitation for reform built up there is an important entry in Winchelsea's court book dated 9 June 1826 when the mayor, jurats and freemen gathered at the 'Guildhall' to hear the precept of the Earl of Liverpool, Lord Warden of the Cinque Ports, requiring the election of two members to serve for Winchelsea 'in the Parliament to be holden at the City of Westminster on the twenty fifth day of June next.' Having received their instructions in the way already described they duly elected unanimously 'Henry Brougham of Brougham Hall in the County of Westmoreland [sic] Esquire and the Honourable Henry Grey, commonly called Lord Viscount Howick of Howick in the County of Northumberland.' In accordance with custom, to overcome the requirement that members should be resident, Lord Howick was elected a freeman.[25] He was the son and heir of Earl Grey. Howick's election at Winchelsea was a necessary safety net to ensure his parliamentary seat for a few days later he fought and lost one of the bitterest contests the county of Northumberland has ever seen.

Four years later Earl Grey became prime minister and led the country through the major crisis of reform. Churchill describes how rebuttal after rebuttal in the House of Lords led to the fall of Grey's government, to his re-election with a vastly increased Commons majority and eventually to impasse. No alternative government was available. The Lords were implacable. 'Feeling in the country became menacing.'[26] When eventually the prime minister and lord chancellor attended the king to press him to create enough peers to ensure a Lords majority for reform and at last obtained his agreement, a threat which was enough to carry the day, both had parliamentary connections with Winchelsea.

10. THE CORPORATION THREATENED

The loss of Winchelsea's members of parliament almost brought about the collapse of the corporation through the wilful action of its own members. However, before dealing with those events and the further threat which followed it is worth examining in general the responsibilities of the corporation during the first half of the nineteenth century and some of the personalities involved.

The chamberlain's accounts for Easter 1800 to Easter 1801 show that income was being received from money collected at the annual fair, from rental for the gaol house and the prison, from the annual licences of two houses and from the king's and town rents. After allowances to some rent-payers the total was £21. 7s. 5d. Expenditure was considerably greater, including salaries for the mayor's sergeant and the chamberlain. The town clerk's account for legal services was the largest amount at just over £19. A mason and a smith had their bills paid as did two labourers for cleaning a well. Two publicans received payments, presumably for corporation entertainment. A proportion of the king's and town rents was paid to Sir William Ashburnham, king's bailiff. There was a bill for land tax, expenses on postage of letters and acts of parliament, an allowance paid to Mary Evans, a soldier's wife, for an unspecified reason and gaol fees for Mary Clarenbold for whom Winchelsea probably remained responsible after her transfer to the House of Correction at Lewes. All this left a deficit on the year of £45.3s.0d. How the deficit was met is not clear. The patron may well have been responsible but the accounts, checked and verified by the corporation members each year, show only a steadily accumulating 'Balance due to the Chamberlain.'[1]

By far the largest part of the corporation's income came from the king's and town rents. Accounting for these became increasingly muddled, leading to a most detailed and methodical review in 1807. Amounts payable by various owners are meticulously listed according to the quarter in which their land was situated. Unfortunately there is no more exact way of identifying the property except where there is some clearly intelligible reference for the modern researcher as there is in the case of Thomas Lloyd Esquire who paid eight shillings and twopence for 'part of the Fryers formerly Pigram's since Holford's and late Mr. Barwell's and Lord Darlington's.' The problem is illustrated by an entry in the sixth quarter for George Stace whom we shall meet shortly: 'for a house and ground formerly Smith's late Haisell's.'[2] Identifying property only by its owners and former owners persisted until as recently as 1943 when the town clerk, Edwin Plomley Dawes, began adding the names of the houses and land to the official records. In the absence of plans, meaningful research relating older entries to present properties is almost impossible.

The history of these rents, now known as the queen's dues is obscure; the accounting and recording of their payment makes a massively complex study better suited to an M.A. thesis than a general account of this kind. I believe that the rents have their origin in the grant made to the corporation by Queen Elizabeth I but the early nineteenth-century corporation members, while happily collecting their nineteen pounds a year, had no documentary evidence of the basis for the payments.

For the fact that we are better informed we have to thank the aforementioned George Stace. As we have seen he lived in the sixth quarter which currently includes the properties between Alards and The Retreat, partially at least known as Cooks Green. Thanks to documents which have recently come into the possession of Winchelsea Corporation it is now possible to be more specific – Stace lived at The Retreat. He was a long-term Winchelsea resident whose variety of service to the corporation is unique. He is first mentioned in the records in 1769 when he was chosen by the mayor to be sergeant-at-mace. Additionally he was a constable, the water bailiff's sergeant and an attorney of the court of record.[3] More is said about these and the other ancient offices in Appendix IV. In 1771 George Stace was unanimously elected a freeman. The considerable significance of such an appointment has already been described – he became a parliamentary voter. We know that Stace owned his own house so the patron of the time, Arnold Nesbitt, would have no hold over him in that regard. But we also know that he was a grocer[4] and that he rented Cruttenden Field, three acres know as Tinker's Garden and part of the cliff from Nesbitt.[5] Possibly Stace's business premises were also the freehold of the patron. If he was prepared to do as he was told that would be quite enough to encourage Nesbitt to seek his appointment to the franchise. Stace obviously proved himself reliable for in 1790 he was further made a jurat in which capacity he served as a magistrate, deputy lieutenant and tax assessor. Quite remarkably in 1794 he was elected mayor, suggesting that he was prepared to support the Barwell/Darlington interest as well. His name just precedes the thirty-six year repetitive listing, usually in alternate years, of Darlington's puppet mayors who had little to do with the town. No other corporation member, certainly since the mid-eighteenth century and almost certainly previously has served in so many of its various positions. What we shall never know about George Stace is the nature of the influence he had which led him to be in private possession of the document already mentioned and generally known as 'Queen Elizabeth's Charter.'

At the mayoring ceremony on Easter Monday 1816, a few weeks before his death at the age of 73, he handed over to the mayor the original document listing the lands officially transferred by the crown to the corporation in 1586. These properties, previously owned by the Greyfriars, the Blackfriars, Farnecombe's Chantry and St. John's Hospital had been administered by the corporation, it would seem quite unofficially, since the dissolution of the monasteries. Much of the land had already been sold before this occupation was challenged by Thomas Talbot and Peter Smith, both of London, who claimed that these were concealed lands and obtained a crown lease. Talbot and Smith's interest had to be bought out for £150 and the corporation's acquisition of the freehold recognised by the issue of the crown grant.[6] When this document was so unexpectedly produced by George Stace it was agreed that its authenticity should be investigated as none present knew anything about it. Later, when it had been declared genuine, the town clerk was ordered to keep the grant in safe custody and to produce it annually at the mayoring to ensure that it was never again lost to the corporation.[7]

We do not know for how long that instruction was carried out; it certainly has not happened for most of the twentieth century but it may well be the origin of the tradition that the corporation's regalia is on display at all mayoring ceremonies. The 'charter' was deposited at the corporation's bank for many years until its transfer in 1993 to East Sussex Record Office for proper safe keeping with the remainder of the Winchelsea archives. The then mayor, Knightley Chetwood, took a great interest in the document at the time of this transfer and presented the corporation with a framed photograph of the first page which includes an original portrait of Queen Elizabeth I within the initial letter. This is now on permanent display in the Court Hall.

Winchelsea observes tradition in all things. The queen's dues, as they are now known, are still collected annually, at the present time by Neil Clephane-Cameron, sergeant-at-mace, acting on behalf of Bernard Dibble, chamberlain. He sends a notification to the householders liable and calls on them to collect amounts as small as 3p in some cases. The total remains at just over £19, no allowance for inflation ever having been made, so the income is of very little value to the corporation but all suggestions that the payments should be commuted in return for a capital sum have so far been strongly resisted. The collection of such an unusual tax from the properties listed in

Appendix VI is a charming survival which is warmly supported by the vast majority of those required to pay.

One further point needs to be made for the modern reader, particularly the Winchelsea property-owning reader. It is not possible to assume that because a house now pays the queen's dues that it stands on land transferred to the corporation in 1586. Payments listed under the names of owners rather than properties have grossly distorted the records. When an owner moved house or bought a second house, particularly in the nineteenth century, a period of eccentric accounting, the payments made were often continued at the new address or paid on one property rather than both. Thomas Turner, for example, in the later years of that century, after living at The Strand, purchased property in Mill Road, paying the total for both from Mill Road. I, too, have experience of this lack of continuity. When my wife and I set up our first married home at Cleveland Cottage, Friars Road in the late 1950s we should have been delighted to pay the queen's dues as did both adjoining properties. What had happened was that two of a terrace of three cottages had belonged to the Cooke family. One was destroyed by fire and Cleveland Place, an inappropriate Victorian villa, was built on the site. When Cleveland Cottage was sold, Mrs. J.C. Rogers, formerly Cooke, continued to pay the dues for both on Cleveland Place, Cleveland Cottage thus becoming lost from the records.

Having the dues and the town rents as its only income led the corporation to a crisis in 1822 when Henry Butler had just taken over as town clerk. It may be that the corporation's income from the patron had finally become inadequate or possibly the books kept by Butler's predecessor had not been handed over. Anyway he was thrown into considerable confusion because he was ordered to draw up the documents to raise a local rate and had no idea how to do so.[8] The town's membership of the Confederation of the Cinque Ports and its consequent exemption from county taxation permitted this. When such a rate was declared, notification was given to the churchwardens and overseers of the poor for the various parishes within the liberty. Their duty was to collect the money due from their area, along with the poor rate, and hand the corporation's part to the chamberlain who would in turn pass it to the treasurer.

The rate demands of the time show the uses to which this money was put, namely: repairing bridges and the gaol, expenses in connection with the gaol including the keeper's salary, the salary of the treasurer, the coroner's fees, 'the charges concerning Vagrants, Soldiers, Carriages, convictions and transporting felons and other general charges.'[9]

Butler was dismayed by the problem facing him. Fortunately Mr. Woods, a Winchelsea grocer and overseer of the poor, discovered that the town clerk of Hastings, Mr. Thompsett, being experienced in such matters, would be pleased to help, and this information was passed to Henry Powell, deputy mayor who would usually conduct day to day business at that time because the mayor was an absentee. Even this suggestion, though, brought Henry Butler anguish rather than relief.

He wrote on 9 July to Thompsett, grateful for the offer of help but deeply regretting his inability to ride to Hastings for a consultation:

> 'I would with the greatest alacrity could I do so but I really cannot by reason of the scurvy which broke out in my right leg the week after Easter [and] has occasioned me to be very lame ever since [so] that I cannot now without the greatest pain and torture get about my house.'

The letter goes on to imply that the magistrates are collecting a rate for the first time. They wish to make the order at the quarter sessions on 16 July. He pleads with Thompsett to send him copies of the appropriate documents by carrier and with disarming honesty concludes, 'I wish to curry the favour of the justices by an anxious attention to their wishes as I was only appointed their town clerk last Easter Monday.' Fortunately his Hastings colleague rose to the occasion, sent the required information for the very reasonable charge of one pound seventeen shillings and a rate was declared on 16 July as required.[10]

Not all parts of the parish were enamoured of this additional taxation. A complaint was later made about Mr. Southerden of Camber, an area then reaching the stage of wishing to establish its independence. It was Southerden's duty to carry out collection from the properties there. If he continued to fail to do so he would have to forfeit his 'goods and chattels.'[11]

With its finances thus secured the corporation moved towards the upheaval created by the Reform Bill. Viewed by the patron and his adherents, all possible interest there might be in the town was lost, even if by electing reforming members under the direction of their patron they had helped to bring this about. What could possibly accrue to them from supporting the affairs of so lame and insignificant a place? The rules of the day were that no meeting of the corporation could be considered quorate unless there were present the mayor or deputy mayor together with at least two jurats and two freemen. What could be simpler then than deliberately to absent themselves so that no corporation business could be transacted and no further trouble or expense be required?

The plan came into force on Easter Monday, 8 April 1833. Notice of the annual hundred court to elect the mayor for the ensuing year had been given in the customary way by 'blowing or sounding of the town horn on this present day at break of day.' At the appointed time of eleven o'clock in the morning the officers were in their place, there were probably a few members of the public, but from among the mayor, deputy mayor, jurats and freemen, just one, Jurat John Tilden. Fortunately for Winchelsea Tilden's colleagues had made no allowance for his tenacity or his determination that their plan should not work. Tilden came from a Winchelsea family and had spent his youth in the town, being listed at the time of the Napoleonic wars as a cripple boy, unable to serve. His father had been a freeman before him and it is likely that they were descended from the Tildens disqualified by Paul Wymond (see p.42). However determined Tilden may have been he was helpless in the face of his colleagues' absence. In accordance with custom he waited one hour and then declared the meeting closed, reconvening it for the same time the following day.[12]

Again the horn was sounded, again Tilden and the officers gathered. Unless they hoped to observe a row the public are unlikely to have wanted to endure another hour's boring wait. The result was the same, no business possible. At 'twelve o'clock noon of this present day the said John Tilden retired.'[13]

He then set about intensive lobbying in the town arguing the vital importance of the corporation's survival, of the continuation of its legal and local government functions, and of Winchelsea's independence which would otherwise be lost. No doubt he was most persuasive but his attempt to acquire a quorum of the former members was only just successful. On 25 February 1834 an assembly was held. The deputy mayor, Joseph Hennah, a long-time resident, attended as did two jurats, Tilden himself and William Lipscomb, and two freemen, George Hill and John Winstone. The impact of their decisions that day was to create a revived organisation assured of a future through the creation of no fewer than thirty five new freemen. In fact only sixteen of those named ever took up their freedom but the effect was the same. Tilden's plan had worked.[14] Life for the corporation continued as before except that control was securely back in the hands of the men of the town. The most important of those appointed on that fateful day was Richard Stileman. He had remained creditably aloof from the corporation throughout its period of patronal domination despite being a leading citizen and landowner. His story will be told in the next chapter. Tilden himself was rewarded with the mayoralty in 1835. Not until the involvement of F.A. Inderwick in the 1880s was anyone to have such a telling influence on the survival of the traditions with which this book began.

Although his report is not dated it was probably in late 1833, before the large influx of new freemen, that Commissioner D. Maude visited Winchelsea making inquiries which were among the preliminaries to the Municipal Corporations Act of 1835. Here was a further possibly fatal threat. Maude interviewed a number of the residents who expressed no interest at all in the corporation or the freedom, believing them useless since the loss of the parliamentary vote. Nevertheless he was eventually informed about the February 1834 assembly. His report defines the limits of the corporation's jurisdiction, lists the officers who are appointed annually and details the procedure for their election. While invaluable for the student these details are too long-winded for inclusion here.[15] The parliamentary background of the borough is explained together with the patron's control, and even the aforementioned attempt to kill the corporation off. The mayor's legal duties are seen as reflecting credit on the borough and are accepted as viable except that finding impartial juries may be difficult. Maude was puzzled about the constantly accruing debt owed to the chamberlain (see p.48) but concludes that he must have been recompensed by the patron even though this is not shown. Most ominously the commissioner suggests that the magistracy for the area should be combined with Rye. Commenting upon the king's dues and town rents he attributes their origin to the fourteenth century when buildings were constructed on waste land within the town. The chamberlain was 'from home' at the time of the visit and had apparently not been contacted since.[16]

This visitation must have left the new and enthusiastic freemen full of apprehension. The removal of the bench to Rye would have emaciated the town's civic duties so much that the corporation might well have ceased to function so soon after John Tilden's valiant efforts to save it. We should remember that in those days there was no incentive at all arising from membership of the Confederation of the Cinque Ports. The Cinque Port barons had not been permitted their 'Honours at Court' to attend the coronation of King William IV and would not be for Queen Victoria. Meetings of the confederation were extremely rare, the longest gap in the nineteenth century being twenty-nine years.

The publication of the bill's contents would therefore have been a great relief. Of the Cinque Ports, Dover was included in Schedule A. It was to be administered by a Commission of the Peace with its parliamentary boundaries retained until altered by further legislation. Hastings and Deal were similarly provided for. In Schedule B, not to have a Commission of the Peace but to retain their municipal boundaries were Faversham, Folkestone, Hythe, Rye, Tenterden and Sandwich. Of Winchelsea and New Romney there was no mention at all.

Since Clause 1 specifically stated that 'the Laws, Statutes, Usages, Charters etc. included in the Act are repealed only for those Boroughs specifically mentioned in Schedules A and B', Winchelsea went on serenely unaffected towards mid-century, led, initially at least, by Richard Stileman.

11. THE STILEMAN STORY

The Stileman family were originally 'Yeomen of Otford' in Kent, moving to Winchelsea at some time in the middle of the eighteenth century. Seven out of eight generations had a boy christened Richard which causes considerable confusion.[1] Richard of the fifth generation (1739-1795) was certainly settled in Winchelsea in time to have his vote as a freeman recorded in 1766.[2]

Richard his son (1787-1844) appears to have enjoyed a relaxed upbringing for the times and to have had the run of the town. In his later years he recalled that he was 'too much and too often with servants and learnt much that was evil in their company.' With the boys of Winchelsea he got on well, claiming their leadership as 'Colonel of the Regiment of Boys'. He felt that boys, like monkeys, learnt vulgar words and dirty tricks by imitation but there was little malice in them. The servants, though, were 'bad instructors'. Stileman's freedom as a youth included being allowed:

> 'to ride Old Drag to the fields in the evening – help with the hay – drink clear water off my hat from the clear ditch. I was never made miserable by being obliged to keep myself clean and was out in almost all weathers.'

During this apparently idyllic existence he came frequently upon the stone-deaf barber whose inability to communicate easily had prevented John Byng from obtaining the local gossip (see p.18). This was Thomas Haisell, a highly skilled man of his craft, specialising in the wigs then so fashionable. Taken into Haisell's shop by his father one day young Richard saw 'among the various appendages in this magazine of powder and soap' a small flaxen wig. The barber, joining in a joke originated by Stileman senior, said he was sure the wig could be made suitable for the boy. This became an obsession with Richard who dreaded the appearance of such hateful headgear. Unfortunately he was unwise enough to tell the servants and a cousin who was staying about his fears. This prompted the arrival of a large box carried by a servant declaring, 'Here's the wig come for Master Richard'. From the box was produced a large, brown frizzled wig which had actually been borrowed from an old man who lived at the end of the garden. The boy was distraught, clung to his mother and was only consoled when the wig was seen being returned to its owner.

Haisell's deafness caused Richard Stileman senior almost equal anguish on one occasion. He wore 'a fine curl like a sausage on each side of his temple. "Take care of my curls, Tom," he instructed. "Yes, sir," said the barber and immediately cut one of them off.'

This evocative reminiscence bemoans the decline of the art of such men as Haisell:

> 'How terribly the tonsor's trade has declined since those days! All gentlemen wore powder, [there were] few who had not their hair dressed every day. I can see the old barber going his rounds with his antique box containing the various engines for torturing the human head into a state of propriety.'

Richard Stileman who lived with his family in a former row of four cottages one of which was still occupied by smuggler Dick Holt and his mother (see p.36) appears to have relished the thought of one day acquiring a grander home. His earliest memory of the house he coveted was the vivid spectacle of:

> 'the solitary figure of a beautiful eagle perched on the window of the Friars ruin... He added a real terror to the awe which invested the precincts of the chapel. When from a position of perfect stillness he thrust his head forward, spread his wings and uttered a shrill cry he made one's young heart jump and one took care to keep a respectful distance.'[3]

(16) The Friars (Greyfriars), shown to the left of the chapel ruins, before Richard Stileman's reconstruction…

These ruins stood in the grounds of The Friars, a house which had been made notorious by the reputation of two former owners, the brothers George and Joseph Weston who were immortalised by W.M. Thackeray in his unfinished novel *Denis Duval.* The criminal activities of their early lives which included extensive fraud, obtaining money by threats (when chief constable of Manchester!), highway robbery and smuggling were set aside when they bought The Friars and settled down to enjoy the life of country gentlemen. So eminent and God-fearing did they appear that George even became churchwarden of St. Thomas's.

However, there was one chink in the armour of their new, anonymous respectability, George had an instantly identifiable 'deformed thumb which was rather like a crab's claw'. This characteristic of the former highwayman was known to a sheriff who spotted it one day and followed the brothers to church, waiting with his men until George and Joseph emerged, bibles in hand.

There followed a violent, exhausting and dramatic chase eventually ending in their arrest as far away as Lewisham. Sentenced to death they were imprisoned at Newgate, escaped, were recaptured and finally were taken, 'kicking and struggling and biting their captors… to the gallows at Tyburn and there hanged' on 3 September 1782.[4] *The Gentleman's Magazine,* however, reported their end much more sympathetically and 'contained a full account of their penitential behaviour at the execution'.[5]

Such ghosts did not deter Richard Stileman. On 27 February 1813 a relation, George Spilsbury, wrote to his brother, 'I am rejoiced to hear Stileman has accomplished his wish of buying The Friars at last – has he thought of peopling it with Stilemans at present?'[6] He may well have done for the following year he married Sarah Curteis. Their family of four sons and six daughters would soon 'people' The Friars with a vengeance.

Richard had ambitions to improve the house which stood in forty-six acres of parkland and in 1819, when one source suggests that there had been a serious fire, he set about knocking it down and building afresh, using many of the same materials. The original design shows, with a few alterations, the castellated manor house which we see today. The architect, J.B. Rebecca, was also responsible for the gatehouse which still stands although recently extended. He labelled all the drawings 'Richard Stileman Esq., Friars, Winchelsea, Kent.'(!)[7]

Having achieved this major development Stileman settled down to the life of a country squire, his wealth and position making him a natural leading figure in the community. He would have nothing to do with Winchelsea Corporation while it was under the thumb of the patron, thus barring him from the local magistracy to which as the principal landowner he would normally have been appointed. He did, however, become a county magistrate, hearing representations from citizens of the eastern part of Sussex. In this capacity he would seek to resolve the problems brought to him by compromise between the parties, calling in the local constables if an arrest were necessary. A serious matter which he could not sort out he would refer to the quarter sessions at Lewes, which he attended.

The complaints were made when he was sitting alone and keeping all his own records. Details have come down to us in a carefully preserved book in Stileman's own hand, providing a wide variety of examples of the atmosphere of life in his times.[8]

During the period covered, 1819-1827 and 1836, the most common problems were violent

...and after. (17)

assaults (he records 63 allegations), underpayment and non-payment of wages (41) and theft (22). The items stolen include four geese, a dog, fruit from orchards, a cart harness, a quantity of hop poles, a fence post, house faggots, a sandy coloured greyhound, part of a hedge, one silver watch, quantities of standing timber and barley, ferrets, a razor, a piece of calico print and a pair of half boots. On one occasion there disappeared from Northiam workhouse 17 pounds of cheese, 6 loaves of bread and several pounds of sugar.

Among the less usual representations made to Stileman were those of riotous assembly, desertion of children, refusal to make provision for a family, refusal to pay the poor rate, dangerous driving, threats of injury, obstruction, verbal abuse, wilful damage and absconding from employment arranged by the parish officers.

The indignation and resentment of those who approach the county magistrate seeking justice and recompense spring from the simply-worded pages. On 23 October 1820 Henry Peckham, a gatekeeper from Beckley, reported how at eleven o'clock on the previous night when he was in bed several panes of glass in the windows of his toll house were smashed. When he emerged to open the gate he found Joseph Filmer of Rye 'with two carts and a whip and stick in his hand'. Peckham later learned that Samuel Green, also of Rye, had been lying in one of the carts. He asserted that nobody else was in the area at the time and he 'verily believes' that Filmer and Green broke the windows.[9] Unfortunately in none of these cases do we learn the outcome so whether the culprits were charged and the windows paid for remains a mystery.

Carts such as those demanding passage through Peckham's tollgate caused numerous problems elsewhere. George Atwell of Winchelsea reported that he was driving one belonging to Thomas Hoad in Dumbwoman's Lane when it was 'run against' by another driven with 'negligence and misbehaviour' by James Whiteman, a carter working for Mr. Woodhams of Udimore. The cart Atwell was driving was 'broken to pieces.'[10]

Bad driving of this kind caused serious injury and provoked a strong complaint from Martha Stocks, a widow of Rye, about a man from Playden whose surname was James. He, she insisted, had violently driven two horses on a public footpath between Leasam and Rye 'whereby Jane Russell about 9 years of age was much hurt by one of the horses running over her'. The lives of 'other of His Majesty's subjects' were put in danger. This was a case of mistaken identity for Stileman has written at the foot of the page 'Not the Person'.[11]

Henry Freeman's complaint of 4 March 1836 reminds us of the responsibilities of the parish officers. A pauper, Maria Freeman, presumably no relation, had been placed as a servant in his household from Lady Day 1836 for one year. She consented to this arrangement and entered his service but on 24 February she absconded without any notice, taking with her the clothes provided for her by the parish officers.[12]

Perhaps less serious, although not to the complainant, Mary Croft, was an incident on Sunday 2 April 1826 when 'some persons maliciously threw a stone down the chimney of her cottage'. She hurried out and saw Thomas Neves and George Foster running away along the road. Challenged they denied doing it, adding cheekily that if they had they would do it again. Mary Croft who, in common with many of her day, signs with a cross, adds, as did Henry Peckham, that there was no one else in the area at the time.[13]

The most sinister entry in Richard Stileman's court book is dated 2 December 1823. Louisa Brooman represented to him that she had been unjustly accused by Mrs. Willard, a shopkeeper from Udimore, of stealing two sovereigns. When she denied this Mrs. Willard threatened, 'to lay her under a fit of sickness until the day of her death unless some recompense were made'. Witchcraft at work![14]

Stileman supplemented his public work as a county magistrate by service to the town as chairman of the vestry meeting of the parish of St. Thomas. In this responsibility he displayed a sense of fair play and compassionate understanding where it was merited. One letter in this vein, sent on 7 September 1827 apologises for his inability to attend a meeting that morning but seeks the co-operation of his colleagues in considering the case of 'Mrs. Philly [Philadelphia] Tree' who appears to be in need of further help from the overseers of the poor because her daughter, who came to Winchelsea to nurse her, is now also ill. 'From her kind and excellent character [she] is well worthy of more than common attention'.[15]

This characteristic consideration encouraged those in need to approach him, hopeful of a sympathetic hearing. Lucy Kite wrote from 'The Preventive Boat, Auchmithie, by Arbroath, North Britton' [sic]. She explained how she and her family have 'since leaving home' [Winchelsea] been required to move frequently at great expense, so much so that she and her husband can no longer afford to take the children with them. Her brother would 'take the boy off the parish' if anything could be paid to clothe him. She pleads with Stileman to intercede with the parish authorities for the payment of the children's allowance a little longer for otherwise her husband is 'resolved to send them home'.[16]

We naturally hope that Stileman helped for that would have been in character, although he could be sharp if crossed. On 19 November 1824, writing from The Friars and regretting that he cannot attend the vestry meeting because of 'the very damp weather', he sets out the case of a man named Richardson who intends to apply again to the parish for help for his boy. Stileman can see no reason why this man should be given any priority but he would not have troubled his colleagues except that Richardson has misrepresented what Stileman recommended at the previous meeting, claiming that he had been told to ask his employer, Mr. Southerden of Camber, for an increase. What Stileman actually said was that if *the boy* did not receive a fair remuneration he should ask for more. Southerden's wages were 'as fair and high as any in the neighbourhood'. On receipt of such a letter the vestry meeting's decision was virtually taken.[17]

Richard Stileman's relationship with Winchelsea Corporation was generally remote at this time because of his failure to become involved. Exchanges between them are, however, occasionally illumined by the records as when, on 4 April 1820 J.E. Wright, town chamberlain, wrote on behalf of the Mayor, Jurats and Commonalty of the Ancient Town of Winchelsea, then as now the corporation's full title, requiring him to reinstate two pieces of land, one at Monday's Market and one near New Gate, which Stileman had fenced in with fields of his own without the corporation's permission as owners.[18]

It is not clear whether the two incidents are connected but on 19 April 1824 Richard Stileman was granted by the corporation a lease on a small piece of land, part of Monday's Market adjoining the king's highway. The lease was for 500 years at an annual rental of 'six pence of lawful money'. That lease is still in place, 3p per annum being paid by the owners of Greyfriars, as the property has been known during most of the twentieth century. (See also Appendix VI.)

We have few opportunities to picture Winchelsea as it was in those days through the eyes of contemporary observers. Stileman is a welcome exception, as we have seen, and so, very briefly, is James Rouse who said of Winchelsea in 1820, 'Such is the state of dissolution to which this once flourishing town is reduced that the grass grown in the streets (though they are all paved) has, on some occasions, produced £4 per annum'.[19] The corporation seldom failed to seize opportunities of this kind to make a little on the side.

And so we come to the Reform Bill and the subsequent Assembly of 24 February 1834 (see p.51) which eventually enabled Richard Stileman to take his rightful place in the Winchelsea community and lead it through the next ten years serving as mayor five times and deputy mayor three times. He died, in office as mayor, on 10 October 1844 aged 57, just twelve days after the death of his beloved wife.

The Richard of the next generation became principal of the London law firm Stileman, Neate and Toynbee. It was his younger brother, Major Robert Curteis Stileman who was elected mayor for the first time within fourteen years of his father's death and was to lead Winchelsea, with a grip as firm although perhaps more benevolent than that of a parliamentary patron, for fifty years through the remainder of the Victorian era and almost to the end of the Edwardian.

(18) The Greyfriars Eagle – late nineteenth century

12. WELLS AND WATER

It is noticeable in the previous chapter that Richard Stileman when wandering the Winchelsea area 'could drink clear water of my hat from the clear ditch'. While such opportunities existed they surely exceeded the availability of fresh water in Old Winchelsea. Although the records are comparatively silent on the subject the large number of clean water sources around the hill of Iham must have been a vast improvement on attempts to extract water through shingle and sand so close to the sea.

Cooper states that water was also scarce at that time in Rye and lists the six wells which so amply supplied New Winchelsea. They were the Pipe Well at the foot of Ferry Hill, St. Katharine's Well on Strand Hill, the Strand Well overlooking the tanyard, destroyed by a cliff fall in the 1840s, the Friars' Well at the foot of the cliff near Greyfriars, the New Well outside New Gate and St. Leonard's Well at the foot of the hill below the former windmill site in the north-west corner of the town.[1]

Winchelsea's best known late twentieth-century well at the foot of the hill, Queen Elizabeth's Well, also sometimes referred to as St. Katharine's Well (the names are confusingly interchanged) is missing from Cooper's list. It stands at the foot of Spring Steps, an ancient steep track which led originally from the town to the quay. The clue to the omission may be not only in the name of the path but also in a report made to the corporation as recently as 1964 by Austin Blomfield, a well known architect from Rye. Calling it Queen Elizabeth's Well he describes how a brick arch had been constructed over it by Messrs. Collins under his supervision and 'The so called "well" has been cleaned out and there is about three feet of water, deep enough to drown a small child, so I advise that bars with chain link fencing attached be put high enough to prevent any child falling in.'[2] This advice has only recently been followed again by the corporation. The first phrase quoted above clearly suggests that this has always been a spring rather than a well. Corroboration comes from the county divisional surveyor's anxiety in 1953 to persuade the corporation to stop the water overflowing and damaging the steps;[3] also from the evidence that a licence was issued in 1877 to Mr. Joseph Davis permitting him to pipe the 'surplus' water to his land on condition that the work was done at Mr. Davis's expense.[4]

The best known of all the wells in Winchelsea legend is St. Leonard's Well. Tradition has it that if you drink of its waters your heart remains in Winchelsea and there you will eventually return. It would have been quite difficult for the Jessup brothers thus to drink when they visited in the early 1950s for after giving the well's position 'in the meadows underneath the north-western hillside just beyond the windmill,' they describe it as 'fenced with barbed wire and its noisome water almost covered by watercress and overhanging brambles.'[5] An admittedly rather brief visit which I made in 1995 showed the track marked on old maps as 'Road leading to St. Leonard's Well' to be a true sunken Sussex lane, gouged out by constant use when muddy. Although where the well should have been there was an area still soft and damp after weeks of dry weather, of the structure there was no sign.

Ford Madox Ford varies the legend by saying that 'whoso drinks of St. Leonard's Well will never rest till he drink again.'[6] When resident in Winchelsea he persuaded his literary associates Henry James, Stephen Crane, W.H. Hudson and Joseph Conrad all to drink in this way. He does not explain why he should wish them not to rest until they drank again, presumably they were supposed to be too anxious to return to Winchelsea and adds rather oddly, 'They are all dead now.'[7] We must assume that St. Leonard's Well was not to blame.

All Winchelsea's public wells were at the foot of the hill, an appalling inconvenience for the ordinary people of the town; the wealthy, of course, sank private wells on their land. It was therefore the cause of much gratitude and celebration when Thomas Dawes Esq., a leading citizen and benefactor who lived at Paradise, later known as Hiham House, offered to provide at his own expense a more convenient well. This is the one still to be seen in Castle Street and the date was 1851 which, as a loose chronological peg, leads us into the second half of the nineteenth century. The provision of this facility at that time comes as something of a surprise to those who assume it to be much earlier, particularly those who have read of its vital importance to the town because it was the only well within the walls when the French were attacking.

In fact it was on 7 January 1851 that the corporation met to consider Mr Dawes's offer. Eager to accept they resolved:

> 'that a piece of ground commencing at the distance of twelve feet from the northern extremity of the western wall of the garden occupied by Robert Coker Nash Davies Esq. [Periteau House] and running twelve feet towards the south and extending ten feet deep towards the highroad shall be appropriated for ever for the purpose… of making a well for the free public use and enjoyment of the inhabitants… without anything being paid now or hereafter for the same. The said well to be constructed at the expense of the said Thomas Dawes and to be hereafter kept in repair without any expense to the Corporation of Winchelsea.'

Presumably such a resolution was adequate in those days to acquire land for nothing. It remains the basis of the corporation's claim to own the site.

After the construction was completed the citizens were anxious to show their appreciation. A public meeting was held at the Court Hall on 28 October attended by the mayor and fourteen residents. A committee was set up to seek subscriptions for a testimonial. By 18 November when a further meeting was held only seven inhabitants joined the mayor but enthusiasm for the project remained high. The sum of nine pounds fifteen shillings and sevenpence halfpenny had been collected. They would buy a silver tankard. Yet another meeting on 25 November, with the attendance slightly up, approved the design and the inscription: 'This goblet was presented to Thomas Dawes Esq. on the – day of – 1851 by the inhabitants of the ancient town of Winchelsea as a token of their gratitude for his having at his own cost constructed a well in Castle Street and given the same to the public of the said Ancient Town for their use for ever.' The presentation was eventually made on 3 December. Residents seem to have been readier to subscribe than to attend meetings for the list of those who contributed contains 38 names, the final amount totalling ten pounds fifteen shillings and a penny halfpenny. Among those included were Mr. R.C.N. Davies and the Misses Stileman, giving the largest amount, one pound, two members of George Stace's family, Mr. Thomas Legg, Mr. E.N. Dawes, town clerk, a relation of the donor, Mr. George Haisell, grandson of the deaf barber, who gave one shilling, and, charmingly, the schoolchildren who collected one shilling and sevenpence halfpenny. No doubt they were grateful that they would no longer be sent down the hill for water.[8]

The part of the corporation's resolution which acquired the land has been fully successful, the part which said they would be required to spend no money in future most certainly has not! The accounts show that as early as 1856/57 William Stace was paid for work on the well on no fewer than nine occasions. These running repairs included providing six links in the chain, repairing the swivel pin, 'grubbing up the well buckets', and eventually completely replacing the chain.[9] By 1888 the pumps had to undergo major repair and restoration including the replacement of frames and bearings, fitting new guides and guide plates and providing a new galvanised rising main. The total cost was eighteen pounds eight shillings and ninepence, a considerable sum.[10] This valuable amenity is thus shown to have been used extensively up to that time, if not for a great deal longer. In fact the corporation tried in 1892 to persuade the Rye Rural Sanitary Authority to take over responsibility for the Town Well. This was refused with advice that as the works were out of repair the well should be closed and locked up.[11]

The corporation's maintenance, despite the original resolution, has included a costly recent restoration. The well is now a much photographed tourist attraction which displays two notices, one reading:

'CAUTION

All persons are strictly cautioned against throwing anything whatever down the town well, as the police have orders to report immediately any act of nuisance so that the offenders may be prosecuted.

Dated the 11th day of July 1872.

By order of the Magistrates.'

and the other:

'Notice is hereby given that the well is to be closed at 7 o'clock in the evening and opened at 6 o'clock mornings and to be closed all day on the Sabbath.

By order of the Mayor'

The Sunday closure sometimes caused surprise and even ridicule. An unidentified and undated newspaper cutting is among the papers of F.A. Inderwick Q.C., six times mayor. Someone has written on it 'Can this be true?!' The piece describes how the 'public pump' in Winchelsea is 'prohibited from working on Sunday.' The pump it says is locked up and a notice placed on it to the effect that it will be closed 'from 7.30 on Saturday night till seven on Monday morning. No water to be drawn on Sundays. By Order of the Mayor.' The indignant journalist concludes by declaring, 'It might restore the Mayor to his senses if his head was placed under the pump for a few hours.'[12]

The last time a detailed examination of the mechanism of the Town Well was made was in the 1970s. The cover was taken off, the walls found to be in reasonable condition and a bucket of water when drawn up seemed perfectly clean. The depth of water was over eighty feet below the well-head, making the level about the same as that of the water table in the fields surrounding the town.[13]

After Winchelsea Corporation lost all its local government functions in 1886 the water situation, if the reader will pardon the pun, became somewhat fluid. Initially it was resolved that the income from the queen's dues would be used to maintain the wells and water supply which was how the 1888 bill (see above) was met. Additionally an officer, Mr. Ernest Freeman, was appointed to keep the Town Well and the springs clean at a salary of one guinea per annum. There is pictorial evidence that at about this time a water carrying vehicle still made deliveries in German Street.[14] When responsibility passed to the Rye Rural Sanitary Authority the corporation failed, as with the Town Well, to persuade them to take over its water and sewage services. They did, however, send the Medical Officer of Health who found the drainage system most unsatisfactory:

'the surface water and water used for domestic purposes [are] being allowed to drain into cesspools attached to privies thereby causing a constant stirring up of the contents with fermentation very prejudicial to health.'[15]

This inspection was provoked by an outbreak of diphtheria at Factory Buildings which we now know as Barrack Square. As a result of this two residents, Edward Jenkins aged 4 and Charles Buttenshaw aged 29 died. Their deaths were attributed to just such conditions as the Medical Officer described.[16]

By 1891 the authority had taken the very positive step of preparing a Winchelsea Drainage and Water Scheme. It was originally planned to pipe the water from a strong spring at Road End Farm, Udimore. The water had been analysed; this source would be cheapest, the problem of having the sewage and waterworks in the same field could be overcome, and there would be no need for a shaft, only a reservoir. The authority had even invited applications for the post of keeper of the waterworks to which former Police Constable Holden had responded. We must presume that this plan involved development of the land beyond the Ferry Hill hairpin where the sewage works now stands.[17] However, the reservoir eventually built was on the site of Waterstone Cottage in Rectory Lane where a commemorative plaque in the garden states 'Water was brought from Newgate Spring into

(19) The Town Well when in full use

Winchelsea Nov. 1895.' Rye Rural District Council, by then the responsible body, had probably decided that having water supply and sewage disposal at opposite ends of the town was more prudent.

The use of the Newgate Spring to provide the town's water was not achieved without some serious objections. Residents gave evidence that since at least 1872 they had been drawing supplies there. That problem was, however, easily overcome – the pump would be left in place so that they could continue to exercise that right should they wish to do so. The reduction of the supply of water to riparian landowners below the spring was not so easy to solve. Major Stileman agreed with the proviso that water should be supplied to The Friars for a fixed price. Miss Brisco eventually agreed a twenty-one year lease and, bearing in mind that hers was only a lifetime interest, the authority decided to proceed.[18]

Responsibility later passed from the Sanitary Authority to Rye Rural District Council which on 31 August 1895 sealed the contract with Messrs. Burnham of Rye for the construction of the Rectory Lane reservoir. One member asked whether that would be the end of the Winchelsea water question. The chairman feared it would not. How right he was.

The matter was taken up by Dr. William Martindale who lived at Glebe Cottage and had been mayor in 1893. He was a prominent pharmacist who in 1883 published *The Extra Pharmacopoeia*, a listing of new and available drugs. This work, later edited by his son William Harrison Martindale, also in his time Winchelsea's mayor, has been regularly updated, is still affectionately known as 'Martindale' and is in such regular use to this day that a CD-ROM version has now been issued. The doctor's enthusiasm for sorting out Winchelsea's water and drainage problems at all costs was to cause the local authority considerable expense and annoyance. Whether the residents appreciated his zealous concern on their behalf we do not know but it seems unlikely. Local worthies declared that Winchelsea was a very healthy place, the residents had been drinking the water for years and it had not killed any of them yet. Ford Madox Ford portrays Martindale in fiction as an unthanked and unappreciated benefactor.[19] Ford certainly had plenty of opportunity to observe this for he was Martindale's son-in-law.

The Martindale protests climaxed at two meetings of Rye Rural District Council in September and October 1896. At one there was a long debate about water-levels near the New Gate spring. Martindale claimed that the level of the spring was nine inches below that of a ditch draining three nearby cottages. Therefore there was a serious chance of contamination. This was fiercely denied by the surveyor who had the members' support.[20]

At the other meeting there were no fewer than three items raised by Dr. Martindale. A Local Government Board inspector had visited the site, examined the levels and confirmed the measurements claimed by the council. One member protested that Martindale was only a private citizen and asked whether he 'could bring down as many inspectors as he chose and saddle the authority with the expense. This will go on for ever!' Another letter dealt with at the same meeting complained that some householders (the principally protesting councillor was one of them) who were within the statutory distance of the main drains had failed to connect with them so that it was impossible to flush the water-closets and drains. The third letter claimed compensation for damage caused by the drains being placed on Martindale's land. As he was such a strong advocate of the scheme, and the only owner to make such a claim, this, as far as some members were concerned, was the last straw.[21]

An examination of the evidence, including his concern over the type of piping being used, suggests that there was considerable justification in what Martindale said. His arguments were reinforced by a case of typhoid occurring in Winchelsea at the time, but the council insisted that it was 'imported'. However he was quite unable to press his case without making himself unpopular. Even the newspaper sub-editors poked gentle fun at him with headlines such as 'Mr. Martindale again to the fore' and 'Once again!'

Winchelsea's water problems would not go away for a long time, if, indeed, they ever have. In 1897 G.M. Freeman Q.C. complained bitterly that the owners of large houses could get water to their top tanks only when Holden was pumping. 'Holden must pump every day.' Holden understandably wanted more money to do this but was refused.[22] There was also much concern at that time about the Strand pump which supplied the trough through an inlet at the bottom. People were thought to be taking water from which horses and dogs had already been drinking.[23]

In the following year there was a fire in Barrack Square caused by a defective chimney. It may have been smouldering for two days. Five Winchelsea men attended although the newspaper article does not make it clear whether they were firemen or local volunteers. They 'subdued the outbreak by cutting away the roof and rafters, there being no hose and but little water available.'[24]

1914 saw a public inquiry at the Court Hall seeking sanction to borrow £250 'for the purpose of the water supply of Winchelsea.' A reserve pump at the waterworks was badly needed for when the existing one broke down there was no backup.[25] The situation hardly seems to have improved between the wars. On 17 March 1939 the *Sussex Express* reported that Hastings Fire Brigade, attending an outbreak in Winchelsea, 'could not obtain an adequate supply of water through their hoses. A report was urgently requested by the parish council into the condition of the mains and hydrants. The frequent lack of pressure was a serious problem.[26]

In the 1930s Winchelsea went so far as to acquire its own 'fire engine' which was kept in the Lower Court Hall. This was a somewhat ungainly contraption consisting principally of a large red cylinder on four wheels from which water was pumped with an action like a Second World War stirrup pump. Cecil Barden can remember it being used only once when the generator shed in Col. Goldschmidt's garden caught fire. The Court Hall double doors were thrown open, the machine manhandled out and dragged amid much excitement through the streets. However, by the time it reached The Mount, the fire was already out.

In 1959 damage to pavements, noted by the residents, turned out to have been caused by exploratory work in connection with relaying the mains.[27] Even this apparently had little effect for I well remember in the early 1960s, when my wife and I were living in the town, standing with a telephone in one hand and a bottle of dirty water in the other complaining to an officer of the Hastings Water Company:

'I have run the water for ages and the bottle still has a deep layer of sediment.'

'It's perfectly drinkable, sir.'

'If I bring it to your office, will you drink it?'

Long pause. 'Er. No!'

The use of the pumps and wells is long ended. Most have disappeared. Two old pumps in Tanyard Lane near Queen Elizabeth's Well were removed in 1961 in connection with a road-widening scheme. The county engineer contacted the parish council who had no objection to the removal of the pumps but thought they might be corporation property. The mayor, Mr. Thomas Bruce, replied that he had no idea to whom they belonged. They were certainly not appropriate exhibits for the museum. With practical common sense he suggested that the parish council should sell them for scrap and share the proceeds with the corporation![28]

While dealing with Winchelsea's water problems over the years it is perhaps worth recording

(20) Queen Elizabeth's Well
showing Thomas Wicks of the Oast House resting before carrying his bucket of water up Spring Steps.

that the community's attitude to the arrival of other utilities was generally resistant. In 1888, in reply to an inquiry asking the price per thousand feet of gas to consumers, Walter Dawes, town clerk, stated 'There are no gas works at Winchelsea. The town is lighted by petroleum lamps.' This was not as explosive an arrangement as it may sound – we would know them as oil lamps.[29]

In 1919 G.M. Freeman, mayor, wrote to the town clerk about the government's proposal to 'divide the whole country into a few vast districts worked by single [electricity] stations.' He thought the cost of labour and materials prohibitive and doubted whether many houses in Winchelsea would take the supply 'as most of the larger houses have their own private lighting.' However, just to be on the safe side, he thought perhaps the corporation members should be consulted.[30] We do not know the outcome because those were the days before records were kept of private meetings. The gable-ends of the little building which held Tower Cottage's generator can still be seen in the enclosure between the garden and Strand Hill.

Objections to the intrusive nature of overhead electricity lines were raised strongly in 1933 by Freeman's son, Anthony. The Hastings Borough Electrical Engineer wanted wayleave for overhead lines across Freeman's land to the settlement at Dog's Hill 'also known as Winchelsea Beach,' where electricity was badly needed. With an appreciation of environmental matters rather ahead of his time Anthony Freeman would have none of it.[31]

The telephone, too, came in for its share of objection. Florence, Lady Swinburne rented The Retreat in 1923. 'At that time there was no telephone in the village.' A friend spent a weekend with Lady Swinburne and her brother, went back to London, pulled some strings and within a few days 'a line was run out from Rye.' This provoked a letter from solicitors acting for the owner, Lady McIlwraith, insisting that 'the telephone [should] be at once dismantled as it ruins the old world amenities!' Lady Swinburne's brother, Mr. Moffatt, enjoyed the joke and replied to the solicitors by using the offending 'phone.[32]

The assumption that The Retreat's temporary 'phone was the only one in the town was not, in fact, correct and, however many others shared Lady McIlwraith's objections, progress could not be resisted. By the time *Deacon's Directory for Rye and District* was published in 1929 twenty-four numbers were listed for Winchelsea, Winchelsea Beach and Icklesham. Among these were:

Winchelsea 1	A.H.T. Finch (the postmaster). This number is also listed for the public call office opposite.
Winchelsea 10	Walter Alford, Station Road.
Winchelsea 13	H. Baird, Periteau.
Winchelsea 8	Mrs. C.S. Campion, Strand Plat.
Winchelsea 7	Robert Cooke, Holford's Farm.
Winchelsea 6	G.M. Freeman K.C., J.P., Greyfriars.
Winchelsea 5	Lt. Col. E. Goldschmidt, The Mount.
Winchelsea 19	A.J. Jempson, Luxford, Icklesham.
Winchelsea 11	Dr. E.T. McDonnell, Winchelsea.
Winchelsea 3	W. Merricks, Icklesham.
Winchelsea 21	Robert Nichols, Yew Tree House.
Winchelsea 17	A.V. Owen, 2, Keith Row.
Winchelsea 18	J. Parsons, Strand Garage.
Winchelsea 25	The Police, Winchelsea.
Winchelsea 14	Lord Ritchie of Dundee, Mariteau.
Rye 161x	John R. Skinner, Backfields, Winchelsea.

and, as the reader may have guessed,

Winchelsea 12	Lady McIlwraith, Tower Cottage.

13. CAREY, COURTS AND CORONERS

The year 1851 which saw the construction of the Town Well saw also the birth of John Carey who, during the next seventy-three years, was to give devoted service to the town in many ways. His particular interest for us is that just before his death Deacon's of Rye published a little volume of his reminiscences. Through this window we are able to view the Winchelsea of the mid-nineteenth century as it appeared to a growing boy.

Carey was born in Barrack Square and initially went to the school from which School Hill takes its name, the schoolmistress being Mrs. George Hearnden, wife of the postmaster. When he was five there is no doubt that in such a tight-knit community he would notice the excitement generated by the end of the Crimean War. The *Rye Chronicle and Advertiser* reported on Saturday 7 June 1856 under the headline 'Peace Rejoicing at Winchelsea':

> 'The day set apart for the general rejoicing on the celebration of peace was observed in this ancient town by the closing of all shops and a general suspension of business and in the evening, by the direction of our respected and energetic Mayor G. Robins Esq., the Town Hall was illuminated and many of the respectable houses in this place participated in a like feeling on the restoration of a blessing which can alone make happy a people and bring prosperity to a nation.'

The paper went on to take a swipe at its home town by adding:

> 'Would that this humble but spirited borough [of Winchelsea] had been better imitated and better supported by her more prosperous neighbour where, we hear in shame, that all was apathy, gloom and darkness'.[1]

The schooling which John Carey received cannot have lasted long for by the time he was nine he had a job at Crutches Farm where, during hop picking, he carried a forked stick to lift the branches clear of the horses, wearing a crêpe veil over his face to avoid scratches. The pay was fourpence for a twelve-hour day from 6 a.m. to 6 p.m.

Like many boys of the time he flitted from job to job as opportunities arose, helping his parents in a bakery business which they took in 1861, working as a dairyman doing both milking and daily delivery, carrying fruit with a horse and van for a market gardener from Doleham, particularly to the Hastings shops, and acting as 'brickey's labourer' for James Croft; at this job he particularly enjoyed standing on the bottom of the ladder and whistling! Eventually Mr. Samuel Griffiths engaged him as a stud groom at Hiham House, in which position he became the proud wearer of a uniform including 'a top-hat with cockade, top-boots and bright buttons.'

Carey's youth was not free from trouble. When living at Doleham he would travel home, presumably on foot, to meet his friends on Sundays. On one occasion they played single sticks, a form of fencing using a branch with the hand-hold guarded, lashing away so fiercely that they caused considerable damage. Fleeing from the keeper they jumped a dyke and hid in woods. Of course, in those days the keeper would know perfectly well who they were whether they escaped or not and a summons duly arrived to appear before the magistrates at the Court Hall. Young Carey was deeply apprehensive but his father seems to have taken a relaxed view of the whole thing for he handed him a sovereign (a gold coin worth just over a pound) and said, 'You will be fined.' Carey senior was speaking from personal experience of Winchelsea justice for he had spent 31 May and 1 June 1849 in the Court Hall cells, although the gaol book does not list the offence. His prediction

(21) The Castle Inn, former home of John Carey – now a private residence.

turned out to be correct, the boys each had to pay sixteen shillings whereupon Carey, seemingly braver by then, produced his coin, 'dabbed it down' and said 'Let's have my change, please.' The other boys he recalled as having to go to the cells until their fines were paid.[2] The court records, dated 4 October 1864, list the offenders as Blackall, Field, Carey and Higter, four boys of Winchelsea, each charged with destroying property and taking poles belonging to Mr. Benfield, farmer, on his property at the cliff. This was the area now occupied by Lord Ritchie's house and garden at The Roundel. The boys are said to be not employed, untrue in Carey's case, and aged 'from about 12 to 16.' He may have received more change than he recalled sixty years later for the punishment is listed as 'Each of them fined six shillings and sixpence to be paid immediately or before 12 tomorrow.'[3] While awaiting his trial in the court room Carey was amused by the case of two men who were charged with stealing walnuts at The Friars. One said, 'Not guilty but I was there.' This plea was to no avail – he was instantly sentenced to one month in prison.[4]

The court which tried John Carey still had wide powers of punishment and influence and had to deal with a great variety of cases. The justices of the peace were the mayor and jurats who took themselves and their duties very seriously, although such a survival in so small a town did occasionally invite ridicule, as when Dante Gabriel Rossetti was staying at the New Inn in 1866 and happened to observe the ceremonies performed on the occasion of the opening of the quarter sessions.

Rossetti saw the procession 'of about seven persons including the Mayor in splendid robes of scarlet lined with sables and three officials in blue robes one of whom was the parish barber and another the carpenter.' After this preliminary had been observed 'in the street by a mob of one female child and by ourselves from the inn window' this 'mob of three' hurried to witness the proceedings. The officials, as many as fifteen plus a dog belonging to one of the constables, vastly outnumbered the public. When the mayor, the same Samuel Griffiths who had employed John Carey as groom, had been informed that there were no cases to be heard that day he gave a strong lecture about the earlier appearance of a man who had been found drunk in the streets. His worship clearly believed that such a lecture to the assembled company would ensure no similar transgressions in the future. Writing to his mother, Rossetti concludes, 'This may give you some idea of the pleasant doziness of the place, which is more to my taste I think than any other I know. Everyone is eighty-two if he is not ninety-six.'[5]

In fact Rossetti's observation of the court was not necessarily typical. While much of its jurisdiction might well be viewed flippantly from the distance of almost a century and a half, let alone by an irreverent on-the-spot spectator, much more involved human tragedy, serious offence and severe punishment.

Selecting almost at random from a wealth of material we deal first with the typical case of Albert Marchant who was caught poaching on Major Robert Stileman's land at The Friars. The major had the good grace not to appear on the bench himself. The case, on 11 February 1868, was conducted by his colleagues Charles Robins, deputy mayor and Jurat Dr. R.V. Skinner. Charles Harmer, gamekeeper, gave evidence that, on the night of 7 January, he had heard shots and seen the defendant come from 'certain land in the occupation of Robert Curteis Stileman where he had been unlawfully in pursuit of game with a gun.' Harmer waited for the support of William Mitchell whereupon they followed Marchant's footprints in the snow and tracked him to the old chapel. He ran towards the New Gate but they were able to catch him and take the gun away. When questioned Marchant claimed that he was taking the gun to his brother. Unfortunately for him his brother later vehemently denied this! Found guilty, Marchant was treated very lightly for the times being fined five shillings with fifteen shillings costs with fourteen days hard labour if he could not pay. The gun was confiscated.[6]

Such a punishment was certainly lenient compared to that meted out, albeit forty years earlier, to one Thomas Bennett, also known as Thomas Seldon, a labourer of the parish of St. Thomas. The unfortunate Bennett was a nineteenth-century 'flasher' who had been convicted by the magistrates for 'wilfully, openly, lewdly and obscenely exposing his person in the public streets and highways.' For this offence, the magistrates' powers being limited, he was committed to the town gaol until his case could be further considered by the quarter sessions. At that hearing he was declared to be 'an incorrigible Rogue and Vagabond' within the meaning of the relevant statute. His two previous offences were taken into account and he was sentenced to be 'stripped by the middle upwards [there must be an unconscious irony in that] and affixed to a cart's tail.' He was then to receive six lashes on his naked back at each place within the town that the town crier made the appropriate pronouncement. The punishment was to commence at 12 noon the following day. The town constables were ordered to attend. After this procedure Bennett must serve six weeks at the House of Correction, Lewes, 'there to be kept to hard labour.'[7]

The court dealt not only with committed crimes but also possible eventualities. On 21 January 1868 Dr. R.V. Skinner told a sitting of the quarter sessions that he was prepared to declare upon oath that he had reasonable grounds to know that 'riot and tumult in the Ancient Town of Winchelsea may occur at any moment.' Skinner's fellow magistrates took the threat very seriously indeed and proceeded to swear in forty-nine special constables to deal with it.[8] No reason for this is given in the court records and one is tempted to observe that there would not be many men left to cause riot and tumult. However a study of the local press reveals that the action was taken in common with towns all over the country. In Sussex Rye and Eastbourne had similarly appointed specials during the previous week. The threat was posed by the Fenians. Their terror campaign on the British mainland provoked the *Sussex Express* into publishing on 18 January a special supplement in which it thundered, 'No man in his senses can possibly believe that it will be sufficient to murder an occasional policeman, to blow up a few powder mills or gasometers, to establish an independent republic in Ireland.' The Fenians' actions were compared to a school rebellion in which 'the utmost which can be achieved is accomplished when a few desks have been destroyed, a few books torn up and the ink spilled out of the inkstands.' However, places such as Winchelsea were taking no chances. The *Sussex Express,* in the same article, regretted grimly 'that a handful of desperadoes can throw a great country into a state of alarm and confusion... they have effectively roused it to self-defence.'⁹ The passing of 130 years does not seem to have brought a solution of this problem any nearer. Of those sworn in that day who have descendants of the same name still living in Winchelsea Henry Streeton and George Dunk are obvious examples. Thirty of the truncheons purchased for the use of these recruits remain on display at the Court Hall.

Rather more routine for the court but producing a dramatic climax was the case of Thomas Street and James Brighton, heard on 14 September 1876. These men had premises at Camber, within the liberty and therefore under Winchelsea's jurisdiction. They were charged with selling alcohol without a licence. George Jeffery, superintendent of police, told the court that 'witnesses who could give evidence would not without being compelled to do so.' They were Hugh O'Neil of St. Leonards, William Turley of Camber and William Hounsell of Udimore. They were eventually so compelled and Hugh O'Neil's proof of evidence describes how he went to a shanty kept by the principal defendant, Street, at Camber. He saw a woman, Mrs. Brighton, and two others playing cards. There was beer on the table. The witness asked for bread and cheese for which he paid twopence. He sat by the fire, later asking for a pint of porter. Mrs. Brighton told him she had none but had stout. This he ordered and paid threepence. Having received no change from the shilling proffered he had another pint. Part of this he told Mrs. Brighton he wanted to take away so she helped him put it in his bottle. He gave this bottle to Police Constable Masters and swore in evidence that it was the one produced in court. Street had been observed at the same hut earlier. Both Brighton and Street were found guilty, the former being fined £5 plus costs, the latter £10. Mrs. Brighton was not charged.

The sting in this story arises from subsequent events. Street had a very active and tenacious solicitor, William Savery of Hastings, who lodged an appeal against his conviction to the High Court of Justice in the Queen's Bench Division. The evidence that Street was ever responsible in law for these premises was unsatisfactory. The magistrates who had conducted the trial were required to set out the case in detail in writing. Street agreed to submit to the jurisdiction of the higher court and Savery, or so he claimed, visited the justices personally to arrange bail of £20 for his client. The whole process of reaching a High Court hearing might take a year when witnesses could well be unavailable or unreliable. The magistrates felt strongly that they were being hoodwinked by a delaying tactic which would lead to Street paying no penalty for a crime of which they, particularly with their local knowledge, were convinced he was guilty. They pulled no punches. Street's arrest was ordered for non-payment of his ten pound fine. He was committed to the House of Correction at Lewes for one month's hard labour. The constables who were sent to find 'goods and chattels' which could be seized to pay the fine had given evidence that after a diligent search they could find no such property.

William Savery, having been outflanked and outmanoeuvred, was deeply offended. He wrote to the town clerk, Walter Dawes:

'Sir, I am exceedingly surprised that you should have caused my client Street to have been taken… To say the least of it, it is a breach of good faith which I shall not forget.

W. Savery'

Street served his sentence. Winchelsea's magistrates were not to be trifled with.[10]

About a year earlier Robert Curteis Stileman and David Skinner as justices heard the distressing case of Emma Partridge of Coastguard Cottages, Rye Harbour where her husband was stationed. Until three years previously he had served at Devonport of which town his wife was a native. The posting to Rye Harbour had told on her mind in such a way that she was in a highly unstable condition. Her husband in evidence:

'About six or eight months after we came here she became different, thinking everyone was against her. At times she has been violent. She has knocked me about the head at different times. She has threatened to knock my brains out. She follows me about when I am on duty, watching me. Yesterday she threw some hot water at me. I am certain she is of unsound mind. I have not the means of keeping her under proper control.'

Additionally the poor woman appeared to be obsessed with a delusion that she was pregnant, sending for the midwife without cause.

Having to deal with such a situation must have been a problem for James Willton, the coastguard chief officer. Nevertheless his observations to the court were direct and sympathetic. On numerous occasions he had had to report Emma Partridge to his superiors for interfering with the work of the station.

'Last Tuesday about five o'clock in the evening I was sent for to Partridge's house. On my arrival I found some broken crockery lying on the floor of the kitchen. Partridge said she had aimed a blow at him with a poker she was still holding.'

He had thrown her on the floor where she was lying crying. She did not appear hurt. Mr. Willton went on to describe how they had tried to persuade her to go to her mother's in Plymouth or to take a house at Rye, all to no avail. There was no suggestion that anyone had treated her unkindly.

In the face of this evidence Major Stileman countersigned Willton's statement upon oath that Emma Partridge 'is not a pauper and is not wandering at large but is deemed a lunatic and is not under proper care and control.' Henry Masters, police constable, then took her to the Sussex County Lunatic Asylum at Haywards Heath where the medical officer signed her admission form with a note that on arrival she had 'one small bruise on left side and large bruise on back of right leg.'[11]

The wealth of human distress and tragedy which lies behind the stark pages of documents of this kind is reflected even more in the records of the Mayor of Winchelsea's duty as coroner. This was a testing and demanding office which had to be undertaken almost immediately upon report of a death within Winchelsea and its liberties requiring his investigation. The inquest was always held the following day at some convenient venue near the place of death and involved the coroner and the jury viewing the body as well as hearing evidence. On one occasion a mayor was summoned home from holiday in Bath and made it just in time, a not inconsiderable feat.

The inquest papers deal with sudden deaths from natural causes, many drownings, death by fire, particularly of children, a number of children suffocated when in bed with parents (those were the days when large families had few rooms), several suicides and, more unusually, a boy killed by the sails of a windmill, a schoolmaster who died suddenly while conducting a school party from London round the town, a doctor who died of an overdose of laudanum, and in 1860 the murder of William Sands although the verdict records only that he was killed by a person or persons unknown; the circumstances are not revealed.

From this wealth of information I shall concentrate on three cases. The first occurred rather before this book's main period in 1787 with Thomas Marten, mayor and coroner, hearing the case at the New Inn. The circumstances are similar to several other inquests and reflect the social circumstances already dealt with when water-supplies were available only from wells at the foot of the hill. Clearly water for drinking and cooking took priority over water for washing. On this occasion the jury heard that a child, James Edmeat aged 6, was sent at about six o'clock on the previous evening to wash his legs in the River Brede. While he was doing that 'it so happened that accidentally and by misfortune he slipped into the water near the Strand sluice and there suffocated and drowned.' The jury, not knowing how he came to fall into the water and having no evidence that it was anything other than an accident, gave their verdict accordingly, supported by the coroner.[12]

The other two cases happened more than a hundred years later. They encapsulate the appalling human tragedies with which the coroner's court had to deal and, by coincidence, were conducted by the two men who served Winchelsea best during the latter part of the nineteenth century, Major Robert Curteis Stileman and Frederick Andrew Inderwick Q.C.

The major, on Saturday 10 November 1883, conducted the inquest into the death the previous day of David Laurence. Laurence was a carpenter working for his father, George, of the same trade, and also serving both as assistant overseer of the poor and as treasurer of the corporation. As assistant overseer he had had a predecessor earlier in the century of the same name and almost certainly the same family (see p.29). A married man aged 35 with three children he was much respected in the town or these public offices would not have been his. It was Laurence's financial responsibilities as assistant overseer and rate-collector which, without any relative or friend having more than the slightest knowledge of his problems, brought about his downfall.

The Union Auditor was due at Rye on the Friday morning to examine the accounts of the various parishes. David Laurence had received formal notification that he was to attend at one o'clock with the books for St. Thomas's. He would be accompanied by his father and by Walter Fuller, farmer and grazier, who were at that time the overseers. George Laurence visited his son's home at 9.30 a.m., told him he should be particular not to be late for the audit and arranged to meet him in plenty of time. Walter Fuller forgot the appointment during the morning, arrived similarly at noon to say that it had slipped his memory but he would be back as soon as he had changed his coat. The two overseers, arriving back together, found that David Laurence had gone out. His wife had no idea where he had gone. They went unsuccessfully in search of him, eventually hurrying to Rye taking the parish books with them. The interview must have been a painful one for it brought George Laurence confirmation that something was seriously wrong – the accounts showed one hundred pounds owing to the parish.

The auditor told them there was nothing which could be done until he had interviewed the assistant overseer. They hastened back to Winchelsea and renewed their search with greater urgency. Sadly it was his father who found him, hanging from the rafters of a shed in the garden of his (the father's) house. He was quite cold. George Laurence called for help from Walter Fuller and Harry Catt, gardener to Mr. Inderwick. Together they cut the body down and gently laid it on some deal planks where Dr. Skinner examined it before it was taken home in the evening.

Harry Catt's evidence at the inquest shows him to have been the last person to see David Laurence alive. Catt was in Rectory Lane, opposite the Rectory gate when Laurence ran past him towards his father's house. Catt asked him the time – about twelve.

Dr. Robert Vaile Skinner's evidence dealt with the time of death, very shortly after Catt saw him, and the deceased's character. The doctor knew him well and had always considered him 'a very sensible well conducted man.' He had no means of forming an opinion as to why he should commit suicide and had certainly never considered him likely to do so.

Clues trickle out from the other evidence. George Laurence said, 'For several weeks he has avoided me and appeared strange in his manners,' while speaking glowingly of his earlier record both as a workman and family member. Walter Fuller was more specific, 'About a month ago he said he had had a call [a bill] come but he had been too busy to get his collections in and doubted whether he would be able to meet it. I gave him a small cheque which he asked for till the following market. He partly repaid me. Nothing has passed since. He was quite capable of keeping the books but on looking at them today I find they are about two months behind.'

The jury, gathered as always at short notice by the chamberlain or sergeant-at-mace, posts later to be held by John Carey, regretfully recorded that David Laurence 'not being of sound mind killed himself by hanging.' Perhaps it is worth recording that the jury contained many who appear in this story or whose family names are featured: George Barling (foreman), Robert Voller, Obadiah Easton, Walter Thorpe (who succeeded Laurence as corporation treasurer), Richard Stace, Albert Cooke, William Carey, James Croft, Thomas Turner and William Mitchell.[13]

The corporation's funds were not affected by David Laurence's tragic mismanagement. His appointment during the previous three years records that his annual salary was three guineas, that all monies must be paid into the London and County Bank at Rye and must only be paid out with cheques signed by the mayor or deputy mayor and one jurat, countersigned by the treasurer.[14] In the accounts there is a tell-tale change of hand at November 1883 but no apparent discrepancy or problem.

The inquest at which Mr. Inderwick officiated concerned a death on the morning of Saturday 4 November almost exactly a year earlier. On the following Monday afternoon the coroner, jury and witnesses gathered at the home of John Battam, Winchelsea's special constable for the Camber area. Inderwick had wanted to meet Walter Dawes, the town clerk, at 9 a.m. to make the necessary arrangements but Dawes was not available and the two men drove to Camber together after the coroner's arrival on the 1.20 train from London.

The story which unfolded before them was one relatively commonplace in the annals of the sea but deeply compelling in the drama of its development. News had reached Winchelsea Coastguard Station at 3.30 a.m. that signals of distress had been seen at Camber. Benjamin Burr, commissioned boatman R.N., set about raising a crew for the lifeboat *The Storm Sprite*. It took him an unusually long time. Only at 5 a.m. had he the full complement of thirteen, six coastguards from Winchelsea Watchhouse, two from No. 31 (Martello) Tower at Winchelsea Beach, together with five volunteer sailors and fishermen from Rye Harbour. As they gathered in the teeth of a storm of awesome strength, with Burr in command, the decision was taken to sail the boat to Camber rather than taking it there by road. The launch would save time but would also be extremely dangerous. Every man's lifebelt was checked and properly buckled, the foresail was close reefed, the cork lines

(22) John Carey (in top hat), chamberlain and sergeant-at-mace
pictured in Mill Road during the 1919 peace celebrations. Immediately behind him are
(left) G.M. Freeman K.C., mayor, in the robes of a coronation baron, and Dr. John Rutherford Skinner

were stretched across the boat to give it self-righting capacity. The evidence suggests that the boat was hauled out using a fixed hawser with both masts stepped before ropes were used to swing it round as the sails were hoisted, impetus thus being gained to clear the surf and set sail for Camber. Such a straightforward account conceals a wealth of courage, skill and seamanship.

All went well until they were within about seven hundred yards of the wreck which by then was plainly visible. As they tried to negotiate shallower water, a heavy sea broke into the boat, immediately followed by another which turned her over. Both masts snapped. The men were not lashed in. Some clung on, others were thrown into the water. The situation was largely saved by the coxswain's presence of mind in immediately dropping the anchor to prevent the boat being carried away from its struggling crew. *The Storm Sprite* behaved exactly as designed and righted herself. Twelve men were accounted for in the boat after the life-and-death scramble which followed, and Edward Robus, a Rye Harbour man on his third volunteer lifeboat duty, was sighted apparently swimming towards the shore. By then they had been carried in among the keddle nets (large fishing nets fixed on poles) so even had they realised that Robus needed help they could not have manoeuvred towards him. The drenched and exhausted twelve had no alternative but to ride at anchor until daylight. During this time they thought they saw Robus safely ashore and walking along the beach.

Alas it was an illusion. George and Charles Southerden, fishermen who also operated the Camber rocket apparatus, were patrolling the shore when they saw something in the sea. Charles waded in on a lifeline and dragged Robus out of the water. His lifebelt, like the lifeboat, had performed exactly to specification. It was supporting his body but his head and legs were hanging down below the surface. Coastguards quickly gathered and spent forty five minutes unsuccessfully trying to revive him for George Southerden said he had appeared to move after being laid on the beach. The crew of the wrecked vessel had been brought ashore in two journeys by a Camber boat.

It must have been a sombre scene as fifteen men gathered in one room of a simple house having heard the evidence and viewed the body. The jury recorded as its verdict that Edward Robus was accidentally drowned through the upsetting of the lifeboat *The Storm Sprite*. The circumstances are made all the more poignant by a rider added by the jury strongly recommending that some compensation should be granted if possible out of the funds of the R.N.L.I. They urged that the case should be laid before the inspector of lifeboats. Edward Robus's death had left destitute a widow and six children. Their duty done the jureymen dispersed to their homes and jobs in Camber; the coroner and town clerk hurried back to Rye.[15] The impact of this tragedy was largely confined to Robus's family at Rye Harbour and the people of the village. It was to be a further forty-six years before a successor lifeboat, the *Mary Stanford*, in another dramatic capsize close to the same spot brought to the same little community a disaster which shocked the nation. But by that time the area was outside Winchelsea's direct jurisdiction.

John Carey's service to Winchelsea and the corporation long survived the demise of its courts and its coroners. He was appointed town crier and sergeant-at-mace after Edwin Laurence fell to his death when a ladder rung broke while he was painting Higham Cottage.[16] The Laurence family seems to have been dogged by tragedy. Later Carey was appointed chamberlain as well. He carried the maces on numerous public occasions, most memorably for him the installation of six Lord Wardens. It was a great sadness to him to be too ill to perform his duties when, in 1920, Winchelsea was honoured for the first time by an official visit from the Lord Warden.

However, the people of the town knew Carey best as sexton and gravedigger, jobs which he combined with helping in various ways at the Rectory. Blanche Patch, daughter of the rector, remembered him as a charming companion to the children who, when he was not cleaning shoes, working the pump which supplied the house with water or helping the gardener, would play cricket with them on the lawn. She also recalled his leading role in the concerts held regularly at the Court Hall.[17] These were highlights of the Winchelsea social calendar.

Carey was forced to give up all his positions in 1921 through persistent ill health. The rector of the time, commiserating with Alfred Osman, mayor, because this indisposition meant the mayor was having to collect the king's dues himself, wrote:

> 'Poor old Carey – he will never again, I fear, carry out his duties in person as Sergeant-at-Mace and Collector and I don't think he can live long. He is, I believe, quite resigned and if he is not to get better no one can wish him to live on as he is'.[18]

In fact he lived on for another three years after being succeeded by his great-nephew, William Bennett. It was during that time that the memoirs were published.

14. THE CORPORATION THREATENED AGAIN

The demise of the courts and the coroners actually took place on 25 March 1886 but much by way of representation, debate and lobbying had gone before.

In 1876 the Municipal Commissioners were on the warpath again and it became clear that an anachronism such as a town of approximately six hundred inhabitants having its own rating and judicial independence could not much longer survive the sweeping local government changes which were taking place. Henry Stringer, Town Clerk of New Romney, first alerted Winchelsea to the danger that Sir Charles Dilke was proposing legislation doing away with such authorities as Winchelsea and Romney Marsh. Hurried consultations took place resulting in the sensible decision that they would keep their heads down until the precise proposals were known.[1]

The axe was eventually poised in 1883 but by then Winchelsea was fortunate enough to have as a resident at Mariteau House Frederic Andrew Inderwick Q.C. His considerable influence was to save the corporation as a body with meaningful responsibilities if not as a local authority. Inderwick, born on 23 April 1836, was educated privately and at Trinity College, Cambridge, later becoming a student of the Inner Temple and being called to the bar in 1858. His legal career was a highly specialist one in the divorce courts which became the Probate, Divorce and Admiralty Division. There he developed into a natural and distinguished leader but displayed a kindly sympathy in cross-examination which was uncharacteristic of his profession. This resulted in his being, in more important or sensational cases, 'reinforced by some conspicuous figure from the common law bar.'[2] Inderwick's colleagues and friends felt he must be destined to become a judge. When he was passed over there was considerable surprise and some resentment which provoked a good deal of press comment.[3] He also had parliamentary ambitions, being a reforming Liberal barrister in the Whig tradition of Lushington and Brougham (see p.47). Unsuccessful at Cirencester in 1868 and Dover in 1874 he eventually became the last member for the Borough of Rye from 1880 until 1885. At the general election of that year he stood for the newly created Rye Division of Sussex but was not elected. Outside his legal and parliamentary careers he pursued an intense interest in history, his books on the subject including *Sidelights on the Stuarts, Interregnum,* and *The Story of King Edward and New Winchelsea.*[4]

As we have seen, F.A. Inderwick's position as mayor and jurat brought him responsibilities as magistrate and coroner where his natural understanding shone through.

> 'He was always regarded as one who tempered gentleness with justice... his unbiased opinions upon all matters that came before the bench caused his judgments to be regarded as correct but there have been times when the kindliness of his nature has shone out as a worthy characteristic of so great a man.'

Well may that sentiment have applied at the inquest on Edward Robus. Mr. Inderwick in turn attracted sympathy from his fellow residents for his family was struck by tragedy, two sons predeceasing him. The affectionate respect which he inspired was well expressed after his untimely death from cancer in 1904 by a Winchelsea resident who said, 'We cannot tell how much we have lost. He did not die to get a good name. He gained it while he lived.'[5]

Frederic Inderwick's membership of the House of Commons at the time of the passing of the Municipal Corporations Act of 1883 was fortuitous indeed. As a government supporter he was able to persuade his colleagues that to strip Winchelsea Corporation of all its powers and thus destroy it would make it impossible for the town to remain a head port of the Confederation of the Cinque

Ports, an unthinkable outcome to us and to Inderwick but not a matter which would have raised more than an eyebrow outside Winchelsea, there being little interest in the confederation at the time. Seaford and Pevensey lost their corporate status under the same statute and submitted to being members no longer. Many of the unreformed corporations affected by the act were far less important than Seaford and Pevensey and had either ceased to exist or had been tainted by corruption. At least, during the negotiations, Winchelsea had the reassurance of a letter from the Local Government Board stating that Sir Charles Dilke 'wishes me particularly to say that there has been no imputation of malversation of funds in the case of Winchelsea'.[6]

Meetings and inquiries resulting from Inderwick's lobbying took a considerable time and it was as late as two months after the second reading that the vital clause was added. On 2 May 1883 he wrote to Walter Dawes, town clerk:

'My dear Sir,

Unreformed Corporations

The government will consent that the Corporation of Winchelsea shall remain as it is, collecting and distributing the corporation funds [the queen's dues] without any interference of the Charity Commissioners, also I <u>think</u> making and collecting the rates and retaining its position and privileges as an Ancient Town of the Cinque Ports.

The criminal and licensing jurisdiction will, however, be taken away as it has in fact been taken away from all other Unreformed Corporations.

This will save the honour and dignity of the Ancient Town and obtain for it a position not accorded to any other Unreformed Corporation in the kingdom.

Yours respectfully,

F.A.Inderwick'[7]

Within five days the new clause, actively supported by Lord Randolph Churchill, had been added to the bill by the House of Commons in committee with the Lords making no objection. It showed the above letter to have been correct in all respects except responsibility for the rates. The word 'think' had been underlined with good reason.

The clause reads:

'Saving as to Winchelsea. In the event of a charter not being granted to Winchelsea the property of the Corporation of Winchelsea shall continue to be held, managed and enjoyed as heretofore, in like manner as if a scheme of the Charity Commissioners, in pursuance of this Act, had provided for such holding, management and enjoyment, and for that purpose the Corporation of Winchelsea shall continue undissolved in like manner as if it were constituted by the same scheme and, not withstanding anything in this Act, Winchelsea shall continue to be entitled an ancient town of the Cinque Ports.'[8]

And so it remains to this day, for Winchelsea did not seek a charter as did her neighbour Lydd at the same time. Legally the corporation is an Exempt Charity established by act of parliament and not subject to the jurisdiction of the Charity Commissioners. The freemen who are its members are appointed by the existing freemen and from them are chosen the mayor and the jurats, almost exactly as happened in medieval times and entirely without the intervention of modern concepts of democracy.

His particular success in saving the corporation is of great importance to Winchelsea but, of course, Mr. Inderwick's prime responsibility as an M.P. was the town he represented, Rye. There his influence and involvement in many matters were warmly appreciated. One result of his supportive action is still a conspicuous feature of the local scene. The River Rother and the Harbour of Rye were, in the early 1880s, in a pretty parlous state, leading the Board of Trade to reduce their legal status to that of a creek annexed to the port of Folkestone, 'But, owing to the representations of Mr. Inderwick, the borough member, Rye has been allowed to retain its registration privileges'.[9] Readers seeing the registration letters RX proudly displayed on local vessels should spare a thought for Frederic Inderwick and his wonderful record of public service.

The passing of almost three years between the Municipal Corporations Act receiving the royal assent and its coming into force allowed Winchelsea plenty of time to consider how it

(23) Frederic Andrew Inderwick Q.C., M.P.

would react and what would be the practical implications. The continued administration of the corporation's finances was to be achieved by handing full responsibility to the chamberlain. He would collect the queen's dues and use them to pay the bills which it was assumed would be greatly reduced. Nevertheless a certain amount of asset stripping was suggested, particularly the sale of the standard set of weights and measures which had been used to ensure the fairness of local traders. Fortunately no buyer was found and the complete set remains on display in the Court Hall. Assurances were received that there would be no further direct demands on the town for contributions to the police or lunatic asylum rates. For this Winchelsea would fall within the general East Sussex rating area for the first time. Exemption from stamp duty was sought and eventually granted on the documents needed for the installation of freemen. Exemption from income tax was also negotiated as all the town's income would be used in maintaining its property. Winchelsea's magistracy was to be joined with Rye and a number of serving jurats were accordingly transferred to that bench.

In this connection the last sitting of the Winchelsea general quarter sessions of the peace was held on 7 January 1886 before 'Frederic Andrew Inderwick Esq. Q.C., Mayor, Robert Vaile Skinner and Robert Curteis Stileman Esquires, Jurats and Justices.' The last grand jury was duly sworn in. The sitting set a rate for the ensuing quarter but no further business was brought before the court.[10] It is perhaps worth pausing to consider the make-up of this last grand jury whose duty it would have been, had they had any, to make representations to the justices about matters of concern within the town. Many of these men find their way into this story in other connections and they represent a sturdy and reliable citizenry always ready to do their civic duty. The names are:

Charles White (Foreman) master mariner of Castle Street
Charles Barling, overseer, grocer and draper, German Street
Obadiah Easton, shoe repairer, leading Methodist, Friars Road
Robert Voller, gardener for F.A.Inderwick, Mariteau House
Walter Fuller, overseer, later jurat, farmer and grazier, Mill House, Mill Lane
Walter Thorpe, assistant overseer, corporation treasurer, Friars Road
Andrew Johnson, baker, Mill Road
John Carey, parish clerk, sexton and verger whom the reader has already met
Henry Streeton, sailor, carrier (daily service to Rye), beer retailer, The Salutation Inn
William Mitchell junior, carpenter, Mill Road
George Hearnden, postmaster, chamberlain, Castle Street
Albert Cooke, butcher, Castle Street, apartments – Derwent Cottage (Haskards)
Charles Jenkins, dairyman, Castle Street
Alfred Wilson, grocer, High Street
Richard Stace, blacksmith, High Street
Edwin Laurence, plumber, sergeant-at-mace, turnkey and town crier, German Street
James Croft, builder, bricklayer, Cooks Green
Edward Piggott, Factory Square (Barrack Square)
Alfred Cooke, farmer and grazier, Friars Road
Joseph Davis, grazier, The Strand
Richard Ratcliffe, butcher, Mill Road
William Stevenson, gardener, North Street
Thomas Wicks, carrier (Thursdays and Saturdays to Hastings), St. Thomas's Street

I am most grateful to Eric Streeton, great-grandson of Henry, for his help in compiling this list.

The last case of all came before the magistrates rather than the quarter sessions on 9 February 1886. James Hardie, a ship owner, was charged with keeping a dog not under control. The case was dismissed but he was ordered to pay thirteen shillings and sixpence in costs. The hand in which the gaol book was kept is not an educated one, almost certainly that of the gaoler, and the spelling is poor, but he it was who wrote 'paid' with a flourish after James Hardie's entry and thus brought to an end many centuries of legal jurisdiction within the town.[11]

Of all the events connected with the ending of this jurisdiction the most extraordinary took place at a corporation meeting held a month before the final quarter sessions. The minutes record the following resolution:

'Mr. Skinner proposed and Mr. Smith seconded that after the Twenty Fourth March next the Town Hall will no longer be required by the Corporation and that Mr. Piper be informed thereof. Carried unanimously.'[12]

And that is exactly what happened. Jesse Piper, successor of the king's bailiffs and freeholder, resumed possession of the building. During the next four years private corporation meetings were usually held at the mayor's home and the Easter Monday mayoring ceremony was held at the school in St. Thomas's Street. However, behind the scenes much was going on which will feature in the next chapter.

Winchelsea was well prepared for, perhaps resigned to, the changes which it expected as a result of the Municipal Corporations Act. It was totally unprepared for, and extremely angry about another statute which caught the town and its legal advisers unawares at the same time. This was the Divided Parishes Act of 1882, sometimes better described as the Surrounded Parishes Act. The purpose of this legislation was to permit the annexation of parishes by those which wholly surrounded them as the parish of Icklesham surrounded St. Thomas's, Winchelsea. A clause permitted inhabitants aggrieved by such annexations to lodge objections within a specified time. However, Winchelsea's residents were given no such opportunity. The Local Government Board told the Guardians of the Rye Union that the act had come into force and before anyone in Winchelsea had been alerted to what was happening 129 houses had been transferred to Icklesham.[13] The only ones excluded were those of the Camber area to which the act did not apply.

Such surreptitious stealth was considered to be far from the spirit of the act and the resulting anger led to petitions, protests and demands for a meeting with Sir Charles Dilke. Sir Charles opined that as the legislation had been implemented a meeting could serve no useful purpose. Winchelsea persisted. The matter came before the Court of the Queen's Bench which, to the dismay of the residents decided in favour of the amalgamation.[14] Still reluctant to give up their efforts Winchelsea's citizens chose Mr. James Davis to take legal action in a test case against having to pay the poor rate to Icklesham.[15] This also failed. A former corporate town had to suffer the indignity of coming under the jurisdiction of a village. It would not take long for this to cause acrimonious repercussions.[16]

These came when the Local Government Act of 1894 followed the previous legislation logically by creating the civil parish of Icklesham to include Icklesham, Winchelsea and Rye Harbour. Apart from some isolated properties such as The Watch Houses, Holford's Farm, Harbour Farm and the old Ship Inn, Winchelsea Beach as we now know it did not exist. It must be said that, however aggrieved Winchelsea may have felt, this arrangement had in it a delightful natural justice for was it not from the parish of Icklesham that King Edward I took the majority of the land for the establishment of New Winchelsea six centuries earlier? The hill of Iham was returning home under the reforming eye of late nineteenth-century legislators.

Winchelsea's hurt pride made the initial stages of the new council very difficult. When the arrangements for its first elections were announced it transpired that there would be only two polling stations, one at Rye Harbour, the other at Winchelsea Court Hall. If Icklesham residents wished to vote they must walk or ride to Winchelsea.[17] Rye Rural District Council was told, 'There is a strong feeling at this [the Icklesham] end of the parish that we have been used very badly.' Intriguingly the speaker, Mr. Bates Barling, went on in supporting evidence to claim that the Icklesham voters were 'almost exclusively of the labouring classes whilst the Winchelsea voters were more of the leisured classes and could easily go a little further to vote.'[18] Whether or not this was correct, the protest was well justified and the position of the polling stations clearly affected the vote. In the true tradition of the grand jury's willingness to take part in local government there were twenty-four candidates for eleven seats. The full results were:[19]

Elected:

E.Ashdown (Rye Harbour) foreman of stoneworks	141
J.R.Skinner (Winchelsea) surgeon	139
T.Wicks (Winchelsea) carrier	126
C.Barling (Winchelsea) grocer	123
Frank Caister (Rye Harbour) shipwright	116

T.Clarke (Icklesham) market gardener		96
W.Fuller (Winchelsea) farmer		95
T.J.Davies (Rye Harbour) farmer		93
A.W.Cooper (Icklesham) farmer		92
Richard Saunders (Rye Harbour) labourer		91
T.Pryer (Winchelsea) independent		89

Not Elected:

Rev. T.T.Churton (Icklesham) vicar	86
R.Baker (Icklesham) saddler	85
C.Wood (Icklesham) farmer	69
O.Lemmon (Icklesham) grocer	66
John Harman (Icklesham) coachman	62
R.Voller (Winchelsea) gardener	60
C.Carey (Winchelsea) licensed victualler	58
F.Crisford (Icklesham) farmer	35
J.A.Steer (Icklesham) blacksmith	32
A.Wilson (Winchelsea) grocer	31
E.Freeland (Winchelsea) farm bailiff	28
A.Eldridge (Winchelsea) fisherman	25
C.White (Winchelsea) independent	23

The Icklesham villagers must have deeply resented a system which would permit the election of all four Rye Harbour candidates, five from Winchelsea and, because many of them could not leave their work long enough to vote, only two of theirs. But things were to get worse. At the council's second meeting the chairman referred with shock and sympathy to the death of Mr. T. Pryer, a Winchelsea member 'in whom we have lost a good friend'. Instead of automatically electing Rev. Mr. Churton, vicar of Icklesham, who had been next in the poll, the council voted by six to two that Robert Voller of Winchelsea, sixth of the unsuccessful candidates after five of Icklesham, should fill the vacancy. The meeting waited while he was fetched and congratulated. The feelings of Messrs. Clarke and Cooper who had proposed and seconded their vicar can well be imagined.[20]

In view of this the reader will not be surprised that Icklesham Parish Council's first chairman came from Winchelsea. However, the distinction of the man chosen precludes criticism on grounds of bias. Wherever he lived he was the right man for the job. Dr. John Rutherford Skinner came of a distinguished Winchelsea medical family. His father and brother also served the town as general practitioners over many years. The new chairman in carrying out his medical duties would tour the area on horseback visiting his patients at all times of the day and night. His devotion to his work was so greatly appreciated that those who benefited eventually clubbed together and bought him a Daimler. Nevertheless, the doctor found it difficult to change his ways and this splendid vehicle spent most of its time covered in sheets.

As the council's operation got under way Dr. Skinner found himself faced with debates on such items as the acquisition of allotments, the improvement of footpaths and public lighting, matters typical of those which have preoccupied the members throughout its existence. In dealing with more controversial topics he showed great skill and impartiality particularly when faced with fierce demands, from Icklesham of course, that the parish should be divided into three wards to prevent any repetition of Winchelsea's attempt to manipulate and dominate. This was supported by

Rye Harbour and despite trenchant opposition from at least two Winchelsea members was finally agreed by the county council and put into effect.

The council's decision to meet at the Court Hall was made a matter of common sense by Winchelsea's geographical position within the parish. A request to the mayor, Major Stileman, for the use of the building was agreed and a charge of two shillings and sixpence per meeting was made to cover the custodian's expenses.[21] Although the major confined his original permission to his personal term of office, the Court Hall and other venues within the town became the council's regular meeting place and have been throughout the vast majority of its first hundred years.

The changes here described forced Winchelsea, albeit reluctantly, into partnership with neighbouring communities. Its attempt to exercise undue influence over the area, most of which had for so long been within the Liberty of Winchelsea, was, even in the comparatively short term, a failure. In the process attitudes began to change.

15. THE COURT HALL

We must now consider how the mayor could be in control of the Court Hall and permit the parish council to meet there when the last we heard was that the corporation did not wish to occupy it any longer. It seems to have been pure coincidence that the building began its known existence as the residence of Reginald Alard whose family were king's bailiffs,[1] and that the freeholder to whom it was returned, Jesse Piper, was also successor to the bailiffs of Winchelsea.

The history of such an old building is mostly surmise and speculation. There may well have been a substantial structure on the site long before King Edward I built New Winchelsea. In support of this various authorities quote the thickness of the lower walls, the nature of the arch over the garden gate and the little alcove in the corner of the garden. The most direct evidence, though, is the dungeon which used to incarcerate the bailiff's prisoners long before the rooms at street level assumed a similar function. It lies below the western room of the ground floor and is now filled with rubble. The topmost section of the arch over its entrance can be seen behind the flowerbed against the building in Hiham Green. This cellar's construction is of very early date and the design, described by Inderwick as a vaulted cavern,[2] is quite different from the basic one used for Winchelsea's wine-stores in the late thirteenth century. W.M. Homan, who made a detailed and definitive account of the cellars,[3] was the last person to attempt serious study of such an unusual variant from the norm.

In March 1933, by arrangement with the mayor, Mr. A.V. Owen, Homan made an excavation in the south-west corner of the interior of the building. He discovered that six feet six inches below the present floorboards there is a stone flagged floor. The steps leading down to it from the entrance visible in the west gable appear to stop at this floor. It is a box-shaped structure, not at all like Inderwick's 'vaulted cavern'. Homan thought this to be a common medieval design providing no definite evidence except that it was clearly of an earlier date that the late-thirteenth-century wine cellars under so many of the town's other buildings. He supposed that it had been part of Reginald Alard's original construction. The rubble he reported as being of 'comparatively recent date' but, uncharacteristically, he carried out no investigation to find clues as to how long it had been there.

On completion of his work Homan replaced and screwed down the floorboards in such a way that future access would be possible but cupboards have since been built over the spot. At the time the corporation members were considering whether opening up this cellar would add to the building's interest to the public but Homan opined that this would be much too expensive and so the situation remains to this day. The mayor himself must have had considerable doubts about the project for Homan's report ends, 'I hope my excavation has not caused you another sleepless night. It was really quite harmless and in the interests of the town.'[4]

With this medieval cellar beneath it throughout, the building has been extensively altered over the centuries. There is evidence of former arcading on the south (High Street) side and the arches now containing the windows could well have given access to an open lower floor, a not uncommon arrangement in similar buildings.[5] Inderwick assumes that the little doorway through which the mayor and members of the corporation squeeze their way with as much dignity as possible each Easter Monday morning was an interior door leading to another upper room on the north side. An alternative theory is that it was once the access door which brought prisoners from the dungeon to beside the justice seat without their having to pass through the body of the hall.[6] Pevsner states that the building was once larger to the east and the west. If all these theories are true it was a substantial building indeed! There seems, however, to be common ground about the magnificent roof-structure which is dated as being part of the major fifteenth-century alterations.[7]

Although, like Homan, he is somewhat scathing about the late-nineteenth-century restoration with which we shall deal shortly, Ford Madox Ford succeeds admirably in characterising the building as being a 'singularly dignified' one. Of it he says, 'It is grey, old, four-square and absolutely sincere'.[8] This perceptive observation, to which might be added a comment on the Court Hall's intrinsic simplicity, remains essentially true.

Of the Court Hall's uses there are as many theories as there are of its shape and appearance. As the king's bailiff's residence the upper room may well have seen the entertainment of visiting royalty. In pre-reformation days it came into the hands of the ecclesiastical authorities, its rental being used to endow lamps and candles in connection with the chantries of St. Thomas's Church. As such it was confiscated by Henry VIII and later transferred into the ownership of the corporation under Queen Elizabeth I's grant of land in 1586 (see pp.48-49) at which time Edward Weekes was the tenant in occupation.[9]

More than three quarters of a century later it became the town's court hall under a resolution passed on 15 February 1665, 'At this Assembly it is ordered, concluded and agreed that the Court Hall of the Town of Winchelsea shall be taken down and a new Court Hall made in the chambers over the…' (here there is a tantalising gap in the records). A committee was appointed to oversee the work with penalties to be incurred if it were not completed by 'Easter Day next' in time for the mayoring.[10]

Another century was to pass before the prison was transferred to the same building, thus providing us with the most dramatic of its uses during the main period of this story. The prison was on the lower floor with the present garden-area as an exercise yard. Those on remand and those convicted of lesser offences were held there, more serious offenders being transferred to the House of Correction, Lewes. The nineteenth-century gaol books list for each prisoner not only the crime and length of sentence but also parish of residence, trade, age, height, hair-colour, eye-colour, complexion of face, 'body stout or slight', and distinguishing marks. The offences are varied and provide in summary a revealing insight into the responsibilities of local justices. They include felony, trespass, vagrancy, breach of the peace, assault, larceny, debt, stealing, insult, deserting wife, breaking church windows, transgression of fishing laws, drunken abuse, destruction of property and taking poles (John Carey and friends – see pp.67-68), selling beer without a licence, using bad language, taking beach, concealing tobacco, deserting children, poaching, demanding wages not due, unlawfully in possession of goods, begging, selling leaven weight, rioting and disturbance, threatening to throw overboard, selling beer on a Sunday before time, refusing to go to sea when ship was ready, acting as a pilot when not qualified, working an engine without a proper signalman (1878), ill-treating a horse, unlawfully igniting a fire in the high road, wandering without means of subsistence (George Wood of Holloway), 'leaving his carriage in the road' (John Piggott, fly driver, 1883), and keeping a dog not under control (James Hardie see p.79).

Not all these were punished with prison sentences but a considerable majority were including an offence, committed by Edward Warden in 1859, of damaging a house in Rye. A bracketed note against his entry reads, 'This prisoner was attended to every week and the scriptures read, also prayers and exhortation, by Charles Robins, magistrate.'[11]

It is doubtful whether the warders had the same concern for the personal and spiritual welfare of their charges. Security was their main preoccupation, particularly as their wages were stopped in the event of an escape. The gaoler's remuneration was sixpence per day per prisoner plus his expenses. Since up to nine prisoners were sometimes held this came to a considerable sum which he would no doubt have to share with those assisting him. Nevertheless the loss of one shilling and sixpence a day would have been a considerable blow when John Farr, Absalom Gillion and George Beam broke out three days after being convicted in 1825.[12]

Security concerns are reflected in the purchase of handcuffs, staves, body-irons and pistols for the use of the gaoler and constables; also in permission being granted to obtain estimates for 'raising the prison yard wall and fixing ironwork thereto to prevent escape.'[13] Reasonable care of the prisoners is, however, suggested by expenses claimed which include payments for coals and wood, straw, washing, bedding, beach for the yard, soap, brooms, sawdust, candles, earthenware, mutton, oatmeal, water and water crocks (in 1830 water for one year cost five shillings) and for cleaning the privy.[14]

At some time between 1810 and 1812 a transaction took place which we can only assume was one of the corporation's many ways of attempting to remain solvent. The freehold of the Court Hall was sold to Sir William Ashburnham who held the title of king's bailiff. Sir William began charging an annual rental of £12 for the building as did his successors and eventually Mr. Piper to whom, as we have seen, the corporation proposed surrendering occupancy.[15] The mayor and jurats retained full responsibility for the building's maintenance and repair. Nineteenth-century sketches and photographs show that during the years it was used as a prison all the present windows and doors on the ground floor street frontage were blocked up with the exception of one barred grille and an access door where the garden gate now stands (see p.45). Of the gaol's interior we have no information except the clues given us by the surviving cell doors and barred openings. An estimate for major work by 'Carpenters, Bricklayers and Smiths' dated 26 November 1822 allows for taking up part of the floor of the 'Inner Gaol', 'to put fillets over all the joints in the planking round the prison to keep out the wind', 'to put a cover over the privy seat in the yard', 'to cut away for a doorway between the two prisons', 'painting the walls and whitewashing [them] and taking out the earth to lower the floor in outer prison'. Intriguingly the specification also includes for carpenters' work 'in making the market house a place for the prisoners to be in a day'. We do not know where the market house was but it was presumably outside the Court Hall compound. The considerable expense of this work £62.14s.4d. must have drained the corporation's reserves considerably.[16]

Little was done over many following years to keep the prison in repair and eventually the authorities declined to allow its use. In 1879 William Wheeler was accused of ill-treating a horse and assaulting Police Constable Relfe while in the execution of his duty. After being charged Wheeler was taken to Rye lock-up. Inspector Dennis informed the bench that he had received orders to this effect from Col. Mackay, the Chief Constable. The magistrates were not amused at having a Winchelsea prisoner held outside their jurisdiction when there was sufficient accommodation in the Winchelsea gaol. The town clerk was instructed to write to Col. Mackay:

> 'to know when and by whom the Winchelsea gaol was condemned as unfit for use as a lock-up house as the Winchelsea authorities [have] received no notice of this being the case'.[17]

The exact nature of the colonel's reply we do not know but from this time on, as we have seen in the case of James Hardie, the gaol book reads more like a court book and we have to assume that the decision was upheld and the cells not used after 1879.

A short while previously, while still in active use as a court-house and gaol, the building was already attracting much interest from antiquarians. In 1873 the annual meeting of the Sussex Archaeological Society was held there. The members travelled by special train from Lewes, stopping at all stations until on arrival at Winchelsea the number in the party had reached about one hundred. This phalanx walked to the town, safely negotiating Ferry Hill, and was shown The Friars, St. Thomas's Church (where the rector gave a talk on the history of Winchelsea), the ancient gates and, of course, the Court Hall which was also to be the venue for luncheon. It very soon became clear that there would not be room for everyone to sit down. The chairman regretted that they had not brought a marquee but tactfully avoided blaming the secretary who had made the arrangements, blaming instead those who had inconsiderately failed to book their places in advance. The situation must have been satisfactorily sorted out for later proceedings included warm congratulations to Mrs. Jarrett, landlady of the New Inn, on the meal provided.[18]

(24) The Court Hall upper room when in use for concerts, showing the stage.

And so we approach again the time when the corporation wanted to have nothing more to do with the Court Hall and surrendered it. On first receiving notice Mr. Jesse Piper wrote to the town clerk alleging that the corporation had 'permitted encroachments to be made on the Town Hall and Gaol by suffering certain buildings to be erected against the wall thereof'. He required that these should be removed and the building left in a state of tenantable repair. When pressed to elaborate he specifically mentioned a lean-to stable placed against the wall. This was probably used by the town clerk who invariably hired a horse to travel from Rye to meetings and court sittings. Challenged to produce the tenancy agreement, Piper could not do so but he claimed that since the corporation had on all but one occasion taken complete responsibility for maintenance they must have an obligation to leave the building in reasonable condition.[19] The exception is an interesting one. Mrs. Ogle, Piper's predecessor, had in 1869 made a contribution of £10 towards the cost of constructing the stone steps which now provide access to the eastern door of the upper floor.[20] After further negotiations it was clearly shown that the structures complained of had been in position long before Mr. Piper became owner and he accepted responsibility.

On resuming possession he put the building up for sale. It was bought by James Dearle Padgett, a freeman, jurat and resident whose declared objective in the purchase was 'to prevent it falling into the hands of the papists'. F.A.Inderwick and the town clerk, Walter Dawes, were deeply unhappy about the course events had taken. Their feeling was that to lose the Court Hall, a building which, with its predecessor, had been the focal point of Winchelsea's civic history for almost six hundred years would devalue the corporation's continued existence, so hard earned by Inderwick, and cost the town any semblance of civic focus and dignity in carrying out its function as a Cinque Port. They approached Edwin Freshfield Ll.D., F.S.A., a legal colleague of Inderwick and a relation by marriage of Dawes. Dr. Freshfield was senior partner of the firm bearing his name, solicitors to the Bank of England. He was also a deeply committed antiquarian with a special interest in the Levant, 'with which he had long family associations'. His 'intimate knowledge of the East' led to his becoming president of the Byzantine Research Fund.[21] Freshfield expressed a generous willingness to help and agreed to approach the owner. By 23 June 1890 he was able to write:

'My dear Mr. Inderwick,

Mr. Padgett has agreed to sell me the Town Hall for £350.

When the purchase is completed I should very much like to have a talk with you as to what we shall do to preserve it for the Old Corporation.

Thank you for drawing my attention to it. If there was a decent – but now I am treading on dangerous ground.

Yours ever sincerely,

Edwin Freshfield'[22]

What we should infer from the last paragraph will always remain a mystery, but it may well have been connected with the reliability and commitment of those so ready to abandon such a vital part of Winchelsea's heritage.

The transition completed, the Court Hall was transferred on 29 September 1890 into the ownership of the corporation, or rather of its nominated trustees. The trust deed laid down that the uses to which the building might be put should be under the control of the mayor with the general intent 'that the said premises may for ever hereafter be of the nature of a Town Hall for the Ancient Town of Winchelsea and the Liberties thereof'.

The original plan was that the lower rooms should be used as a reading room and library, usually and almost certainly accurately referred to as the Men's Reading Room. The upper floor, apart from being the venue of the corporation's meetings and the Easter Monday Hundred Court, was to serve as a concert hall. Work to change the building from court and gaol to community centre proceeded apace under the direction of Charles Smith, architect, of Rye. The windows of the ground floor were found almost complete and re-set in the old stonework, the fireplaces were cleaned and made safe but otherwise unaltered, the prisoners' plank beds and deal cells were removed. The most dramatic alteration took place upstairs. A false ceiling had for many years been attached to the beams. This was removed and the glories of the roof structure revealed. Although four hundred years old it required virtually no repair. The first-floor windows were replaced and decorated with the arms of the leading families which had held the bailiwick. The little door in the north-west corner was discovered behind plasterwork and a small window inserted in the opening. It was only later that the door was fully reinstated and the steps built to provide the room with a second entrance. When the wooden structure occupied by the mayor and jurats sitting as magistrates was dismantled, a number of painted boards built into it generated considerable interest. They were, with some difficulty, correctly fitted together upon which 'it was discovered that they formed a rude picture in distemper of St. Leonard of Winchelsea in the act of blessing the fruits of

(25) *Tom Collins, caretaker, poses with a visitor in front of the old prison door and bars.*

the earth'. This picture remains on display.[23] The generosity of Edwin Freshfield's gift was supplemented by his financing of the other principal task undertaken, a major repair to the roof tiling. It cost £68.

Remarkably, by Easter Monday 1891 the transformation was complete. The freemen, jurats and officers gathered in the presence of leading residents and members of the public to hold the mayoring ceremony at its traditional home for the first time for several years. F.A.Inderwick was elected mayor. Much was said about the vital part he had played in acquiring the building. Inderwick in turn managed to slip in a good-natured appeal for further funds to provide equipment, the cost of which he estimated at £40. The meeting paused to pay tribute to Dr. Robert Vaile Skinner who had recently died and to congratulate George Hearnden on his reappointment as chamberlain 'in his ninetieth year'. The formal climax was the appointment of Dr. Freshfield as an honorary freeman of the ancient town in recognition of his generosity, a unique distinction at the time.

The ceremony was followed by a luncheon, also in the Court Hall upper room, at which 'Host Down's catering gave the utmost satisfaction'. Among the guests of the mayor and corporation were Mr. Millman, Clerk of the House of Commons, Mr.C.H. Stenning, the area's county councillor and H.J. Elliott, assistant overseer, soon to become the first clerk of Icklesham Parish Council. The town clerk, Walter Dawes, spoke 'in eulogistic terms' of Mr. Inderwick's leadership and his interest in 'all which appertains to the welfare of the place'. In response his worship gave an entertaining account of the history of the building.[24]

Ownership secured and restoration completed, much still remained to be done. A committee was set up to oversee the establishment of the reading room and library downstairs. The rules were duly drawn up. They included that smoking would only be permitted after 7 p.m.; that cards and other games might be played after the same time but not for money or money's worth; and that the committee should have power to fine users for misconduct or to strike them from the list of members.[25] Inderwick's appeal for funds for equipment had an interesting sequel indicative of social change. In 1901 the committee saw fit to purchase from R. Milsom of 28, High Street, Rye, for use in the room, either new or as replacements, three nine and a half inch enamel spittoons.[26]

Upstairs the concerts became important social occasions held monthly in winter and were eagerly anticipated. A platform at the western end served as a stage with raised plank seating helping the view of those at the back. The performances were homely, family occasions in the style of the old time music hall with H.J. Elliott developing a reputation for his style and energy as chairman. The local press would frequently print lists of the performers, their songs, recitations and other musical contributions. These make dull reading but we are able to learn something of the atmosphere of a type of occasion long outdated through an evocative account by the rector's daughter, Blanche Patch, who was later to become secretary to George Bernard Shaw:

'During the winter we had social evenings once a month and the admission charge was twopence. The village postman, the coachman from The Friars and two charwomen were among the artistes. Occasionally I would contribute a banjo solo – in those days of brilliant banjoists I should have been considered, quite rightly, a very bad performer on an instrument which had a disconcerting habit of snapping a string at the wrong moment. The coachman knew but one song which he sang without accompaniment, the refrain being, "Under the trees, with her bowl on her knees, Maria sat silently shelling green peas." He unconsciously added to his success by putting a penultimate "e" into the word bowl! Our postman, comparatively young, would ask when delivering letters at the Rectory if Miss Blanche could come round to the Town Hall, where there was a piano, to run through a song he was proposing to sing, and if I did not play for him Mother would. She was a good reader at sight and loved accompanying singers. The older ladies who attended these social evenings considered that there ought to be some censorship of what was to be sung, regarding me as much too young to decide what was a suitable comic song and what not. One evening my father came along because mother was not well and I could see that he was not very pleased with one of the songs given by the railway porter. However, he restrained himself and it was not until we were leaving the hall that he was heard saying to the offender, "I hope I shall never hear such a song again."'[27]

Ted Streeton remembers rather later concert parties with considerable pleasure. By the time he was a fascinated spectator as a boy professionals sometimes came to take part. He particularly liked one group who came year after year and would step from the magic world of the stage to talk to members of the audience. 'They had no side to them – they were just like us, trying to earn a living'.

In the earlier part of the twentieth century, with the obvious exception of the concerts, public access was largely downstairs. A Winchelsea guide book published in 1915 indicates that the reading room and library were open all day for residents and visitors, serving as a men's recreation room in the evenings. Users were asked to drop a penny in the box provided and to donate books and periodicals when possible.[28]

A *Methodist Recorder* reporter, preparing an article about John Wesley, visited the town in the late 1920s. Although he was mistaken about the room in which the trials had taken place, his account is of interest:

'When I arrived in Winchelsea I looked round for a likely source of information and in a few moments, having paid the sum of one penny, found myself in an old prison which is now used as a reading room. Where there were cells – one of the stout oaken doors may be seen – there are now various relics, including bits of the Wesley tree, some fashioned into little souvenirs. Where the malefactors used to be tried there is a small billiard table, a few cases of rather dusty books and one or two newspapers. The room when I saw it was hardly attractive enough for the purpose of study. Possibly in the winter it is not used a great deal.'[29]

After the reading room was closed in 1931 the use of the lower rooms as a men's club continued for some time. Upstairs, however, with the brief exception of the Peulevé initiative (see p.153), it was not until after the Second World War that a major development led to the establishment of the museum and its regular opening between May and September. Author of the 1947 report to the corporation which paved the way for the project was Captain Herbert Lovegrove R.N. who had come to live in Winchelsea and was taking an intense interest in its history. Only a year later he was to become a freeman and jurat; one of the town's most devoted and distinguished servants of the second half of the twentieth century. He felt very strongly the importance of an attempt to inform and interest the many visitors whom he observed wandering rather aimlessly round the town.

Captain Lovegrove was extremely cautious about the corporation appearing to have any intention to profit by charging for admission. As their official income remained at just over £19 per annum from the queen's dues it would not seem to have been all that unworthy a motive. In fact he recommended what has been the situation throughout the museum's existence, namely that, with the exception of meeting the expenses of the invigilators, all takings should be used in maintaining the exhibits and the building. He also anxiously urged that the residents of the town should be involved; without their interest he felt the project unlikely to prosper.[30] It was much later that this support took an organised form with the greatly valued establishment of the Friends of the Ancient Monuments and Museum of Winchelsea.

The members of the corporation eagerly responded to the idea but were doubtful about whether they had sufficient material for display. The nineteenth-century artefacts observed by the *Methodist Recorder* reporter were still there, particularly including the town horn and the standard set of weights and measures, but the Wesley tree souvenirs had all gone and there was not much else. The mayor, Anthony Freeman, eventually put out an appeal reporting the receipt of bequests and gifts and seeking from residents the loan of items of local and historic interest. There was a considerable response including a gift of pictures of Winchelsea from Hastings Corporation's collection as 'a token of goodwill between fellow portsmen'. The mayor's exhortation included what has always been a major motivation, 'The corporation is very anxious to throw open the fine upper chamber of the Court Hall to the general public as soon as the museum is arranged.'[31] Whatever the interest of individual items and the insight they provide into Winchelsea's history, the room itself remains the finest exhibit.

The museum has, at the time of writing, been open for forty-five years during which time local residents as well as members of the corporation have given much time-consuming and devoted service as curators and invigilators. In a curatorial capacity particular mention should be made of Charles Croggon who, while town clerk, held a supervisory brief on behalf of the corporation for many years; of Josian Andrew, Barbara Murrell, and of Maurice Humphreys whose enthusiastic involvement was cut so tragically short by his illness and premature death. The number of visitors peaked at about eight thousand a year in the early 1970s but is now, as what seems to be part of a general trend, considerably fewer. An unusual feature not on display is the whole set of visitors' books completed over the years. They make an interesting study.

The opening of the upper room and concentration on its maintenance resulted in the sad neglect of the lower floor. In 1965 the mayor, David Homan, wrote to the current users about its dilapidated condition and outlined the corporation's ideas for improvements. He proposed redecoration, the provision of lock-up cupboards (the ones which blocked up his father's access-route to the cellar), window-curtains and hangings for an enclosed storage area. Electric heating was to replace the coke stove which had to go because of the mess it created as did the oil stoves on grounds of safety. The organisations using the lower part of the building were the youth club, the county library, the girl guides, the old people's club and the Winchelsea Produce Market.[32] It is worth noting that in those days although no longer, while the museum was open, the public were allowed to visit the outer room of the lower floor.

In the thirty ensuing years many further improvements have been made including, amid not inconsiderable controversy, the provision under the 1869 stairs of a lavatory for the use of members of the corporation and staff on duty. While fairly basic, it is a considerable improvement on the unroofed privy seat in the exercise yard which the prisoners at one time had to use! A tea and coffee bar has been provided and new lighting, partly concealed, installed by Mr. Reginald Packard, has greatly enhanced the atmosphere of the rooms.

The use of the Lower Court Hall remains personally controlled by the mayor exactly as it was when the parish council applied to Major Stileman a hundred years ago.

(26) The Court Hall, 1997

16. CENSUSES AND ROLLS

Within a few days of the 1891 mayoring ceremony and celebratory luncheon there took place the most recent census in Winchelsea for which full details are available for public inspection. The enumerator was H.J. Elliott who served Winchelsea in so many ways. His painstaking records show the road in which each property stood, although only a very few houses are individually identified; the names of the occupiers; their relationship to the head of the household; whether they were married, single or widowed; age last birthday; profession or occupation; whether they were employed or employers; and place of birth.

Such precise details are unavailable for the twentieth century because they remain closed for one hundred years, but it is clear that the total population of the town has remained unusually constant over the nineteenth and twentieth centuries while its nature has changed out of all recognition. The trends which have led to Winchelsea becoming principally a community of the retired can be identified in the nineteenth-century censuses.

Kenneth Clark made an analysis of the 1851 records which, he observed, provide us with 'an accurate snapshot' of Winchelsea in that year. He notes many leading citizens and their occupations, particularly drawing attention to the landowners whose farming interests provided a very high proportion of the work available.[1]

Despite its inclusion of less personal information, I have chosen the census made ten years earlier for the purposes of this study, providing as it does a gap of fifty years for a comparison. The results of my detailed analysis for the area covered by the town, The Strand/Tanyard Lane and Station Road/The Ferry are included as Appendix IV.

Before 1841 the returns were largely a counting of heads. In 1801 when the first official census was taken, it was only the permanent residents and not the garrison who were included. The overseers of the poor carried out this work until 1831 and were allowed more than one day on which to make the count. The *Victoria County History of Sussex* has published the total number of residents of the parish of St. Thomas's and the Winchelsea liberties as follows:

1801	*625*	1841	*687*	1881	*613*
1811	*652*	1851	*777*	1891	*686*
1821	*817*	1861	*719*	1901	*670*
1831	*772*	1871	*679*		

These figures would have included the settlement of Camber.[2]

Occasional additional information can be found in such sources as the church registers where it is recorded:

> 'By an account of the population taken on the tenth day of March 1801 under the authority of Parliament it appears that this parish contains one hundred and six houses or tenements occupied by six hundred and twenty five persons whereof two hundred and eighty five are males and three hundred and forty two females and that seventy-six persons are employed in agriculture, seventy one in trade and the remaining four hundred and eighty consists of women, children and others not falling under the above descriptions'.[3]

Similarly the corporation minutes noted on 28 June 1831 that the recent account of the population had shown that the parish included 143 inhabited houses occupied by 172 families.

There were five uninhabited houses. Forty-five families were chiefly occupied in agriculture, forty in trade. 363 males and 409 females made a total population of 772, a decrease on the return made in 1821.[4]

The reader wishing to make a detailed study of the figures in Appendix IV will see that, while far from startling, certain trends are clear. The average age of adults is rising as is the number of households. It should be noted that in 1841 adults only had to declare their ages to the nearest five years. Falling are the size of families, the numbers per household, the numbers of uninhabited dwellings and the number of children of school age. The vast majority of those listed in 1841 as born in Sussex would have been born in Winchelsea itself. Sadly they were not asked to be so specific. Even in 1891, however, the comparatively static nature of the population is well illustrated by 238 declarations to that effect. I doubt whether in 1995 more than half-a-dozen residents could make such a claim.

In 1891 there was a most noticeable fall of almost fifty percent in the numbers employed in agriculture, a statistic almost matched by an increase in the number of domestic servants. The cause of the latter development was noted in Pike's *District Blue Book* for 1885, which, when referring to Winchelsea, noted that 'recently several private families have taken up residence there.' The Inderwicks at Mariteau House merited special mention.[5] Despite this there was virtually no change in the numbers of those listing themselves as of independent means.

Even such bare entries reveal for us something of the circumstances of those whose names are recorded although regrettably there is no space here to examine in detail the enumerator's returns. In 1841 there were only two principal houses. The entry for The Friars gives its occupants as William Bennett, gardener, his wife and two children together with three female servants. The Stileman family were counted at their London home. Katherine Gybbon, a relation, is, however, recorded as living elsewhere in the town and keeping two servants. Resident at Cleveland House were Katherine Woodhams, her two daughters, three visitors and four servants. As suggested above by the summaries of earlier censuses, the vast majority of cottages either relied on agriculture for income or were the homes of those providing services for the town. The postmaster, Richard Wilson, lived in Friars Road, then known as Cleveland Street, where no fewer than nine men gave their occupation as agricultural labourer. William Stace, the blacksmith, lived and worked in the High Street with his wife and nine children. George Haisell, hairdresser, son of Thomas (see p.53) also had his premises in the High Street. William Bray, veterinary surgeon, worked from his home in Mill Road; Richard Osborne kept the Castle Inn where he lived with his daughter, a servant, and George Willard aged thirteen, pot-boy. The parish records of St. Thomas's provide the best source of information about the poverty so prevalent in Winchelsea at that time but clues are provided by the census which reveals, for example, that one small cottage in Friars Road was occupied by no fewer that sixteen people, George Barden, wheelwright, and his wife, their fifteen-year-old agricultural labourer son Joseph, three more agricultural labourers, William Ockenden, Mitchell Williams and Charles Clarke, with Clarke's wife and their six children.[6]

By 1891 the number of properties occupied by those wealthy enough to provide a focus for services and supplies had considerably increased. The Inderwicks at Mariteau House came into this category as we have seen. The Stilemans continued at The Friars in the persons of Major Robert and his sister Katherine. A leading addition since 1841 was The Rectory (now the Old Rectory) where lived Henry Patch, rector, his wife, their son John (who was later to succeed his father in the living), five other children, a cook, a nurse and a housemaid. Cleveland House may have fallen on harder times for the head of the household, Mary Luff aged 61 and of independent means, lived there with three unmarried daughters and a son aged 19; no servants are listed. They may, of course, have lived out. Also into this category fell The Mount, home of Mrs. Frances Padgett, widow of the purchaser of the Court Hall, Sea View House (Strand Plat), occupied by Sarah Smith, widow of independent means, and Glebe Cottage, the home of Dr. William Martindale, his wife Maria and their daughter Mary aged 17. Their other daughter, Elsie, was later to marry Ford Madox Ford. One would expect Periteau House to be included in this list. It was, indeed, a focus for the provision of services by the town's tradesmen, but not only as a private residence for Mrs. Maria Skinner, recently widowed on the death of Dr. Robert Vaile Skinner, was also using the property as an asylum for 'lunatics', for so the census listed them. The household included her son Ernest who had succeeded his father as a general practitioner, her nephew John, also a doctor and soon to become the first chairman of Icklesham Parish Council, four lunatics, four attendants and four servants.[7]

In the absence of any formal censuses such as these, clues about the size of Winchelsea's population between the thirteenth and eighteenth centuries are rare. In 1724 there are said to have been only thirty-five to forty families living in the parish of St. Thomas.[8] In 1652 Winchelsea was 'all rubbish and a few despicable hovels only standing' (see p.16). It has been calculated from a religious census that in 1576 there were 150 residents,[9] a notable decrease from eleven years previously when a Certificate of Commissioners indicated that Winchelsea had 109 households, 12 vessels (1 hoy, 6 cockboats and 5 lighters) and that the vessels were operated by 10 mariners and two fishermen. At the same time Rye had 530 households and 66 vessels. It is interesting to note that at a period when it could be expected that Winchelsea would lag far behind her fellow eastern Cinque Ports, Hastings had no more than 280 households and Pevensey only 64.[10]

We have already seen (p.10) that there was a major decline in Winchelsea's population during the fourteenth century. Before that we have an outstanding point of reference in the meticulously prepared rent-roll which was produced in 1292 listing those to whom sites had been allocated in the new town. Like his predecessor, W.D. Cooper, Frederic Inderwick was fascinated by this document. In *The Story of King Edward and New Winchelsea* he comments particularly on the predominance of clergy and those associated with the churches and friaries. Of those providing for Winchelsea's defensive needs he noted various smiths, stonemasons, a lance-maker, an armour-maker, several gatekeepers, a pikeman, and a trumpeter. The general traders were represented by ten bakers, six butchers, five cooks, four cobblers, several coopers, two water-carriers, two barber-surgeons, reapers and carters or cart-makers, a thatcher, two horse-breakers, two bird-catchers and many others.[11]

Despite the temptation to follow this exploration further, it is the total number of households listed which is important to us at present. There were 682 which Homan believed would represent a total population of between four and six thousand, a very large town for those days.[12] Cooper records the preamble to the rent-roll as saying, 'These are the places set out, enfranchised and on which a rent has been put in the new town of Winchelsea, which is just now built by the mayor and twenty-four jurats and by Sir John de Kirkeby, Bishop of Ely on the part of our Lord the King.'[13]

Understandably the survival of this document, of which there are two copies at the Public Record Office, created a great deal of interest in 1992, the seven hundredth anniversary of its compilation. The town clerk gave a talk at the Easter Monday Hundred Court during which he suggested that, while no equivalent was possible for it would be an invasion of privacy, an attempt might be made to compile a residential roll for 1992 as part of the celebrations. This project came into being in the autumn when a letter was delivered to all the approximately 240 homes within the area of the original roll. When compared with the nineteenth-century censuses this number of households illustrates well that, despite its reputation for antiquity, at least half Winchelsea's present properties have been built in the twentieth century. The residents were told of the proposed celebratory residential roll and invited, if they wished to be included, to return a form giving their name(s) and address, together with a copy of W.M. Homan's plan of the town as originally laid out, on which the position of their home could be indicated. It was explained that, were the residential roll ever to be published, the most likely opportunity would be in this book which was at that time in the very early stages of planning and research. The names would be entered, as in the original, according to the quarter in which the respondents lived and would generally be shown as surname with one christian name, following the earlier precedent. There can, of course, be no closer comparison for the 1292 list was of heads of household only.

The form sent to residents included an invitation, on an entirely voluntary basis, to submit in a section headed 'Additional Information' such details as the nature of their work, whether they were retired, service to the town of Winchelsea and the wider community, length of residence, relationship to former residents etc. Many responded in some detail and I have benefited from numerous leads thus indicated, information about individual properties and family connections being the most common. It became clear, for example, that there are still descendants of the Stileman and Skinner families living or owning property in Winchelsea, something of which I was not previously aware. The confidentiality of these forms has been, and will continue to be, carefully preserved.

One hundred and fifty-six returns were eventually received and the resulting roll is published as Appendix I. While the return of the forms was awaited a major celebration of the seven hundredth anniversary of the rent-roll took place at the Court Hall on 21 November 1992. A luncheon hosted by the mayor and mayoress, Knightley and Mary Chetwood, was attended by the mayors of all fourteen member towns of the Confederation of the Cinque Ports, including the Speaker, Councillor John Ciccone of Rye, with their consorts. This was a warm and convivial occasion, indicative of the camaraderie which has developed in recent years among confederation representatives. The town clerk spoke about the rent roll and each mayor was presented with a copy of the most detailed version of W.M. Homan's plan, together with a commemorative certificate.

A detailed analysis of the residential roll was later undertaken. The incomplete nature of the survey and the confidential contents make any direct comparison with the original rent-roll impossible. However, it became clear that there were quite striking ways in which the outcome could be related to the nineteenth-century censuses. The most notable of these was the concept of retirement. In 1841 there was no such thing. If you were not supported by a private income you worked your full lifespan or went to the workhouse. By 1891 eleven of the 570 residents declared themselves to be retired from quite ordinary jobs, one each of army, bailiff, blacksmith, cab driver, farmer, gardener, grazier, innkeeper, navy, police constable and tea dealer. In 1992, of the ninety-three people who made any reference to their occupations, no fewer than fifty-five said that they were retired, a massive increase which has clearly dominated the social development of the town in the twentieth century. There are other trends which it seems reasonable to deduce from these returns. With the renewed qualification that the residential roll is incomplete, these, when reduced to pure statistics are:

The percentage of those who refer to their occupation and say that they are retired:

| 1841 | 0.00 | 1891 | 1.92 | 1992 | 59.10 |

The average numbers of persons per household:

| 1841 | 5.44 | 1891 | 4.91 | 1992 | 1.92 |

The average number of children in households where there are children:
     1841   3.36   1891   3.13   1992   1.60

The percentage of households with children:
     1841   70.10   1891   44.10   1992   12.25

One further trend becomes clear but is not quantifiable in the same way. In the late nineteenth and early twentieth centuries wealthy professionals such as Frederic Inderwick and George Freeman had a London residence as well as one in Winchelsea, but the wider ownership of second homes was something far in the future. The 1992 residential roll returns show fifteen persons and families declaring their Winchelsea properties as second homes. Others may have this status but not have mentioned the fact. Yet more are highly likely to be among the approximately 84 properties from which no forms were received. This development has probably not yet affected Winchelsea as much as it has many country communities, largely because so many of the current 'weekenders' take an enthusiastic and active interest in the life of the town, but it is one which may well have a considerable impact in the future.

17 . ARTISTS AND AUTHORS

1891, year of the gift of the Court Hall and year of the census, saw also the first visit to Winchelsea of Ford Madox Ford. He came courting, the object of his affections being Elsie Martindale, elder daughter of Dr. William Martindale, a prominent pharmacist who was freeman, jurat and soon to be mayor of the town. Martindale's campaign to improve Winchelsea's drainage and water supplies we have already noted.

Ford was eighteen, elated by the publication of his first book and the smoking of his first pipe of tobacco. He travelled by train. His recollection takes us no further than 'old fashioned' Rye station where he noticed bright placards and vividly recalled the 'singularly fine grey ashes' of his pipe.[1] Elsie was a former schoolfellow at Praetorious School where Ford had been captain of cricket. They were so much together that she became known as 'the captain's wife'.[2] It was in the long term to be an unhappy relationship.

Ford's importance to us is that of all the artists and authors connected with Winchelsea in the nineteenth and early twentieth centuries by their subject matter, residence or family ties, he is the most intimately involved and provides us with a focal point not only through his acquaintance with many distinguished authors resident in the area in his own time but also because he was the grandson of Ford Madox Brown, an artist who had supported and encouraged the Pre-Raphaelite Brotherhood, a group closely associated with the town earlier.

To begin the sequence which leads us to Ford and beyond to authors of the later twentieth century we must look first at the work of J.M.W. Turner and his dramatic watercolour with Strand Hill and the town as background. Although the picture was finished much later, its origins lay in his observation of a regiment on the march during the Napoleonic wars. The column is making its way up the hill through Strand Gate and we can see St. Thomas's Church, the ruins of Greyfriars Chapel, buildings in the High Street and the Roundel, although their positions seem controlled by artistic rather than factual requirements. In the foreground the detail is precise, demonstrating an exact draughtsmanship which anticipates the Pre-Raphaelites. Early studies for the picture, included in Turner's *Liber Studiorum* which also includes two studies of the Pipewell Gate, show a soldier speaking to a woman resting on a bank beside a road, and later two women with bundles and two soldiers with a baggage wagon in the distance. The final version has a woman apparently unwell, accompanied by two friends, one of whom is comforting her. Two baggage wagons make their way towards Strand Hill as do serried ranks of soldiery, two of whom have stopped near the woman. The brooding skyscape which overpowers the scene is symbolic of war and the zig-zag lines of troops have been said to suggest the pattern of lightning in the storm. Such allegorical interpretations were to be developed by the Pre-Raphaelites as was his water-colour technique in immersing paper containing a carefully drawn outline in water to permit the speedy application of background colour on which the detail would be superimposed. This they termed the 'wet white ground'.[3] Turner's use of the area for inspiration is further illustrated by his *Rye, Sussex* which portrays dramatically the bursting of a temporary dam constructed during the building of the Military Canal. Rye and Camber Castle appear in the background.

The Pre-Raphaelite Brotherhood, which drew much from Turner's influence and example, was founded in 1848 by John Everett Millais, William Holman Hunt, Dante Gabriel Rossetti and others. The three named were all former students of Sir Joshua Reynolds whose artistic techniques led them irreverently to dub him 'Sir Sloshua'. They wanted to return to the style of the Florentine

COPYRIGHT BRITISH MUSEUM

(27) Winchelsea during the Napoleonic wars as portrayed by J.M.W. Turner

painters before Raphael and to precise literal detail. Ford describes the movement's purpose as, 'a thing in its inception, as perfectly clear, as simple and as sharp cut as a ray of sunlight driven through the gloom of a cellar from a keyhole in a door'.[4] There is no space here to study the artistic significance of the Brotherhood but the Winchelsea connections of its leading members are well worth noting. Rossetti was a regular visitor whose feelings about the town and amused observation of its civic procedures we have already noted (see pp.68-69). Hunt, too, came often and later lived at Pett where he hoped to be able to work in solitude. His artistic skill was greatly admired, adulated by some. Burne-Jones wrote of him, 'There entered the greatest genius that is on earth alive, such a grand-looking fellow, such a splendour of a man, with a great wiry golden beard and faithful violet eyes.'[5] He was also described as 'a kindly and unswerving evangelical Christian, with all the discipline and convention of a man who had risen from relative poverty by his own effort and talent.'[6] Whether these characteristics would have made him a lovable grandfather is perhaps doubtful, but that view of him would be of great interest to us because his second marriage, to Marion Edith Waugh, produced a son, Hilary, who married Gwendoline, daughter of George and Annie Freeman of The Friars and sister of Anthony Freeman of Wickham Manor. Hilary's daughter, Diana, left us revealing insights into the eccentric life of the Freeman family in a highly acclaimed book *My Grandmothers and I.* Her revelations we shall examine later.

Holman Hunt's close friend John Everett Millais is reputed to have stayed twice in Winchelsea, presumably at some length and notably in 1854. The impact made on him is reflected in his choice of local settings for his paintings. Millais followed Turner in choosing a view of the town from the north-east as background for *The Blind Girl.* Replacing phalanxes of soldiers and stormy activity we find here a tranquil country scene in which the blind girl sits at the roadside with her child companion. Behind them the light of a rainbow surmounts the hill of Iham where the topography and buildings, true to Pre-Raphaelite ideals, are much more faithfully reproduced than by Turner.

It seems a shame that this view, immortalised by such distinguished artists as Turner and Millais, has been allowed to become obscured in recent years by large trees which have grown on the adjoining hillside. However vitally important trees and their preservation may be, it should still be possible for the modern artist and visitor to see and appreciate Winchelsea's dramatically steep ascent to its principal medieval entrance.

Elsewhere within the town Millais concentrated his attention on the church where *My First Sermon, My Second Sermon* and *The Random Shot* were painted. The story is told of how Millais, spending much time contemplating a setting for the last of these, was challenged by the verger who demanded to know his business. On being told that Millais proposed to paint the church this worthy retorted, 'You need not hang about any longer for the church was fully done up last year'.[7] Church attendance in the area during his stays seems also to have caused Millais some embarrassment. On one occasion he heard Rev. J.J. West, rector of St. Thomas's and a notable preacher, make most disparaging remarks about painters and the shortcomings of their work.[8] On another the vicar of Icklesham, conscious of this illustrious member of his congregation, used it to illustrate man's limitations beside those of his creator, saying of some spiritual quality, 'No, my brethren, he cannot paint that'.[9]

The Millais family's association with Winchelsea continues to the present time. Sir Ralph Millais, his grandson, and Lady Millais lived at Saffron Gardens, School Hill, and their son, Sir Geoffroy Millais, still lives in the town. Together they took a leading part in preparations for an exhibition entitled *Millais Artist and Man,* held in St. Thomas's Church in 1988.

Millais greatly enjoyed his stays in Winchelsea at Glebe and the New Inn. The former, one of the town's most distinguished properties, was also visited by William Makepeace Thackeray who used it as the rectory in his novel *Denis Duval.* Millais himself showed Thackeray the tomb of Gervase Alard which later featured in the book. Like his friend, Thackeray was entranced by Winchelsea and must have had plenty of time to appreciate it for he stayed at The New Inn while writing *Denis Duval.*[10] His daughters reported of him:

> 'He came home delighted with the old places; he had seen the ancient gateways and sketched one of them, and he had seen the great churches and the old houses, all sailing inland from the sea. Winchelsea was everything he had hoped for and even better than he expected.'[11]

Into *Denis Duval* Thackeray wove real characters and incidents. The most important from Winchelsea's point of view are the Weston brothers, supposedly respectable residents of The Friars who, as we have seen (p.54), finished on the scaffold. In the story they are guardians of Agnes, the love of Denis's life. When one of the brothers is accompanying Denis and the rector, who has a valuable box as luggage, the other Weston holds up the coach and is shot in the face and injured by Denis. After that the young man had enemies in the town! The Winchelsea setting of the story is atmospheric but largely unspecific and seldom permits the identification of actual places or properties although Magazine Cottage is supposed to have been Denis's home.[12] Scenes such as those depicting the boy's schooldays at Peacocke School in Rye and the spreading through the area of news of the outbreak of the Napoleonic wars give vivid insights into the life of the times and I found myself much disappointed that I was not able to follow Denis's adventures in the navy because the book was left unfinished on Thackeray's death.

I have already mentioned the Winchelsea connections of Holman Hunt and Millais. It was their Pre-Raphaelite colleague and friend Dante Gabriel Rossetti who, through his great admiration of Ford Madox Brown's work, wrote to him seeking to become his pupil. Brown agreed and thus was drawn into the circle of the Pre-Raphaelites. Although he consistently declined to join them his influence was considerable. Brown's own connection with Winchelsea was mainly through his descendants. His younger daughter, Catherine, married Franz (or Francis) Hueffer and it is as Ford Hermann Hueffer (pronounced Hoofer or Huffer) that their son, Winchelsea's principal literary connection, was known when he lived in the town. His father, an emigrant from Germany, was a distinguished writer on music and one-time music critic of *The Times*. The premature death of Francis Hueffer in 1889 brought his son more under the influence of his grandfather with whom the family moved to live. Despite the problems generated by anti-German feeling during the First World War, Ford continued to use his original name throughout his service as an officer in the British army and changed it only in 1921 when the war was over.

Ford married Elsie Martindale on 17 May 1894 despite fierce opposition from her parents which provoked an elopement in circumstances similar to those in which his grandfather had married his second wife. Ford and Elsie lived first at Aldington near Romney Marsh but, with family relationships improving, Dr. Martindale purchased a property in Friars Road, now known as The Little House but then somewhat curiously to the modern ear called The Bungalow. The name is actually taken from the Hindi and means a building with a verandah. The Bungalow was made over to Elsie and the couple moved in in 1901. The house had been built in 1782 by General Prescott, later to become Governor General of Canada, in exact imitation of a Canadian frame house. Originally it had a verandah at the front but despite this and other minor alterations it remains largely as it was in Ford's time. A commemorative plaque now adorns the building, placed there by Charles Kinross, Ford's friend and a subsequent owner.

Katharina Forbes-Dunlop remembered as a child observing Ford and his wife about the town. His demeanour she recalled as 'solemn, quick moving, giving a grey appearance', regretting that he was generally too preoccupied to notice a polite 'Good morning' from the children. His wife 'usually wore long, floating yellow garments so we called her "The Mustard Pot". She usually swept past us unnoticing and we didn't really like her.'[13]

Dr. Martindale died in 1902, found at his London laboratory where he had almost certainly committed suicide. Two years later the improvements in family relationships which had been developing were shattered by Elsie's accidental discovery that Ford had become the lover of her younger sister, Mary. Such news would have devastated the doctor and it has been suggested that his suicide may have been partly provoked by his earlier unrevealed knowledge of the affair.[14]

The marriage did not immediately break up but in 1907 Ford decided that country life was no longer a sufficient stimulus for an intellectual mind and moved to London, visiting Elsie at weekends. The following year The Bungalow was sold and the couple became permanently estranged, though she would never divorce him. Both are recorded as making comments on life in Winchelsea which are relevant to trends we have noted elsewhere. He said that he had tired of the town 'to which genteel families come in search of health and quiet which they find in abundance'. She left because life at Winchelsea was becoming 'artificially fashionable'. Ford wrote to his mother, 'We have definitely unfurnished The Bungalow and stored the furniture – so there's an end to Winchelsea'.[15]

This air of finality does not reduce the affection with which Ford, for a time at least, viewed the town. His book *The Cinque Ports* contains two chapters on Winchelsea which, while not entirely reliable historically, are certainly appreciative. The second begins:

'I know of no place more prodigal of pleasant impressions than this old town, which offers itself so open to the sky upon its little hill. Consider it beneath a summer sun and it recalls the May-day riot of colour and bright laughter of a medieval township. Under a grey sky it will make you ponder on the cracks and crannies of the castles of the old time before us'.[16]

Elsewhere he wrote, 'It is an infectious and holding neighbourhood. Once you go there you are apt there to stay'.[17]

Ford's reputation, both professional and personal, has not generally been high over the years. As he is so important among Winchelsea's literary and artistic associates it is a pleasure to note that the balance has been redressed by Alan Judd's informative and extremely readable biography first published in 1990.

Of all Ford's literary friends who lived in the area or visited during his residence at Winchelsea we shall concentrate here on the two whose connections were the closest, Joseph Conrad and Henry James.

Conrad and Ford were collaborators, an arrangement initiated by Conrad who felt he needed help with the intricacies of a language not his own. To further this co-operation he rented, for a time at least, a little cottage in Friars Road almost opposite The Bungalow. He must have been rather a severe presence of strong square build with a walk betraying him as 'a sailor who never seems to find solid earth a footing after sloping deck'.[18] Katharina Forbes-Dunlop, a little girl of seven living opposite at the house then known as Etterby and now as Tamarisk, was fascinated by the figure she observed through the open cottage door writing industriously. One day as she sat on his doorstep

(28) The Little House, formerly The Bungalow, once home of Ford Madox Ford.

innocently watching he suddenly asked what she was going to do when she grew up. Eagerly she replied, 'I want to write books like you'. Conrad told her sternly that it was the men who wrote books and the women who looked after the men and kept them well fed. He then sent her off to ask her mother to teach her to make rice pudding. This unusual request was agreed and an appetising rice pudding borne across the road and greatly appreciated. The child was then instructed, 'Now remember, all girls must be able to cook.' In her professional career as headmistress of a school for girls she claimed to have ensured that this stricture was observed.[19]

Ford's collaboration with Conrad earned considerable disapproval in the literary world for he was assumed to be taking advantage of the older man to further his own ends as a writer. More acrimony ensued when Jessie Conrad strongly objected to Ford's biography of her late husband.

These events have some parallel in Ford's relationship with Henry James who lived at Lamb House, Rye. James was already recognised as a great writer and Ford sought to claim or develop a greater level of friendship than James sought to give. 'The Master' tended to keep him at a distance and on occasions 'was quite likely to dive into a ditch or bolt behind a tree to avoid meeting Hueffer whom he had observed approaching along a country road.'[20] Nevertheless the association brought James to Friars Road to fall, like Conrad, under the observant eye of Katharina Forbes-Dunlop. She was particularly fascinated by his use of a bicycle on which he would travel many miles, usually followed by a manservant. On his arrival outside her home, James, presumably preoccupied in thought, would dismount and walk away, leaving the bicycle to crash dramatically to the ground, to be picked up by the manservant.[21]

James's long residence in Rye led him to write about the area directly and indirectly in a way that Conrad never did. The Winchelsea of the turn if the century James described as a 'high, loose, haunted square....There are ladies in view with sun bonnets and white umbrellas.'[22] He put the town in fiction as well for *The Third Person,* a short story set in Marr which was reputedly Rye, in fact contains the description:

> 'It was in the middle – or what passed for such – of the big, blank, melancholy square of Marr; a public place, as it were, of such an absurd capacity for a crowd, with the great ivy-mantled choir and stopped transepts of the most nobly planned church telling of how, many centuries ago, it had for its part, given up growing'.[23]

Surely St. Thomas's, Winchelsea.

Ford recalls James's visits to Winchelsea with perception and affection:

> 'I can still see his sturdy form as, arranged in a pea-jacket which nobly enhanced his bulk, wearing one of his innumerable cricket caps, emphasising his steps and the cadences of his conversation by digging his cane into the road, he stumped under the arch of the sea-gate up the hill into Winchelsea, lugging behind him on a ten yard leather lead his highly varnished dachshund, Maximilian. The dog would gyrate round his master. Mr. James would roll his eyes; he would be slightly out of breath. There would be a gentle snifter of rain... In the great square, round the great half fallen church the rain would run in light drifts. He would dig his cane point into the grass verge and exclaim: "A Winchelsea day, my dear lady. A true Winchelsea day... This is Winchelsea, poor but proud." Waspishly patriotic we would point to the red-roofed pyramid across the marsh and exclaim, "That's your Rye. It's *pouring* there... Rye... Not rich but dirty," These were the only occasions on which we stood up to The Master. And he never heard.'[24]

Such insights flow from Ford's pen, locally about H.G. Wells, Stephen Crane, Galsworthy, Kipling, Coventry Patmore and many others; nationally about such as D.H. Lawrence whose early writings Ford published when editor of *The English Review*. The first examples of this work were sent to Ford by a young lady of Lawrence's acquaintance at the time that he was teaching in Croydon. She and Lawrence were entertained by Ford who recalls their being unused to the ways of his household. They openly asked the housemaid whether the young lady should keep her hat on and the manservant waiting at table which knives and forks they should use for the various dishes. Ford later visited Lawrence's home and tells of a circle of family and friends in which religion, literature and philosophy were constantly the subject of conversation with Lawrence's father interjecting as he sat at the table counting the miner's wages he had brought home. Ford describes Lawrence's background as totally failing to prepare him for the ways of the world, the residents of the row of houses he lived in being so law-abiding that no policeman was ever seen there and so poor that no burglar was ever attracted.[25]

My study of Lawrence's life and works took place many years ago. I can recall finding nothing remotely as illuminating as this.

Ford's departure from Winchelsea in 1908 broke the thread linking the artists and authors connected with the town during the previous hundred years. Other artists had been his contemporaries, notably William Padgett and Edward Sachse, both Royal Academicians. A little later came John Mallock a notable resident who is acclaimed as a painter in references within Winchelsea's archives and was elected a freeman; also Reginald and Kate Wilkinson, husband and wife. Reginald was another who achieved the distinction of exhibiting at the Royal Academy. Padgett and the Wilkinsons are commemorated in the churchyard and of the five only Mallock does not feature in the reference books known to me.[26]

During the later twentieth century such literary and artistic associations have been many and varied but there is no similar link. We shall therefore note a few examples of those who have been resident.

In the early 1920s the American poet Conrad Aiken lived at Lookout Cottage. Aiken, a contemporary of T.S. Eliot, had established something of a reputation in his home country where 'He was reviewed regularly and seriously by critics and fellow poets'. In England, however, recognition was gained with much greater difficulty. A collection of his narrative poems, *Punch*, published in October 1921, did not sell and attracted little attention. Aiken was drawn to the area by its association with Henry James, by its likeness to that of his home town, Savannah, Georgia and by the hope that his children could obtain a good education there. Though depressed by his lack of success he seemed to enjoy life at Winchelsea. 'We are comfortable here, it's a lovely place, rent is cheap, views and walks and tennis and beer are plentiful.' His stay, though, was short for by February 1924 he had bought Jeake's House in Rye, with which town he became principally connected.[27]

Robert Nichols stayed considerably longer. I am grateful to Miss Josian Andrew who, during a conversation at Lord's, drew my attention to the First World War poet's residence at Yew Tree House. This was later readily corroborated by the present Lord Ritchie of Dundee whose sister Margaret, then a teenager, was much smitten by the romantic figure of a recognised published poet and war veteran. 'She was inclined to pursue him round the place.'

Nichols was greatly concerned about the encroachment of the sea and the threat it posed to the bungalows at Dog's Hill, Winchelsea Beach. He went so far as to interrupt the mayoring ceremony on Easter Monday 1930 to request a hearing seeking the help of the mayor and

(29) The inundation at Winchelsea Beach which cause Robert Nichols so much concern.

corporation in raising money to tackle the problem. He was permitted to attend a special hundred court a week later to put his case. After the meeting the mayor, Anthony Freeman, wrote to say that, while members had sympathy for any who had developed land in ignorance of the clear danger, the corporation could not be responsible for an appeal which would be misleading because it could not bring a long-term solution of the problem.[28] This was a diplomatic response from men who privately thought these bungalows, which they described as shacks, should never have been put there. The then Lord Ritchie of Dundee no doubt incurred his daughter's displeasure by feeling that the best thing that could happen was for the sea to wash them away.

The unfortunate predicament of these owners had been largely brought about by the financial demands of the great depresssion. William Crump, a man both determined and down to earth, who then owned Holford's farm and other land in the area, was forced to realise this asset by selling off plots, mostly for holiday use. In those pre-control days some purchasers proceeded to import old railway carriages and even parts of trade vans with which to make holiday homes. To use the words of Alex Finch, 'Winchelsea Beach became a shambles.' The new Battle Rural District Council eventually took strict enforcement action which even included destroying them by fire but by that time Crump had sold out altogether.[29]

William Crump did not get on well with the men whom Nichols approached for help. Alan Cooke recalls that the farmer once appeared before Rye magistrates on a comparatively minor motoring charge and was deeply offended at being fined the maximum amount. In the chair had been G.M. Freeman who later ordered hay from Crump and was sent, without much hope of success, a bill considerably above the normal amount but coinciding exactly with the cost of the fine. Quite apart from his land sales, William Crump took advantage of the potential for developing land for golf by laying out a small course near Dog's Hill. He made no formal arrangements but would keep an eye open for players and charge them a fee. One day he approached a gentleman and asked for payment. On being told, 'I'm Lord Ritchie of Dundee,' he responded, 'And I'm William Crump and you owe me half-a-crown.' That time he got his money in full!

Robert Nichols was a close friend of Robert Graves and Siegfried Sassoon. One contemporary critic certainly rated him alongside them as a poet while acknowledging that the literary potential of young men whose current writing was so deeply affected by their experience was difficult to foresee.[30] Another, quoting Nichols' description of the time before a man's first experience of combat:

> Nearer and ever nearer…
> My body tired but tense,
> Hovers twixt vague pleasure
> And tremulous confidence.
> Arms to have and to use them
> And a soul to be made
> Worthy if not unworthy;
> If afraid, unafraid.'

comments, 'These last four lines sum up the gospel of the soldier before his initiation into war more aptly and perfectly that many volumes of so called battle psychology have been able to.'[31] Clearly his was a major talent, an opinion confirmed by his commemoration among the First World War poets in Poet's Corner, Westminster Abbey.

We know little else about his residence in Winchelsea but must assume that the corporation forgave him his interruption because on Easter Monday 1934 the same Robert Malise Bowyer Nichols was elected a freeman. However, he attended no further meetings in that capacity and his name then disappears completely from the corporation records. He died during the Second World War but the circumstances are not known to me.

A prolific resident writer with much experience of the life of the town in mid-century was Pamela Barrington, wife of Charles Barling the grocer, three generations of whose family served Winchelsea, first in German Street and later in Hiham Green. She wrote many novels both as Pamela Barrington and using her husband's name. A number of them were translated into other languages and it is said that at least one of her books includes, with their names changed, real Winchelsea characters such as Don McKenzie, landlord of the New Inn. Unfortunately I have yet to discover which title offers such revelations. I should like to read it!

In 1971, Malcolm Saville, a much loved and extremely popular author for children, came to live at Chelsea Cottage in Castle Street. My wife and I still have our copies of many of Saville's books which we so enjoyed as children, notably *Mystery at Witchend, Seven White Gates* and *The Gay Dolphin Adventure*. The last mentioned is set locally and has its climax built around the sea breaking through at Dog's Hill; the event which caused such concern to Robert Nichols. Malcolm Saville's cousin, Michael, now lives at Winchelsea Beach, his home overlooking the area which flooded, and he is an expert on the history and development of that community.

Apart from using local settings in fiction, Malcolm Saville wrote *Portrait of Rye* and while resident in the town re-wrote and edited *The Story of Winchelsea Church*. His work brought that publication readably up to date and includes as neat a potted history of Winchelsea as one could wish to find. Saville greatly enjoyed personal contact with his young readers and many came to Winchelsea when he lived there. An article about him published in *Sussex Life* tells the story of one such visit beginning with two youngsters walking hesitantly down Castle Street to spy out the land, plucking up the courage to ring Mr. Saville's bell, being engaged in a long, friendly conversation and leaving, happily waving and clutching their copies of his books, duly autographed.[32]

And so from those who wrote in Winchelsea to one who wrote about it, selected for his important literary connection. Antony Mackenzie Smith of Backfields, Rectory Lane discovered in 1992 in the British Museum Reading Room, *Specilegium Poeticum,* a collection published, probably privately, by Manley Hopkins, father of Gerard. The collection includes *The Winchelsea Shepherd,* written about 1850, a long poem describing the life of the shepherd who has spent all his working years in the fields around the town. In response to a question posed by the poet, 'What's yon dim mass?' the shepherd replies:

> 'Tis Camber Castle, yon grey wall,
> Near where those colliers float,
> Some times a ewe or lamb will fall
> Into its brambled moat.
> I go there twice, my daily round,
> I go there wet or dry:
> My cottage stands beneath the mound
> That bears Winchelsea high.'

This hardly compares with the deeply influential poetry of Hopkins' son, whose adoption of the Catholic faith caused his father such anguish, but it serves as a timely reminder that for hundreds of years between the departure of the sea and the arrival of the wealthy and later the retired, Winchelsea's economy was almost entirely reliant upon agriculture. Mr. Mackenzie Smith appends a note to the poem pointing out that emphasis on the middle syllable of Winchelsea which is necessary to make the last quoted line scan was the local pronunciation of the name.[33]

Another Book of Sussex Verse, published in 1928 includes *The Ancient Town* by I.M. Holmes. Mrs. Holmes, a niece of William Gladstone, was the wife of Basil Holmes, mayor in 1925. She and her husband lived at Three Kings, Mill Road and it was in their memory that their daughter Edith and her two brothers presented Harbour Field, Winchelsea Beach to Icklesham Parish Council. Her poem commends itself to us by warmly enthusing on the beauties of Winchelsea. It opens:

> 'Show me the town in Spring, the "ancient town"
>   That is no bigger than a village street,
> Yet winds about in squares of far renown,
>   With old-world houses where the corners meet.'

and concludes:

> Oh wondrous little town, how fair thou art!
>   Beloved by nature – hard to spoil today.
> You know the reasons why you hold the heart.
>   Be simple and contented while you may.'[34]

Finally we note the topical and witty poems of L.P. Polhill. Mr. Polhill, was born in 1912 at 2, Hillside Cottages, opposite the bottom of Strand Hill, and recalls with great amusement the cyclists who crashed dramatically into his family's garden when trying to negotiate the hill. He now lives at Three Oaks and retains a razor sharp memory about the Winchelsea of his youth. In 1986 he wrote strongly supporting the strictures of the then mayor, Noel Eccles, against the dropping of litter in the town and suggesting that the penalty for littering Winchelsea's streets was once death by hanging. It is true that in days long gone mayors imposed the death-penalty on wrongdoers but it has actually never been shown that this offence was included!

With his letter Len Polhill enclosed a number of his poems. One, dated 1956, draws attention to the provision of guttering on the south side of the Court Hall. Apparently rainwater had been disgorging straight onto pedestrians below. The poem, after suggesting that the building dates from the time of King Edward I's construction of New Winchelsea, ends:

> 'Eight centuries have well nigh passed
> And men are heard to mutter
> We've noted something wrong at last
> King "Ted" forgot the gutter!'

A complaint in verse by the same author, aimed at the editor of the *Sussex Express and County Herald,* draws attention to the use of a word to describe Winchelsea which certainly grates on my ear and no doubt on that of many residents. It reads:

> When next you send Reporters
> To an ancient Cinque Port town
> May they sense an air of dignity
> Respecting past renown.
>
> …
>
> Where jurats don their stately robes
> And mayor his honoured cloke
> Inhabitants of course there are
> But these aren't *village* folk.'[35]

18. THE STILEMAN STORY CONTINUED

In the same year, 1908, that the Hueffers put the furniture from The Bungalow into store and went their separate ways, there occurred the death of Major Robert Curteis Stileman J.P., D.L. As we have seen, the major, in the absence from the town of his three older brothers, succeeded his father as Winchelsea's 'squire' and first became mayor in 1858.

He was educated at Tonbridge School where his academic prowess is said not to have been greatly revered. Reputed to have sown a considerable number of wild oats in his youth, he suffered a serious riding accident and while recovering repented of his former way of life and became deeply religious. His commission was in the West Kent Militia and later he was a forceful and enthusiastic officer in the Cinque Ports Volunteers. The extent of Major Stileman's public service was legendary, including time-consuming attendance as a local and county magistrate, nineteen terms of office as mayor, forty-nine years' membership of the Rye Board of Guardians, chairmanship of the area's Conservative Association, managership of National Schools, including St. Thomas's, Winchelsea, founder-membership of Rye Rural District Council, and, for a time, a Deputy Lieutenancy of the county. At the time of his death he was the senior member of Winchelsea Corporation, having been made a freeman on 11 August 1857, and the only survivor of those who had been magistrates by virtue of their position as jurats before the Municipal Corporations Act of 1883 came into force (see p.78).[1]

Major Stileman succeeded his father at The Friars where he and his sister Katharine, also unmarried, kept an alert, stern eye on all that happened in the town and provided open house for any of their eight brothers and sisters who might wish to visit with their families.

The long period covered by the major's 'reign' saw plentiful incident and change. During his first mayoralty there occurred the scandal, shock and excitement created by a murder, that of Susannah White by her husband John. Theirs was a volatile relationship which ended in her mysterious death by stabbing near the railway line to Rye Harbour. Tragically seven children were left motherless. John White was eventually arrested, covered in mud, at Wittersham, having earlier been seen near Camber Castle. Regrettably the inquest papers have not survived within the Winchelsea archives but Major Stileman would undoubtedly have presided as coroner for the incident took place within the Liberty of Winchelsea and we know that the proceedings concluded with a verdict of wilful murder against White who was then remanded to Lewes for trial at the assizes. Town Clerk Edwin Dawes became involved in detailed discussions about the case, particularly as regarded professional opinions on the defendant's sanity. No doubt rumour and gossip abounded. The trial was held on 24 March 1859 and resulted in a verdict that White was guilty on the lesser charge of manslaughter. He was sentenced to be imprisoned for the rest of his natural life.[2]

Major Stileman would also have been present at the Court Hall in 1860, as deputy mayor, for the reading of a proclamation by Queen Victoria 'For the Encouragement of Piety and Virtue and for the preventing and punishing of Vice, Profaneness and Immorality'. To this end Her Majesty, on the advice of the Privy Council, required all persons in authority to set an example by their own piety and virtue. Specifically banned by the proclamation were the playing of dice, cards or any other game whatsoever, privately or publicly on Sundays. The document goes on to require and command all the queen's 'loving subjects', 'decently and reverently to attend the Worship of God on every Lord's Day'. To ensure active encouragement of this requirement not only were all 'taverns or other Public Houses' forbidden to sell alcohol on the Sabbath but no resident or visitor was permitted to be within those buildings during the time of divine service.[3] This edict would have received the uncompromising support of Robert and Katharine Stileman.

In 1863, during the major's second period of office as mayor there was widespread celebration of the marriage of His Royal Highness the Prince of Wales, later King Edward VII, to Princess Alexandra of Denmark. John Carey remembered this as one of the grandest days that Winchelsea ever had. Winchelsea has always been good at celebrating and on this occasion the corporate spirit shown under the major's leadership was impressive. A splendid dinner was given at the Court Hall including the largest round of beef they could find, other joints, pickles and boiled potatoes. The meal was open to anyone who came along with their own knife, fork and plate. Carey recalled that everyone had helped in some way, his own contribution being to assist Mrs. Fuller in peeling a bushel of potatoes.

Riotous games and contests later took place in the street outside with the Court Hall wall lit by Chinese lanterns. In the corner of the churchyard a long scaffold-pole was erected, heavily greased and with a leg of

(30) Major Robert Curteis Stileman J.P.

mutton at the top with the legend 'Who gets me has me!' Attempts to remove the grease and climb the pole were comically unsuccessful until a boy called Blackhall disappeared briefly to return with his trouser pockets filled with grit. The pole was thus climbed and the mutton claimed. Those marvelling at this ruse were told he learned it when at sea in a coal ship. In the road nearby were water-filled tubs with oranges floating in them, competitors 'bobbing' for the oranges having to do so with hands tied behind their backs. A third game was described by Carey thus: 'Six boys on the churchyard wall [were] grinning through horse-collars for prizes, and, talk about mouth, you could drive a toy wheelbarrow inside some of them!'[4]

Ten years after his encouragement of this animated scene Robert Stileman, again in office as mayor, spoke at a dinner given during a visit to Winchelsea of the Sussex Archaeological Society (see also pp.85-86). The major, with characteristic patriotism, responded to a toast to the 'Army, Navy and Reserve Forces' by saying how gratifying it was to those attached to the services to know that they were appreciated. He remarked that 'the army, although small in numbers in times of peace, formed the nucleus of a force which could soon be raised and sent to any part of the world to defend the honour of the country'. This was warmly greeted by his audience. Whether consciously or unconsciously referring to Winchelsea's origins, he continued by expressing the hope that 'it might not be necessary largely to extend the army, but they also hoped that the navy – the principal arm to which the country looks for defence – may always be maintained in the highest state of efficiency (loud cheers)'[5]. Maybe this was a salvo at threatened defence cuts.

Among those listening to the major's words was Rev. Edward Whitehead, recently inducted as rector of St. Thomas's. The previous year, 1872, Rev. James John West M.A. who had owned and held the living for forty-one years, had somewhat precipitately departed. Robert Stileman's long-running conflict with Mr. West would have been a constant talking point within the parish.

Much is made in comments on the Stilemans' influence in Winchelsea of the fact that they had 'very strong and very narrow religious views which she, in particular, rammed down people's throats in season and out of season'.[6] The major went so far as to build his own conventicle in Rookery Lane where he would preach to any who chose to come and to his servants and estate workers for whom attendance was compulsory. This building is now the garage of 2, Strand Plat. These servants and estate workers had to submit to a strict regime quite apart from being told where they must attend worship, a regime which drew not a little sympathy from others in the community. They were, for instance, absolutely required to be teetotallers, a restriction which they sometimes failed to observe when the major and his sister were away in London. On one such occasion the Stilemans' butler, gardener and under-gardener came before the magistrates charged with being drunk at the Bridge Inn. They were fined a very small amount and the press were asked not to report the case so that the major should not hear of it.[7] Such stern discipline did not prevent the family showing appreciation of those who served them loyally and well. In St. Thomas's churchyard is a stone engraved:

> 'Sacred to the memory of William Bennett late of this place who died 15 June 1865 aged 70 years. This tablet is erected as a token of esteem and regard by the family of the late Richard Stileman Esq. with whom he lived beloved and respected for upwards of 60 years. Also Mary, widow of the above who died February 6th 1883 aged 90 years'.

William Bennett was gardener at The Friars and lived in the Gate Cottage. Such a public tribute seems considerably ahead of its time. Perhaps if the major had learnt of the drinking charge it would never have been made!

His kindness and consideration to Winchelsea's less fortunate residents was noted and appreciated by many. Alex Finch wrote of him:

> 'The major was one of the old type of gentlemen and every year at Christmas he and his housekeeper used to call on all the poorer people and take them a small Christmas present. He also allowed them to go into what we called Friars Cliff and take any broken down tree limbs for firewood.'[8]

Len Polhill, too, recalls that rook pie was a favourite and available addition to the diet of the Winchelsea poor. The rooks would have come from Friars Cliff but whether or not they were acquired with permission he cannot remember!

Major Stileman's involvement with the parish church and Rev. Mr. West appears to have proceeded with reasonable normality during the early years of his leadership in the town but by 1864 he had ceased to serve as churchwarden and attended vestry meetings only on secular matters notably when seeking approval for the closing of a footpath on his land![9] Later his name disappears completely from the parish records.

It has recently come to light from three letters purchased at auction that Robert Stileman's father, among others, had taken up the cudgels against Mr. West very early in his incumbency. The dispute appears at that time to have been purely doctrinal. Spokesman for those who had ceased attending St. Thomas's was David Laurence, one of the churchwardens, who sent a bitter complaint to the Bishop of Chichester and later acknowledged the bishop's response by agreeing that Mr. West could be given details of the objections. He rather ruefully observed that it was difficult to be precise on points of doctrine 'because Mr. West preaches extemporarily and therefore he cannot be called upon to produce his Sermons'.

West's response to the complaint was extremely robust. He described 'a most disgraceful scene' following the production 'at the public house… amongst some of the most notorious drunkards in the place' of the bishop's letter to Laurence, following which 'idle and ill-conditioned joking men assembled on the Sabbath to jeer me and my congregation as we came from the House of God'. West had no doubt that opposition to him was being orchestrated by the corporation about which he had recently complained to the prime minister, Lord Melbourne:

> 'and which is entering under the influence of a Mr. Stileman who has lately returned to Winchelsea having been many years absent from imbecility of mind. It would be a great satisfaction of my mind to have a personal interview with your Lordship as I have no doubt you are in entire ignorance of the wickedness of this place.'

The rector was strongly supported by Samuel Cloud, the other churchwarden, who wrote to the bishop reporting 'the most shameful abuse conveyed in Language too horrid and disgusting even to think of' to which he had been subjected by those who opposed West and referring to him as 'a most faithful and devoted minister of Christ and of most exemplary moral character.'[10] Though it does not necessarily undermine his testimony, it seems fair to point out that Cloud had been installed as master of the local school by West and was being paid by him.

The rector's remark about Richard Stileman's many years' absence from 'imbecility of mind' is an astonishing thing to say if there were no truth in it. Certainly as regards Stileman's absence from Winchelsea the documents known to me do not refute it. His service as a county magistrate is recorded between 1819 and 1827.[11] He was not present when appointed a freeman in 1834, nor when the corporation heard an application on his behalf for a lease of land at Greyfriars the following year. He briefly resumed his county magisterial career in 1836,[12] and applied to be registered as a voter for the Eastern Division of Sussex in the same year.[13] The East Sussex Record Office copy of the 1832 Poll Book shows him eligible to vote by virtue of land ownership at Peasmarsh and Winchelsea, but resident at Greenwich and not voting. The Poor Rate ledger for the parish of St. Thomas's the following year lists The Friars, rated at £30 per annum as empty with no payment made[14] and an undated list of voters, probably for 1837 has the legend 'Greenwich, Kent' deleted against his name and Winchelsea substituted.[15] Richard Stileman first attended a corporation meeting on Easter Monday 1837, being elected mayor for the first time twelve months later. The exchange of letters with the bishop is dated 1840.

Len Polhill believes that Mr. West married into the Ashburnham family of Ashburnham Place, Guestling, distinguished local landowners and bailiffs of Winchelsea. This has recently been confirmed for me by Mr. J. C. Morgan of Islington who is researching West's life and work. Mrs. West was formerly Alicia, daughter of Sir William Ashburnham, 5th baronet, in whose gift lay the parish of St. Thomas's. Quite apart from disputes with his parishioners, things were not easy for West during the early part of his incumbency. For a start there was no rectory. The 'parsonage', noted with pleasure by Celia Fiennes (p.17), had stood, set back from the road, beside the Court

(31) Interior of St Thomas's Church in the time of Rev. J.J. West
Note the box pews and the vestry wall blocking part of the north aisle

Hall. This was the home of Rev. Mr. Hollingberry who had the gate placed in the middle of the churchyard's north wall to provide him with the shortest possible route to his services. However, sadly for the town, this building was pulled down during the 1820s. Whatever temporary arrangements Mr. West may have made to live close to his flock, they were inadequate during his wife's illness and in May 1843 he obtained, on the strength of her doctor's recommendation, permission from the Bishop of Chichester to live in Hastings, 'until you can provide yourself with a suitable House, in a healthy situation near the said parish church'.[16] He built that house, now known as The Old Rectory, from which Rectory Lane takes its name.

Rev. J.J. West was a noted preacher with Calvinist views who was greatly esteemed by the Calvinist Independents and the closely related Strict Baptists. This alone would have been deeply disapproved of by Robert and Katharine Stileman as it had been by their father. Several stories about West's preaching have come down to us including one from Sir John Everett Millais (see p.99), and another from the recollections of John Carey who used to hear him when sitting at his post waiting to pump the wind into the old barrel organ which provided the church music. On this occasion the rector used as an example his purchase in London the previous day of what appeared to be a pot plant but was in fact a cut flower inserted in earth. By the next morning it had withered away. 'He told the people, "It was like [you] – it had no root to it"'. Mr. West had been preaching for twenty minutes when some of his associates from outside the town arrived. Carey quotes him as saying, 'Ah, I see I have some friends from St. Leonards. I think I will take my text again; if any of my people want their dinner they had better go because I haven't half done yet!' The sermon lasted about an hour but Carey probably could not see from his position whether anyone left, certainly he does not tell us.[17]

Writing many years later, in 1936, Philip Kent recalled being just one such visitor. He was taken as a boy from Hastings to Winchelsea every Good Friday to hear Mr. West preach. The thing that puzzled him was that all the visitors from Hastings were Particular Baptists. He presumed that the reverend gentleman must have had Calvinistic leanings. 'He was a most eccentric preacher and several incidents occur to me which, as a lad, I thought very humorous'. Unfortunately for us Mr. Kent did not give the details, but he did say that these visits would have been between 1860 and 1870.[18]

Mr. West's alleged personal behaviour and particularly that of his family would have considerably widened the rift with the Stilemans. We learn in most detail of the circumstances from the reminiscences of Dr. Ernest William Skinner who, having known the family as a boy, wrote of the rector's children:

'Blair, the eldest son, became a clergyman and in order to annoy his father, it is supposed, became very high church, but this did not prevent his being imprisoned for assaulting his wife. Arnold, the best of the family, was in the navy and went down with *The Captain*. The last time he was home his father would not allow him in the house, so he came and spent the night at Periteau [the Skinner family home]. Ted, the youngest, used to get drunk in the village public houses with the blackguards of the village. He eventually enlisted in the army, went abroad and died... Violet, the eldest daughter, I once saw outside a little inn in the town sitting in a farm cart while Tom Cogger, a rather disreputable labouring man, brought out a pint of beer to her, which she drank sitting up in the cart. She eventually married quite respectably and was lost sight of for years but long after all the Wests had left Winchelsea she came back one day and called at Periteau and seemed quite all right, but drove off to Hastings in a fly and got drunk at the White Hart and was summoned before the Hastings bench of magistrates. There were three other daughters, one, Flora, I think, was sort of decent, the others as bad as possible. One had an illegitimate child in the house. They used to make the old man drunk at night and then have their friends in.'[19]

Dr. Skinner's passing reference to *The Captain* well illustrates the fascination of a study such as this. I could not resist trying to find out about this ship and what happened that she should sink with Arnold West on board. Fortunately Canon Basil O'Ferrall, resident of Winchelsea and retired naval chaplain, was able to help me. It appears that *The Captain* was the last ship to combine turret guns with full sailing rig. The heavy armour-plating on her turrets and a mistake in calculating the necessary freeboard led to disaster when she capsized with extensive loss of life in a heavy gale off Cape Finisterre on 7 September 1870.[20]

In another incident which the doctor remembered or of which he had been told, Ted West was involved with friends in a 'drunken frolic' at the New Inn after which they were accused of stealing the weights of the church clock. Clearly wishing to make a protest against the magistrates before whom they had appeared, these young men burnt effigies of Major Stileman and Dr. R.V. Skinner the following November 5th in the New Inn yard. One of the maids from Periteau returned to the house much excited and exclaimed, 'It wasn't a bit like Major Stileman but it was just like Master.'[21]

Dr. Skinner also tells us of Mr. West's Calvinistic views, and his monthly preaching engagements in London, recalling him as a rather tall, fine-looking old man with a white beard, the preacher of interminable sermons, not always in a completely sober state. He once heard him, while on the subject of predestination, say, 'You cannot tell who is going to be damned and who is going to be saved – why, my hell-hound sons may be saved for aught I know.'

These recollections of the West family are qualified by the doctor with the words, 'Of course, what I am going to put down is not of my own knowledge and may not be true'. Skinner was certainly younger than the West children, on one occasion being put by Ted West to ride on a pig's back and driven to market while carefully dressed by his mother in a clean linen suit![22] Nevertheless such happenings would have been the talk of Winchelsea and not all he heard as a child could have been unreliable. To guard against the Skinners being deeply prejudiced against Mr. West as the Stilemans certainly were, it seems reasonable to support this information with other documentary evidence.

The family's propensity for violence is illustrated by a report published by the *Sussex Express* on 13 July 1872. Edward West was brought before Winchelsea's magistrates accused of assaulting the parish clerk, Thomas Budden, who had gone with a message to the rectory. When Budden arrived Edward West swore at him, shouted, 'You are all against my father', and attacked him. West was found guilty and sentenced to fourteen days in prison.

The rector's illegitimate granddaughter was also a reality, being, as Skinner stated, 'in the house' but sadly not for long for, as was so common in those days, she died as an infant. The christening, conducted by Arthur R. Carter, minister of St. Mary, Poplar, is the first in the parish registers after the entries cease to be in James West's hand. The inquest was reported by the *Sussex Express* less than a fortnight before Edward West's attack on the verger. Dr. R.C.N. Davies gave evidence that the baby was healthy and well looked after – he opined that it had had a fit and died of natural causes. The verdict accepted his evidence.

Dr. Skinner says of West's departure, 'Things got so bad at last that the Bishop held an inquiry, but luckily the old man died before his living could be sequestrated'.[23] It needs little reading between the lines to deduce that the inquiry and the final break were provoked by Robert Stileman. The parish records show that on 4 April 1872 a vestry meeting was held, following due public notice, for the purpose of holding the annual election of the people's churchwarden and hearing the rector's nomination of his churchwarden. The list of those actually present is not included but the minutes read, 'Mr. C. Neve proposed and Mr. Skinner seconded that Major Stileman be the parish churchwarden. Carried under protest by the rector because [Major Stileman] does not attend the parish church'.[24]

Rev. Edward Whitehead was inducted into the living of St. Thomas's on Wednesday 23 October 1872 having been nominated by John Patch Esq., barrister, of Blackheath, the new patron. Further direct evidence of the long estrangement between the Stileman-led corporation and J.J. West is to be found in a report of the Easter Monday mayoring in the following year. The ceremony, at which Robert Stileman became mayor once more, was followed by a 'cold collation' at the New Inn 'at which the members of the corporation sat down with other gentlemen including the rector. This is the first time for many years that the rector of the parish has dined at the mayoring dinner'.[25]

None of this permits us to draw any definite conclusions, but Rev. Mr. West's personal reputation in Winchelsea certainly did not in any way match the wide esteem in which his preaching was held elsewhere, a point clearly made in *The Christian World* obituary.[26]

During all my researches about James John West I have felt closest to him when talking to Len Polhill. Len was brought up as a Winchelsea Methodist and even fifty years after the rector's death stories about him were legion in that community. On one occasion he is reputed to have thundered, 'If I saw the devil running across the churchyard with a Methodist on his back I wouldn't shout "Stop!" because he'd be running away with his own.' Mr. Polhill showed me, with the greatest pleasure, a poster advertising a commemorative service to be held in the Rectory Lane Methodist Chapel at which Rev. Keith Wood, recently inducted as Rector of Winchelsea, would be the guest preacher. 'That wouldn't have happened in my time.' Or, it would seem, in Mr. West's! Nevertheless, the Methodists of those days readily acknowledged how Mr. West regularly packed his church and his kindness towards elderly parishioners in the wider Winchelsea community.

James John West lies buried just outside the main door of Guestling Church – a tranquil spot after such a turbulent life.

Leaving his enmity with West to follow Major Stileman's later career it is perhaps worth noting, because of the insight it gives into the times, an incident which happened to him, or rather to his carriage, a quarter of a century later. Stileman's coachman, Gaywood, he who sang his one song at the Court Hall concerts (see p.89) was driving Miss Stileman and her companion, Miss Bleasby, near the top of Rye Hill by the King's Head when they were passed by the carriage and pair of Col. Brookfield, M.P. for the Eastern Division of Sussex. The colonel was the Conservative opponent who had brought Frederic Inderwick's parliamentary career to an end eight years earlier. Brookfield's carriage, occupied by two of his daughters and a nurse, suddenly crashed into the side of the other when one of its horses shied, either at the sound of a nearby windmill's sweeps, or frightened by alternate patches of shade and bright sunlight through the trees. Physical damage from the crash was slight but Stileman's horses bolted, terrified, in the process breaking the splinter bar, snapping the pole and breaking the traces. This separated them from the carriage and ensured the safety of its passengers but the unfortunate Gaywood clung tightly onto the reins and was dragged violently to the ground. While passers-by carried the coachman to the porter's lodge of the workhouse where a doctor attended him, the horses were 'pluckily stopped near Playden Church by Mr. Aldridge (traveller for Messrs. Newberry, Battle) who was riding to Rye on a bicycle'. Eventually Gaywood was gingerly lifted into the colonel's carriage and taken to The Friars to be tended by his wife, 'Major Stileman being in attendance'. The newspaper account of this incident concludes by expressing pleasure at the others involved 'escaping any serious result' and hoping that the only sufferer would quickly recover.[27]

So far as we know he did, but Miss Stileman, though as no consequence of the crash, was to live for less than another two years. Katharine Stileman had been the steel in the relationship which had so dominated the town. Her propensity for ramming her religious views down people's throats has already been mentioned. She was certainly stern but could also be kindly and thoughtful. In earlier days she had run a school for the local children. This was held in a wooden building beside the present site of Saffron Gardens, hence the name School Hill. She was reputed to be one of the liveliest of her large family, an entertaining companion, and a great benefactress. Only a week before her death and despite ever more debilitating illness she had found the time and energy to arrange the gift of new, strong boots to every child in the town for the winter. The townspeople certainly missed Miss Stileman but to her brother Robert her death was a devastating blow, followed as it was little more than a year later by that of his sovereign, Queen Victoria, to whom he had also been devoted.[28]

This latter passing brought the possibility of the highest honour available to a leading Winchelsea citizen. It was not to be, but we note with respect that this was through Major Stileman's own selflessness. Winchelsea, being a head port within the Confederation of the Cinque Ports, takes its turn at providing the Speaker of the Confederation. This duty moves, annually on 21 May, from west to east through Hastings, Winchelsea, Rye, New Romney, Hythe, Dover and

Sandwich, then back again to Hastings in a process somewhat quaintly known as 'septennial revolution'. The office is vested in the mayor for the time being of the duty port and if the mayoralty changes during the year the speakership changes as well. A glance at Appendix II shows that during his nineteen terms of office as mayor Major Stileman had been Speaker on no fewer than six occasions. Since interest in the confederation was low at the time, he may not have had a great deal to do in this potentially important position, but his record of six separate terms has not been equalled since and is never likely to be.

The honour which had eluded the major because of Queen Victoria's long reign was that of becoming a Baron of the Cinque Ports, a title originally applied to all freemen of the Ports but later applied only to those representing the confederation at a coronation. For many centuries it was the right of these Cinque Port representatives to carry canopies over the king and queen in the coronation procession. Unfortunately when King George IV was crowned the heavy and elaborate canopies weaved and tottered, as did the bearers, not up to the task. As a result Honours at Court, as this Cinque Port privilege is known, were not granted for the coronations of King William IV and Queen Victoria on the ground that no canopies would be used. The death of the old queen provided a perfect opportunity to breathe new life into the Cinque Ports organisation right at the beginning of the new century. A gathering of representatives readily and enthusiastically agreed to seek the restoration of their ancient right. The case was presented before the Court of Claims by Frederic Inderwick K.C., acting on behalf of the confederation. His quiet persuasiveness and extensive knowledge of the subject convinced his hearers that Honours at Court should be restored for King Edward VII's coronation and it was arranged that, should canopies not be used, other duties would be found.

Major Stileman must have been delighted by this decision. Winchelsea's baron would be its mayor. He was serving his eighteenth term in that office. He would need only to express a wish to continue for another year to achieve this distinction. And yet he knew that without the efforts of his friend, both publicly and behind the scenes, there would have been no opportunity. As the meeting which would select the new mayor approached, Stileman wrote to his colleagues pointing out the vital part that Inderwick had played and expressing the view that they would surely wish him to represent them.[29] Thus Frederic Inderwick was appointed mayor for the last time, and a Baron of the Cinque Ports. In 1903 Robert Stileman succeeded him, Speaker six times and mayor nineteen, but never a baron.

The major's 'reign' was drawing to an end. He continued in office as deputy mayor, keeping his usual watchful eye on all that happened in the town. His death on 17 May 1908, at The Friars at the age of 77, brought to Winchelsea not only a sense of shock and sadness but also one of foreboding and doubt.

19. THE FREEMAN SUCCESSION

Robert Stileman had no heirs interested in Winchelsea. His only surviving brother was William, a retired Indian Army major-general, who was a rare visitor. What was to happen to the extensive Greyfriars Estate and the major's other property? It seemed as though the citizens' worst fears would be realised when it all came up for auction on 26 July 1908.

A considerable proportion of the hill of Iham, both land and buildings, was involved, divided into ten lots. The largest area of park and woodland was offered with the house, the lodge and the ruins of the Greyfriars' Chapel. Other properties for sale included The Old Workhouse, Lookout Cottage, Sea View House (Nos. 1 and 2, Strand Plat) with the major's mission hall, all the Barrack Square houses, Miss Stileman's former school buildings in School Hill, part of The Old Malthouse and a nearby cottage. The other land was principally between Tanyard Lane and the River Brede (at that time there was no other development along the road) and a large area between the top of Sandrock Hill and Wickham Manor. Ominously the auctioneers, Hampton and Sons, included as an advantage of the principal lot, 'This estate must... strongly appeal to Land Companies and Speculators as it presents an Absolutely Unique Opportunity for Profitable Development'. The catalogue goes on to draw attention to 'several thousand feet of frontage to main roads and any quantity of good building stone on the property, free of all building restrictions'. This building stone was in a quarry in the park. It had been worked 'for many years at a Royalty of two shillings per cubic yard of sand carried away.' Current licence holder was the ubiquitous H.J. Elliott in his capacity as highway surveyor but his tenancy lasted only until the end of the year. Other attractions are listed as splendid pasturage, the availability of nearby Rye Golf Course, 'capital' course fishing in the Royal Military Canal, and the large number of rabbits killed on the property. The comfort of estate workers was not forgotten, 'In the garden is a gentlemen's W.C.'[1]

Had property developers succeeded in acquiring all Major Stileman's land and buildings, Winchelsea today would be a very different place. They did not. George Mallows Freeman K.C., a leading resident who had been Stileman's friend and colleague on the corporation was at that time living at Cleveland House. He purchased a considerable majority of the lots with the express purpose of preserving the character of Winchelsea and preventing extensive development. To this intention he stuck firmly throughout his life. He was, for example, greatly upset when Hiham House was knocked down and a large number of smaller houses built on the land. As we shall see, the motive was to preserve a social balance within the community but Freeman thought it went too far and on the death of Charles Walter Campion in 1926, bought Mariteau House to prevent the same thing happening.

Following alterations and improvements to The Friars, carried out under the supervision of the well known architect Sir Reginald Blomfield, Mr. and Mrs. Freeman moved in to what was to be their country home. Mr. Freeman was a small man, extremely short-sighted, but distinguished and decisive. Nevertheless she wore the trousers. Theirs was a strange household, immortalised by Diana Holman-Hunt in her book *My Grandmothers and I*. This she described as 'a venture in autobiography, true in essence but not in detail'. She says that we must not accept characters other than the principals as real and that incidents have been transposed. With these reservations she paints a vivid picture of the eccentric lifestyle of the two households in which she was brought up. The first of these was The Friars for her mother was the Freemans' younger daughter, Gwendoline. Mrs. Freeman keeps a stern eye on her grand-daughter; he is more kindly. The household servants are Mr. Johnstone the butler who depends on the bottle and whose weakness is indulgently covered up by the Freemans, Miss Fowler, Mrs. Freeman's personal maid and Diana's confidante, Whaler, Arthur the chauffeur, Mrs. Hopkins the cook, Hannah, Tilly, Dan the vegetable gardener, Polly who runs away when she discovers she is pregnant and when eventually found is reinstated in the household, and Polly's mother who works in the dairy. Diana leads a superficially strictly controlled but surprisingly independent existence on which her imagination thrives. She explores the marsh and becomes a friend of Timothy who lives in a hut near the beach and has a hook in place of one hand; is driven by Arthur in the car which is one of the very few in 'the village' – it has a container with pennies to throw to 'the gate boys'; prays fervently and loudly in the church for the sacking of her cousin's fierce governess thus occasioning comment from 'the vicar'; performs a list of duties pinned daily to the curtain in her room; becomes intensely curious about Polly's pregnancy and when she presses her grandparents about this Mrs. Freeman fobs her off by saying she has lost 'The Book of Directions'. The overall impression is that while the Freemans give the outward appearance of ruling their household with a rod of iron, in fact they exhibit a considerable tolerance and are accorded affectionate respect.

Among the girl's more general recollections of Winchelsea are included a visit to Mary Millais, daughter of Sir John Everett Millais. Mary sat in the Freemans' pew for *'My First Sermon'* and *'My Second Sermon'*. She also remembers the church having 'deathly beetles watching in the roof', and her grandfather contributing towards the cost of removing them, The Friars' rope-operated lift which it was Arthur's job to work when he was not driving the car, a journey from London during which it took an hour to fill and light the car's oil lamps, and stories of the old monk, a ghost alleged to haunt The Friars and the marsh.

Since William Holman Hunt was so closely associated with Winchelsea as a member of the Pre-Raphaelite Brotherhood it is worth pausing to visit the household of his widow, Diana's paternal grandmother. Here eccentricity also abounds. She is an apparently wealthy woman living a spartan existence surrounded by treasures which she defends with systems of tripwires to keep out burglars. Her only servant is Helen who lives in the basement and has a better reputation for loyalty than for efficiency. Diana's father, Hilary, is in the Indian army and returns home only very infrequently, on one occasion winning her fervent gratitude by instantly removing her, to the headmistress's consternation, from a hated boarding school. Mrs. Holman-Hunt is intensely proud of her late husband's achievements, constantly visits his grave, and gives impromptu lectures to startled listeners at venues displaying his pictures. During her husband's lifetime she had a reputation for lavish entertaining but in Diana's experience this was done frugally with boy scouts called in to help. One set of such recruits insisted on taking the ladies' hats as well as the gentlemen's.

Diana Holman-Hunt is not the only witness we have as to the strange doings of the Freeman household. It was Douglas Turner's job, when employed by Barlings as a boy, to deliver the groceries. He recalled arriving on one occasion at two o'clock in the afternoon. Passing the servants' hall very quietly so as not to disturb Mrs. Ferguson, the cook, he arrived in the kitchen to find Mrs. Freeman there. She put up her lorgnettes and demanded, 'Who are you? And what are you doing in my kitchen?' The cook heard, came tearing along the passage and shouted, 'Your kitchen; how long has this been your kitchen? Don't let me see you here again until we do the menus at ten o'clock tomorrow morning.' It would seem there was one person in the house whom Mrs. Freeman could not dominate!

While George Mallows Freeman (he was always known by both christian names or both initials) was engaged in his professional career at the bar and spending much time at their London home in Bryanston Square, it fell to Mrs. Freeman to fulfil the duties which were expected of them

(32) Easter Monday 1957. Anthony Freeman is sworn in as mayor by Captain E.N. Dawes, town clerk. Also pictured are Lord Ritchie of Dundee (left) and Joseph Rogers.

within the town. The children, however, held her in awe. Margaret Muggridge wrote, 'Mrs. Freeman, the lady who lived at the Greyfriars, would sit at the back of the class. She never spoke but just watched. She was very grand.'[2] Ron Turner, who went to the school considerably later, remembers her in less formal mode. She visited his class every Monday morning to conduct transactions for the school bank. Each child placing a penny in the bank was rewarded with the gift of a chocolate. Len Polhill, too, remembers her as a benefactress who would come to the school at the end of each term to find out which leavers needed jobs and offer to provide them. Mrs. Freeman's formal visits to residents are recalled by Lord Ritchie of Dundee whose parents received one soon after moving into the town to live at Strand Plat. She called at 3.30 p.m. Any later would have suggested that she required tea, any earlier would risk interrupting a siesta. Sitting with a card in her lap, she referred from time to time to the notes on it of subjects it would be proper to raise in conversation. They must have been stilted occasions. She was also liable to put on airs and graces when dealing with tradesmen. Alex Finch remembered that on her first visit to his business she declined to sit on the shop chair while placing her order and he had to bring a better one from his dining-room at the rear of the shop. Rather ruefully he remarked, 'I would not have done it these days but I could not afford to refuse such a request then'.[3]

    Within three years of acquiring The Friars, G.M. Freeman achieved the distinction which had eluded Robert Stileman. As mayor in 1911 he became a Baron of the Cinque Ports at the coronation of King George V and Queen Mary. Conscious of receiving the honour as a representative of the people of Winchelsea, he wrote for them an account of his experiences which was eventually printed as a single-fold leaflet by Adams of Rye Ltd. There is not room here for all the details about the coronation service itself but some of the background and personal information captures the atmosphere admirably. All the barons were booked in at the Charing Cross Hotel the night before 'so as not to get lost'. To say they slept there, much as they might have wished to, would be an exaggeration for until 2.30 in the morning 'a perfect pandemonium reigned in the streets, including every form of trumpet and whistle; and at four began the firing of cannon and the forming up of troops'. The barons left the hotel shortly after 6 a.m. and took their places at 9.30, having earlier been amused by being mixed up in a melee of adjustments to robes, uniforms, helmets and swords, and being complimented on their own uniforms by the Earl Marshal. The duty assigned to them as a replacement for carrying the canopies (see p.116) was to take the standards of the countries of the British Empire as their procession entered the Choir of Westminster Abbey and hold them until the standard bearers returned after the three hour ceremony. The separate processions of the queen and the king passed them twice during this time, the standards having to be dipped in salute on both occasions. The problem was that the standards were nine feet high and their majesties had two resplendent officials on either side of them so there was little room. 'We were very much afraid of poking some high dignitary and being consigned to some terrible punishment. However, all went well,' Mr. Freeman received the standard of Canada from the Earl of Aberdeen. The barons followed the processions out of the Abbey and made their way back to the hotel where they 'fell like famished wolves upon our long deferred lunch'. Freeman concludes, 'It was a unique experience, historic and awe-inspiring.'[4]

While all this was going on the people of Winchelsea were also celebrating coronation day. Unable just to sit watching on television, they did the job properly. In the morning St. Thomas's was packed to the doors for a special service, some members of the congregation having to stand despite all the Court Hall chairs being brought over to supplement the church's supply. The service included a recital of the main events and significance of the coronation. A parade round the town, led by John Carey carrying banners displaying Winchelsea's coat of arms, included the Winchelsea Band and many children splendidly dressed for the occasion. The children then enjoyed lunch at 'the field', presumably the cricket field but possibly the field opposite Rookery Cottages in Back Lane where events were sometimes held at that time. In charge of providing the meal was Mr. Homard of Manna Plat bakery who remarked to Dr. John Skinner on the vast quantities of ginger beer the children drank. The doctor, no doubt viewing the matter professionally, said none of them was any the worse as far as he could see. Lunch for the adults followed at two o'clock. 'Homard did it extremely well, the food was good and well cooked and nicely served and nobody had anything but praise for it.' This was a considerable feat when you consider that 305 people were fed and another twenty lunches sent to the elderly and infirm who could not be there. Toasts were liberally drunk to the king and queen, to the mayor and to Mrs. Freeman, all of which were greeted with enthusiasm. 'The band started to play the anthem at the wrong time but this was a detail; we made them play it again at the right time.' When it started to rain the big tent was cleared, the band put at one end and everyone else squeezed in. 'It must have been very nice and warm especially as they were all a bit drunk.' Later the weather relented and sports were held in the evening. Once again Winchelsea had celebrated in style.[5]

Twenty-six years later, after the coronation of King George VI when Major John Addison Burke was Winchelsea's baron, the arrangements included a residents' lunch in the New Hall and a bonfire and firework display by Winchelsea Mill. Requirements made of participants at the ceremony seem to have been somewhat less rigid than in G.M. Freeman's day for the major's daughter recalls that he always claimed to have been able to absent himself long enough to smoke a pipe in the abbey cloisters during the service and he left London in time to be back in Winchelsea for the firework display.

Whether Major Burke paid personally for the display we do not know but the question of who paid for the 1911 celebrations is answered in reports of the mayoring ceremony on Easter Monday 1914. Col. Barrington Browne proposed George Mallows Freeman as mayor for a year in which he would become Speaker of the Confederation of the Cinque Ports and preside over a Court of Shepway for the installation of the new Lord Warden, Earl Beauchamp. The colonel eulogised about Mr. Freeman's services as mayor in the past 'saying none of them was likely to forget his hospitality in coronation year (applause).'[6]

The installation of the noble lord, a glittering piece of ceremonial, took place on 18 July 1914, just seventeen days before Germany invaded Belgium, drawing Britain into the war for which 'the lights [went] out all over Europe'. Winchelsea's representatives at the court were Jurat Dr. J.R. Skinner, Jurat Alfred Osman and, of course, Mr. Speaker Freeman presiding. The list of those attending the subsequent luncheon includes not only Mrs. G.M. Freeman but also Mrs. Holman-Hunt so both Diana's grandmothers were there. Numerous speeches included Earl Beauchamp's toast, 'I have the pleasure to propose the toast of the Speaker of the Cinque Ports, the Mayor of Winchelsea, and we are fortunate in being able to toast one known far beyond the boundaries of his own ancient town.' Mr. Freeman's perceptive and well-crafted reply included a jocular reference to the fighting propensities of their medieval predecessors and a revealing statement about the ports' current signs of revival:

> 'Dover is going to become a great Imperial Port. Hastings is going to become the Paris of the South. Rye has found refuge in an ancient game in which cannon balls are exchanged for golf balls. Sandwich is going to become the Swansea of Kent whilst Winchelsea folds its hands and sits in the sun (laughter) and reposes upon its heritage of fadeless beauty and eternal poetry.'[7]

As we look back, knowing what was to come, these words achieve a bitter irony. During the next four years Winchelsea was quite unable to fold its hands and sit in the sun; it became once again a garrison town. Of G.M. Freeman's leadership during that awful conflict we shall learn later.

Although Mr. Freeman was not mayor at the time, the friendship cemented between the Speaker and the Lord Warden at the latter's installation undoubtedly led to the first official visit to Winchelsea by a Lord Warden in office. The mayor, Alfred Osman, proudly announced the arrangements in a poster prepared by Deacons of Rye. From it we learn that Rt. Hon. the Earl Beauchamp K.G., P.C., K.C.M.G. etc., Lord Warden of the Cinque Ports, had agreed to attend the Armistice Day Anniversary Service at St. Thomas's at '2 o'clock in the afternoon of' Sunday 7 November 1920. He had also agreed to speak at the Memorial Cross after the service. A large luncheon party was held at the Court Hall beforehand, the mayor and corporation, no doubt prompted by Mr. and Mrs. Freeman, having put great deal of effort into the arrangements. The association with Armistice Day made it a commemorative rather than a celebratory occasion but great interest was created and a large crowd gathered.[8] For John Carey, though, it was sad for different reasons. Growing ill-health prevented his carrying out the duties of chamberlain and sergeant-at-mace on a ceremonial occasion for the first time since his original appointment to the latter position thirty-three years earlier. The maces were carried by Ernest Freeman and Charles Scuffle.

Earl and Countess Beauchamp were deeply appreciative of all that had been done to make them welcome and ensure the success of the visit. The next day she wrote from Walmer Castle, the Lord Warden's official residence:

> 'Dear Mrs. Osman,
>
> Our united thanks to you and the mayor for such a delightful day yesterday, every moment of which we enjoyed. The Lord Warden asks me to send you the enclosed photograph which he has signed. Once more our gratitude for all your kindness and hospitality.
>
> Believe me, yours sincerely,
> Lettice Beauchamp'[9]

The photograph remains in the corporation's collection at the Court Hall. It was to be a further sixty years before another official visit to Winchelsea by a Lord Warden.

Mr. and Mrs. Freeman's gift of land for the construction of the New Hall is further evidence of their benevolence and concern for Winchelsea and its inhabitants. It had for some time been apparent that the Court Hall, as a community centre, was no longer adequate for the town's needs. Much enthusiasm and initiative went into the provision of more commodious and convenient accommodation. George Mallows Freeman wrote on 19 October 1924 from 'Grey Friars' as his home was by then known, saying that he was 'happy to give a site for the Village Hall in the field adjoining the Rectory wall, comprising the present Rifle Range and another adjoining piece of land of equal size'. The only conditions which he attached were that the roof should be tiled and that the

(33) Wickham Manor
Home of Anthony Freeman

design of the exterior should be subject to his approval. The project received a further boost when Lady McIlwraith offered a donation of one thousand pounds provided the townspeople raised the remainder of whatever total sum might be required to complete the work.[10]

The rifle range was pulled down, fund-raising continued successfully, greatly helped by Mrs. Freeman's gift of all the necessary chairs, and the New Hall, as it has always been known, eventually came into use. For sixty-five years it provided the town with good facilities for an enormous range of activities; whist drives, horticultural shows, badminton, meetings of various local organisations such as the Women's Institute, a dining area for the schoolchildren who for many years walked there and back at lunchtime, theatrical performances, wedding receptions, mayoring receptions and many more.

However, there were problems to come and these first engaged the attention of the New Hall Management Committee in 1943 when their annual report contained the following:

'…The outstanding event of the year was the discovery in August by Mr. G. Turner that the walls of the hall were spreading outwards and needed immediate attention. After consultation with the gentlemen members of the committee the chairman (Mr. A.H.T. Finch) called in a firm of architects, Messrs. Callow and Callow of St. Leonards to inspect the place and they advised immediate temporary supports by wire straining cords and took measurements to advise on permanent repairs. The architect proposed these alterations: either to put four solid tie rods through to remain permanently, this would have precluded the use of the hall for badminton in the future, or to pull the walls in with the rods and secure the trusses with iron plates and then remove the rods. This scheme would leave the hall as efficient for badminton as it was before. The committee favoured the second proposal but it was held that as the walls were cavity walls the pulling in was not practicable and the architect afterwards concurred with the suggestion that this part of the proposal should be abandoned and the work be confined to the stabilisation of the roof trusses with iron plates which he assured us would prevent any further spreading of the roof. This scheme is to be proceeded with as soon as the iron plates can be obtained…'

The matter again came before the committee at a special meeting held at Firebrand, Major and Mrs. Burke's home, on 2 September 1943. The minutes record:

'In the course of the discussion it was mentioned that the architect had expressed surprise at the removal of the original tie rods from the two trusses and Major Burke stated that they had been removed to accommodate the badminton club but that the original tie rods were of no use and it was therefore thought harmless to remove them. Mr. Standen agreed with this view. There does not appear to have been any decision of the committee to have them removed…'

Unfortunately the effectiveness of the iron plates lasted only until 1990 when the New Hall was again declared unsafe. After extensive research and inquiries the committee produced a highly detailed and closely argued document which came to the conclusion that the needs of the community could and were being met at various alternative venues. Since the unanimous and enthusiastic support required to raise considerable sums for 'the essential repairs and improvements needed to make it safe for use by the public and to secure the necessary public entertainment licences' was not forthcoming, such an exercise could not be justified.[11] Since then the New Hall has been closed. There is now, however, a major initiative afoot under the enthusiastic leadership of

Roger Neaves, and of Peter Stevens, the cricket club president, to repair the structure and bring the building back into use. An exhibition of the proposals was held at the Court Hall in December 1995. The problem that large amounts must be raised within the community remains but grants are promised and hopes are high.

It is a great pleasure to be able to add before going to press that the New Hall was officially re-opened by the mayor, Robert Beecroft, on 1 November 1997 and is now again in full use.

Mrs. Freeman died in 1928. Diana Holman-Hunt then went to live with her other grandmother whom she knew as 'Grand'. Things were difficult, Grand was suffering from increased senility and eventually was killed in a traffic accident. When Diana returned to visit Greyfriars she found a deteriorating situation. After his wife's death Mr. Freeman sold the family car, a much prized 1918 Panhard Levasseur, and it became Winchelsea's taxi. The old man fell heavily when engaged in trimming fruit trees. He broke his hip and thereafter walked with a pronounced limp. This was probably the occasion on which Diana recalled the estate bell being tolled dramatically to summon help. As the years passed Mr. Freeman's poor eyesight worsened into blindness and Diana once found him sitting in the dark, cared for by a reduced staff and no doubt suffering from the loss of his wife's support. His death came on 10 March 1934.

As with their predecessors the Stilemans, the Freeman family could provide a successor of stature, energy and devotion to Winchelsea. Philip Anthony Mallows Freeman was already deeply involved in the town's affairs. Having been made a freeman in 1918, he succeeded his father as mayor in 1930, the first of nine occasions on which he served. Anthony Freeman, as he was known, for he disliked his first name and particularly his initials, was born on 10 November 1892 and educated at Eton and Oxford. Before the First World War, during which he served with distinction in the Royal Artillery and was wounded, he had already begun farming the 500-acre Wickham Estate at Winchelsea. After the war he shared this work with a partnership in Finlay, Durham and Brodie, merchant bankers of London. A term of office as High Sheriff of Sussex in 1939 preceded Second World War responsibility for the Rye Harbour post of the Royal Observer Corps and later for Winchelsea A.R.P. His intense love of history and concern for the preservation of tradition lay behind a deep interest in Winchelsea Corporation and the Confederation of the Cinque Ports. Anthony Freeman succeeded his father as a Baron of the Cinque Ports when he attended the coronation of Her Majesty Queen Elizabeth II. Later, as a baron, he was a member of the Cinque Ports' representation at the state funeral service for Lord Warden Sir Winston Churchill in St. Paul's Cathedral.

Anthony Freeman followed his father in his firm intention of preserving Winchelsea and the surrounding area in every way possible, particularly by preventing unnecessary and undesirable development on his own property. But he was also able to take a wider national view as is shown by his words at the mayoring ceremony on Easter Monday 1962:

> 'I have just driven down from my fishing in the extreme north of Scotland, nearly 800 miles. Having known this route all my life I am horrified at how one of the smallest but undoubtedly one of the most beautiful countries in Europe has been spoiled, defiled and uglified. I said before that my powers as your mayor are very limited, they are indeed, but so are those of all our authorities. Rural District Councils, County Councils, political parties, parliament itself, are also limited in this vital question. It is for you, ladies and gentlemen, the general public, to insist on this and to act before it is too late to preserve something which belongs to us all and which is being taken away from us by avarice, vulgarity, selfishness and lack of taste and education. Therefore it is

to you....that I appeal to help in every way to preserve the beauty and dignity of this unique old town.'[12]

Strong words indeed and views ahead of his time. Many have now adopted them. Thanks to people like Anthony Freeman it is not too late for Winchelsea but is it too late nationally?

The above speech was prepared on the notepaper of the Navidale House Hotel, Helmsdale, Sutherland where Mr. Freeman had just spent his annual spring holiday salmon fishing. His lifelong delight was in the countryside and its sporting pursuits. In February 1961, writing on some corporation business to his colleague and friend Thomas Bruce who was mayor at the time he appended a note, 'I hope you will come again to shoot pigeons on Saturday at 4.30, I have found another roost in Wickham Cliff.[13]

After his death in 1971 it was found that Anthony Freeman's desire to preserve his town's ancient traditions was reflected in his will. He sought to ensure that his legacy to Winchelsea Corporation for the maintenance of the Court Hall would not accrue to that body if its ancient rights and privileges had been removed by modern legislation. The will bequeathed:

> 'To the Mayor and Corporation of the Ancient Town of Winchelsea (if in existence at the time of my death and not then subject to popular or public election but duly elected or chosen according to ancient procedure or customal on Easter Monday in each year) the sum of Five Hundred Guineas.'

The Wickham Manor estate passed to the National Trust; a marvellous way of ensuring that its future should be in the hands of like-minded people. Until her death in February 1998, the estate continued to be managed, as it was in Anthony Freeman's lifetime by Mrs. Anne Croggon whose career there began when, on her arrival in Winchelsea in 1939 as the guest of Lord and Lady Ritchie of Dundee, she was eager to help the war effort and joined the Women's Land Army. Special mention, too, should be made of John Dunk whose whole working life has been devoted to assisting with the management of this vital part of Winchelsea's heritage.

We shall meet Anthony Freeman again in many connections during the latter part of this book but now we must turn from two of Winchelsea's most distinguished families during the nineteenth and twentieth centuries, to one of its most distinguished houses.

20. TOWER COTTAGE

Tower Cottage stands sentinel beside the Strand Gate, in a prominent position, guarding the principal access to the town, originally from the harbour and now from Rye. The oldest part of the building, overlooking the top of Strand Hill, dates from the early part of the seventeenth century and is two-storeyed, constructed round a central chimney with four flues. To the north of this is a similar later extension, with a third phase dating from about 1870 providing to the east what have since been the main rooms with a commanding view over the marsh towards the sea. The property's name originates from its proximity to 'The Tower' as the Strand Gate was known until the beginning of this century.

The earliest knowledge we have of Tower Cottage is that it is reputed to have provided the quarters of the Duke of Wellington when he visited to review the troops stationed in the area during the Napoleonic Wars. Its reputation during the mid-nineteenth century is less distinguished. Dr. E.W. Skinner tells us that it was the home of Rev. Mr. Brocklebank, Rector of Udimore, and his family who were, he claims, 'just as disreputable as the Wests' (see pp.110-114). Dr. Skinner's father, Dr. Robert Vaile Skinner, served as Admiralty surgeon and agent with responsibility for the coastguards. When Lieutenant Menzies, chief officer at Cliff End, was found to be absent without leave after drawing his pay, Dr. Skinner senior went straight to Tower Cottage and demanded that the lieutenant should return to duty. After Mrs. Brocklebank's original denial of his presence, he was eventually produced, considerably the worse for wear. 'He had been drinking and spending his money with the reverend gentleman and his amiable daughter.'[1]

Tower Cottage's importance in the town, and, indeed, the nation, stems from its occupation by the country's most distinguished actress of her time, Miss Ellen Terry. Deeds which have recently come into the possession of Winchelsea Corporation show that she purchased the property in 1892 for £300 in her married name at that time, Ellen Alice Wardell. The Winchelsea people of the late nineteenth century were initially suspicious of this arrival in their midst. News and fame travelled far less rapidly in those days. A reputation as a brilliant actress in London would carry little weight in a small Sussex town. To the 'society' ladies of Winchelsea, being an actress was still not quite respectable and Mrs. G.M. Freeman would certainly have reflected at considerable length before deciding to call at 3.30 p.m. with her conversation prompt-card.

However, such reserve, for the ordinary people of the town at least, could not survive long in the face of Miss Terry's engaging personality and her enthusiastic involvement in Winchelsea's affairs, particularly its amateur dramatics at the Court Hall. The ice may well have been broken by her generosity for after the death of Miss Stileman she took over responsibility for providing shoes for Winchelsea's children and her gift of furniture for the Court Hall was exceptionally useful.

Henry Irving's fame, too, would have been little appreciated in Winchelsea, his frequent presence at Tower Cottage adding more than a whiff of scandal to any existing prejudice. Their relationship was certainly a close one. On a recent visit I was shown their respective bedrooms with an interconnecting door. As a professional relationship it provided much of inestimable value to Victorian theatre. Anecdotal evidence of their influential presence in Winchelsea's community includes an observation that they would rehearse together 'in the meadow beyond the Rectory garden'.[2]

On one occasion they were members of the audience at a Court Hall concert when a hypnotist failed to persuade anyone present to submit to his skills, whereupon Irving announced that he would give half a crown to any man who would co-operate. This considerable inducement

(34) Tower Cottage

encouraged a young man to come forward. After going through his ritual and making passes over the volunteer's head the hypnotist said, 'You can't speak, you can't move'. Whereupon the subject cried, 'Oh, yes I can,' and jumped up to receive Irving's reward amid loud laughter and applause.[3]

John Carey remembered the couple's always dramatic behaviour. On a bitterly cold winter's night after he, as verger, had locked up the church, Sir Henry called out to him from the New Inn. The moon was shining on the church's east window and Sir Henry and Miss Terry walked over.

> 'It was a grand sight! The great long icicles were dangling over the windows from the ivy, some two feet in length and the moon full, it was lovely. We walked round the church and shouted and clapped our hands for an hour. We were all standing on the altar steps when down went Miss Terry onto the floor. I said, "Have you hurt yourself, Miss?" Her reply was, "No, I did it on purpose because you can't read tablets with the moon on your back."… "Shall I read it, Miss?" "Yes, if you can."'

Whereupon Carey read out to them the memorial to Margaret Jorden on a stone in the choir floor and was rewarded with cries of 'Bravo, Johnny!'[4]

Katharina Forbes-Dunlop's involvement with the actress was more sustained. It began, she recalled, in near disaster. Miss Forbes-Dunlop and her sister, then seven and five respectively, had as a pet a much-loved old brown donkey called Gipsy who was not averse to coming into the house, and certainly enjoyed being ridden. Katharina would ride him, accompanied by her sister on a tricycle in the shape of a horse with flowing mane and tail. One particularly favoured route was down Pannel Lane through the New Gate where they could visit Annie Homard at Newgate

Cottages. They expected to meet no traffic in the lane but one day came upon Henry Irving and Ellen Terry spanking along in a high dog-cart exploring the countryside. Irving, by skilled driving, managed to bring the cart to a halt while Katharina clung to the donkey's mane and her sister and tricycle spilled onto the grass verge but without hurt or damage. 'Gipsy and the horse were nose to nose, staring in dignified silence at one another.'

Henry Irving jumped down and started shouting at the petrified children about the rules of the road. His companion, though, sought to calm him. 'She smiled at me and called out, "Take your little sister home and tell your mother all about it. Nobody is hurt. Come to tea both of you – and the donkey – on Saturday."'

This they did and their friendship began. There was then a lace-making class held in the building which is now The Little Shop on the corner of Castle Street and High Street. It had been established at the very end of the nineteenth century by Mrs. Skinner of Periteau, widow of Dr. R.V. Skinner and mother of Drs. E.W. and J.R. Skinner, all of whom feature elsewhere in these pages. The lace industry had been well established and successful in Winchelsea a hundred years earlier and this revival proved popular among the local girls who attended to learn the skills of lace-making with little wooden bobbins on a big round cushion on their laps. Examples of Winchelsea lace are on show in the Court Hall Museum.

Ellen Terry visited the class one day and asked how many of the girls were to be in the forthcoming school play at the Court Hall. All but one began to tell her about their parts. Katharina would not be in the play for she did not go to the school, she was educated at home.

> 'A few days later, Ellen Terry arrived at our door and asked mother if she would allow her to teach me to dance so that I too could be in the coming performance. Mother gladly agreed and my joy knew no bounds. I worked eagerly under my wonderful teacher for I had much to learn. My mother created a muslin tutu and practised arranging my smooth, straight hair. Autumn came on and the great day dawned – but disaster. I was lying in bed stricken with influenza and full of woe. My mother at once sent round a note to Ellen Terry to tell her that I could not possibly appear that evening. However, she had reckoned without the great actress. Before long there came an imperious knocking on the front door and I, up on my grief filled bed, heard a voice exclaiming, "Of course she must come tonight! Don't you know that a performer never lets her audience down. I have arranged for Harry Neave (the postman) to be here at six. He will wrap the child in a blanket and carry her to the Court Hall. She will dance. After the show he will wrap her up again and bring her home." My joy was unbounded. All happened as the great actress had arranged. I did my dance and made a rapid recovery. It has been one of the joys of my life to have been taught by Ellen Terry.'[5]

Such interest and friendly involvement cemented Miss Terry's place in the affections of the community.

Tower Cottage, during her residence, saw many illustrious visitors and not a few momentous theatrical decisions. Sir Henry once insisted on reading aloud to the gathered company a shortened version of *Coriolanus* which he had prepared for performance. The listeners were dismayed. Miss Terry could not believe that Shakespeare had written it. When they expressed their doubts he seemed quite determined, said it was very fine and resolved to cut it more. 'But the next morning he called out to me from his bedroom to mine, "I shan't do that play." Joy! Joy!'[6]

Dame Ellen, as she became, moved to live at Smallhythe Place near Tenterden and Winchelsea people were most reluctant to see her go. Her popularity undimmed she was frequently invited back, on one occasion causing much amusement when opening a fete by, instead of giving the expected carefully prepared speech, simply announcing, 'It's open!' and proceeding enthusiastically to visit all the stalls to take part and meet the people.[7]

Sadly her declining years were shadowed by growing forgetfulness and dementia. Ford Madox Ford, her contemporary as a Winchelsea resident, had commented on signs of this some time earlier in a letter to his mother but it became pronounced.[8] Fully aware of this disability, she called it her prison. Her death came at Smallhythe in 1928, just a year before that at Tower Cottage of another of its distinguished residents.

Lady Harriett Ann McIlwraith was widow of Sir Thomas McIlwraith, a former premier of Queensland, who had been knighted by Queen Victoria for annexing New Guinea to the crown just hours before the Germans arrived to put their flag on the territory. Unfortunately Sir Thomas's career in public life ended in his being severely discredited at the hands of his enemies and even his descendants think he was a rogue. Hopefully the record will be put right in a history of the McIlwraith family being prepared by Patricia Twaddel of Broadbeach, Queensland. She writes, 'He was a man ahead of his times [who] brought great stability and prosperity to the state of Queensland.'[9] Sir Thomas died in apparent poverty but fortunately for his wife, and for Winchelsea and district, he had settled a generous income on her at the time of their marriage. This security she used both to ensure her own well-being in retirement and to fund projects for the benefit of her adopted community.

There was a marked contrast between the extroverted society hostess, consort of the state premier, and the reclusive eccentric who was known to the people of Winchelsea after her purchase of Tower Cottage. Lady McIlwraith took up residence with her staff, a cook, two maids and two gardeners, in a property much in need of 'modernisation'. She installed one of the town's first electricity generators and the original switches are still in position although not in use. Dr. Ben Chishick, a Rye general practitioner who now owns Tower Cottage and lives there with his family, believes that Lady McIlwraith weighed about twenty stone towards the end of her life. Movement from ground to first floor in her wheelchair was facilitated by the installation of a remarkable rope-operated Waygood Otis lift. The balancing is so sensitive that one can easily imagine an old lady, even one severely disabled, being able to use it on her own, although no doubt she usually expected a servant to do the work. Dr. Chishick uses the lift as a wardrobe in the first floor bedroom and, when showing me round, kindly brought his clothes down to the ground floor and up again to demonstrate its qualities. An engineer from the makers, a firm still in existence, visited Tower Cottage some time ago, 'spent most of the day playing with the lift', and declared that he had never seen one in a private house before. Had he been employed by his company sixty years earlier, he might well have seen another in Winchelsea for we know that Greyfriars had a similar rope-operated lift but we do not know whether it was a Waygood Otis.

Lady McIlwraith was deeply fond of Tower Cottage which she greatly appreciated with one notable exception. She lived there at a time when the presence of motor traffic on Winchelsea's roads was becoming more and more intrusive. This was nowhere more apparent than on Strand Hill where the right-angled bend under the arch, before the provision of a mirror, prompted all cars to sound their horns to warn oncoming traffic, thus causing Lady McIlwraith intense annoyance. For two summers she employed a man to stand at the corner directing traffic thus preventing the hooting. The duty was then taken over by the A.A. who kept an officer there, at her expense, from

(35) Easter Monday 1922.
Mayor James McGowan, Lady McIlwraith's son-in-law, holds one of the corporation's maces.
All those pictured with him feature at some point in this story.
They are (left to right) C.W. Campion, Hon. J.K. Ritchie, Lord Ritchie of Dundee, G.M. Freeman K.C.,
William Bennett (chamberlain), Walter Dawes, town clerk, Basil Holmes, Major J.A. Burke.

9 a.m. until lighting-up time with relief from his colleague whose usual patrol was on a motorbike and sidecar between Hastings and Rye. However, the old lady continued to find the traffic intolerable and eventually had Pipewell built on the other side of the town, living there in summer and at Tower Cottage in winter when things were quieter. The transfer between the two was a ritual carried out in her wheelchair with one servant pushing and another pulling.

Douglas Turner, whose father worked regularly at Tower Cottage, recalled, as do others, the presence of the A.A. man, and was told other stories about Lady McIlwraith's household. The cook and one of the gardeners were husband and wife and lived in the house. The gardener would nip into the kitchen in the middle of the morning and at lunchtime. When he heard his employer making her way to look for his wife he would say, 'Here comes the old bugger!' and make a rapid departure. Unfortunately a quick-learning African parrot had his quarters in the kitchen. The bird picked up the phrase in no time and would say it loudly on the approach of all and sundry. Lady McIlwraith got rid of the parrot!

Her generosity as a benefactress was legendary. We have already noted how she gave £1000 towards the cost of building the New Hall. St. Thomas's Church also benefited substantially, but her major project in the area was undoubtedly the Rye, Winchelsea and District Memorial Hospital. When it was first suggested that a hospital should be built as a war memorial she gave £2000; this was followed by further substantial gifts totalling about £20,000. It is therefore not unreasonable to claim that she very largely paid for it. Lady McIlwraith became the hospital's first president and was made an honorary freeman of the Borough of Rye in recognition. Amazingly her increasing incapacity meant that she only once saw the hospital which she had fostered. When the building was officially opened in 1921 by Princess Louise, Duchess of Argyll, Lady McIlwraith was represented by her son-in-law and daughter, James and Leila McGowan, who also took an intense interest in the project.

Lady McIlwraith, quick to get rid of parrots, was also, as a later resident of Pipewell recalls, quick to get rid of builders. Mrs. Marcia Bruce, widow of Thomas A.N. Bruce, local solicitor, three times mayor and town clerk for two years during Charles Croggon's first mayoralty, tells how Lady McIlwraith's builder, as a condition of her gifts, was to construct the hospital. However, a set of pegs which he had put up at Pipewell fell down. On being called to remedy this defect he submitted a bill for seven shillings and sixpence. Result – no more work for Lady McIlwraith and no hospital to build.

The obituary notice for this distinguished resident, published in the *Sussex Express* on Friday 27 December 1929, is accompanied by a photograph of her with a parrot on her shoulder. The one which swore? This piece, while extolling and listing her good works, remarks that she had been an invalid for many years, adding rather sadly, '[She] had few personal friends.'

The final story concerning Tower Cottage for which we have room here, brings together Ellen Terry, Lady McIlwraith and George Mallows Freeman as mayor. During his long theatrical association with Dame Ellen, Sir Henry Irving discovered a remarkable piece of seventeenth-century ironwork in Nuremburg and brought it to this country for use in one or more of his productions at the Lyceum Theatre, later presenting it to his leading lady who had it fixed to the Strand Gate overhanging her garden where it could clearly be seen from the house. It would seem that she did not consult the corporation as owners of Strand Gate.

The original use of the bracket had been to hang an advertising sign across a narrow street in the town of its manufacture. The buildings were low and the width of the street accounts for the unusual hinged arm which is attached to it. When a cart carrying a high load wished to pass by, the owner of the shop whose wares were advertised, or more likely his servant, had to hurry to an upstairs window and pull the bracket back out of the way to allow passage.

When Lady McIlwraith purchased Tower Cottage in 1914 she thought that, with no such inconvenience involved, she would restore the bracket to a form of its original use by hanging from it a sign announcing the name of her home. Accordingly she applied to the corporation for permission. The idea was not well received. Mr. Freeman replied, after consulting the members and counsel, that permission would not be granted. There was no evidence that Dame Ellen had consulted the then mayor, Frederic Inderwick; the iron bracket, being secured to the corporation's property had become part of that property and might not be used in the way proposed.[10] The decision caused Lady McIlwraith almost as much annoyance as the traffic but she was unable to overturn it and the bracket remained in position, without the name sign, for almost a further seventy years.

Having so decisively established its ownership all that time before, the corporation had the ironwork removed in 1984 and proposed that it should be fixed to the Court Hall where such an important artefact would be more prominently seen. Unfortunately by then it was seriously corroded and in poor condition but thanks to a generous grant from the Ironmongers' Company, recognising the bracket's artistic quality and historic importance, a painstaking major restoration by Mr. R.A.R. Moseley of The Forge, Appledore, holder of the Bronze Medal of the Company of Blacksmiths could be afforded and was duly undertaken.

Charles Croggon, having begun these negotiations as town clerk, continued them as mayor, needing all his customary tact and persistence to obtain the necessary planning and listed building consents. Eventually the bracket was skilfully and carefully attached to the Court Hall by John Turner, to designs and specifications by his brother Peter, far above the old door from the yard to the prison, and clearly visible from the road.

Then came the sting in the tail of this tale. The corporation proposed to hang from the bracket a sign with the legend 'Court Hall Museum' in just such a way as Tower Cottage's owner had wanted to use it all those years before. This was duly done but the spirit of Lady McIlwraith must have been at work for each time a gale blew the sign became dangerously dislodged. Despite adjustments this continued to happen. In the interests of safety the sign was removed and now stands somewhat ignominiously in the Court Hall but the bracket remains securely in place, preserved for all to see.

(36) The Court Hall iron bracket

21. THE FIRST WORLD WAR

Lady McIlwraith purchased Tower Cottage in the months leading up to the outbreak of this awful conflict. However, fifteen years previously we have the first evidence of a military presence in Winchelsea since Napoleonic times. In 1899, as Katharina Forbes-Dunlop and her sister were playing outside their home in Friars Road, old Mr. Easton, shoemaker and stalwart Methodist who lived opposite, called out, 'Do you want to see the soldiers?' The girls ran down Rookery Lane to the raised pavement leading to The Lookout, a vantage point exactly as it is today.

> 'We managed to get in front to lean over the railings so we had a splendid view of the soldiers coming down the High Street on their way to Folkestone or Dover to embark for the Boer War in South Africa. The crowds of villagers behind and around us shouted and cheered as the columns of men passed. They were singing and whistling and all was excitement. So carried away was my little sister that she snatched off the little scarlet felt slipper she was wearing. The soldiers looked up smiling as she tossed the little red shoe down at them. One soldier caught it, waved it back at her, called out, "My mascot!" and tucked it into his pocket. I often wonder what happened to it. I hope it brought him good luck in the far away fields of South Africa.'[1]

If it did, he was probably of an age to need it again as a good luck charm during the First World War when Winchelsea was once more a garrison town. Miss Maud Peel, owner at that time of The Armoury, recorded that almost one hundred years after the Battle of Waterloo, her home was again occupied by the commanding officer of the troops billeted in the town, then Captain Parnell, this time Captain Parker. Later in the war the property was rented by Brigadier General Sir H.E. Burstall of the Royal Canadian Army against whose name she has pencilled 'in command of the troops at the front', and later still it was used on his last leave by Major and Mrs. Walthew, the major losing his life on his return to France towards the end of the war. However, The Armoury was not exclusively the quarters of officers; three 'Tommies' were billeted there for a time when almost every house in the town provided accommodation for garrison soldiers. Those at The Armoury were from Lancashire.

> 'The musical sing-song of their voices, and north country expressions soon proclaimed the land they came from. Well mannered and well behaved they were; and delighted with the Lancashire fare of oatmeal porridge we added each morning to their government rations. Theirs was voluntary service for their country. They had not "had to be fetched". Most truly one hopes these good, orderly lads lived to return and came back uncrippled. "We've been well done by in many other places," said they to my cook, "but we've never been done as well as here. We would like to stay longer." And for our part we were sorry when the time came for them to leave.'[2]

Winifred Homard, too, remembered the garrison occupying Winchelsea during this period. She lived with her large family at Newgate Cottages, her sister being a particular friend of Katharina Forbes-Dunlop. The Homards were poor, father's income as a shepherd being supplemented by mother's casual earnings in service. During the war the presence of the troops ensured that there was much need for her work in the households being used for billeting. On their departure these soldiers marched through the town on their way to the trenches just as their predecessors had marched to the Boer War. Many were at Wickham Farm, near Winifred's home; one farm building which had the luxury of a wooden floor being used as the officers' mess. The Homard family made further income by selling flowers from their garden for the officers' dining table. The Wickham troops dug trenches all round the area, a particularly substantial one being along the bank of the Royal Military Canal from the beginning of Sea Road to Pett. There was additional excitement for the Homard boys and girls because a suspected spy lived on the road to Icklesham, a Mr. Phipps, generally referred to as Old Phippy. He talked with a German accent and provoked further speculation by giving the children chocolate and asking questions about the soldiers' movements. Phipps was even thought to be in the habit of signalling out to sea from his cottage window, but suddenly he vanished, heard of no more, thus confirming in the children's minds all they had suspected.[3]

Douglas Turner particularly recalled that at this time the town was shorn of civilian young men who were away serving their country, only elderly men being left as members of the permanent community. This brought the women together and led to the formation of the Winchelsea branch of the Women's Institute. The school, too, suffered and was without one teacher throughout the war. The need for extra allotments to enable families to grow more of their own food was met when Mrs. G.M. Freeman negotiated this use for land at Wickham Farm owned by her son Anthony who was himself away at the war. Douglas thought it was a very long way to have to walk with his mother and the pram to the bottom of Sandrock Hill and along a path to their plot. Mrs. Turner grew so many carrots that, unable to use them all normally as vegetables, she made carrot jam to avoid wastage. The children were less than enthusiastic!

Police Constable Muggridge moved during the war from Rye to the police house in Mill Road, now known as Peelers. His daughter Margaret was deeply impressed on their arrival to find that the toilet was indoors, an unexpected luxury. P.C. Muggridge, as part of his job, was responsible for assisting the commanding officer in finding billets. He would send his daughter ahead of him to inquire of householders how many men they could take, thus enabling the task to be undertaken smoothly.[4]

The war which brought about this disruption seemed to Winchelsea's residents to be very far away but they followed its progress with intense interest through the newspapers. External signs of the conflict, other than the presence of the garrison, were few, although Margaret Muggridge recollected seeing gun-flashes from France when watching at The Lookout and their sound is said to have been audible in the area. The impact was more closely felt, though, through reports of death and injury to men known to them, an experience shared by the vast majority of communities. Nevertheless, considering the very large numbers of its men who enlisted, Winchelsea was comparatively lucky in the small number of deaths. There were some civilian casualties as well. Despite the fishing fleet being restricted to an area between Dungeness and Beachy Head there were a number of incidents which would have shocked local communities, most notably the mining of the *Margaret Colebrooke* with the loss of all but one of the crew of seven.

Another reminder of the proximity of the war would have been a military funeral held at St. Thomas's on 25 August 1917. Almost exactly a month earlier *H.M.S. Ariadne,* a minelayer steaming down Channel fully loaded with 400 mines, had been sunk by a single torpedo from a German submarine, U-boat UC65, three miles west of the Royal Sovereign light vessel off Beachy Head. The body of one of her marines, described in the parish records as 'An unknown Royal Light Infantryman, aged about 40' was washed up at Winchelsea Beach. His standard Ministry of Defence tombstone stands in the south-west corner of the churchyard engraved 'A Royal Marine of the Great War. H.M.S. Ariadne. Known Unto God.' Very Rev. Canon Basil O'Ferrall, a former chaplain with the marines, has been investigating this stone with a view to discovering more about the

(37) Troops pose in front of the Court Hall c.1915.

circumstances and possibly identifying the occupant. At the time of writing the mystery is deepening rather than becoming clearer. Neither the Royal Marines' Association nor the Royal Marines' Historical Association has any knowledge of the grave. According to their records only two marines went down with *Ariadne* and both are buried elsewhere.

Probably the most dramatic manifestation of the enemy threat was the dropping of bombs at Pett by a Zeppelin a few months earlier on the night of 16/17 March 1917. The alarm and excitement thus created can well be imagined. The Zeppelins had been a danger for a long time; one of Mrs. Homard's daughters wrote to her on 15 September 1915 from Kensington with the message, 'We are all well and safe but the Zeps have tried to get here every night so far'.[5] However, a threat to London was as remote to Winchelsea people as the battles in France and an incident close by came as a rude awakening. The bomb was dropped from one of the Germans' new 'height climber' Zeppelins, specially lightened and equipped with oxygen supplies for the crew. This permitted flight at an altitude of 20,000 feet, far beyond the capacity of any contemporary British fighter 'plane. Robert Kohl, the officer commanding L39, crossed the coast at Margate that night with three others. He travelled south-west, going out to sea again at St. Leonards, a route which would have taken him directly over Pett where he dropped six bombs, damaging two houses. After meeting unexpectedly strong winds on his homeward journey Kohl was forced far off course, eventually being brought down by anti-aircraft guns near Compiegne with the loss not only of his aircraft but also all seventeen crew; not a great return for damage amounting to £163 and no casualties at Pett. The lightness of the damage did not, however, deter large numbers of sightseers who collected souvenir pieces of the bombs from a field crater.[6]

Winchelsea Corporation's records of the period are no more than the normal formalities noting proceedings of the annual mayoring ceremony, but the war twice had sufficient impact to merit a mention. On 5 April 1915 the mayor, George Mallows Freeman, informed the assembled company that no less than £270 had been collected in Winchelsea and forwarded to the County War Patriotic Fund at Lewes; a magnificent response by so small a community.[7] Five months later a special corporation meeting readily approved an agreement prepared by the mayor with the garrison commanding officer to hire the upper room of the Court Hall to the military for only a peppercorn rent. At the same time the members prudently resolved to insure 'The Town Hall' against aircraft bombardment.[8]

The parish council records would almost certainly have provided much more detail but sadly they are believed to have been destroyed by the mother of a clerk who died shortly after the Second World War, leaving Icklesham Parish Council with no surviving minutes before 1950. Examples taken from the records of other local parish councils show that at Udimore they had no allotments such as those to which Douglas Turner had to trudge so frequently and could only rely on local farmers to allocate more land for potato-growing. Nevertheless they noted that almost all cottagers saved their own seed. Pett, too, was anxious about potato production and resolved to purchase a 'Bucket Sprayer' at a cost of one pound for public use in the prevention of potato disease. Pett was also much alarmed by the Zeppelin raid referred to above and feared that the bombs might have been attracted by the presence of searchlights. Not unreasonably a request was submitted that such searchlights should be moved further away from residential property.[9]

As the end of the war approached, Margaret Muggridge's mother, intensely patriotic and fervently hopeful that the slaughter would soon cease, had a Union Jack fastened to a clothes prop ready in her bedroom some considerable time in advance.

'When the armistice was signed, November 11th 1918, she was in the post office when the news came through on their telephone and we, only being nextdoor, had the first

(38) Disappointed recruits 'Willing but Won't'
(l to r back) unknown, Albert? Barden, Neddy Field, Mrs Homard – Castle Inn, George Gaywood, Ernest Freeman – decorator.
(seated) Dickie Homard – baker, Jack Gallop – carpenter and builder, 'Smiler' – painter

flag out. People in the road said somebody had got news and, of course, it soon spread.
I was still at school and there used to be a bell on the roof, us kids pulled it like mad.
It's a wonder we didn't pull it down.'

Several of the boys went to the rector and asked for a half holiday but he, rather brusquely,
turned them down. Mr. Douglas was not alone in feeling instinctively that this was not an occasion
for celebration.[10] Westfield Parish Council's chairman some months later expressed the opinion that
festivities were out of place, although another councillor thought an enjoyable afternoon of sports,
followed by tea for the children, would not be inappropriate.[11]

Suitable ways to commemorate the sacrifice of those from the town who had served their
country became a major preoccupation for the people of Winchelsea during the months which
followed. First to take the lead was Charles Walter Campion of Mariteau House, a former mayor
who was serving as a churchwarden of St. Thomas's. He issued a leaflet headed 'Local War Memorial
for Winchelsea':

> 'It is proposed, if funds permit, to erect a Cross in the Churchyard, in accordance with
> the Resolutions moved by the Mayor and adopted by a Public Meeting held at the
> Court Hall on 24 January. Upon this Cross will be engraved the Names of our own
> fallen Soldiers, and, as it will be the only visible record in Winchelsea itself of all that
> happened in the Great War – of England's danger, England's effort and England's
> triumph, and of the part played by Winchelsea men in the Defence of their Country –
> the Committee appeal to every member of the Parish to take some share, however
> small, in raising the necessary funds. Each householder is therefore requested to write
> on the Form overleaf what sum he and the members of his household are willing to
> give or promise for this purpose.
>
> On behalf of the Committee
>
> February 1919   C.W. Campion' [12]

Mr. Campion's apportionment of all danger and all credit for victory to the English was an
eccentricity which his readers would probably not have remarked upon. Funds were readily
forthcoming, and the cross, at which the mayor, corporation and representatives of the Royal British
Legion, with the clergy and congregation of St. Thomas's gather still to observe a two minutes'
silence each Remembrance Sunday at 11 a.m., was dedicated, as we have seen, during the visit of the
Lord Warden, Earl Beauchamp, the following year. The First World War names, read out on such
occasions, are:

Archibald L. Baldwin
William P. Freeman
Robert Griffin
Henry Patch
Noel Patch
Frederick G. Penny
George T. Snashall
Norman Streeton
Edward Watson

The cross has also been engraved, 'We pray you also remember Basil Lees Inderwick of the
Canadian forces buried at Winchelsea January 28, 1915.'

As it turned out the memorial cross was not to be 'the only visible record in Winchelsea itself'. As the result of an entirely separate initiative undertaken by Mr. and Mrs. Campion there is, in the upper room of the Court Hall, a memorial tablet recording the names not only of those men of Winchelsea who died but also of those who served, a total of one hundred and nineteen, with fatalities indicated by red crosses. Winchelsea was indeed lucky that so high a percentage of its men returned. Anyone making a close study of the two lists will note that there are discrepancies among the deaths recorded. Currently the reasons are not known.

The Campions set about raising the money for this second tribute by hosting a garden fete, organised by the Winchelsea

(39) Winchelsea war memorial when new.
Note that the roof of Hiham House, demolished soon afterwards,
can be seen in the background.

Women's Institute, at Mariteau House during the summer of 1919. This raised the considerable sum of forty two pounds five shillings which was supplemented by further voluntary work and individual contributions. The 'tablet' was designed and made by Mr. A. Austen and dedicated at a social evening held at the Court Hall on Tuesday 1 December 1921. Mrs. G.M. Freeman welcomed the invited ex-soldiers and their wives, Mrs. Campion gave an account of how the money had been raised, and G.M. Freeman K.C., formally accepting the tablet on behalf of the corporation, 'said that those men who had served in the Great War had had a great chance of serving their country and had accepted it nobly'. Celebration certainly seems to have been deemed appropriate on this occasion for the formalities were followed by 'an excellent concert' given by the ex-servicemen with refreshments served liberally in the interval. The evening concluded with the hearty singing of *Sussex by the Sea, Old Lang Syne, Rule Britannia* and *God Save the King.*[13]

The tablet may be inspected by all who visit the Court Hall to this day but it would not be quite true to say that it has been in its position ever since. In 1975 the mayor and corporation decided, on the grounds that it was not an appropriate exhibit for what had become essentially a museum, to move this memorial to the Lower Court Hall where gatherings of Winchelsea people would be more likely to see it. A storm of protest ensued, led by Alex Finch, Charles Potter and Douglas Turner representing 'the older residents'. Their anger was provoked by a feeling that to move the board from its original position was inappropriate and an insult to those commemorated. A meeting between the disputing parties failed, because of a misunderstanding, to sort things out and a petition signed by eighty-one residents was then submitted. This outlined the history of the tablet and objected that it was now 'in a most unsatisfactory position near bags containing rubbish.'

Charles Croggon, town clerk, with his usual tact, responded to the petition with an assurance that the corporation's representatives at the consultation meeting had in fact agreed to the request to replace the memorial upstairs, reserving only the right to consult the full corporation and to site it differently following a major reorganisation of the museum. This was done and the board was placed, close to its original position, on the opposite side of the same window, an action which brought an appreciative and conciliatory letter of thanks from the objectors. As part of the most recent museum reorganisation the tablet has now assumed a position of considerable prominence behind the mayor's chair.

The earlier controversy caused the mayor of the time, Donovan Cole, considerable upset. He felt that the matter had been blown up out of all proportion and had served unnecessarily to exacerbate feelings of resentment among long-established residents for the activities of the corporation.[14] In realising that such feeling existed he was certainly correct although it was to be only another five years before the situation was eased by the appointment of Douglas Turner as a freeman.

The provision of First World War memorials within the town was not completed even by the tablet although the last had a wider dedication to the men of the Cinque Ports and the ancient towns of Rye and Winchelsea. Presented by Lord Blanesburgh this took the form of three stained glass windows by Douglas Strachan in the north aisle of St. Thomas's Church, dedicated by the Archbishop of Canterbury in 1933 at the third of a series of services which brought St. Thomas's to national attention. Of these we shall learn later.

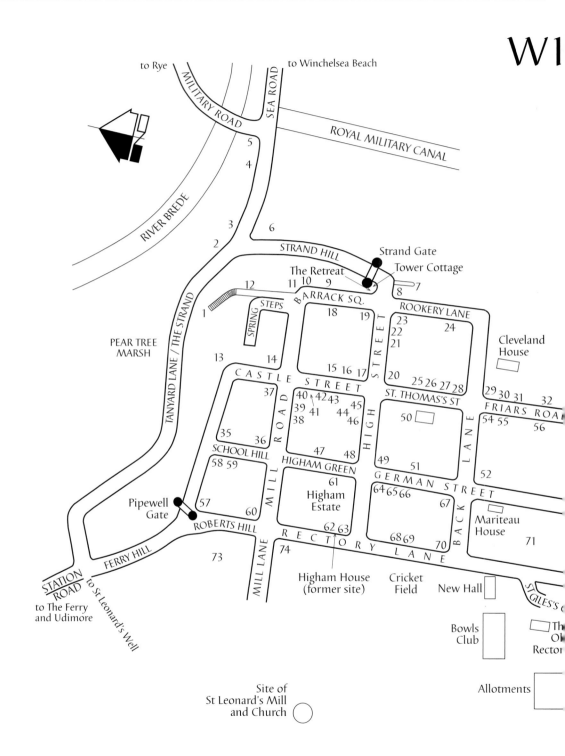

to Rye

to Winchelsea Beach

MILITARY ROAD

SEA ROAD

ROYAL MILITARY CANAL

RIVER BREDE

5

4

3

6

2

STRAND HILL

Strand Gate

Tower Cottage

The Retreat

11 10 9

8 7

12

BARRACK SQ.

SPRING STEPS

ROOKERY LANE

1

PEAR TREE MARSH

TANYARD LANE / THE STRAND

18

19

23

22

21

24

Cleveland House

13

14

15 16 17

20

25 26 27 28

29 30 31

32

CASTLE STREET

HIGH STREET

ST. THOMAS'S ST

FRIARS ROA

54 55

56

37

40 42 43

39 41 44 45

38 46

50

35

36

47 48

49 51

52

SCHOOL HILL

MILL ROAD

HIGHAM GREEN

GERMAN STREET

58 59

61

64 65 66

67

BACK LANE

Mariteau House

71

Pipewell Gate

57

60

Higham Estate

62 63

68 69

70

ROBERTS HILL

RECTORY LANE

FERRY HILL

73

74

MILL LANE

Higham House (former site)

Cricket Field

New Hall

ST GILES'S

STATION ROAD

to St Leonard's Well

to The Ferry and Udimore

Bowls Club

Th O Rector

Site of St Leonard's Mill and Church

Allotments

HELSEA TOWN

1 Queen Elizabeth's Well
2 Hillside Cottages
3 The Old Malt House
4 The Bridge Inn
5 Strand Garage
6 The Old Workhouse (Strand House)
7 The Lookout
8 Lookout Cottage
9 Cooks Green
10 The Mount
11 Alards
12 The Roundel (residence)
13 King's Leap
14 Five Chimneys
15 The Armoury
16 The Town Well
17 Periteau House
18 The Barrack Houses
19 The Stone House
20 Firebrand
21 Finch of Winchelsea (now the post office and the Tea Tree Restaurant)
22 Nesbit
23 Strand Plat
24 Rookery Cottages
25 Haskards
26 St. Thomas's Rectory (former school site)
27 Nelgarde
28 Glebe (Cottage)
29 White Cottage
30 Cleveland Cottage
31 Cleveland Place
32 Etterby/Byways (now Tamarisk)
33 The Little House
34 The Lodge (Gate Cottage)
35 The Five Houses
36 Manna Plat
37 Salutation Cottages (formerly Inn)
38 Three Kings
39 Peelers
40 The Old Post Office
41 Castle Cottage
42 The Castle Inn
43 St Anthony's (formerly part of Keith Row)
44 Magazine House
45 The Little Shop
46 Magazine Cottage
47 formerly Barlings (grocers)
48 The Court Hall
49 War Memorial
50 St. Thomas's Church
51 Wesley's Tree
52 Trojan's Plat
53 Public Conveniences
54 1 Friars Road
55 2/3 Friars Road
56 'Conrad's Cottage'
57 Moneysellers
58 Saffron Gardens
59 Pound Cottage
60 The Orchards
61 Higham Cottage
62 Westway
63 Firin
64 The New Inn
65 White Close
66 Ballader's Plat
67 Yew Tree House
68 Methodist Chapel
69 Waterstone Cottage
70 The Oast House
71 Truncheons
72 St. John's Hospital (surviving gable)
73 Pipewell (dwelling)
74 Telephone Exchange

Chapel ruins

Greyfriars (The Friars)

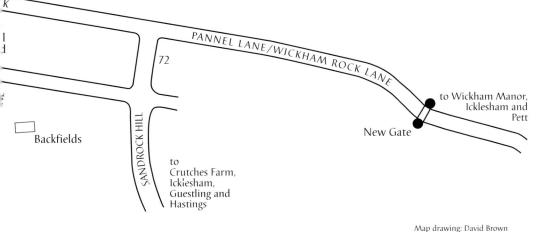

Map drawing: David Brown

22. WINCHELSEA, VICTORIA, AUSTRALIA

It was at the beginning of the war whose victims and survivors were thus commemorated that Sir Arthur Stanley, Governor of the State of Victoria, paid a visit to Winchelsea in that state and, knowing the English town of the same name, asked how it came to be used for the Victorian township. This sent researchers scurrying to the Melbourne archives where they unearthed a letter written in 1851 in which 'His Honour the Superintendent (C.J. Latrobe)' informed the Surveyor General in Sydney that he had, subject to the appropriate permission, given the name Winchelsea to 'a township on [the] right bank of the River Barwon on the main line of a road from Geelong to Colac, also some suburban allotments on the opposite bank'. The researchers concluded that Mr. Latrobe had used the name of the ancient Sussex town.[1]

In those mid-nineteenth century days the original name of 'The Barwon' soon fell out of use and Winchelsea 'became the home and dwelling place of station hands, shearers and a few tradesmen who also catered for the needs of the outlying population which consisted of graziers and farmers.'[2] So far as is known to the residents of the two communities, these are the only two places in the world to bear the name of Winchelsea.

Sir Arthur Stanley contacted the mayor of Winchelsea, England, George Mallows Freeman K.C., who was immediately attracted by the idea that some special relationship should be initiated. By the time the arrangements were made the war had been in progress almost two years and for most of 1915 troops of the two countries had been fighting gallantly side by side in the Dardanelles campaign and particularly at Gallipoli. The symbol of the association was to be a flag of the Cinque Ports, specially made by 'a Winchelsea lady, the sister of the late well known landscape painter William Padgett'. The use of this design was doubly appropriate because Winchelsea uses as its arms those of the Cinque Ports. When sending the flag to Mr. Freeman, Miss Padgett wrote:

> 'It has cost very little money but a very great deal of thought, work and care… I feel very honoured to work this for Australia for the sake of the magnificent sacrifice and help that country has given us and thank you very much for giving me the opportunity of doing my bit for them.'

The mayor quoted this tribute in his letter to Sir Arthur enclosing the flag and it was clearly greatly appreciated by the governor and by the councillors, officers and citizens of Winchelsea, Victoria. Formal resolutions of gratitude were passed, special permission was obtained for the flag to be used officially in Australia and, after one unfurling ceremony had been abandoned because of appallingly wet weather, it was flown for the first time on 4 August 1916.[3]

This was not the only flag to be involved in the early stages of the association between the two Winchelseas. The parochial school of Winchelsea, Sussex sent the local state school of Winchelsea, Victoria a Union Jack and received the Australian flag in return. The school log book for 28 January 1916 records:

> 'A handsome flag has been sent from Winchelsea in Australia for the school flagstaff. It was presented at noon today by the Mayor and unfurled by the Mayoress. After cheers had been given for King George, for the donors of the flag and for Mr. and Mrs. Freeman, the children marched past and saluted.'[4]

This led naturally to letters being exchanged, firstly on a fairly regular basis but later much less frequently, as is illustrated by one sent on 24 May 1933 from England to Australia:

'Dear Scholars,

We are writing to you again after a very long time. We are very proud of the flag you sent us and we hope you are of the one we sent you. As it is Empire Day today we put our flags up and saluted them, when afterwards we sang the National Anthem, we went in and sang our school song and Land of Hope and Glory. When the flag was sent to us, none of the scholars who are at school now were here, but the oldest vaguely remember the letters.

I remain, a sincere fellow scholar.

Gwendoline Bertha Ball'[5]

The link between the schools, as well as the communities, was further strengthened by the visit three years later of James and Leila McGowan, Lady McIlwraith's son-in-law and daughter, during James McGowan's third term as mayor. On 7 December 1936 they were formally greeted at the Winchelsea Shire Hall by Shire President Alex McLellan. As we have seen, Winchelsea was the centre for the surrounding country, giving its name to the local authority, a shire being roughly equivalent to a district council in England. Speeches of greeting were followed by visits to the schools where Mr. McGowan gave the children a message from the pupils of his Winchelsea, to the churches, the children's playground and the soldiers' memorial. A year later Major John Addison Burke sent as a gift to the shire an inscribed china bowl bearing the arms of the ancient town of Winchelsea as a memento of the coronation of King George VI and Queen Elizabeth. Major Burke, as mayor, was Winchelsea's baron on that occasion and it was a striking relevance to the relationship between the two towns that he had the privilege of receiving the Standard of Australia during the coronation service just as his predecessor, G.M. Freeman, had received that of Canada.[6]

(40) Air crash near Wickham Manor – 1930s. With the wreckage – George Cook (left), whose daughter was sponsored by Winchelsea, Victoria and Jimmy Homard.

The Second World War prompted further backing for Winchelsea, Sussex from its Australian counterpart, notably the sponsorship of Georgina Cook whose father, George, was killed on active service in 1943. The money came from the Patriotic Fund Committee and an inquiry much later asked for news of Georgina who had married and become Mrs. Ford.[7] Additional practical support came during the period of strict rationing which followed the war. Winchelsea's gratitude was expressed in a letter from Major Burke's wife:

'Dear Friends,

I am head of the local branch of the Women's Voluntary Service so it falls to me to take charge of and distribute your most generous and most welcome gifts to the old people and the children of our Ancient Town. We had six cases sent to us and I was able to give really lovely "lots" of good things to 152 different households. I hope you will have had letters from many of them thanking you – I can assure you your kindness touches us very deeply. We had a very unpleasant time during the war along this coast within sight of France and our beautiful old town had two big bombs on it, but our old people were wonderful. Very few left their homes. Again thanking you for all your wonderful gifts and for your kind thoughts and good wishes.

Yours truly,

D.M. Burke [8]

Of that 'very unpleasant time' we shall learn more later.

It was in 1960 that the next official visit from England to Australia was undertaken on behalf of Winchelsea Corporation by Freeman Anthony Hugh Thomas. Mr. Thomas, a Winchelsea resident in his younger days, was made a freeman on Easter Monday 1939. The war took him away from the town but he has lived nearby for many years, notably at Smallhythe where his wife was curator of Ellen Terry's Smallhythe Place for the National Trust and where he led the development and running of the adjoining theatre. As a non-resident freeman Mr. Thomas has not been eligible for the mayoralty but in 1962, in view of his living close at hand, he was invited to re-join the corporation as a jurat so that his wisdom and advice would be available. He served in this capacity until 1995. Appointment to the freedom of Winchelsea is, however, an appointment for life and at the time of writing Mr. Thomas has held this position almost 57 years, a record in the nineteenth and twentieth centuries, and, in view of the age at which residents are invited to become freemen these days, one which is most unlikely ever to be broken.

Mr. Thomas wrote to the then mayor, Captain Herbert Lovegrove, giving him an account of the visit and commenting on the obvious prosperity and attractiveness of Winchelsea, Victoria. Although there is not room here to give details about those named, the letter illustrates extremely well that the relationship between the two communities had developed on a personal as well as an official level:

'… As I arrived at the Shire Hall, a solid, stone Victorian building, the Cinque Ports flag was run up, which I considered a very nice thought, and I was received by six Shire Councillors headed by the President, Mr. Guye, a very fine old man just retired after twenty years in the Victorian parliament, the last six as Minister of Transport. There were about a hundred people present and I felt very much like the Duke of Edinburgh. A terrific spread had been prepared which I could hardly do justice to, owing to the number of hands I had to shake and the fact that the temperature was over ninety. It was interesting to meet at least six people who had been to our town, and I promised to convey greetings to people there, especially from Councillor Stribling [owner of the Mercedes which had brought Mr. Thomas from Geelong on the coast where his ship had docked] who wanted to be remembered to Stone, Mrs. Burke and Mrs. Cookson and was so sorry to hear of Cookson's death. Also the boy Nash, now a very smart young army chemist, who had got special leave from Melbourne to be present, wished to be remembered to "Councillor Freeman" and sent positively affectionate messages to Mrs. Burke… '⁹

It was Winchelsea, Sussex's seven-hundredth anniversary celebrations in 1988 which next brought the special relationship to prominence in the two Winchelseas. The recognition of seven centuries of history created great interest in both communities and not a little respect from our Australian friends who had just marked their national bi-centenary and were about to celebrate their own 125th anniversary, the shire having been established in 1864.

An invitation for Winchelsea, Victoria to be represented at the Service of Thanksgiving on 16 July 1988 was responded to with enthusiasm. Although the itinerary of the official party did not permit attendance at the service itself, Councillor and Mrs. Barrie Gregory, with former Councillor and Mrs. Irwin Parsons, arrived at the Court Hall on 6 July to be greeted by the mayor and mayoress, Jurat and Mrs. Guy Hughes, members of the corporation and leading residents, among them Mrs. Petronilla Barclay, daughter of Major and Mrs. Burke, who has herself twice visited Winchelsea, Victoria.

In a gracious and entertaining speech Councillor Gregory spoke of the cordial association of the two Winchelseas, offered warmest congratulations on the anniversary, explained that Dr. Errol

(41) The former Shire Hall, Winchelsea, Victoria
photographed by Ken Chetwood whose daughter stands near the door.

Pickering would represent the shire at the service and presented a specially commissioned picture of Winchelsea, Victoria at the beginning of the twentieth century painted by Robert Coy, an artist living in nearby Lorne. Mr. Gregory explained that artistic licence had been used to emphasise important features, particularly the Barwon Bridge which was a striking landmark for all who lived in or visited the township and which for this reason had been made considerably larger than life. Also included were the Church of England church, by a remarkable coincidence also St. Thomas's, the United Church formerly Presbyterian, the school and the Barwon Hotel. Some houses along the river bank suggested the settlement as it then was but the vast majority had been left out to avoid cluttering the scene. In the background the countryside and hills were brown from drought as they had been when the picture was commissioned the previous March. It was in these hills and right to the coast at Geelong that disastrous fires raged in 1983 as a result of the careless dropping of a cigarette in tinder dry conditions. Tragically for one family but mercifully in general, only one life was lost. Winchelsea, Sussex's official records show that on the occasion of those fires a letter of sympathy had been sent by the mayor, Douglas Turner, to the President of the Shire, deeply regretting the destruction.[10]

Councillor Gregory also presented the mayoress, as President of the Women's Institute, with a bell to call the members to order at the beginning of meetings. This beautifully crafted artefact had been sent by the members of the Winchelsea, Victoria branch of the Countrywomen's Association, Australia's equivalent organisation.

During the years following these presentations the flag of the special relationship was kept flying, on one occasion literally, by Jurat Knightley 'Ken' Chetwood who visited Winchelsea, Victoria three times in conjunction with stays at the home of his daughter Jane who lives about fifty miles away at Lara Lake near Geelong. In 1989 he presented to the shire a glass goblet engraved with the arms of the Cinque Ports by Mrs. Margot Bruce, a Winchelsea, Sussex resident. Also etched into the glass were the dates 1288 - 1988 in recognition of the recently celebrated seven hundredth anniversary. The gift was accompanied by a copy of Peter Turner's video of the celebrations including the visit of Councillor Gregory and his party described above.

On his return Ken Chetwood reported to his colleagues on the warm reception he had been accorded with introductions to shire councillors in the council chamber and a day's guided tour of the area.[11] On the two subsequent visits he was greatly privileged, first as deputy mayor and then as mayor, to be invited to be guest speaker at the Australia Day celebrations, in preparation for which he made a point of learning the words of *Advance Australia Fair*. His speeches displayed a close interest in the history of both communities, drawing attention particularly to Australia's connection with the Confederation of The Cinque Ports through the Lord Wardenship of Sir Robert Menzies and the interest shown in Ken's third visit by the present Lord Warden, Her Majesty Queen Elizabeth the Queen Mother whom he told about it when attending a reception at Walmer Castle, her official residence. On his 1994 visit, in the knowledge that the Cinque Ports flag presented by George Mallows Freeman had attained the ripe old age of 78 and was somewhat the worse for wear, Mr. Chetwood gave his hosts great pleasure by presenting them with a replacement specially made by the Admiral's flag loft at Chatham Dockyard.

These contacts left the mayor with a great curiosity about Superintendent C.J. Latrobe who later became the first Governor of Victoria. What was his connection with Winchelsea, Sussex which would lead him to recommend the adoption of its name in a far distant land all those years before? As a result of much research it transpired that Charles Latrobe who retired after a life of travel to live at Clapham House, Litlington in Sussex, formerly the home of 'Prinny' and Mrs.

Fitzherbert, had a cousin, Edward Latrobe Bateman who was an artist and a member of the Pre-Raphaelite Brotherhood. The close connections of that group with Winchelsea have already been described and the fact that Bateman emigrated to Australia with Thomas Woolner and Bernhard Smith, seen off at Gravesend by Dante Gabriel Rossetti, William Holman Hunt and Ford Madox Brown seems to seal the connection beyond reasonable doubt. Even if Latrobe himself had no great connection with the ancient town, his cousin and his friends would have spoken enthusiastically about its characteristics which they so admired.[12]

On the same occasion that the new flag was presented, Winchelsea, Victoria reciprocated with a proposal that the relationship should be placed on a more official basis. The Shire President, Councillor Lindon Crossland, handed to Ken Chetwood a letter with this suggestion:

> 'It is with great pleasure that I write to invite the town of Winchelsea, England to enter into a formal affiliation with the Shire of Winchelsea. The Council of the Shire of Winchelsea resolved at its meeting on 8 December 1993 to commence a formal sister town relationship with Winchelsea, England to build on the growing awareness and appreciation of each other's culture and people… Would you please place my request before your Council and convey my warmest greetings to the community of Winchelsea, England on behalf of the Shire of Winchelsea.'

The mayor promised to recommend this most warmly and on his return it was indeed accepted with enthusiasm. The full text of the letter can be seen in the Douglas Turner Room of the Lower Court Hall as part of a special display devoted to Winchelsea, Victoria and including the Robert Coy picture and other memorabilia.

Shortly after the formal association had been cemented the shire of Winchelsea ceased to be a shire, being amalgamated under local government reorganisation with the shire of Barabool and part of the City of South Barwon to form Surf Coast Shire. This is the rough equivalent of what happened to Winchelsea, Sussex when Battle Rural District Council, in whose area it stood, became part of the much larger Rother District Council under the Local Goverment Act, 1972. Exactly the same reasons were given, the Chief Executive Officer of Surf Coast Shire writing in his first annual report, 'One of the advantages of restructuring councils is that more cost-effective solutions can be found and I am confident that in this respect the Surf Coast Shire will deliver.'[13] Let us hope that, for the sake of the residents of our sister town, he is right. Whether that is how things have turned out in England twenty-two years after similar legislation came into force it is not the purpose of this book to comment!

Anyway, a reassuring letter was received in August 1995 from the mayor, Councillor Noel Bates, sending greetings from the new shire and particularly the residents of Winchelsea. It would seem that the special relationship is safe. He said, 'In an effort to retain the history of the former shires a historical centre has been established at the offices in Winchelsea where memorabilia is to be kept for future generations.' Councillor Bates intriguingly added, 'The possibility of a cricket match between the two Winchelsea Cricket Clubs is an interesting prospect.'[14] That would certainly hit the headlines!

The connection between the two communities was further confirmed during Ken Chetwood's third visit in November 1996 when he was presented with a framed letter from 'The Mayor and Council of the Surf Coast Shire' drawing attention to the eightieth anniversary of the initiation of the arrangement. This was formally handed to the mayor on Easter Monday 1997 and is now included in the Lower Court Hall display.

May the twenty-first century see continuing interest in connections between the two Winchelseas and men like George Mallows Freeman, James McGowan, Anthony Thomas, Ken Chetwood and their Australian equivalents, particularly Barrie Gregory in recent years, emerge with the leadership and enthusiasm to ensure this.

(42) Winchelsea, Victoria

23. RESIDENTS AND RIVALRY

Shortly before Katharina Forbes-Dunlop waved the soldiers farewell on their way to the Boer War and her sister returned home without one felt slipper, there arrived in Winchelsea Miss Maud Peel, former owner of The Mermaid in Rye and a niece of the late Sir Robert Peel, in search of a new home. She had seen advertised for sale by auction a dwellinghouse, shop and premises in Castle Street. Attractions of the property included 'A partly walled Garden with Wood Lodge, Van Lodge and Stable with Loft over; also a piggery adjoining. The spring water is laid on and there is also an underground rainwater tank.' A second lot was for sale as building land with a frontage of eighty feet to Castle Street.[1] This property we now call The Armoury and we owe to Miss Peel its complete renovation and the fact that the potential building land remains undeveloped. When she first saw the property its condition and circumstances were unfortunate indeed.

This was once one of Winchelsea's most thriving businesses, a bakery which served the town and the area efficiently and profitably. John Sharp, the proprietor, was energetic and enthusiastic; also the owner of St. Leonard's Mill where he ground his flour. He greatly increased his sales, built a large brick oven against the north wall of the house to allow extra production, and on his death the whole flourishing concern passed to his son of the same name. Sadly John Sharp junior inherited his father's business but not his acumen. Sales fell, areas of property were sold off, even the mill was disposed of to help support the family. This tragic decline was observed silently but with deep sorrow by John Sharp senior's widow. By the time that even her home was in the hands of Messrs. Vidler, Son and Clements, the only visible sign of the premises' former use was 'one sad cottage loaf, resting on its side against the misty pane of a bow window [looking] out onto the street.'

When Miss Peel arrived, accompanied by the estate agent, she was prepared to find the property in a state of dilapidation, but not for the scene of human distress on which she stumbled. Only her own words can adequately paint the picture:

> 'When the house agent led me down two steps to the brick floored bakehouse, now known as the drawing room, there, seated and silhouetted against the dark, dusty background, was a lonely figure, the aged mother of the owner, a bowl on her knee over which she was peeling potatoes. A black cat, tail stiff and erect, moved around her, eyes on the intruders, indignant at the untimely interruption, but the bent figure, her head covered with a coloured kerchief, moved not. Silently and unheedingly she continued her work, not even raising her head when, with a few words, I apologised for the intrusion. Poor soul! How could she in any sort respond with her sore heart and so soon to leave the home to which she had come in the days of her joyous youth, proud of her husband, of his work, and of the position he had made, and now to go forth and end her days among strangers, far from friends and home, and in an unknown country.'[2]

Having purchased the home so painfully left by the old lady, Miss Peel set about a major restoration and reconstruction, living opposite at The Castle Inn while the work was done, and leaving The Armoury much as we see it today with the Castle Street frontage quite transformed. She became a pillar of the community, supporting the church particularly, and acquired, apparently as a charitable exercise, 'the barrack buildings and their pestilential hinterland'.[3] 'The barrack buildings' are now the comfortable homes of Barrack Square and the 'pestilential hinterland', once used for drilling the garrison, remains largely garden land, although there has been some development.

Maud Peel was recalled by Douglas Turner as one of Winchelsea's many eccentrics. She was extremely deaf and used an ear trumpet. The maintenance of her property, like its history, was something of an obsession. She would sit in the little conservatory beyond the room in which Mrs. Sharp peeled potatoes, with a large board on her knees, writing and drawing instructions not only for major alterations but also for minor daily work. When the workmen were carrying out her instructions she would appear with her ear-trumpet and require Mr. Ellis or the foreman to shout into it if she wanted to know exactly what was happening. There were never fewer than two men from Ellis Brothers of Rye on the site full time and if they completed the work on their daily instruction sheet by ten o'clock in the morning they had to sit in their shed until it was time to go home. For almost a year Douglas himself was one of these employees. During this time The Armoury cellar was discovered by accident. Miss Peel was being urged to put up the rents of the Barrack Square houses which she had restored and let but she did not want to do so, instead taking away half the gardens to make them less valuable. A man by the name of Toby Knight was digging deep post-holes for the fence along the new boundary. One day he rushed into the shed where Douglas and his colleagues were sitting and shouted, 'I've lost my bloody shovel. It's gone down a bloody great hole!' He had cut through the top of a previously unknown cellar which contains, near the foot of the steps, a polished, scooped-out stone which Douglas thought 'was used to hold holy water in the days when Catholics worshipped in secret.' Whether he was prompted by the owner's imagination we do not know.

All Miss Peel's extensive alterations and improvements did not serve to make the house any warmer in cold weather but the old lady who was very careful with her money in all but building and restoration had her own solution to this problem. Douglas Turner remembered:

'She used to wear voluminous skirts that dragged on the ground. She had a single burner oil stove. The old gardener used to trim it and light it every morning before she got about and put it in the conservatory ready for her. She'd go out there, take up her drawing board, lift up her skirt and put the stove underneath. We said it was Winchelsea's first example of central heating.'[4]

Mrs. Bethell, Len Polhill's grandmother who was Miss Peel's housekeeper, also became involved in such frugality – she had to make a pint of milk go an exceptionally long way!

Maud Peel sought out the history of her property through extensive research. She drew detailed plans of the barrack area during the Napoleonic Wars, claimed to have identified part of her garden as the site of the Presbytery of the Knights Templars,[5] surmised about the one-time use of the area for bear-baiting, and traced major families which had occupied the land over the centuries. This led to a wider study of Winchelsea's more general history during which she made extracts from the church registers, compiled notes about leading citizens and developed a theory that the octagonal structure so clearly to be seen at the corner of The Stone House at the top of Strand Hill was once the base of an ancient wayfarers' cross.

Miss Peel's recollections of the Winchelsea of her day have been invaluable in the compilation of this book and some are referred to elsewhere. The reliability of her writings about earlier times is not so clearly established. On her death the volumes containing copious notes and a typescript summary of her findings came into the possession of her contemporary devotee of the town's history, William Maclean Homan.[6] His methods were quite different. He relied on the scholarly study of original documents, assisted by an agent, Miss Gwyneth Wise, who, on his behalf, visited the Public Record Office and other repositories, making detailed transcriptions and sometimes

(43) The Armoury before Miss Peel's restoration. The large exterior oven can be seen on the left.

translations. The extent and value of Mr. Homan's researches are beyond question. They are painstakingly detailed, academic and authoritative, the two best known being the layout of New Winchelsea, derived from the 1292 Rent Roll (see p.7) and of Winchelsea's medieval cellars, to almost all of which he managed to gain access to make plans and drawings.[7] He felt that Miss Peel's work was based by contrast on a romantic imagination and could not be relied upon for he wrote in the front of her summary account:

> 'The following was written by Miss Maud Peel who died in 1939 when over ninety years of age. She owned the house known as The Armoury in Quarter No. 7, Winchelsea, from 1897 until her death and resided there. Unfortunately hardly any of her notes on Winchelsea are in accordance with reliable documentary evidence and her historical outlook is derived from most unreliable and incorrect sources. W. Maclean Homan, 2, Friars Road, Winchelsea. 10 August 1940.'[8]

Whether this was unnecessarily dismissive is a matter of opinion. What is not in doubt is that Mr. Homan was better qualified to judge that any other twentieth-century student of Winchelsea's past.

William Maclean Homan was a Norwegian who brought up his family in Scotland. They later emigrated to South Africa, a country which Mr. Homan much loved, and where he set up in business. In the late 1920s Mr. and Mrs. Homan returned to England and set about finding somewhere to live. Their daughter, Mrs. Helen Goldie, took an afternoon coach-tour while staying at Tunbridge Wells, as a result suggesting to her parents that Rye was a place where they might

(44) St Leonard's Mill, Winchelsea

consider settling. They went to stay at The Mermaid. On the first morning they were there Mr. Homan went out for a walk, returning to announce, 'I've found a place much nicer that Rye where we could live.' He eventually bought numbers 2 and 3, Friars Road but always used them as one house and had the front door of No. 3 removed. Later he also acquired No. 1 which, after his death, became the home of his son David who was later both Mayor of Winchelsea and Chairman of Icklesham Parish Council. No. 2/3 is still Mrs. Goldie's home.

On taking up residence in Winchelsea, Mr. Homan senior, whom I remember as a rather stern, bearded figure gazing out from his doorway on the town he so loved, used his talents as engineer, linguist and historian to immerse himself in Winchelsea's past. He compiled a massive collection of documents and information on which he based his *History of Winchelsea 1292-1800* which well illustrates his radical views for he was no respecter of reputation or tradition. Sadly this and other major works such as *The Churches of Winchelsea* have never been published but they are available in typescript on the shelves of the search room at East Sussex Record Office where Mrs. Goldie arranged for all her father's papers to be transferred after his death in 1956. A full list is included as an appendix in *Winchelsea Corporation Records* published in 1963. The Homan papers include original documents, maps, plans, account books, transcripts, photographs, drawings, unpublished writings and copious notes, the whole archive a tangible tribute to a man who dedicated so much time to throwing light on Winchelsea's past.

Not all his scholarly writings remain unpublished. A booklet entitled *The Founding of New Winchelsea* has had a wide circulation and is the definitive work on this important event which, as we have seen, had considerable national as well as local importance. Mr. Homan contributed widely to such publications as *Sussex Archaeological Collections*, *Sussex County Magazine* and *Sussex Notes and Queries*.

However, his involvement in the town was also actively practical. His enthusiastic exploration of the Court Hall cellar has already been described (p.83). He became the corporation's honorary archivist and was the first curator of the museum established at the Court Hall in 1950. In earlier years he pursued his desire to further the preservation of ancient buildings by leading a major appeal for restoring St. Leonard's Mill during the 1930s. This magnificent structure was in an appalling state of disrepair and needed extensive work. In order to facilitate the receipt of grants Anthony Freeman, as landowner, gave an undertaking to the Society for the Protection of Ancient Buildings that the mill would not be demolished or removed from the site for thirty years, although he specifically required that it should not be open to the public. The local appeal attracted strong support from Lord Blanesburgh, Lord Ritchie of Dundee, Mr. Freeman himself, Miss Maud Peel and many others. Miss Peel, writing to Mr. N.P.W. Viner Brady, joint organiser of the appeal with Mr. Homan, made the suggestion that when the mill was again in full working order it should be used to pump the clear water of St. Leonard's Well up to the town. Obviously Winchelsea's water supply still fell short of the residents' hopes.[9]

This restoration of the mill was at least partly completed; there seems to be some doubt whether the sails were actually re-affixed, a difficult and expensive exercise. The machinery, however, was definitely in place at that time. It was not until further work was carried out in the 1950s that the consultant architects recommended its removal to permit the insertion of a framework reinforcing the external structure. This allowed the superficial appearance of the building to be maintained but almost certainly contributed by very considerably lightening its weight to the final destruction which befell the mill in the great storm of 1987. Another theory is that it was not so much the reduction in weight but the extreme rigidity created by 'the Forth Bridge' of reinforcing girders which brought the structure down. Earlier a few slats would have been blown away thus allowing the tempest to pass it by. The mill was the most important of Winchelsea's landmarks wiped off the map on that violent night. Now all that remains is a plaque reading:

> 'On this site stood St. Leonard's Windmill, destroyed in the great storm of the 16th October 1987. The windmill was built in 1703 on the site of the ancient Saxon church of St. Leonard on which you are now standing.'

W. M. Homan would have been bitterly disappointed had he lived to view the scene. He would have been almost equally disappointed that the date on the plaque is incorrect and should have been about a hundred years later.

Other keen subscribers to the windmill appeal included the Miss Beddingtons, two elderly ladies who can be numbered like Miss Peel among Winchelsea's more eccentric residents. They lived in some luxury in adjoining houses but were not on speaking terms. For how long this estrangement persisted is not clear but the present Lord Ritchie of Dundee certainly remembers being told as a boy that these ladies had little communication with each other. Ted Streeton, too, recalls the animosity between them. On one occasion they co-operated sufficiently to leave together for London in the local taxi. By the end of the day, however, things had become so strained that one returned to Winchelsea in the taxi and the other by train. At one time they kept a chauffeur and limousine but even this hardly improved the situation. Len Polhill, too, remembers that when the chauffeur, Mark Winter, was taking them to Hastings arguments grew so intense by the time they reached Icklesham that one got out and walked back to Winchelsea while the other completed the journey.

The Misses Beddington were both resident from about the beginning of this century; Miss Maud converted Ballader's Plat a grocer's shop owned by the Barling family into her home and Miss Beatrice lived at White Close next door In accordance with society custom of the time the elder sister, Maud, was referred to simply as Miss Beddington. Miss Beddington died in 1939, the same year as Miss Peel, and Miss Beatrice in 1943 so they were long-term residents looked upon with some awe and exercising a powerful but kindly influence within the town. Margaret Muggridge paints a lively picture of their lifestyle and of that influence:

'Some of us girls used to go to a knitting class at Miss Beddington's house. [She was] a little Jewish lady who lived in German Street facing the tree John Wesley preached his last outdoor sermon from. It was a lovely house and she kept a butler, a funny looking man with a face like the old advert for monkey soup. Also a housekeeper, a widow who had lost her only son in the war. Archie Baldwin's name is on the memorial in the church, poor soul! Miss Beddington used to supply the wool and we knitted socks which we were allowed to keep. I once knitted one and my sister the other. She knitted so tight I doubt if any soldier got his leg into it. When we went home Miss Beddington gave us a rock bun which lived up to its name, some kids threw them over the wall to the sheep. Further along the road was another Miss Beddington and she was interested in historical things and had a studio at the top of the house with baskets of clothes, lovely velvets etc. and we had a play occasionally at the Town Hall…'[10]

Later she recalled her family, recovering from 'flu, being brought a jelly in a basin, sent by Miss

(45) A scene from one of Miss Beatrice Beddington's plays – her maid is pictured on the right.

Beddington and delivered by the butler. Unlike the rock buns the jelly was greatly enjoyed.[11] Miss Beatrice was a particular friend of Ellen Terry and would encourage her to return to Winchelsea after her move to Smallhythe. On these occasions Dame Ellen frequently supported local good causes such as the Red Cross at charitable events in the garden of White Close and at recitals in its music room.

Len Polhill recalls that Miss Beddington ran a boot club, successor to the provisions earlier made by Miss Stileman and Ellen Terry. The children took their twopences which she kept in the bank and in time arranged for them to be measured for and provided with new shoes. Not to be outdone, Miss Beatrice organised a coal club into which pennies and twopences would be paid, resulting eventually in Walter Alford's arrival to deliver to the participating families. Despite the need to earn a little extra money whenever possible, Len's family were shocked when Miss Maud Beddington, an enthusiastic amateur artist, arrived at their door one day, remarked that Len's younger brother was a good looking boy and asked whether he might pose in the nude on her hearthrug. Permission was refused!

The Misses Beddington were generous contributors to all Winchelsea causes and their names invariably appear on subscription lists, particularly those of St. Thomas's Church. When the church authorities decided to raise further funds by offering reserved seats in return for a premium payment, these ladies were among very few who felt their position in Winchelsea society to be such that they could properly apply. They also helped the New Hall with donations following the rejection of a controversial plan to provide the additional community accommodation which Winchelsea was felt to need at that time by extending the Court Hall over the present garden area. Although at least one of the jurats was involved in the early stages of the scheme, it seems an architect was employed even before the corporation as owners had been officially consulted. There was dissension among those forming the committee involved so the matter was referred to Lady McIlwraith as potentially the main contributor. We have reason to be grateful that she instantly vetoed the idea of extending the Court Hall and so the New Hall came to be built.[12]

Among those resident in Winchelsea at the time was Leonard Peulevé with his wife and family. Madame Peulevé was headmistress of St. Thomas's School and, led by the father, the family became involved in opening the upper room of the Court Hall to the public with various corporation artefacts and items associated with Winchelsea on display. Among the boys engaged to show people round during the holidays was Ron Turner who recalls that Leonard Peulevé, formerly a garden architect, designed and laid out the Court Hall garden as it is seen today after the possibility of its being built over came to nothing. During this work he discovered, beneath the present lawn area, a mosaic pavement, possibly Roman. No doubt it will eventually be once again revealed.

Another who would have shown visitors round was Leonard's son, Henri, a St. Thomas's chorister and later a pupil at Rye Grammar School. Henri Peulevé's military career is today commemorated in a Court Hall Museum display prepared by Jurat David Bourne with the active encouragement of Miss Vera Atkins. The tribute records how Henri, bi-lingual as a result of the family's frequent moves between England and France, and one of the first TV cameramen at Alexandra Palace, joined the Royal Electrical and Mechanical Engineers at the beginning of the 1939-1945 war, later being recruited into the Special Operations Executive. After breaking his leg the first time he parachuted into France, he escaped to Spain and eventually made his way back to England after several months in a Spanish gaol. On his return he set about organising and equipping highly efficient teams of resistance members for sabotage operations, frequently leading them himself with conspicuous gallantry. In March 1944 he was captured, saving the lives of his associates by steadfastly refusing to give any information under interrogation. Attempting escape for the second time he was shot in the thigh, being left on recapture to remove the bullet himself with a spoon. Transferred to the concentration camp at Buchenwald he successfully escaped in April 1945, capturing two S.S. men in the process and taking them with him to reach the safety of the American lines. Major Henri L.T. Peulevé DSO, Chevallier de la Legion d'Honneur, Croix de Guerre, Médaille de la Resistance, died in 1962 and is buried in the Anglo-American cemetery in Seville, Spain.

(46) William Maclean Homan

His remarkable story has been kept alive by another Winchelsea resident, Miss Vera Atkins, who first came to the town to visit her aunt, Mrs. Mendl, in about 1925. Miss Atkins' part in the story of the S.O.E. in which Henri Peulevé served was a critically important one. As a W.A.A.F. officer she became personal assistant to Col. Maurice Buckmaster, head of F section, and 'earned the formidable reputation of being the real power behind the operation.' A *Daily Telegraph* report dated 6 May 1991 about the newly dedicated S.O.E. memorial at Valencay says of her:

> 'She is almost 83, and although spry and spruce, with a memory that is the filing cabinet of a clandestine army, she sees her efforts to gather her agents at the dedication of the memorial as the final act of her war.'

The memorial, at which Her Majesty Queen Elizabeth the Queen Mother laid a wreath that day, was made possible largely by Miss Atkins' efforts. After the war, knowing that about five hundred agents had been despatched to France and that at least one hundred were missing she set out to trace what had happened to them. This incredible piece of detective work formed a major part of the basis for the inclusion of names on the Valencay memorial. The same *Daily Telegraph* article highlighted her remarkable service by reporting:

> 'Atkins and Buckmaster have been written into popular culture as Miss Moneypenny and "M" of Ian Fleming's James Bond books, but the fictional characters are a trivialisation of their models.'

A much more fitting recognition came when, as one of his last acts in office, President Mitterand appointed Vera Atkins to be a Commandant of the Legion d'Honneur, the highest rank of the order. This remarkable honour to a Winchelsea resident was locally noted by a special inscription in the official record of Winchelsea Corporation.[13]

Henri Peulevé's fellow Court Hall guide, Ron Turner, like his brothers Douglas, Leslie and Norman, has spent his whole life in Winchelsea. As the firm of Turner Brothers, builders, they served the town outstandingly and extensively for many years. Ron remembers the Winchelsea of the late 1920s and the 1930s when life in the town was played out at a slower and much more relaxed pace. The notes which he has very kindly given me highlight much that illustrates the contrast with the present day. Mr. Wheeler lived at Gate Cottage by the entrance to the Greyfriars drive and worked in the estate gardens. It was his wife's task to open and close the gates every time a vehicle wanted to go through. Nearby, in the cottage once rented by Joseph Conrad to be near his collaborator, Ford Madox Ford, lived Mrs. Collins who took in washing. At Byways, opposite, Mr. Cooke and his family ran a taxi business, their home having once been called Etterby, where lived the Forbes-Dunlops. In St. Thomas's Street at Haskards, formerly Derwent Cottage, lived Mr. and Mrs Cook with their son who later married a Miss Brook and moved to live in one of the Rookery Cottages owned by G.M. Freeman. Their daughter, Georgina, was the girl sponsored by Winchelsea, Victoria after her father's death in action. Mr. Cook senior worked on the Greyfriars Estate, his wife taking in paying guests one of whom was Beatrice Potter. Mr. Brakefield ran the blacksmiths' business at Forge House but in his son's time, as cars replaced horse transport, petrol pumps were installed and it became a garage. In the barrack houses, paying the rents which Miss Peel wanted to keep as low as possible, lived Mr. Whiting who worked as a carter at Mill Farm, Mr. and Mrs. Burt – he was the verger -, Mr. C. Barden, roadman and keeper of the Lookout, Mr. F. Barden, labourer, Mrs. Ball, Mr. Jones, chauffeur to Mr. Mallock at The Mount, Mr. Heywood who worked for Walter Alford, coal merchant at The Ferry. Mr. Smith, insurance agent, Mr. Weller, plumber, and Mr. Whiteman, farm worker.

Mr. Heywood's boss, Walter Alford, served the town for many years through his business and his time as member, later chairman, of Icklesham Parish Council, earning the gratitude of vast numbers of residents. My wife and I remember him struggling uncomplainingly through the low doorways of Cleveland Cottage carrying hundredweight sacks of coal for the property has no rear entrance. That was as his years advanced. Of a kindness shown in his earlier days Margaret Muggridge wrote:

> 'One other memory I have of Winchelsea was of a girl who came to school who had T.B. I should think. Anyway she was ill and always very breathless. In the end she died. She was one of a large family and I believe the father was in the army. The family must have been poor as Walter Alford, our coal merchant, brought her coffin up to the churchyard in his coal cart, poor girl. I made a cross for her with flowers and leaves and my mother bought some white ribbon to tie on. The same family had an older sister who fell off Camber Castle and was badly injured. There was not much state help for people in those days.'[14]

At No. 2, The Orchards in Mill Road lived Mr. and Mrs. Williams, Mrs. Williams being the author, Patience Strong. Her husband purchased Mariteau House and employed Turner Brothers to convert it into five properties.

Ron Turner's recollections of the post office are particularly vivid for he once worked there. The business was moved from Castle Street to High Street in 1924. There, Alexander H.T. Finch, who had moved to the town as a small boy in 1903, presided over Finch of Winchelsea, a business which had a grocery store on one side and the post office and telephone exchange on the other. Winchelsea was quite a focal point for postal services in those days for the Royal Mail van was garaged in a building on the site which has since contained the automatic telephone exchange, at the beginning of Mill Lane. Each evening this vehicle, driven by Mr. Hickmott, set off to Rye and later up through the country to the main sorting office at Reigate, picking up the mail from post offices on its route. On the return journey it dropped the mail off and reached Winchelsea at 5.30 a.m.. the night's work completed. Ron had to report for duty at 6 a.m. to sort the mail brought by Mr. Hickmott for the Winchelsea area. From that time until ten at night he shared responsibility for the post office counter and the manual telephone exchange with Miss Brooks. Their complex shift system provides an interesting contrast with most modern working arrangements:

> 'I worked 6 a.m. until 8, then I'd go home for breakfast until 10, in from 10 -12, lunch from 12 – 1 and I'd stay until 2 so that Miss Brooks could go for her lunch and then three days a week I would stay on until 6; the other three days I would go home from 2 – 4 and then go back from 4 – 10. Sundays I worked from 8 until 1, and the other Sunday from 1 until 10.'

On Sundays the shop was not open, of course, but the telephone exchange had to be manned. By the time Ron was an operator there were about eighty lines. All connections and ringing were done manually. He recalls that they were kept quite busy, frequently having to use considerable initiative routing calls around the country to reach a required destination but initially all calls had to be carried out of the town on one of the two lines to Rye or another two to Hastings. Anthony

(47) Alexander H.T. Finch

Freeman of Wickham Manor was by far the most frequent telephone user. Ron still remembers many of the numbers quoted on page 66; at the time he knew them all by heart. But what of the hours between 10 p.m and 6 a.m. when neither Ron Turner or Miss Brooks were on duty? If anyone wanted to make a call into or out of a Winchelsea number during the night, Alex Finch, the postmaster, had to get up and deal with it. Devotion to duty indeed! [15]

Alex Finch, despite what must have been large numbers of disturbed nights, became deeply involved in Winchelsea life. Between 1935 and 1943 he served the corporation as chamberlain, taking considerable pleasure in the ceremonial duties involved but unfortunately he then had a serious disagreement with the mayor, resigned, and a short time later was elected Chairman of Icklesham Parish Council. As the dispute smouldered this regrettably heralded a period during which relations between the corporation and the council were particularly strained.

The survival of Winchelsea Corporation with its mayor, jurats and officers, while Winchelsea is a ward of Icklesham Parish Council, the minor authority carrying all local government responsibility for the town, is a situation bound to cause misunderstanding. Outside bodies understandably cannot grasp that if a town has a mayor he is not leader of the local authority. Even officers of Rother District Council make such errors to this day, addressing letters to the town clerk as 'Clerk of Winchelsea Parish Council'. The strong disagreements there used to be between the corporation and the council are fortunately a thing of the past, and we hope will remain so. In recent years the two bodies have worked together most effectively in Winchelsea's interests, a trend encouraged by the increasing number of residents serving both. In giving an account of problems which have arisen in the past I, having had a foot in both camps, tread, with either foot, on difficult ground! Looking at the matter historically I can see quite clearly that the friction which has arisen when the corporation does something disapproved of by members of Winchelsea's long-established families, or something which is perceived as being outside the limited responsibilities which the corporation actually has; this friction is the direct descendant of the strong feelings which existed within the town when the citizens lost control of the corporation and the franchise it controlled two hundred and fifty years ago. As such it is part of what makes Winchelsea different and any rivalry there might be should be tempered with respect for the tradition which ensures the unique nature of the town's civic status.

An example of these problems arose in the early 1950s when, under Alex Finch's chairmanship, the parish council was seeking an allotment site. There were already allotment gardens in Tanyard Lane but some tenants had been given notice; the land formerly rented by Miss Peel had been acquired by Battle Rural District Council for the Spring Steps houses and another site was badly needed. Agreement was difficult to reach. The parish council even threatened compulsory purchase of a site at Mill Farm.[16] Eventually, having declined previously to enter into negotiations, Anthony Freeman as landowner suggested that Douglas Turner, in his capacity as a parish council member, was the only person with whom he was prepared to discuss the matter. These gentlemen sorted it all out, coming to an admirable and, on Mr. Freeman's part, generous arrangement. The Cricket Field Allotments were established at a rental which it was the owner's wish should apply in perpetuity. This has since been honoured by the National Trust. The parish council constructed the necessary fencing and Douglas Turner managed the site on the council's behalf for well over thirty years.

In 1954 Douglas Turner was involved in another dispute, this time not as negotiator but as complainant. His letter is worth quoting at some length because it not only explains a specific problem, it also robustly states the basic cause of the friction.

Castle Cottage,
Winchelsea,
Sussex.

The County Surveyor

22 March 1954

Dear Sir,

On Saturday last, March 20th, the Winchelsea Corporation planted an oak tree on the green directly in front of my house, and erected a most unsightly iron fence some six feet in diameter and six feet high around it. This is an eyesore at the moment but in a few years will shut out all light and sunshine from the front rooms of my house. It is also over the main drain connections to adjoining property and the G.P.O. underground ducts.

I am given to understand that permission to plant it was given by your department. You are doubtless aware that the Winchelsea Corporation does not represent the people of Winchelsea in any respect as it lost its powers under an act passed some 120 years ago [71 years actually but the point is made]. Its members are not elected by the electorate but fill vacancies themselves. The local government representatives apparently were not consulted. As a ratepayer and elector I consider this should have been done. If you gave permission for an oak to be planted on this site I fear a grave mistake has been made. I should be grateful if you would take immediate steps to have it replanted in a more suitable place...

Yours faithfully,

Douglas H. Turner' [17]

(48) Douglas Haydn Turner

The then owner of The Armoury fired a similar salvo. This was a coronation oak. It was moved.

And so we pass to the life of service which Douglas Turner devoted to the town of his birth. I am indeed fortunate that before Douglas's death in 1994 he recorded for me his reminiscences about Winchelsea in the twentieth century. Particularly relevant to us here are the contrasts he drew between the Winchelsea of the 1920s and the present day. He listed the businesses which existed in the town just after the First World War: four pubs, three grocers, a dairy, a pork butcher, two shoe-repairers, a baker, a greengrocer, a market garden, a plumber and decorator, two butchers, a post office stationer and newsagents, a blacksmith and an ironmonger. By contrast there are now a post office, a restaurant, two pubs, a corner shop and a butcher's; considering the trends of the late twentieth century Winchelsea is extremely lucky still to have these. Douglas pointed out that the 1920 businesses were supported largely by providing for the needs of eight principal houses and of those serving them who occupied many of Winchelsea's cottages. These houses were Greyfriars, Cleveland House, Mariteau House, Periteau House, Hiham House, The Mount, Backfields and Yew Tree House. Of these, Greyfriars was until recently a county council old people's home, although it has now returned to private use; Cleveland House has remained a single dwelling, Periteau has been divided into three dwellings, having been a 'lunatic asylum' in those earlier days, Backfields, too, has become three separate dwellings, Mariteau five, The Mount three and Yew Tree House three. Hiham House has been knocked down and many smaller homes built on the site. The trend is clear, as it is with transport provision within the town. There are no figures to show the present number of motor vehicles in Winchelsea and serving it.

Mr. Turner reckoned that as late as 1928 its entire transport needs were met by eight cars, one taxi, one bus, two horsedrawn flys and two carriers.

Douglas Turner was singularly well qualified to make such comparisons. He was born in the house now known as 2, High Street, next door but one to the Court Hall, on 3 June 1909. In 1916 he moved with his family to Castle Cottage which eventually became home for mother, father and eight children. Tragedy required them to exhibit the sturdy independence necessary in those days for Mrs. Turner died and the oldest sister, Evelyn, then aged 15, had to give up her job in service with Dr. John Skinner at Backfields and take over responsibility for the family.

Douglas was to live at Castle Cottage for the rest of his life. He served the church as choirboy and server, the cricket club as fixture secretary and player, the New Hall Management Committee as secretary and eventually as a trustee, the Gardeners' and Allotment Holders' Society as secretary and latterly chairman, the Friends of Winchelsea Church as a council member, St. Thomas's School as a manager, later governor and Icklesham Parish Council as a member representing Winchelsea Ward for thirty-seven years. His working life, too, was devoted solely to the town and the area, first as grocer's delivery boy, then as a plumber and eventually as a director of Turner Bros. His intense enthusiasm for gardening was also provided for within the town, in the garden of Castle Cottage but more extensively at the allotments and at the home of his eldest son, John. Douglas was a member of the auxiliary fire service throughout the Second World War. In 1980 he was invited to become a freeman and join the corporation. We have noted circumstances which meant that his acceptance was far from certain. His friend Alex Finch, for example, had always urged him to have nothing to do with that body, but fortunately for Winchelsea he rejected that advice.

> 'I adopted the attitude, if you can't beat them join them! You see, up until the Second World War they'd always been the upper ten, they didn't want any working people. I was really astounded when Kenneth Whitehead who was mayor came here one day and asked me if I'd like to be a freeman – astounded that I'd been asked. I thought, "Well, it's a very good opportunity, why shouldn't you take it?" And I enjoyed it.'[18]

Thus came a new lease of life for Douglas and Elsie, the wife he had first met when delivering groceries to Mariteau House where she was the kitchenmaid whose duty it was to take them in. By the time he had been freeman and jurat five years Douglas had served twice as deputy mayor and twice as mayor. With Elsie as consort he filled these offices with distinction within the town and was an active ambassador throughout the Confederation of the Cinque Ports, ensuring with enthusiasm that Winchelsea was always represented at functions and that the town played the fullest possible part in confederation affairs.

What is extraordinary about Douglas Turner's service to Winchelsea is that it represents single-minded devotion to a community and lifelong residence within it almost unknown since transport developments permitted and encouraged fluid movement of the population. When elected mayor he confidently claimed to be the first holder of that office who had crawled round every bathroom in the town. Had he chosen his words carefully he could also have claimed to be the first person born in Winchelsea in the twentieth century to become mayor. (Anthony Freeman was born in 1892).

The citation which hangs in the Court Hall explains why he is held in such affectionate regard:

> 'Many have served Winchelsea with distinction in the twentieth century, some devoting themselves to its people through their professional lives, some as elected

representatives, some through voluntary involvement with organisations and some as members of the corporation but no one else has dedicated a whole life to the town as Douglas Turner did, serving in all four capacities. The mayor and members of Winchelsea Corporation, wishing to pay tribute and feeling that there should be some permanent recognition of this unique record, have named the inner room of the Lower Court Hall the Douglas Turner Room in his memory.'

And so it will remain.

Nevertheless the last word in this chapter will go to Alex Finch. On his retirement it was the town's wish to honour and recognise his exceptional service as postmaster. The passing of the years had not entirely removed old wounds. The corporation's only record of this is distinctly cool. The minutes record:

> 'Proposal for testimonial for Mr. A.H.T. Finch who has been postmaster for 43 years reported. Agreed that this should not be organised by the corporation. The mayor is prepared to support it by his name if it is organised by someone else'.[19]

In fact the matter was taken up by a small committee under the chairmanship of Sir John Shaw K.C.M.G. The grateful residents raised the generous sum of £120, a cheque for that amount being presented to Alex Finch during a party at Sir John's home, 2, White Close.

Let us hope, whatever may be the rights and wrongs of that dispute, that all concerned will ensure such ill-feeling does not persist in the future. There are a number of possible circumstances in which Winchelsea will need to show a united front to the outside world.

(49) The circus comes to Winchelsea – 1920s

24. ST. THOMAS'S CHURCH

The Church of St. Thomas the Martyr has played a vital part in the story of Winchelsea; its dominating central position within the surviving part of the town makes it a natural focal point for residents and visitors alike. This appears to have been the definite intention of those who planned New Winchelsea although in earlier years two other parish churches served the town. The Church of St. Leonard, sited to the west where the windmill stood until 1987, was within the walls but not within Winchelsea's jurisdiction for it principally provided for the community of Iham or Petit Iham, once a limb of Hastings within the Confederation of the Cinque Ports. Boundary stones marked CH (Corporation of Hastings) can still be seen in nearby fields. The likelihood is that any remaining parts of this building, which had long been in decay, were destroyed when the windmill was moved to this prominent position.[1]

The Church of St. Giles was a far more integral part of the community, sited where we now see the Old Rectory and St. Giles's Close. Here it was that the churchyard overflowed into Deadman's Lane after the worst of the French raids. We can be much more precise about the final disappearance of its remains for Rev. Drake Hollingberry left a delighted account in the parish records of how he managed to get rid of them. In 1777, in parts at least, the walls stood several feet above the ground. Far from the reverential care which would be lavished upon them now, the rector ordered that these walls should be knocked down and the foundations dug up. He availed himself of the opportunity partly to cover the expense by selling the stone for the construction of Rye's new harbour at Winchelsea Beach. When the land was later ploughed an unexpected problem occurred. The ploughshare 'struck against something so firm that it became necessary to use a mattock.' On investigation the obstruction turned out to be a bar of lead, five more eventually being found together with some sheet lead. The rector assumed that these must have been at one time part of the church roof. He sold them as well, raising a further twenty-three pounds ten shillings and sixpence, thus completely covering his costs. Mr. Hollingberry's satisfaction at the outcome is implied in his note: 'the rector is now in possession of a pleasant and level garden made from a heap of ruins and a roughter.' (a rough enclosure)[2]

Of the early days of St. Thomas's Church itself there is much speculation. No authority doubts the cathedral-like architectural excellence of the plan, some are unsure about whether it was ever completed. Materials of the highest quality were certainly available for such work in the late thirteenth and early fourteenth centuries; timber in the great forest of Anderida which covered the Weald of Sussex, stone from Caen in Normandy and the ruins of Old Winchelsea which provided a quarry still accessible at low tide.

> 'Competent authorities assure us that the workmanship of the stonemasons – particularly... in the moulding of their arches – stands unsurpassed in Gothic architecture. And they had their fun, too and have left for us to enjoy many small heads of unknown vanished men and women who smile down at us with sightless eyes.'[3]

The quality of the timber used is well illustrated by an account reporting that in 1903 the original roof timbers of the church 'are of an integrity so thorough that a village carpenter who recently climbed up to test them blunted all his tools in the enterprise.'[4]

If the building was completed it stretched to within a few feet of the western churchyard wall and Wesley's tree. Circumstantial evidence attributes the loss of the vast majority of the structure to the depredations of the French raids and the ravages of the Black Death. By the time these had ended and any attempt to reconstruct the church might have become practicable, the population had so dwindled that no useful purpose would have been served. Thus we are left with the sanctuary, the choir with its side aisles and the ruins of the transepts; a building of unusual shape and particular impact, although it is twentieth century alterations which have so greatly enhanced this latter quality.

The almost complete disappearance of the nave and of any archaeological evidence of its construction is accounted for by Mr. Hollingberry's entrepreneurial enthusiasm for making use of materials which were not in his view being useful. The stonework of what may have been a separate campanile tower, and of the nave foundations, was sold along with that of St. Giles to be used in constructing the new harbour.[5] At that time fragments of tessellated flooring were uncovered, the best evidence there is of the building's completion for such flooring would be unlikely to be put down unless the nave roof were on.[6] A detailed archaeological examination in 1850 showed no traces of the nave foundations 'excepting those of the great central piers and a small portion of wall at the south-west angle of what was the southern aisle'.[7]

Following the death of their deeply respected rector, Drake Hollingberry, the parishioners of St. Thomas's experienced for the only time that I have so far discovered the effects of having an absentee incumbent. The loss of their two services each Sunday and the constant presence to which they had become accustomed caused great resentment resulting in a petition to the Bishop of Chichester.[8] Some of them might well have been even less happy when, in 1831, Rev. J.J. West became rector. However, here we shall pass by his controversial career for it has been fully dealt with elsewhere. (see pp.110-114)

During the main period covered by this book there have been a number of major restorations, the first of them taking place in the middle of the nineteenth century, largely at the expense of Thomas Dawes, donor also of the Town Well. For many years the sanctuary had been home to 'unsightly old framing and pewing, put up to support what was once the dignity of the mayor and jurats of the place.' The removal of these pews revealed not only the piscina and sedilia on the south side but also the door to the sacristy on the north. Together with the corporation pews was swept away a three-decker pulpit with preaching level, reading level and clerk's desk which had stood centrally, thus obscuring the view of the sanctuary. This was replaced by the present stone pulpit on the north side of the chancel steps and the oak lectern on the south. The removal of the box-pews in the body of the church was also planned but not carried out until much later. These alterations were enhanced by the opening up of the windows on both sides of the sanctuary which had been filled with bricks and plaster. With acumen and foresight, W.D. Cooper comments in his account of this work '[The Chancel's] effect would be improved if [these windows] were filled up with stained glass.'[9]

We catch a glimpse of the church during the time of one of Mr. West's successors, Rev. Henry Patch, through the pen of his daughter Blanche:

'On Sundays at Winchelsea we children sat and, in the winter shivered, in old box pews. These pews were high, and when we knelt down, facing the expanse of dividing wall, we would sometimes insinuate the edges of a hymn book through the cracks in the wood. On the other side knelt a family of grown up sons, and if one of them gave the hymn book cover a tug we would call that catching a fish. Occasionally they would slip sweets over to us, usually sugared almonds. When the pews came to be dismantled, I was told that the books in the Rectory pew had to be put to one side as some of the messages written in them were not intended for general circulation. The only heating in the very lofty building was a hideous stove in the middle aisle with a black pipe to carry off the smoke, and probably the heat with it. Our pew had a quite useless oil stove, but, as we grew older, we added to our comfort by carrying hot-water bottles and rugs to church. Probably others in the congregation were doing the same thing. Anyway, an objection from either of my parents would have been unlikely, both of them being of quiet and practical tempers.'[10]

Rev. Henry Patch was rector from 1883 until 1901, the living having been purchased by his father from the estate of James John West. His daughter's assessment of his character was born out by Miss Maud Peel, a leading parishioner, who wrote '[He was] no great preacher but deeply loved and respected for his faithful service to the church and his parishioners.'[11]

The major work done very early in the twentieth century proposed, among other things, underfloor heating for the church, necessitating taking out the box pews which Blanche Patch found so uncomfortable, the removal of the vestry which was then at the west end of the north aisle, its walls partly obscuring the tombs, the construction of the present vestry, cutting away the ivy from the exterior and the restoration of the tombs. The architect, J.P. Micklethwaite, felt that the ivy was causing irreparable damage to the walls and must be removed although he felt a less harmful creeper should be grown to maintain the appearance of the building.[12] The rector, Rev. J.D.H. Patch who had succeeded his father, was also strongly in favour of the ivy's removal and he wanted no replacement. Much controversy surrounded this part of the work, and an outcry was raised by many who thought it a desecration to change the appearance of the church so drastically, thus ruining, as they saw it, its attractiveness for artists. This school of thought considered the ivy's impact on the structure far less than had been suggested. Many years later they were supported by W.M. Homan who, on examining the walls, declared that those which had earlier been covered with ivy were in better condition than those which had not because of the protection it afforded.[13] However, the rector won, despite fierce attacks. Philip Webb, co-founder with William Morris of the Society for the Protection of Ancient Buildings, was a particularly severe critic. An attempt was made to enlist Ellen Terry's help in preventing the ivy's removal[14] but she, sturdily independent as always, wrote giving Mr. Patch her full support.[15]

The restoration of the tomb of Gervase Alard in the north aisle caused even greater upset. This work was made necessary by the earlier extensive application of whitewash and a major structural fault. Philip Webb sent his friends to keep an eye on what was happening. One of them, Sidney Cockerell, wrote:

> 'We walked over to Winchelsea and saw those glorious tombs being shamefully scraped; too late now to smash the head of either parson or architect against an angle of them. There is a race of hereditary parsons called Patch who will not be satisfied while there is any interesting thing remaining in that old fragment of a church.'[16]

This quite ignores the fact that constant application of whitewash had almost obliterated part of the carving.

The structural fault involved the instability of the tomb's heavy canopy which could only be corrected by its removal and re-setting:

> 'During the work the effigy was removed and the grave below it opened. The coffin was apparently composed of stone slabs, the sides being two feet high, and was covered by a stone arch. The floor of the coffin was about 4' 6" below the present floor level…

and the body was enclosed in a roughly cylindrical leaden shell about one eighth of an inch thick. This lead casing got broken during the work. The total length measures about 6' 7" so whoever the person is who is buried there, he must have been a man of unusual size.'[17]

Mr. Homan consistently challenged in his writing the normal attribution of this tomb as that of Gervase Alard, admiral of the fleet under King Edward I and a member of Winchelsea's leading family of the time, but this remains the generally held belief.

The breaking of the casing caused considerable morbid interest. The rector's sister recalled:

'Before [the reconstruction] could be started the workmen had to open the tomb and in due course came on the admiral's skeleton wrapped in lead. News of this find soon got around and sightseers began to arrive. My brother was obliged to tell the workmen, who were probably making a profit out of their find, that the exhibition must stop, and the tomb was then surrounded by some sort of hoarding. The last visitor was Lady Maude Warrender. She tried to persuade my brother to let her see the remains, but he succeeded in showing her that it was quite illegal to permit the general public to view bodies buried in consecrated ground, even though they had been buried for many years.'[18]

The tomb restorations were carried out at the expense of Frederic Inderwick in memory of his late son, Godfrey. Sadly Mr. Inderwick senior did not himself live to see the work completed.

(50) Work in progress on the restoration of the Alard tombs.

However rigorous the repair work done, it could not remove unsightly graffiti, largely initials, carved there by members of the public to the great annoyance of the church authorities. Since 1902 a large poster had been displayed in the south aisle: [19]

ST. THOMAS'S CHURCH, WINCHELSEA
CAUTION – INJURY TO TOMBS

By Statute entitled Malicious Damage to Property Act, 1861, it is provided that any person who shall destroy or damage any statue, monument, or other memorial of the dead, painted glass or ornament, or work of art in any Church, Chapel or other place of Divine Service, shall be liable to imprisonment for not exceeding six months with or without hard labour and if a male under 16 with or without whipping, and will be liable, in addition to the above punishment, to pay for the injury done.

Any person found damaging the tombs or monuments in this Church (either by cutting names or initials or otherwise) will be prosecuted according to law and will be held liable to pay for the damage caused thereby.

The public are requested to assist the undersigned in carrying out the law in order to protect the Ancient and Valuable Monuments of this Medieval Church.

F. A. Inderwick, Mayor
J. D. H. Patch, Rector
Herbert J. Elliott } Church
Walter Fuller   } Wardens

In the early 1920s further major work was carried out, this time under the direction of H.P. Burke Downing F.R.I.B.A. He particularly recommended repairs to the external roof where several areas of tiles were liable to slip because they had been fixed with iron nails which had since rusted, and on the external stonework, including that of the transepts which he thought would collapse if not given urgent attention. The most important internal work involved the removal of the kingposts (similar to those supporting the Court Hall roof) in the sanctuary. These had been added long after the original construction and Burke Downing reported that they had diverted the original roof stresses and load-bearing structure in a dangerous way. They were removed, and the roof restored to its present, much more satisfactory, appearance.[20]

For the survival of these details, and many more about the life of the church, we are indebted to the records kept by Arthur Vernon Owen (1899 - 1982) who was churchwarden from 1926 - 1934. A.V. Owen was made a freeman of Winchelsea on 16 April 1928. His election to the mayoralty in 1932 was hailed by the *Sussex County Magazine* as 'a striking example of what youth can achieve'.[21] At the time he was a solicitor with the firm of Langham and Douglas in Hastings, and was deeply involved in all aspects of life in Winchelsea where he lived at 2, Keith Row (now St. Anthony's) and later at Nesbit in the High Street. He left the town in 1934 to join Currey and Co. in London where he became a partner and spent the rest of his working life. Despite his absence from the town Mr. Owen continued to be an actively interested member of Winchelsea Corporation until his death, at which time he had been a freeman for more than fifty-three years, a record only beaten in modern times by Freeman A.H. Thomas (see p.142).

A box of Mr. Owen's papers was handed by his son to the then town clerk, Charles Croggon. When later sorted and listed these were discovered also to include many documents dealt with by his predecessor as churchwarden, Charles Walter Campion (1839 - 1926).[22] Campion, the younger brother of William Henry Campion of Danny, Hurstpierpoint, lived at Mariteau House and was also a freeman who had served as mayor in 1909. His career lay in parliamentary administration. Called to the bar of Lincoln's Inn in 1866, he became secretary to the Speaker of the House of Commons and later served as Examiner of Standing Orders. The papers which these gentlemen preserved provide not only an account of the church restorations but also reveal much information about the major gifts of Lord Blanesburgh which were dedicated at three important services between 1929 and 1933, services which brought St. Thomas's to national attention in a way which had not happened since medieval times.

In those times the windows of St. Thomas's had been filled with glorious stained glass, providing a colour and warmth of light much in contrast with the stark uniformity of the modern clear glass. Just one example of the fifteenth-century glass remains to be seen today, in the north window of the sanctuary where four surviving medallions were re-set in the early twentieth century. It was Lord Blanesburgh's burning ambition completely to return the church to the splendour of its earlier days by providing the stained glass which he felt would achieve this.

Rt. Hon. Robert Younger P.C., G.B.E., Baron Blanesburgh of Alloa, County Clackmannan (1861 - 1945), a life baron, was the fourth son of James Younger of the well-known brewing family of Alloa. A barrister, he became a judge and eventually a Lord of Appeal, on which appointment he took his title. For many years a Winchelsea resident, he bought Greyfriars after the death of G.M. Freeman having, like his predecessor, formerly lived at Cleveland House. A bachelor with wealth which he used to such beneficial effect, he had many local as well as national interests. Locally he was president and later life vice-president of the Hastings Music Festival.[23] Nationally he was involved in setting up the League of Nations after the First World War and retained an intense interest in its work and aims about which he would hold discussion groups at the home of Miss Maud Beddington. Len Polhill was one of those who attended. He remembers Lord Blanesburgh with the deepest respect and retains a pang of regret that his lordship should have lived to see the collapse of the organisation to which he devoted so much time and effort.

Lord Blanesburgh's grand design for St. Thomas's began after a tragedy of national impact had taken place within three miles of Winchelsea and within the former liberty on 15 November 1928. On this fateful night the Rye Harbour lifeboat was called to the aid of the Latvian steamer the *Alice of Riga* which was reported drifting and taking in water off Dungeness. On the firing of the maroon, launchers and crew rushed to their duty with all the speed and urgency expected of those dedicated to the saving of life whatever the conditions and danger involved. At the third attempt the *Mary Stanford* was launched into the teeth of the storm. Five minutes later a message came from the coastguard that the crew of the *Alice* had been taken aboard another vessel and help was no longer needed. Desperate efforts to recall the lifeboat by signal and loud hailer were defeated by the tumultuous gale. Three and a half hours later, attempting to return into the mouth of the River Rother, the *Mary Stanford* was overturned by a gigantic wave and all seventeen members of the crew were lost. 'The close-knit community of Rye Harbour that day lost an entire generation; eleven children were left fatherless and nearly every family in the village was touched by the tragedy.'[24]

The needs of the people of the village required that inquest, inquiry and a national appeal should be followed by memorial. In Rye Harbour church, a tablet of Manx stone; in the churchyard a magnificent statue of a lifeboatman heading the grave, unveiled by Lord Blanesburgh in 1931, and

(51) The churchyard with grazing sheep – late nineteenth century.

at St. Thomas's, Winchelsea a beautifully designed and inscribed stained glass window, met the need to keep the memory of these brave men alive. Thus began his lordship's plan. The man chosen to carry it out was Douglas Strachan Ll.D., H.R.S.A., an artist already famous for his stained glass work in the War Memorial at Edinburgh Castle and the St. Dunstan's window in St. Paul's Cathedral. His first window at Winchelsea depicts the lifeboat forging its way through the angry sea while figures on the shore anxiously watch its progress. At the foot are the names of those who died and an inscription by Sir Henry Newbolt which includes the words: 'In the darkness of their supreme hour they stayed not to weigh doubt or danger but freely offering their portion in this life for the ransom of men they had never known, they went boldly into the last of all their storms.'

This moving tribute was unveiled at a service held on Saturday 6 July 1929 in the presence of a large congregation including the mayors and corporations of Winchelsea and Rye, led by Anthony Freeman serving his first term. Among those also present were many relatives of those who died, other residents of Rye Harbour and, of course, the donor, Lord Blanesburgh who was accompanied by the Attorney General. The service was conducted by Bishop R.S. Fyffe, Vicar of Westfield and formerly Bishop of Rangoon, assisted by the rector, Rev. C. Carey Taylor. In pointing out the relevance of having such a memorial in Winchelsea, the bishop recalled the neighbourliness which existed between the two communities arising from centuries of maritime association.[25]

That maritime association is further reinforced by an obelisk standing near the south-west corner of St. Thomas's churchyard commemorating another disaster which stunned the nation and involved far greater loss of life. The inscription reads:

'In the memory of Henry Coventry aged 18 years [here there are two other illegible names] and of the 287 passengers and crew of the Northfleet who were drowned off Dungeness on the night of January 22nd 1873'

(52) St. Thomas's Church – featuring the great chestnut which fell in 1987.

The *Northfleet,* a sailing-ship bound for Hobart in Tasmania with more than three hundred emigrants, anchored for the night about two miles off Dungeness after encountering very bad weather in the channel. As the passengers slept the crew on watch suddenly observed a steamer bearing down on them at full speed. No amount of frantic shouting could divert her. She smashed into their vessel cleaving her massive timbers below the waterline and sailed off into the night without making any attempt to stop to help the victims of her negligence.[26] The horror of the ensuing scenes can hardly be imagined. The names recorded on the St. Thomas's obelisk are those of bodies washed ashore on the coastline of the parish. It was eight months before, after world-wide inquiries, the culprit, the *Murillo,* was arrested off Dover. This was the incident which provoked legislation requiring all vessels to carry their name clearly displayed on both sides of the bow and on the stern.[27]

The congregation attending the lifeboat memorial window service would have noticed work in progress on the windows beside it and those at the eastern end of the church. These were eventually dedicated on Saturday 9 May 1931 in memory of members of Lord Blanesburgh's family. On the same day and with the same dedication there came into use a new organ built by J.W. Walker and Sons 'whose ancestors have been building organs since the time of Milton'. This service was conducted by His Grace the Archbishop of Canterbury, the Most Reverend Cosmo Gordon Lang D.D. Of the many people attending who feature elsewhere in this story, Douglas Turner carried the cross at the head of the Bishop of Chichester's procession, and his brother Ron, with Dick Wood, carried the Archbishop's train.

An evocative account by Maud Stepney Rawson records:

'[The day] dawned slowly. Not even a western breeze could dispel the high canopy of grey cloud enveloping town and church, wooded hills and marshland. A curious hush prevailed throughout the place. Owing to tireless organisation and forethought the final preparations were carried out in complete tranquillity. The mowers gave the last touches to the already trimmed turf of the churchyard, loving hands laid fresh, bright flowers on many a grave, a group of parishioners was busy arranging vases of white lilies and cherry blossom on both altars... Just after noon the grey pall dispersed, the sun rode out and turned the fabric of the church, with its bosses of wild yellow wall-flower, into a cloak of grey splendour, studded with gold. The sea became a sheet of pale lapis lazuli; the footpaths, roads and valley streams silver ribbons in the green countryside.'[28]

The occasion more than matched the setting. Hundreds of Lord Blanesburgh's guests arrived by special train from London and by car from all over the country, and the choir of the Temple Church, with their choirmaster George Thalben Ball, sang magnificently and for the first time outside London, an honour greatly appreciated by Winchelsea. In concluding his sermon the archbishop addressed himself directly to the people of the town:

'When you behold the beautiful proportions of your church, and your eyes rest upon the radiant colours of these windows, when your ears listen to the tone of the organ, you will indeed be holding communion with God. Then lift up your hearts to Him in thankful worship. Thus we enter into the true meaning of the dedication of these noble gifts to the glory of God, for through them we laud and magnify His holy name.'[29]

The completion of Lord Blanesburgh's grand design for St. Thomas's came on Saturday 21 October 1933 when the final three windows, those in the north aisle, were dedicated. Again there was a nationally significant gathering of guests, this time including the Lord Mayor of London; again the Archbishop of Canterbury officiated; again the choir of the Temple Church sang, but on this occasion an additional feature was that the service was broadcast on the National Programme by the B.B.C. These three windows are a memorial to the men of the Cinque Ports and the Ancient Towns of Rye and Winchelsea who gave their lives in the great war of 1914-1918, and together with the windows were dedicated a memorial plaque naming those of Winchelsea who died, and an altar designed by Mr. H.S. Goodhart Rendel. The window designs represent the elements of water, earth and air in commemoration of the service in that conflict of the navy, the army and the Royal Flying Corps. They were unveiled during the proceedings by Admiral of the Fleet Sir Charles Madden, Field Marshal Lord Milne and Air Marshal Lord Trenchard respectively.

The archbishop's address movingly recorded:

'We meet today to make our reverent remembrance of those men who, on land or sea or in the air served their town and their country. They were for the most part just plain men of Kent and Sussex passing quietly through this transitory life. Then, suddenly, inexplicably they were drawn into the maelstrom of war... their bodies lie in the town which girds their homes or in foreign graves but their names, and more than their names, their spirit, liveth for evermore.'[30]

And so the transformation of St. Thomas's during almost five years' work came to fruition. Not all critical assessments of the effect have been complimentary. Certainly the result does not imitate the medieval windows which were much milder in tone but the overall effect is stunning. Of his specialist medium Douglas Strachan wrote:

'The fact about stained glass is that it is simply light itself, and the artist in glass is one who modulates its tones with the light it emits; I say "emits" because good stained glass gives the impression of being itself the source of light.'[31]

So it is at St. Thomas's.

Any reader who goes to look or to look again at these windows should not miss their best kept secret. If you stand to one side of the Alard tombs and look behind the apex of their canopies you will see the most exquisite rendering in stained glass of the seal of Winchelsea.

Within seven years of their completion the windows came under threat of enemy action as the country was again plunged into war. Understandably this caused Lord Blanesburgh, who had invested so much so selflessly in the enterprise, great anguish. He felt that the windows were 'recognised far and wide to be quite irreplaceable' and thought they had 'earned for the church in many quarters the title of "the twentieth century Chartres"'. The mayor and corporation were enlisted to support the removal to safety of the windows, or as many of them as possible. Unfortunately the rector objected. One of the few letters on this subject which have survived, from the mayor, Anthony Freeman, to the Archdeacon of Hastings, begins: 'You will be as annoyed as I was to hear that the cat is fairly among the pigeons – our turbulent priest has entered a legal objection to your faculty.' The letter goes on to commend the bishop's active support in trying to persuade the only possible contractors to undertake a job towards which they were showing some resistance.[32] However, all this happened in 1944, presumably provoked by the threat of the V1 and V2 'flying bombs' and either the rector won or the legal proceedings took so long that the war ended with the outcome unknown and the church undamaged. Thus these magnificent windows remain an inspiration for us and future generations. They are a fitting memorial, not only to those to whom they are dedicated, but also to their donor and their artist.

The post-war years have witnessed the distinguished incumbencies of Rev. R.M. Ware and Rev. C.G. Scott. On Rex Ware's induction in 1959 the patron was still Rev. J.H. Patch. The *Sussex Express* reported: 'An unusual feature of the service was the scarlet robed mayor [Captain Herbert Lovegrove] reading the Deed of Presentation on behalf of the patron who was unable to travel from Devon for the service'.[33] The advowson has since passed into the hands of the Guild of All Souls. It is worth noting that Geoffrey Scott, at the time of writing recently retired, during his incumbency became the first rector since Drake Hollingberry also to be Vicar of Icklesham. Geoffrey Scott's successor, Rev. Keith Wood, was inducted and installed on 25 June 1996 and the story of St. Thomas's thus continues under a new incumbent.

25. THE SECOND WORLD WAR

Of the impact of war on ordinary citizens such as that described by Archbishop Lang in his 1933 sermon, we have an excellent example in the experience of Gwyneth Wise. She was not a Winchelsea resident but during most of the 1930s had, as a record agent, carried out research on behalf of William Maclean Homan who was at the time so busily steeping himself in Winchelsea's history. Miss Wise was paid three shillings and sixpence an hour and was often apologetic in accepting payment for work she so much enjoyed. Letters passed frequently between them for he was a demanding correspondent; on one occasion she said that he must have imagined her buried under the volume of his letters. She visited the Homans at Winchelsea, met Mr. Homan at the British Museum for discussions and generally enjoyed his confidence not only as a professional researcher but also as a critic of his work. The lively exchanges between them end on 6 January 1940 with a letter headed '881487 Sergeant Wise, c/o Officer i/c W.A.A.F. Personnel, A. & A.E.E., R.A.F. Station, Boscombe Down, Amesbury, Wiltshire.' It reads:

'My dear Mr. Homan,

Your registered letter made me feel most horribly guilty! I had received both your previous letters although I didn't get the first until just before Christmas as the Post Office for some reason hadn't posted it on and it had been lying in my flat. I had meant to write to you ever since but I am so frightfully busy now that it has always been put off hoping things will be slacker later.

I have been down here since the end of October, having been working at the Air Ministry previous to that. I am Senior N.C.O. here with about 40 W.A.A.Fs under me. We are terribly short of administrative staff and I work about 14 hours a day. Still the work is very interesting and I am very happy here. We are supposed to be getting another sergeant soon which will let me have some time to myself and make things a bit easier. At the moment I am distinctly weary!

It is frightfully difficult to realise there is a war on. Things like food rationing and the blackout don't worry us and I find myself so wrapped up in the petty happenings of our own little world that I barely have time to do more than glance at the headlines of the papers.

I am returning you St. Giles' deed. I feel very contrite that I have not been able to do anything about it. That is the reason why I haven't written before as I always hoped to be able to get down to it. I took a look at it just now and could get even less from it than I did in the summer. The part of my brain which tackled such problems seems to have packed up altogether. Everything previous to last September is as remote now as if I was in a different lifetime!…

All good wishes for 1940.
Yours very sincerely,
Gwyneth Wise[1]

Miss Wise's feeling that she was living in a different world must have been shared by Winchelsea's citizens. Uppermost in their minds during the summer of 1940 was the invasion threat, fiercely and frighteningly renewed for the first time since Napoleon's plans foundered as impractical. Hitler's Operation Sealion allowed for landings to be concentrated on the coast between Rye and New Romney with the shores of Rye Bay as the main beachhead.[2] Winchelsea would have been in the forefront of the battle. This threat provoked diverse reactions. The families which had been sent from the expected bombing of London were whisked away to safer areas. Thousands of sheep on Romney Marsh were evacuated by train before any plans were made for local people; the 'sheep train specials' carried 85,000 of them away as far as Yorkshire and in the long run this had a profound effect on the economy of the marsh, not least that much of the vast area ploughed for food production has remained in that use.[3] Romney Marsh had been the scene of defensive work since as early as 1938. Douglas Turner was one of those involved:

> 'They sent all the blokes on the dole out there, we didn't have any work at the time. We had to dig holes and put poles up to stop aircraft landing – thousands of poles. You got eighteen pence for digging the hole and a shilling for filling it in. The poles were mostly saplings cut down from the woods out Beckley way.'[4]

Ted Streeton, who worked on the same job, remembers the pay as being rather more generous but you had to earn it – the foreman came round with a dipstick to make sure the depth was right.

The sea was allowed to flood large areas of Pett Level with astonishing results in encouraging the return of wildlife. The whole of Winchelsea Beach became a prohibited area, part of the Rye Defence Area, with those like Percy Ide needing to enter it for such essential duties as feeding the remaining stock being issued with passes by the officer commanding the garrison.[5] Alex Finch, too, had one of these passes. After quoting his identity card number the document declared that he 'is a genuine postal official and conducts legitimate business at Winchelsea Beach. Stamped by the East Sussex Constabulary and the orderly room of the Royal Irish Fusiliers (Princess Victoria's) it is firmly endorsed 'Must NOT go onto the actual beach and will only visit during hours of daylight.'[6] Some of the residents forced to leave their homes were billeted at Cleveland House and Petronilla Barclay remembers, when home from her school which had moved to Devon, being engaged in filling palliasses with straw for the displaced residents to sleep on.

Instructions and exhortations were heaped upon the population. One pamphlet entitled *Beating the INVADER* recounts how 'Where the enemy lands, or tries to land, there will be most violent fighting. Not only will there be battles when the enemy tries to come ashore, but afterwards there will fall upon his lodgments very heavy British counter-attacks.' Civilians were told that they must leave their homes if ordered but for any left in the immediate neighbourhood of the fighting:

> 'Keep indoors or in your shelter until the battle is over. If you can have a trench ready in your garden or field so much the better. You may want to use it for protection if your house is damaged. But if you are at work or if you have special orders, carry on as long as possible and only take cover when the danger approaches. If you are on your way to work finish your journey if you can. If you see an enemy tank, or a few enemy soldiers, do not assume that the enemy are in control of the area. What you have seen may be a party sent on in advance, or stragglers from the main body who can easily be rounded up.'

'Carry on' and 'Stand Firm' are phrases punctuating the document. Those not too close to the battle must continue life as normal and not attempt to leave their district; those in the area of the fighting must take their orders from A.R.P. (Air Raid Precaution) Wardens, the military, the police and the Home Guard in uniform; they must immobilise vehicles, beware of faked orders or those impersonating British officials, take careful note of official bulletins and not attempt to add to any stock of food they might have been able to make.[7]

Of course, all this brought back to Winchelsea the garrison last in occupation a quarter of a century earlier. A number of units were stationed in the town and a surviving plan shows that, of these, D Company of the Durham Light Infantry used The Armoury as their officers' mess, Glebe as sergeants' mess, Yew Tree House as the hospital, Firebrand as company headquarters, the Court Hall and Periteau House as billets and the cricket field as a parade ground.[8] The renewed military use of the Court Hall is illustrated by a inventory of the 'Recreation Room' made when it was taken over by E Company of the 30th Queen's Regiment. The room had already suffered. An account of its condition reads: [9]

> '5 window panes broken
> 12 window panes cracked but serviceable
> Plaster fallen off walls
> Woodwork near window sills damaged and broken
> Stonework near window sills chipped and broken
> Ceiling defaced with numerous holes'

Among the listed contents, in true military style were:

Billiards Table	1	Cloth loose at one end and pockets broken
Chairs wooden	6	1 slightly damaged
Chairs basket	3	groggy
Clocks grandfather	1	u/s
Boards dart	1	
Table ping pong	1	
Boards shove halfpenny	1	
Boxes donation	1	empty

Any amusement we might obtain from such survivals is instantly dispelled on realising the nature of the involvement of the troops using these woefully inadequate facilities. A letter dated 29 August 1942 from the mayor to the Officer Commanding the First Battalion, Royal Regiment of Canada reads:

> 'Dear Sir,
>> As Mayor, I wish, on behalf of The Ancient Town and Corporation of Winchelsea to express thro' you our admiration for the outstanding gallantry displayed by all ranks of the Royal Regiment of Canada on the occasion of the recent attack on Dieppe and to add our deepest sympathy for all those who fell in the Cause of Liberty.
>> Winchelsea cherishes an imperishable memory of the ties of affection and good comradeship born and fostered during the period of The Royal Regiment's sojourn among us.
>> The case containing your Regimental Badges and Crest presented by you to our Ancient Town occupies a place of honour in the Court Hall and will serve as a permanent reminder of our association with you and Glorious Canada.
>>> I remain
>>>> Yours sincerely,
>>>>> Ernest Goldschmidt (Lt. Col.)
>>>>> Mayor'[10]

The display case can still be seen at the Court Hall. Perhaps it should be treated as a memorial to those who died at Dieppe.

(53) Lord Blanesburgh with evacuees at Greyfriars.

The writer of the above letter, Ernest Zven Goldschmidt, was another of Winchelsea's larger-than-life characters. He was the son of Jenny Lind, 'the Swedish nightingale', and resolutely declined at any time to anglicise his name although a number of his correspondents inadvertently did this for him. The colonel was a fierce patriot who could be seen at the beginning of the war stumping round the town asking all the young men such as the present Lord Ritchie of Dundee whether they were going to join up and go to 'fight the Bosch'. Col. Goldschmidt and his wife lived at The Mount and the view taken of him as something of a caricature of a typical military gentleman was reflected in the young people dubbing him 'Colonel Damnit'. He was already in his seventies which perhaps accounts for his not being involved with the local Home Guard, a duty undertaken by his predecessor as mayor, Colonel Wildeblood, who recruited Malcolm Ritchie and set him to moving sandbags. The colonel, among other lectures, instructed his men in how to make Molotov cocktails but when he tried one out in a demonstration it singularly failed.

This lack of proficiency may have been at least partly responsible for additional training when an army unit joined the Winchelsea home guard for a combined exercise sometime in 1941, an event which had an extraordinary sequel during the widening and re-aligning of the junction between Rectory Lane and Sandrock Hill more than thirty years later. A mechanical digger working on the scheme suddenly exposed 36 of these devices one of which broke, releasing considerable quantities of smoke as phosphorous came into contact with the air. The police, the fire brigade and a bomb disposal unit were called, the Molotov cocktails being eventually carefully removed to a field in Pett where they were blown up. Understandably the incident provoked speculation, the local press report concluding, 'There were several army and civil defence units in the area around Winchelsea during the war and Rye Police think that the bottles were probably buried as rubbish by one of the units.'[11]

Percy Ide, however, was able to be much more specific. He had buried them! Ide, landlord of the Bridge Inn during the war, on seeing the report contacted the paper and 'owned up'. It was as a member of the Auxiliary Fire Service that he had attended the exercise:

> 'About 300 Molotov cocktails were made out of old beer or milk bottles filled with petrol and phosphorous. An old car was left across the road at Sandrock Hill and we all stood at the top of the Rectory Lane bank and chucked these fire bombs at it. The idea was that it would be good practice at stopping a tank or some other German vehicle. The car, the roadway and the hedges were soon all blazing and we firemen had to go and put it out. At the end of the exercise there were still about three dozen bottles left over and I asked my chief officer what to do with them. He told me to bury them where we were, on the bank at Rectory Lane, and if the Germans did invade we could dig them up and throw them at them.'[12]

Winchelsea Home Guard's meetings were held at the Old Workhouse (now Strand House) and Lord Ritchie remembers, at the height of the invasion scare, having to go down Pannel Lane and take up a position in a field one lonely, moonlit night. At that time the availability of weapons was very limited. The most startling example of their later presence in the town was when Alec Brakefield accidentally almost shot his friend and brother-in-law Alex Finch through the wall of their adjoining homes when his rifle went off while being cleaned.

Lord Ritchie describes Ernest Goldschmidt as:

> 'Very fire-eating, and his wife was a gentle soul and was always trying to pour oil on troubled waters. They used to come and play bridge and he got into rages when he made a hash of his hand. She would say, "Ernest, calm down, don't worry, you're doing all right, Ernest"'.[13]

Regardless of such shortcomings causing some amusement, the colonel's commitment to Winchelsea and all aspects of its life was absolute. He sat on numerous committees, taking particular interest in the New Hall, its construction and maintenance and was always willing to offer his services and help. While it is sad to report, it was quite in character that his forthright, inflexible, brusque manner partly caused the rift with Alex Finch, town chamberlain which has already been described.

These characteristics are further illustrated by the colonel's attitude to flag days held in Winchelsea. In 1942 he received a request to permit a house-to-house collection in aid of the Soldiers', Sailors' and Airmen's Families Association. Winchelsea had a tradition in such matters; there were three annual flag days, Alexandra Rose Day, Poppy Day, and Red Cross Day. Such traditions he would not abandon. Nevertheless the special circumstances of the war led him to consult the Chief Constable and the Clerk of Battle Rural District Council, both of whom provided what he felt to be vague and unsatisfactory replies. In the margin of the District Council's response he wrote:

> 'As I have had no support from the Chief Constable or Battle I propose to ignore them and continue with only our three recognised days – I have forbidden all other house to house collections and resent outside interference. E. G.'[14]

Perceptive readers will have noted that the colonel and his correspondents were presuming a jurisdiction for the mayor to which in fact he had no right. Nevertheless such presumptions greatly increased the colour and interest of Winchelsea's civic involvement with the war effort and appear to have had general support from the residents of the time. With the parish council's records lost it is difficult to assess its members' activities or feelings on the matter.

The colonel was fond of annotating documents such as the above letters which came into his possession. Another would have made him and the vast majority of his fellow citizens apoplectic; a pamphlet entitled *Stop Bombing Civilians* issued by a body calling itself the Bombing Restriction Committee deplored in some detail the bombing of civilian targets by the allies. True to form and understandably he scrawled on the front 'No mention is made of London, Coventry and many other of *our* cities' and at the end, 'Only just retribution and well deserved'.[15]

Two months before his letter about the Dieppe raid Col. Goldschmidt, as mayor, had taken the salute at a church parade on United Nations Day, 14 June 1942, an occasion inspired by the prime minister's wish to honour our allies, particularly those who were not part of the Commonwealth. The event was hurriedly arranged, heralded by two letters from the Ministry of Information sent only six days in advance. One announced:

> 'The government has decreed that Sunday 14 June shall be observed as a day of Salutation to the Allied Nations by the British Commonwealth of Nations… It is proposed that the general theme of the day shall support a royal or government message which will be publicly proclaimed by the mayor or chairman of the council in every locality throughout the country. It is hoped that local authorities will be able to arrange a church or other parade representative of the Services, Civil Defence units, workers and all branches of the community… the parade should culminate in a salute to the Allied Flags.'

The list of flags to be saluted commenced, of course, with the United States of America and the Union of Soviet Socialist Republics, followed by the names of twenty other nations. Conscious of the problems, and desperately seeking to clarify them in advance, the ministry sent a follow up the same day:

> 'If a strictly official salute were being organised, only the flags of the Nations on this list would be saluted. Lack of flags etc. will in almost all cases make this impossible and it has been agreed as a compromise that where the flags are unobtainable the saluting base may be dressed with the Union Jack, bunting, and as representative a selection of the allied flags as is available. In this case the National intention to honour all the allies should be very fully publicised to avoid any possibility of misinterpretation. Should any query be raised, it can be explained that the omission of any of the allied flags is due not to ignorance or oversight, but to lack of material.'

It is not difficult to imagine Col. Goldschmidt, resplendent in his mayoral robes, standing stiffly to attention on the saluting base beside however many flags could be found and later thundering out Mr. Winston Churchill's message (marked 'SECRET – not to be divulged in advance) part of which read:

> 'Let us pay this tribute to the valour and sacrifice of those who have fallen and the endurance of those who fight today. Let us remember everyone, man, woman and child, who in the oppressed and tortured countries works for the day of liberation that is coming. In this ceremony we pledge to each other not merely support and

succour till victory comes but that wider understanding, that quickened sense of human sympathy, that recognition of the common purpose of humanity without which the suffering and striving of the United Nations would not achieve its full reward.'[16]

All must have met the colonel's demandingly high standards. Lt. Col. R.F. Ware M.C., commanding 16th Battalion, Durham Light Infantry included the following message in his Part One Orders on 17 June:

'The Mayor and Corporation of the ancient town of Winchelsea desire to thank the commanding officer for his co-operation on United Nations Day and to congratulate the Guard of Honour on their fine and soldierly appearance on that occasion.'

Unfortunately the appearance of the men of the garrison was not always 'fine and soldierly'. The same orders contain the following stricture:

'Cases are still being reported of Motor Transport drivers being seen with their caps off, [battledress] unbuttoned, or smoking, and of passengers sitting on or leaning over the tailboard. Such practices will cease.'[17]

Throughout the earlier part of the war the already mentioned threat of invasion and also that of air raids, were very real. In July 1941, Lt. Col. Hedley Basher, commanding officer of the 1st Royal Regiment of Canada, later to serve at Dieppe, outlined the arrangements made for the allocation of the residents to public shelter accommodation which had been provided. The church bell had been chosen as the signal for action stations. In the event of the population being confined to shelters for a considerable time one A.R.P. warden and a first aider were allocated to each shelter, stretcher equipment being provided, rescue parties were detailed and the emergency hospital would be fully staffed under the direction of Mrs. Wildeblood and the Duchess of Bedford (then resident at Mill Farm House). Mrs. Burke was to arrange for some at each shelter to be responsible for cooking and looking after the children. A gas decontamination centre was available in the town provided the water supply was functioning. Arrangements were in hand for latrines to be set up and screening to be provided in each shelter, for emergency water tanks, for paraffin stoves and brick ovens, for hurricane lamps and for tarmac floors to replace the existing earth ones. Alex Finch had made arrangements for flour supplies, the baking of bread and for supplies of meat, milk and vegetables sufficient for a ten day period.[18] In fact no such long-term confinement of the citizens took place but there were many air raids and we shall concentrate here on the most serious and dramatic attack on the town which took place on 13 January 1943.

At the time Douglas Turner was serving with the Auxiliary Fire Service whose Winchelsea base was at the garages opposite The Orchards in Mill Road. There were about ten men in the unit including Jim Buttonshaw who was one of the drivers, Percy Ide, Charles Standing, electrician to the unit, Fred Trill, Ernie Trill, Albert Turner, Douglas's cousin, and Percy Carter. They operated throughout the area, covering Icklesham and Rye in emergencies and using an old Chevrolet car which towed their water-pump. Four full-timers manned the station, part-timers being collected from work or other duties when possible. Their most gruesome call-out came after an attack involving two Messerschmitts which approached the town from Winchelsea Beach, straight into the field of vision of a bofors gunner in the emplacement beside Strand Gate. This structure has never been demolished and remains as a reminder of Winchelsea's fortified state during the Second World War. The gunner, with the aircraft full in his sights, let fly. The enemy

(54) Castle Street after the bomb, 1943.

machines took urgent avoiding action, ducking beneath the gun's trajectory and 'scuttling back towards the coast'. One of them went too low and flew into electricity wires along Sea Road. The impact cut off the cockpit canopy and the pilot's head. The aircraft crashed at Castle Farm. Douglas and his A.F.S. colleagues, responding to the resulting call-out, found the head in a nearby field. The national news that day announced the shooting down of an enemy fighter at Winchelsea and the local press claimed that the aircraft had earlier machine-gunned a group of Land Army girls, two of whom were injured.[19]

The next day the raids resumed. Two bombers, coming in along the line of the River Rother towards Rye, veered off across the marsh towards Winchelsea. They dropped a string of one thousand pound bombs, one scoring a direct hit on a house in Tanyard Lane, another landing on its side in the allotment gardens where the Spring Steps houses now stand and ricochetting into Castle Street where it exploded in the middle of the road between Salutation Cottages and Five Chimneys. Other bombs dropped at Winchelsea Beach.

A casualty list compiled on the day by R.A. Lusty, Officer in Charge of the Rural District Casualty Information Office, shows that Mrs. Violet Morris, aged 37 of 2, Salutation Cottages was killed, and her husband William seriously injured, as were their neighbours Frederick Barden aged 83 and his daughter Emily of 3, Salutation Cottages and Marion Humphrey aged 54 of Five Chimneys. A further thirty-six residents were treated at Rye Memorial Hospital, the Royal Sussex Hospital, Hastings, or at Winchelsea's own first aid post, situated at Moneysellers in North Street where Mr. Walter Alford was air raid warden and Mrs. Finch-White was in charge of 'cooking and first aid'.[20]

Much property was devastated. Two cottages where the butcher's shop now stands were totally destroyed, Salutation Cottages, The Old Post Office, Five Chimneys and Castle Cottage were severely damaged, with the roofs of many other Castle Street and Mill Road properties affected. The Turner family at Castle Cottage had a lucky escape. Douglas was just about to go back on duty when the siren went and he heard cannon fire. Already wearing his heavy fire service jacket, he hurried upstairs to fetch Peter who had been left in his cot as he was recovering from pneumonia. At the moment the bomb exploded Douglas was leaning over the cot. Splinters of glass from the windows became embedded in his jacket but did not penetrate it. The register plate of the fireplace downstairs, along with large quantities of soot, fell into the pram where Peter would have been but for his illness. Douglas, carrying Peter, led Elsie, John, and Jane to his mother's in Mill Road before returning to duty. The severe damage to their home included the complete collapse of all the ceilings in the newer part of the house at the back but the much older ceilings of the front rooms were not affected. The family had to live elsewhere for nine months.

On that morning Lilah Smith, amid the ensuing chaos, calmly recorded in the school log book:

'Attendance this morning was only 27 out of 52 and this afternoon 25. Bombs were dropped before morning school, wrecked several houses and caused some casualties. The school building received some damage – broken windows, a lampshade and ceilings and one door fastening and cupboard were broken. The Director of Education recommended that school should be kept open despite the low attendance.'[21]

William Maclean Homan, whose experience as a civil engineer kept him much in the forefront as an adviser during the war, was soon on the scene of the incident compiling reports and plans. Five Chimneys he reported to be 'damaged but repairable'; Salutation Cottages 'could be repaired as soon as possible'; The Old Post Office 'pulled down as unsafe. Medieval timbered house – should be rebuilt'; Castle Cottage 'ancient timbered house – should be repaired'. However, things were to get much worse before they improved. Inexplicably, within ten days of the incident, supposedly under orders from the Works Engineer of Battle Rural District Council workmen arrived:

'To strip tiles and in some places tile battens from several hundred yards of completely undamaged and mostly new roofs, as well as from the walls of several slightly or partially damaged houses in Castle Street... The foolish act of stripping these perfectly sound roofs, substantially constructed, has naturally not only caused very extensive damage to the houses by exposing them for three and a half months to the weather but has made the houses appear much more derelict and has been liable to prejudice Ministry officials and others, thus unjustly causing the condemning of houses to demolition.'[22]

Winchelsea was outraged. We must presume that the only possible excuse for such an act could have been that the properties were empty and the building materials needed elsewhere. Unfortunately the surviving records known to me do not show which houses these were or which were eventually repaired or demolished.

Several families like the Turners were left homeless by the bombing, and a lack of alternative accommodation within the town led Col. Goldschmidt to join Mr. Homan's protests but particularly on the subject of property requisitioned by the military. A month after the raid he wrote to the Billeting Officer of the district council:

'Dear Sir,

Since the recent severe air raid on Winchelsea many of our townspeople are still homeless and have had to depend on others for hospitality and shelter. I am informed by the Police that "Moneysellers" – a house near the Landgate is empty and suitable for the accommodation of say 8 – 12 persons. Though commandeered by the military it has been vacant for the last year – surely this appears to constitute a quite unnecessary hardship for the victims of German Brutality.

As Mayor I request that you will be good enough to take *immediate* action to ensure the occupation of "Moneysellers" [by] the unfortunate people who have been made homeless. The officer commanding troops here has promised to assist in every way.

I remain, Sir, Yours truly,
E. Goldschmidt
Mayor[23]

And so the war proceeded as, for the ordinary residents, a strange mixture of patriotic fervour and despair that the end seemed far away. Ernest Goldschmidt did his best to fan the patriotic fervour by drawing the attention of the 1942 mayoring ceremony to a message received from *H.M.S. Winchelsea*. She was a destroyer of 1,120 tons, launched in 1917 and eventually scrapped in 1960. The first to bear her name since 1794 she won battle honours in the Atlantic, at Dunkirk and in the North Sea. The colonel also, characteristically, issued a stern warning against complacency, advised his hearers to stand on the tips of their toes and be ready for whatever the year might bring, expressing the firm opinion that 'the tide is beginning to flow our way'. Spoken six months before the victory at El Alamein, those words were both optimistic and prophetic.[24]

The area was vastly active. The village of Camber, like Winchelsea Beach, had been closed to the public, the Rye and Camber Tramway and the Romney Hythe and Dymchurch Railway were in constant military use, the Pipe Line Under The Ocean terminal was being constructed under the greatest and most successful secrecy at Dungeness, and the loss of fishing boats and their crews in Rye Bay brought further tragedy to local families. The approach to D-Day produced even greater action, the Rye harbourmaster on one occasion recording the departure of no fewer than 86 landing craft in 35 minutes. For the presence of these craft fuel tanks had been built on the nearby golf course, refuelling of them being carried out by a pipeline under the river from the rail terminal at Rye Harbour.[25] Landings from assault craft were practised on Camber Sands while nearby other troops, unaware of why they were there or why confined to their camps so strictly, were under canvas somewhere between Rye and Northiam. One of them was Lt. Col. Henry Dormer, Winchelsea's mayor at the time of writing. Returning as he did to the area many years later, he has not yet been able to identify where he stayed under such secrecy.

A far more immediate impact on the local residents was created by the launching of the V1 and V2 flying bombs. Douglas Turner recalled the first he saw:

'I was on duty in the car park of the Pipemakers in Rye one morning about four o'clock and I saw the first "doodlebug" coming. I couldn't make any sense of it at all. This thing came in with flames spouting from its backside'.[26]

The first line of defence against this terrible new weapon was moved to the coast between Beachy Head and St. Margaret's Bay with 'the largest concentration of artillery in the country, manned by 1300 gunners, between Camber and Rye Harbour village'.[27]

At about the same stage of the war Douglas Turner and his A.F.S. crew had another dramatic call-out, this time to Pett Level where a Flying Fortress had crashed. Early in the war the area had been allowed to become flooded by the sea to make enemy landings more difficult. Unfortunately for the potential rescuers the officer in charge of the area had earlier trodden on a mine and with him went the plans of the Winchelsea Beach and Pett Level minefields. The A.F.S. party from Winchelsea were joined by their chief officer from Battle who commented simply, 'Well, we've got to get out there somehow, haven't we?' and led the way. Douglas and his men followed:

> 'He was one of the sort of blokes that where he'd go, you'd go, a natural leader. We didn't tread on any mines or I wouldn't be telling this story. The crew of the 'plane all survived – they bellylanded. The water wasn't very deep and we brought them all back.'[28]

Between 12 August 1940 and 19 April 1944 there were forty-one raids on the parish of Icklesham (no separate figures for Winchelsea are available). Four residents were killed, Mrs. Morris on 13 January 1943 as we have noted, one during a machine-gun attack the previous month and two when a high explosive bomb fell in October 1942. Ninety-six bombs fell of which twelve failed to explode, as well as hundreds of incendiary bombs. There were eight separate machine gun attacks by planes on the area. Forty three residents were injured, almost all in the January 1943 incident.[29]

As the war drew finally to a close, sites in Winchelsea which had been fortified were returned to normality including a weapons pit in Rectory Lane and the sandbagged emplacement round the Town Well. The strong-point at The Lookout from which the guns had blazed at enemy aircraft in unison with their colleagues the other side of Strand Gate was demolished and the area reinstated at

(55) Victory Parade in the High Street, 1945.

the cost of the Ministry of Defence. The plans, drawn up under the supervision of the Officer Commanding the Royal Engineers, East Sussex, show that the town benefited from not only the reconstruction of the public shelter as it is today but also provision of a new stone wall between The Lookout and the Strand Gate with full repairs and reinstatement of the wall in front of the shelter, the steps and the handrail on the raised path.[30] The seat provided at that time (1946), looking down Strand Hill through the gate, has only recently had to be replaced. The new one was provided in memory of Mrs. Doris May Avery, a former resident of nearby Tower Cottage.

As a final act of remembrance the names of Donald Alford, George Cook, Robert Jenkins, Anthony Stuart and Harry Willeard were added to the war memorial cross in St. Thomas's churchyard.

Donald Alford was one of Walter's sons. George Cook lived at Rookery Cottages, worked on the Wickham Estate and made a table still in use at the Court Hall. He is pictured with the crashed aircraft (p.141) and it was his daughter who was sponsored by Winchelsea, Victoria after his death. Of these five I have so far learned most about Harry Willeard, the son of Tom Willeard, the local postman, and a friend of Ron Turner's. Harry was a private in the Queen's Royal Regiment and was badly burned at Tobruk. On 22 May 1943 he wrote to his half brother, Robert Collins, from 'India Command'. He had heard about Winchelsea's worst bombing the previous January, thought the town must be looking pretty dilapidated, and expressed great relief that The Castle was still there. The letter described his living conditions and the intense heat, adding fervent hopes that the war would soon be over so that he could see again the family he so missed and rejoin 'the crowd at The Castle'. A few days after writing the letter he was sent on a mission into the jungle with two native scouts and never seen again.[31]

26. ARCHIVES AND REGALIA

As we pass from the ending of the Second World War into the second half of the twentieth century it becomes opportune to consider the remarkable story of the recovery of Winchelsea's archives which happened in the early 1950s. No historian of Winchelsea had had the opportunity to base his work on these exceptionally valuable documents. Cooper used the records of the Sussex Archaeological Society, Inderwick and Homan used Cooper and their own research. It may well be that Homan was shown the court books in the later years of his life but his *History of Winchelsea 1292-1800* had been completed in 1942. Winchelsea's records were then lost and had been for two centuries.

The most likely reason is that they were taken to London in the mid-eighteenth century to be used in evidence in connection with a massively complex legal dispute known as the Winchelsea Causes involving the control of Winchelsea's parliamentary seats. After this use they were probably set aside at a solicitor's office and forgotten. The absence of these books and the vacuum thus created in the recorded knowledge of the town was a considerable irritation to Anthony Freeman who felt strongly that Winchelsea was belittled by being unable to match her fellow ports in the confidence of certainty about events of the past. In 1946 he first began making inquiries of archaeologists and historians who might be able to help in solving the mystery. He made no progress until seven years later when, at the suggestion of a friend, he visited a firm of solicitors in Lincoln's Inn. The *Sussex Daily News* in its account of the 1954 mayoring ceremony reports:

> 'Mr. Freeman said he went to the office expecting to find a few papers. Instead he found a priceless collection of documents including a number of large minute books of the courts of the "Hundred" and other courts covering the period 1527-1721. There were also a quantity of large manuscripts written in medieval French and Latin and books of extracts. Almost every page was decipherable. Mr. Freeman added that a great deal of research was necessary but it was hoped shortly to have a number of the documents on view. One result of the research [undertaken already] was that they [would be] able to add the names of 260 mayors to the panels in the Court Hall.'[1]

On 27 August 1953 Mr. Freeman signed, as mayor, for Messrs. Trower, Still and Keeling of 5, New Square, Lincoln's Inn, London, a receipt for the books.[2] This discovery drew, within a few days, delighted congratulations from Major Max Teichmann-Derville of New Romney, a distinguished antiquarian and Freeman's close friend, who offered advice and strongly recommended that these records should be 'transferred to proper muniment rooms in the care of qualified archivists.' He added, 'I see from *The Times* that Sussex County Council (sic) are now advertising for a County Archivist at £1025 per annum so that Sussex records will be properly preserved.'[3] Miss K.M.E. Murray, Principal of Bishop Otter College at Chichester and constitutional historian of the Cinque Ports added her own congratulations, also recommending a permanent deposit at the County Record Office and expressed considerable interest in examining the books.[4]

Unfortunately the corporation members, less experienced in such matters and delighted at the recovery of such precious archives, were reluctant to part with them again and initially proposed that they should be kept in a locked chest in the Court Hall.

However, wiser counsels were eventually to prevail. The *Sussex Daily News* article quoted above drew a quick response from Francis W. Steer F.S.A., County Archivist, who wrote three days after its publication earnestly offering the facilities of his department which was 'anxious to receive documents on long-term loan... and to co-operate with other authorities who have important historical documents in their custody.' This co-operation would include detailed cataloguing. While pondering this suggestion, Winchelsea Corporation, much to Mr. Steer's delight, invited him to become their honorary archivist. He visited Anthony Freeman to discuss the matter and later stayed in Winchelsea while compiling a preliminary report on the bundles and items other than the books; the report ran to eight closely typed pages. In his opening paragraph Mr. Steer stated, 'I was unable to see any records in the custody of your Town Clerk on this occasion.'[5]

This was Anthony Freeman's next problem in his pursuit of the town's historic papers. Edwin Plomley Dawes was in office as town clerk and his family, represented by his father, his grandfather and his grandfather's cousin had held the position continuously since 1826 with other family members including his great-grandfather having served before that. Surely, Freeman felt, Dawes must have somewhere the records which would fill the still existing gap between 1721 and 1883. He somewhat cautiously raised the subject first in a letter dated 28 August 1954.

'My dear Edwin,

I am rather relieved that the County Archivist at Lewes has undertaken to examine and epitomise the great mass of Winchelsea Corporation records which I discovered last year.

This, however, only carries us up to [1721]... Is it possible that there may lie in your office records proceedings and minute books of a date later than that and indeed the whole of the nineteenth century? I do hope it would not be a great labour for you to look for these, but perhaps at some time you could make a search and let me know...

Yours ever

Tony

Captain Dawes replied, 'When I get time I will certainly make a search and let you know what books and records I have in connection with the "Antiente Towne of Winchelsea".'[6]

Unfortunately the time did not materialise. The matter was raised at corporation meetings, with varying degrees of tact, on four different occasions during the rest of the 1950s but the standard response became, 'I will ask a member of my staff to have a look.'

We know this because in 1955 the mayor started keeping a book which recorded the proceedings of corporation business meetings. These had previously passed unminuted because the town clerk did not attend most such meetings and kept records in the Hundred and Assembly Book only of formal courts. When Capt. Herbert Lovegrove first became a corporation member in 1948 he must have been surprised to discover this unbusinesslike practice and it was on his initiative as deputy mayor that the omission was corrected. This unfortunately was not achieved without the town clerk becoming somewhat agitated that others would be keeping records outside his control. He was eventually placated by a paragraph in the explanation prefacing the book:

'that when the Town Clerk was present and took minutes at any meeting of the corporation, his record should be taken as a true record of the meeting in preference to any minutes which might also be taken by the mayor or deputy mayor'.[7]

Meanwhile the rediscovered archives were causing great interest. In 1956 Captain Dawes received a letter from the History of Parliament Trust seeking permission to examine the sixteenth-century records in as far as they related to the parliamentary history of the borough in Tudor times.

A Mr. Gabriel visited Winchelsea to carry out this inspection and the secretary of the trust's Education Board later wrote: 'The documents proved exceptionally interesting – more interesting I am told than those of any other of the Cinque Ports.'[8]

Such comments convinced the corporation that proper professional care was essential and a resolution to that effect led Mr. Steer as County Archivist, in acknowledging receipt, to write:

> 'The records will remain the property of the Corporation of Winchelsea but will be held by me, acting for the County Records Committee, in safe custody at Pelham House, Lewes. The records are reclaimable, in whole or in part, by the Corporation of Winchelsea at any time and are open for inspection… during normal office hours.'[9]

That remains the basis on which Winchelsea's archives are deposited, now at The Maltings, and they are added to from time to time as further documents come to light or cease to be in current use.

The next important development was the catalogue. Mr. Steer's letter went on to say, 'The records will be catalogued in detail and the catalogue printed as soon as circumstances permit.' This most useful book, copies of which are still available from the Record Office, assists researchers by summarising the subject-matter of the more difficult pages of earlier years. It was published in 1963 by which time the editor, Richard F. Dell, had become County Archivist. He acknowledged: 'Above all it is to Mr. F.W. Steer, County Archivist of West Sussex and Honorary Joint Archivist of the Cinque Ports, that credit for this volume is due'.

The list and the collection of Winchelsea's records were as full as they could be at that time but regrettably this was made possible only by the death in 1962 of Captain Edwin Plomley Dawes who had never got round to hunting for, or asking his staff to hunt for, 'the missing link'. On hearing the sad news Francis Steer sought permission to visit Dawes and Prentice at Rye to conduct the long-delayed search. There he found:

> 'the missing eighteenth-century court book, several nineteenth-century volumes of minutes of the corporation and a good [many] loose documents. It would have been tragic if these had turned up after we had gone to press.'[10]

Richard Dell was somewhat alarmed that Edwin Dawes's surviving partner, Noel Prentice, favoured the documents being kept at Winchelsea. This was not agreed by the corporation and they were duly transferred to the East Sussex Record Office.

These latest books were not needed for work on the Mayoral boards in the Upper Court Hall; the information in Cooper, the notes and minutes kept since his day, and the books up to 1721 had enabled the inscription of the names to be completed. It is clear, though, that this was not done under Anthony Freeman's supervision for in November 1960 he wrote to the mayor:

> 'Upon our inscribed panels in the Court Hall there are painted the names of mayors from Easter 1649 to Easter 1660. The "reign" under which they served is described as "The Commonwealth". This is historically, also legally, incorrect. The proper term for this unfortunate period is "The Great Rebellion" or, which I prefer, "The Interregnum". I do not suggest that the names of the mayors of this period should be removed as they were recognised in their office by the Act of Amnesty and no proceedings were taken against them although I believe the mayor of 1660, illegally elected, was displaced… The word "Commonwealth" was the invention of the so called Parliament. After the murder of King Charles I on 29 January 1649 "Parliament" had no legal existence whatsoever – hence its own title of Commonwealth is illegal and incorrect for us to use since we are a royally constituted body.'[11]

A glance at the boards is enough to show, not only that the change was made, but also the tell-tale patch left by the deletion. Anthony Freeman's staunchly royalist and traditionalist views carried the day.

    And so from archives and the information they reveal, to artefacts. A Municipal Corporation, as Winchelsea was for hundreds of years, acquires and uses the trappings of office which represent its dignities and responsibilities. Most publicly noticeable are the maces, carried before the mayor on all official and ceremonial occasions. Winchelsea's are old and small. Their insignificant appearance beside the elaborate maces of many of the Cinque Port towns has frequently been remarked upon, but originally they served a totally different purpose. While strictly ceremonial eighteenth-century maces such as those of Hastings and Rye are intended to emphasise the dignity and importance of the mayor and of the town's authority, Winchelsea's, dating one from the late fifteenth century and the other from the mid-sixteenth, were carried to defend the mayor from attack. Anyone wielding them would find that their weight and balance make them singularly effective for such a purpose. Some other Cinque Port towns, notably Rye, still possess these smaller maces but no longer use them. Winchelsea, probably more through penury than love of tradition, continues proudly to use its ancient maces and holds its head high when doing so. In recent years, when placed ceremonially before the mayor's seat, the maces lie on a specially designed cradle made by one of my former colleagues, John Smith of the staff of William Parker School, Hastings. This incorporates a carving of the ship side of the town seal and is a piece of outstanding twentieth-century craftsmanship to match the medieval.

(56) The medieval seal of Winchelsea

Obverse or ship side   *Reverse*

    The seal there depicted is an even older survival, dating from the thirteenth century. This has had a chequered history. It served the purpose of all seals, to authenticate documents on behalf of the corporation. The impression was obtained in wax and a clear print required the exertion of considerable force. Unfortunately good examples still attached to documents are rare but there is a collection of display versions in the Court Hall. The obverse of the seal depicts a Cinque Ports ship and the reverse the churches of Winchelsea. The ship is similar to those on other Cinque Port seals and has been much discussed and analysed. W.M. Homan thought such vessels could not possibly have been used in battle but only for transport of people and goods, others have even queried their seaworthiness. Contemporary accounts suggest that the Cinque Ports ships were able to give a more than satisfactory account of themselves against enemies of considerably larger size and were used for that purpose ruthlessly and without provocation. Ships of remarkably similar construction are still used in Portugal as river cargo vessels. Considerable research on this subject has been carried out by Jurat David Bourne who believes that both the Cinque Ports ships and the present Portuguese ones are descendants of the Norse longboat.[12]

The seal displays, round the edge of the ship side, a legend which, when translated, reads 'The Seal of the Barons of our Lord the King of England and of Winchelsea.' This part of the original was once stolen to prevent the sealing of documents authenticating a disputed parliamentary election in the town. A replacement, of exquisite eighteenth-century craftsmanship, was made and used for about 150 years. Eventually the original which had somehow come into the possession of Mr. W. Denne and his descendants was returned through the good offices of F.A. Inderwick's son Walter who, as a token of the corporation's gratitude, was presented with the eighteenth-century copy.[13] This, too, was eventually returned to the corporation which therefore now has both versions and another of different design which is intended for documents signed by the mayor.

The last person to use the seal as originally intended was my predecessor as town clerk, Charles Croggon, who reported that an attempt to gain an impression in heated sealing wax was a messy business not conducive to the well-being of the Wickham Manor kitchen stove. When preparing for the sealing of Winchelsea's return on the occasion of the installation of Sir Robert Menzies as Lord Warden of the Cinque Ports in 1966 he, with some relief, arranged for it to be done by an expert at the College of Arms, noting that it was achieved by heating a plastic material far more stable than sealing-wax. Nowadays the corporation must still authenticate legal documents with the seal but does so using a printer's die.

Two of the other surviving artefacts need special mention. One is the town's 'silver oar' Of it a 1915 guide book to Winchelsea says:

> 'The Silver Oar of the Corporation which dates from the fourteenth century and gives
> to Winchelsea the right to search vessels passing up and down the Channel is almost
> unique, London alone having a similar specimen.'[14]

Several other sources state this as a fact but beyond knowing that it was the water-bailiff's sergeant who carried out such duties we have no further details. It is not actually an oar at all but a small mace. This caused some surprise when the National Maritime Museum asked to borrow it for an exhibition they were planning in 1966. After initial enthusiasm the Curator of Presentation wrote:

> 'From the description it does not appear that the Winchelsea sergeant's mace has any
> maritime significance, let alone being shaped like an oar; I wonder how it got the
> name… [Have you] ever looked to see if the mace unscrews to reveal an oar inside?'

It does not, and the National Maritime Museum lost interest.[15]

The second item is a far less prepossessing small wood and brass object with the brass section now loose in its setting. This was the badge of office of a town constable. Winchelsea appointed six such officers, whom we would know as specials, up to 1886, although their activities and responsibilities were considerably reduced after the introduction of the full-time county constabulary. The Very Reverend Basil O'Ferrall, formerly Dean of Jersey and now a Winchelsea resident, told me after my talk about the corporation's regalia at the 1994 mayoring ceremony that such symbols of office were in use by constables in the Channel Islands until comparatively recently. When an arrest was to be made the offender was tapped on the shoulder with this symbol of the constable's appointment, after which he was supposed to come quietly!

Finally we come to the insignia of those still in office in the town. The mayor's badge and chain were presented in 1905 by George Mallows Freeman K.C.[16] The badge includes a representation of the ship side of the town seal and the chain is made of gold links on which are engraved the names of those who have held office as mayor since 1852. Space on the front and back of the links recently ran out so, in order to avoid having to add new links and have the chain eventually dangling round his worship's knees, new names are being engraved on the link edges.

The deputy mayor's badge was presented to the corporation by another of Winchelsea's most distinguished servants of the first half of the twentieth century, Major John Addison Burke whose wife, at the same time, presented the mayoress's badge.[17]

Of the present mayoral and jurats' robes we are far less certain. His worship certainly wore scarlet when Queen Elizabeth I visited Winchelsea and when Dante Gabriel Rossetti observed the opening of the Quarter Sessions in 1866. However, a photograph of the mayoring ceremony in 1922 (see p.130) shows not a robe in sight. James McGowan, mayor in that picture, later presented the mayoral robe.[18] Of those worn by the jurats, and their hats, we have no similar knowledge. A recent inspection showed the majority of them to have exceeded their useful life and to be beyond repair. They may well have to be used for many more years!

It has, however, been possible to do something for the town's chamberlain and sergeant-at-mace. Their gowns, when seen alongside those of their fellow Cinque Ports macebearers looked until recently distinctly shabby and new considerably more elaborate costumes with jackets and knee breeches have been designed and made by Julie Ede. The first use of these at the 1995 mayoring prompted me in the prologue to this book to describe the officers as 'resplendent' in their uniforms. Before that day the word would not have been appropriate.

(57) Bernard Dibble and Neil Clephane-Cameron
in the new uniforms, Easter 1995

27. BASTIONS AND BY-PASS

The bastions, of course, are Winchelsea's three surviving medieval gateways; the by-pass an unfulfilled twinkle in the eye of residents and engineers for more than ninety years. The story of one follows naturally from the story of the others.

Least seen of the imposing town entrance gates because of its remote position is the New Gate. For a casual driver or pedestrian from visible Winchelsea the sudden appearance of this imposing structure at the foot of a steep slope in Pannel Lane on the way to Pett serves dramatically to emphasise the original size of the town. This is the entrance at which, according to legend, the French and Spanish were so treacherously and disastrously admitted in 1380. It protected the low southerly point where the natural, though reinforced, eastern cliff defences met the man-made western ditch. Very few authorities attempt to date the structure although Cooper describes it as one of the two remaining original gateways which would place its construction in the late thirteenth century.[1]

As early as 1415, when the town had shrunk to the area which, principally, it still occupies, plans were made to exclude the New Gate completely from the defended area, a wall being built which very considerably reduced the protected land 'because the site is now too large for the inhabitants and to enclose all of it would be unbearable.' That wall extended from the southern side of the Greyfriars' site across to beyond the eastern side of what is now Rectory Lane and then northwards to Pipewell Gate.[2] It is believed later, when it had outlived its usefulness, to have provided much stone for the construction of Camber Castle. The original strength and durability of the New Gate must have been enormous for once it served no defensive purpose there can have been little motive for its preservation or maintenance. However, it miraculously survived the neglect of centuries and the depredations of those similarly seeking building materials until its value was recognised in the 1920s by a request that, with the two other gates, it should be scheduled as an ancient monument.

The Board of Works sent an inspector to examine them. W.H. Martindale, a freeman living at The Elms, Icklesham and son of Dr. Martindale, mayor in 1893, had submitted the request for scheduling. The inspector's report stated firmly that repairs must be put in hand before responsibility could be accepted by the board. Martindale wrote to the mayor, Lord Ritchie of Dundee, asking whether there was anyone generous enough to make the New Gate safe. Martindale himself was at that time paying for repairs to the Court Hall. No individual was found but a public appeal was launched for the restoration of 'St. Mary's Gate'. This name appears nowhere else in the records and by 1925 when a nine page detailed schedule of works was agreed with Breeds and Son of Rye the name New Gate was again being used.[3] The recommendations included raising the level of the roadway by twelve inches to prevent undermining. It seems the corporation did not agree to this, but accepted Breeds' quotation of £200 for the remaining items, less than half the cost estimated by the Board of Works.[4]

Since those days the structure has been maintained by the corporation, advised and financially assisted by various government departments which have from time to time had responsibility for ancient monuments. As a result it continues to stand, a lonely sentinel, provoking from modern traffic, because of the sharp angle the road takes beneath it, a regular sounding of horns which would have intensely annoyed Lady McIlwraith had she lived nearby.

While the southern bastion has but two names, one relatively obscure, the north-western has regularly been known by three – Pipewell Gate, Land Gate and Ferry Gate. This was originally the route to the land (the Udimore ridge) where a ferry-crossing of the River Brede was necessary and also the way for citizens to reach the Pipe Well. Dating here is much easier because John Helde, mayor in 1404, supervised the rebuilding of this entrance and helpfully added a shield on which his name is engraved. The need for expensive work in 1951 led to a somewhat startling but understandable suggestion that ownership of the gates should be transferred by the corporation to the Ministry of Works. That body had written the previous year drawing attention to the need to remove an iron bar which was causing corrosive damage and to consolidate the stones round a breach in the vaulting. No reply was received. On being reminded of the matter and conscious of the potential cost, the town clerk, Edwin Plomley Dawes, suggested that the ministry should assume 'guardianship'. This was rejected both by the department on the rather surprising grounds that the gate was of 'local rather than national' importance, and eventually by the corporation who, whatever the problems might be, declined to relinquish the traditional ownership of centuries.[5] The repairs were carried out, as have been numerous others since, with assistance provided with the costs by the appropriate government department or establishment, although between the early 1980s and the time of writing the level of such grants has reduced from 75% to 40%. Fortunately the corporation has been regularly supported by East Sussex County Council, Rother District Council, Icklesham Parish Council and the Friends of the Ancient Monuments and Museum of Winchelsea, thus permitting proper maintenance of such important and irreplaceable buildings.

Circumstances fortunate for the corporation meant that by far the biggest work needed during the twentieth century on the Strand Gate was paid for entirely by the highway authority, East Sussex County Council. This gate, Winchelsea's best known and most photographed, stands, as has already been described, at the top of the steep hill which led originally to the 'strand' beside the harbour. Cooper thought it contemporary with the building of New Winchelsea,[6] other sources place it as late as 1390 but whatever may be the truth of its actual date, the Strand Gate's bluff embodiment of the spirit of the ancient town is beyond question.

In 1955 an unthinkable situation occurred which threatened the possible collapse of the structure, or at least of its eastern towers. The problem was revealed when scaffolding was erected to permit an investigation into whether it would be practicable to construct a footpath outside the gate, thus avoiding the extreme danger to pedestrians caused when they had to walk through the arch under constant threat from vehicles. Those conducting the examination discovered that the Strand Gate was being undermined by surface water from the road. The corporation immediately called on Mr. C.H. Dobbie, a distinguished consulting engineer, who was later to become a Winchelsea resident. The summary of his full report makes the situation quite clear:

> 'The Strand Gate is in a dangerous condition due to its situation on the edge of a cliff at a sharp bend on a steep hill. The cliff face has been worn into a ravine by the discharge of road water from an old culvert and pipe so that the foundations project into space for the very tower most likely to receive the impact of vehicles. The situation becomes progressively more dangerous. Remedial measures are suggested which also would allow of the construction of a footpath.'[7]

Fortunately Mr. P.R. Anscombe, County Divisional Surveyor for East Sussex County Council, reached precisely similar conclusions and very substantial work to shore up the cliff, support the towers and build the pedestrian way was undertaken at his authority's expense with the corporation's full support, led by Anthony Freeman, freeholder of the adjoining affected land.

Because of New Gate's remote site and Ferry Hill's reconstruction to by-pass Pipewell Gate, it is Strand Gate which has suffered most from the pressure created by the ever increasing intrusion of modern traffic. Robert Goodsall, writing soon after the above works, was pleasantly surprised to find that this particular bastion had survived at all:

> 'Although the arch width is that normally found in medieval gateways, it certainly presents a problem for modern day traffic and it is fortunate that Winchelsea has had sufficient civic pride to prevent this fine relic of her past from being sacrificed to convenience, something which might well have happened at any time during the last two centuries when the city fathers of other places such as Canterbury and Chichester were enthusiastically pulling down their ancient gateways in the cause of modern progress.'[8]

Perhaps during his visit Goodsall admired, as did many residents of that time, the skill of East Kent Bus Company drivers who would sweep through the arch, their vehicles unerringly leaving a few inches to spare on either side. Of course, not all drivers were as knowledgeable or as skilful; accidents and incidents became more and more frequent. The first of which we have full documentation happened considerably earlier. On 26 May 1949 George Goodsell of Oxford Road, St Leonards was driving a Plummer Roddis furniture van through Strand Gate when he felt an impact. On stopping he found that he had struck a hook, one of the ancient gate hangings, making a groove three feet long and an inch deep high on the side of the van. As the arch was between ten and eleven feet wide and the vehicle only seven feet, it might have been assumed that with greater care all would have been well. However, Plummer Roddis took an action in the county court for the recovery of a twenty eight pounds fifteen shillings repair bill. The threat of action caused consternation among the members of Winchelsea Corporation and on receipt of counsel's advice that there could be no question of negligence they decided to defend the case. When it came to court the *Evening Argus* reported:

> 'An action against the Mayor and Commonalty of the Ancient Borough of Winchelsea was described by Judge F.K. Archer at Hastings County Court as "an ungracious one". Sued for a sum greater than their yearly income, Winchelsea "Corporation" were given judgment with costs… Judge Archer observed: "This was a most ungracious action to have been brought. I should have thought Plummer Roddis and Company would have been pleased to make good the damage to their van without saying a word about it. But they have done so and I will not enlarge upon it." The judge commented, "The driver succeeded in doing something that has never been done before. Millions of vehicles must have passed through the archway and never before has one got hooked on it."[9]

Members of the corporation were greatly relieved to receive the £83 which it had cost them to defend the case. They have never since been sued, but that did not stop vehicles damaging the arch, becoming stuck in it, or causing problems trying to back up when drivers realised they could not get through, on a fairly regular basis. Records were kept by local residents. These show that most problems were caused by continental vehicles and those with drivers who had not been to Winchelsea before. Captain Herbert Lovegrove was called to one incident in April 1962. An articulated lorry belonging to Ross Garages of Cardiff was well and truly wedged in the arch. The driver did not know the route and complained bitterly that the signing and warnings were totally inadequate, an assertion to which the police gave support but even so it was to be another nine years before definite major action was taken. Messrs. Hartnells of Brede were called with heavy lifting gear

(58) Pipewell Gate contends with modern traffic.

and the vehicle was pulled out with considerable difficulty. One handrail post on the raised footway was alleged to have been damaged in the operation and another, beside the mirror, was broken 'by the pressure of the crowd of people watching operations'.[10]

An accumulation of incidents of this kind inevitably led to increased demands for a Winchelsea by-pass, agitation in favour of which had been going on for most of the twentieth century, initiated by George M. Freeman in 1904.[11] However, it was not the development of the internal combustion engine which first caused problems for road-users in the area; they had existed since medieval times when all self-respecting travellers would go by sea rather than attempt to negotiate the impenetrable forests of the Weald or the treacherous coastal ways. The ever-changing topography of the area made the situation worse. In 1760 Thomas Turner was making his way to Winchelsea in the hope of taking a shop which he had heard was to let. Passing through Rye in appalling weather, he discovered that the tide was out 'and I, a stranger, was afraid to venture through, so that I turned back and rode to a public house about two miles back where I hired a guide.' All this was to no avail. The shop turned out to be already let.[12]

The problems faced by road travellers in Sussex were highlighted some thirty years earlier by Daniel Defoe who wrote:

> 'I have seen one Tree on a Carriage which they call here a *Tug* drawn by two and
> twenty Oxen; and even then 'tis carry'd so little a Way, and then thrown down and left

for other *Tugs* to take up and carry on, that sometimes 'tis Two or Three Years before it gets to *Chatham;* for if the rains come in, it stirs no more that Year, and sometimes a whole Summer is not dry enough to make the roads passable. Here I had a Sight which indeed I never saw in any other part of *England:* Namely that going to Church at a Country Village not far from Lewes, I saw an antient Lady *and a Lady of very good Quality I assure you,* drawn to Church in her Coach with Six Oxen, nor was it done but out of mere Necessity, the Way being so stiff and deep, that no Horses could go in it.'[13]

Thomas Turner had probably observed similar difficulties but, had he attempted his journey between Rye and Winchelsea fifty years later, the way across the marsh would have been comparatively safe for he could have used the Military Road constructed with and beside the canal during the Napoleonic wars. This provided a well-defined route but hardly adequate for early twentieth-century motor vehicles and it was still under military control. Great resentment was caused because the substantial tolls charged were not used to improve the surface which was described as early as 1910 as being 'in an execrable state' and two years later by a passing motor-cyclist on a February weekend jaunt as 'a shocking road, all ruts and holes and a perfect sea of slush.'[14] A survey carried out in 1924 revealed that during a six-day period 2,735 motor-propelled vehicles passed between Rye and Winchelsea as against 396 horse-drawn vehicles. Requests to the county council to take over the road and put it in good order were not well received. A petition on the subject from Winchelsea residents drew little response, the only tangible result being a proposal that all vehicles other than private cars should be banned from using the road, thus reducing wear and tear. Understandably this produced a furious response from the public transport lobby.[15]

Nevertheless it was the passage of traffic through Winchelsea rather than near it that really precipitated the initial demands for a by-pass all those years ago. G.M. Freeman's 1904 representations were almost certainly on the same lines as his remarks at the 1907 mayoring when he:

'Alluded to the dust nuisance in the town and urged upon members to bring before the County Council a recommendation to the effect that noticeboards should be put up to request motorists not to drive through the town at a higher rate than ten miles an hour. The property along the main road was greatly damaged in consequence of the dust raised by motorcars and he thought steps should be taken to remedy the evil.'[16]

It was in those days that Alex Finch recalled rushing to see if help was required when cars got into trouble attempting the ascent of Strand Hill, frequently earning a penny or twopence for pushing the reluctant vehicle. One particular steam car would not respond even to the efforts of a number of small boys and, while the owner continued his journey by train, was left in a yard at the foot of the hill. Here it became a considerable attraction, eventually being taken away to prevent further deterioration. 'Goodness knows if it ever went anywhere after we had done with it.'[17]

Steps were not taken despite Mr. Freeman's strictures and on 13 June 1919 the first official entry in the corporation's records appeared:

'The Town Clerk was ordered to write to the Clerk of the Rural District Council (Highways) calling attention to the Traffic through Winchelsea and suggesting the diversion of the traffic over the existing road through Winchelsea to a new road to be constructed for about half a mile from the bottom of Land Gate Hill until it joins the Hastings main road.'[18]

The town clerk did not seem too clear about his brief so in a letter to him some three weeks later Lord Ritchie of Dundee explained exactly why members were so concerned:

'After a lull during the war the dust and noise created by motors is again becoming a nuisance to those who live in the principal streets of the town and will shortly become intolerable. The great bulk of the traffic is passing from Rye to Hastings and vice-versa. It enters the town by a steep and dangerous hill at one end and leaves it by another steep and dangerous hill at the other end. The climb at the one end and the descent at the other are a cruel strain on horses and the conditions generally are a serious handicap to passengers and all who are interested in the road transport of the neighbourhood. The remedy is obvious and its cost would not, I imagine, be very great. It would mean widening the present road for a distance of about 300 yards between the foot of Strand Hill and the foot of Land Gate Hill and making a new road for a distance of about half a mile from the latter point until it joins the Hastings Road in the neighbourhood of the Rye R. D. pumping station [at the foot of Sandrock Hill].'[19]

Following the resulting submission there must have been some definite, if slow, progress for in October 1927 the mayor actually produced at a corporation meeting the professionally produced plans of a by-pass 'for heavy traffic'. This would run from above Crutches Farm round the north of the town to join the Military Road to Rye beyond the River Brede. The project had even been costed, the estimated total being £27,750. Members' opinions are not recorded but the minute ends: 'The Mayor stated he would communicate with the Chairman of East Sussex County Council thereon.'[20]

Typically in this whole saga these plans were still in the pipeline twelve years later. The *Sussex Express and County Herald* carried an article headed 'DEMAND FOR WINCHELSEA BY-PASS. ALARMING ACCIDENT FIGURES.' It was stated that the plans 'have been drawn up and approved by the East Sussex County Council and by the Ministry of Transport, and in fact the by-pass is listed in the County Council's town planning scheme as an approved road. But the delay in commencing its construction is causing concern'. The route was the one shown to the corporation in 1927 and the road was stated to be sixty feet wide. In a dramatic interview Major Burke, then deputy mayor, quoted the 1936 and 1937 reported accident statistics on the short stretch of the A.259 through Winchelsea, 21 incidents, 20 people injured and 2 killed. He cited particularly a collision between two lorries and a car in the High Street 'near the junction where the children come out from school'. He pointed out the tremendous dangers involved in heavy lorries negotiating Ferry Hill and Strand Hill, commenting that a greatly increasing number of lorry movements was being generated by growing industrial development at Rye Harbour.[21]

In 1944 things were being made even worse by the constant military traffic and the mayor, Anthony Freeman, was becoming desperate. He wrote to Mr. R.E. Knocker, Seneschal of Dover Castle and Joint Solicitor of the Confederation of the Cinque Ports:

'For the last forty years since my father, whom you knew so well, first inaugurated the question, we of the town of Winchelsea have been seeking a by-pass road. For all these years we have been defeated either by local bodies or various Ministers of Transport. Since the appointment of the prime minister as Lord Warden of the Ports the matter has taken on a somewhat different aspect; and I desire to seek his help to achieve our end as I feel that suitable representations by him will work the oracle with any ministry.'[22]

(59) The Rectory Lane/Sandrock Hill junction before the much needed re-alignment.
The surviving gable of St. John's Hospital is also shown.

Mr. Freeman proposed sending a petition supported by all the ports and the Ancient Town of Rye. Whether it was ever sent I have yet to discover. If it was, Mr. Churchill clearly had more important matters to attend to at the time.

The by-pass saga next surfaces in the corporation's files in 1962 when the Ministry of Transport published a diversion order for a south-easterly route running from Strand Bridge, along beside the canal, climbing Friars' Cliff and rejoining the A.259 at the Rectory Lane/Sandrock Hill junction. There was never any positive progress on this proposal.[23]

The first practical steps to improve the situation were taken in 1971 when it was proposed in response to a growing number of incidents, particularly at the Strand Gate, to alter the official route of the A.259 to follow Rectory Lane, Ferry Hill and Tanyard Lane. The great advantage of this proposal was that it would allow the junction at the top of Sandrock Hill to be re-designed so that through traffic was fed along Rectory Lane and kept away from the town and the Strand Gate. No amount of signpost alteration or additional warnings had earlier been successful in persuading heavy lorries to turn left at that point and deviate from what appeared to be the principal route.[24] In the absence of any actual plans to build a by-pass this was the most sensible suggestion to date but there was still considerable local concern about the implications of the proposal. This took tangible shape in a petition organised by Mr. J.D. Wood and signed by large numbers of residents, complaining that the proposed trunk route was more dangerous than the existing one and extremely difficult to improve as the Icklesham to Winchelsea stretch had recently been improved. Any such diversion with associated work was a waste of money in view of the fact that the only solution to Winchelsea's traffic problems was a by-pass.[25] Much heated debate followed with the parish council and the corporation strongly supporting the new trunk route. Eventually the *Sussex Express* was able to report 'Winchelsea Accepts Trunk Route Change. But fight for by-pass will continue'. At the end of a public meeting:

> 'The organiser of a petition protesting against the re-routing said he would ask people who had signed to retract their objection – as long as the Town Council (sic) continued to press for a by-pass. Said Captain Lovegrove, "Make no mistake – we will continue to fight tooth and nail."'[26]

The petitioners' fears about improvements to the new route seemed justified when, in 1973, the county council proposed the complete closure of Strand Hill to vehicular traffic in order to protect Strand Gate from further damage and provide a quieter environment for residents, The residents clearly did not want a quieter environment on those terms. The proposal was greeted with outrage and a feeling that the principal motive was to allow cheaper improvements at the foot of the hill by permitting removal of the hump and thus improving safety in Tanyard Lane. The proper way to achieve that was to build a by-pass. For the parish council, the corporation and the residents, here acting with complete accord, to lose the regular route from the town to Rye, an alternative route for emergency vehicles, and the town's dramatic principal entrance for tourists, among numerous other reasons, made the idea ludicrous. Fortunately, after fierce protest, it was consigned to the waste paper basket where Winchelsea felt it belonged.[27]

In the face of this it was not long before the next set of by-pass proposals appeared. The local authorities and the public were asked to comment on two alternatives. Route A ran to the west but was much less radical than the 1939 proposal because it left the existing road near the foot of Sandrock Hill and rejoined it at the Tanyard Lane/Station Road junction, thus providing no relief from the dangers of Tanyard Lane or for its residents. Route B ran to the east and south of the town, almost exactly similar to that recommended twelve years earlier. An exhibition was held at the New Hall, with a later public meeting and the opportunity for residents and organisations to comment in writing. Of the organisations, a majority favoured Route A, of the individuals 86 preferred Route A and 106 Route B 'while eight rejected both alternatives on the basis that a longer by-pass embracing Rye and Icklesham was the only possible lasting solution to traffic problems in the area.' Such an indecisive result led naturally to indecision and the matter was shelved yet again with no action to be taken until the results were available of a feasibility study into 'trunk route needs between Lewes and Folkestone'.[28] When that study was completed, four years later, the Department of Transport declared itself in favour of Route A because there was no likelihood of a major reconstruction of the trunk route on a new line.[29]

A further five years later the whole process started again. More plans, another exhibition and another public consultation. This time there was no southern and eastern route but several western and northern alternatives. One (the green route) began half way along the Icklesham straight, swept across to Winchelsea Station and along beside the railway to enter Rye near the Martello Tower. Two more (the brown and blue routes) began on the Winchelsea side of Crutches Farm, brown joining green at Winchelsea Station and blue curving round Winchelsea to join the Royal Military Road on the way to Rye. A further alternative (yellow) was to begin both these possibilities much closer to the foot of Sandrock Hill.[30]

The reader will by now not be surprised to hear that the results of the consultation were inconclusive. When Winchelsea Corporation voted, four members favoured the green route, two brown, one blue and three yellow/blue. At the parish council and among the public the outcome was similar, the main result being the sensible suggestion that it really was not possible to consider the matter without knowing where the Rye by-pass was going.[31] Nevertheless the Department announced that its preferred route was the green; it then declared in favour of a route through Rye which followed the line of the railway, thus splitting the town in two. There was another enormous row with Rye winning decisively.

After another six years, with Rye's route likely to be to the south and consequent amendments to the Winchelsea line provoking banners proclaiming 'Save these Rye houses from the Winchelsea by-pass' it was decided that earlier traffic forecasts had been an underestimate and that a dual carriageway rather than a single would be required. More public exhibitions and consultations followed in 1990 (Hastings Eastern), 1991 (Rye and Winchelsea) and 1993 (Guestling Thorn and Icklesham). Once these additional elements were added to the equation Winchelsea Corporation came out in favour of a route right along the Brede Valley beside the railway. At no time does this seem to have had any realistic chance of implementation.[32]

All these proposals and counter-proposals were leading nowhere. Eventually an 'A.259 Guestling Thorn to east of Rye Round Table Conference' was arranged to be held at Icklesham Village Hall in January 1995. The purpose was to obtain a consensus of interested parties on a route to cover the whole of this section of the road. With no round tables, far too small a venue with overflow portakabins and television links, and ill-will predominating over goodwill, things proved difficult. Despite the best efforts of the chairman, Mr. Robin Wilson, the result was not consensus but conflict. The various communities stuck to the routes which they favoured, the Save the Brede Valley Action Group objected strongly to the Icklesham and Winchelsea routes and the conference was for a time disrupted by those from outside the area with only an interest in preventing the building of any road at all.[33]

At yet another exhibition the conference solutions were displayed but, except for Guestling Thorn and Rye, these were alternatives, one of the Winchelsea suggestions being to tunnel under the town. This provoked further stormy reaction and large numbers of placards in Winchelsea windows with the legend NUMBY (not under my back yard), and the formation of a Winchelsea Residents' Association under the chairmanship of John Gooders. Most recently this part of the road has been taken out of the government's road-building programme for the foreseeable future.

So where do we go now? Certainly not along a Winchelsea by-pass. Since attempts to resolve the matter have already taken well over ninety years, perhaps that is not too surprising. A pamphlet of historical information, published in the 1920s by the owner of the Golden Galleon in Rye, after announcing that in 1921 'HORSELESS WAGGONS firft ply for hire from *Haftings* unto *Rye*' adds an undated but obviously much earlier prophecy that 'A GREAT COAFT ROAD fhall run from *Devon* unto *Dover* upon a new *Rhee Wall*'[34]

Perhaps it will only happen and relief for Winchelsea's traffic problems result when somebody is as decisive as Winston Churchill would have been had he received, had time to consider, and decided to support Anthony Freeman's petition.

28. COUNCIL HOUSING AND CLOCHEMERLE

At the same time that Winchelsea's archives were being rediscovered and the Plummer Roddis pantechnicon was becoming impaled on the Strand Gate, the future of the town as a viable community was under urgent consideration. Long before, in the 1920s, when Miss Peel was still making the Barrack Square houses available for ordinary working people by keeping their rents down, the Rural District Council had recognised the need for low-cost housing by proposing to build on the area currently occupied by Pipewell and adjoining land, above Ferry Hill. Lady McIlwraith considered this an inappropriate site and offered to purchase it for the construction of a second home to which she could move in summer to escape the traffic noise. In return she would demolish Hiham House, a large and expensive old house where her son-in-law and daughter were living and use the land to build houses for renting. The plan was carried out and Hiham Green, Hiham Cottages and Hiham Bungalows resulted. When Lady McIlwraith went to view the first two properties completed, now known as Firin and Westway, she is reputed to have declared that they were much too grand and ordered that the remainder should be less expensive.[1] These homes were sold in 1945, their tenants having first option.

This undertaking was intended to protect Winchelsea from the growing tendency for cottages to be acquired by wealthier outsiders to the detriment of those who needed jobs in the area just as much as the area needed to be able to provide such jobs. However, the impact upon Winchelsea's historic appearance and one of its oldest buildings caused outrage. The incident provoked G.M. Freeman to purchase Mariteau House when it later came onto the market to ensure that it did not meet the same fate. Miss Peel, although she hid behind the pseudonym 'A Lover of Winchelsea', wrote forcefully to the local press in an attempt to enlist support against the project:

'Dear Sir,

Will you kindly afford space in your valuable paper to make known a plea for the oldest inhabitants of this historic town; those I mean who were born here and whose families have lived here from generation to generation and who are filled with dismay at a scheme proposed by a comparative newcomer which, if carried out, will entirely efface the present aspect of one of the central quarters.

By long association the town is their town. They are truly attached to their birthplace. They are proud of her beauty, of her historical interest... They gratefully welcome efforts to preserve her history, her old buildings and her old landmarks and now they are faced with the disaster of standing by while a sojourner here, arriving a stranger from the colonies, destroys entirely the whole face of one part of their town...'

Miss Peel elaborated her theme with an evocative and imaginative word-picture of the part of Winchelsea then threatened. She did, however, acknowledge Lady McIlwraith's 'great liberality to aiding every philanthropic undertaking'.[2] It was also true that her family joined in such philanthropy. Ron Turner remembers going to Hiham House at the invitation of the McGowans. They gave Christmas parties for the children of the town in the conservatory there 'with a Christmas tree going right up to the roof' which made a great impression on him.[3]

Miss Peel lost the day. Hiham House and the Christmas parties were no more. It has to be said that many of the inhabitants to whom she imputed such idealistic motives were probably extremely glad to seize the opportunity of acquiring homes at reasonable cost, whatever might be the objections to their siting.

However, construction of the Hiham Estate delayed further consideration of exactly the same problem by only ten years. This time the catalyst was the appalling condition of the Salutation Cottages in Mill Road, so bad that Anthony Freeman had given an undertaking that, once the council had found his tenants alternative accommodation, the cottages would not be used for human habitation until they had been re-converted into one dwelling. In fact they were later re-built as three. The overcrowding involved, quite apart from other conditions, can be illustrated by the list of tenants who were: At No. 1 with twelve in his family, Mr. Creasey; at No 2 Mr. Streeton with a family of three; at No. 3 Mr. Brown (3); No. 4 Mr. Hickmott (5); No. 5 Mr. Sills (3). These were not the only families in need and the site proposed was on the Mill Field to the east of Rectory Lane, an assurance being given that no land within 350 feet of the mill would be used. The mayor at the time was James McGowan whose then home had been lost to provide housing earlier. He had no objection, and the parish council fully supported the site but some members of the corporation most certainly did not. The Clerk of the Rural District Council, C.T. Chevallier, writing to the mayor on 7 April 1936 attempted to clarify the situation:

'At a Town Planning Inquiry, held last summer by the Ministry of Health, into the proposal of Mr. [Walter] Alford to build cottages along Station Road, on very low lying ground, this Council was successful, as in similar cases hitherto, in resisting such development, but the need for working class houses at the Winchelsea end of the parish was strongly emphasised, and it was also stated that it was practically impossible to buy land for such purpose along the higher ground – that is to say along the island site of Winchelsea, although the demand was great.

A member of the parish council was present and undertook to support this council's efforts, and presumably the Winchelsea representatives have had a voice in the parish council's recommendation.

It is further noted that the petition which has been submitted by the Deputy Mayor does not appear to be very representative of all classes as, indeed, all the signatures appear to be those of sixteen of the more cultured and leisured residents and in four cases of their wives…'

He went on to urge the mayor to bring the support of the parish council to the attention of his colleagues and gave an assurance that the development would conform with Winchelsea's layout in 'squares'.[4]

None of that would have placated William Maclean Homan who was positively vitriolic on the subject, even more so than the deputy mayor and his supporters. Homan wrote in an unpublished article entitled *Winchelsea in the time between the two World Wars*:

'About ten years ago a determined attempt, without any justification, was made to build Winchelsea half a dozen council houses. Fortunately for the town this evil scheme was defeated though it had the support of some inhabitants who saw a chance of getting cheap houses at the neighbourhood's expense. The site on which it was hoped that the Council Houses would be erected was the best in the Town and one must only glance for instance at the hideous jumble of shoddy Noah's Ark type buildings at Icklesham to realise that they would have harmed Winchelsea.'[5]

With regard to the site, these views might today attract much support, architecturally and aesthetically there might be some sympathy, but socially, backing would seem most unlikely. This stage of the battle was, however, won by Mr. Homan and his supporters.

The intervention of the war ensured that the matter was again delayed ten years, a detailed assessment of Winchelsea's housing needs being produced in 1946 for Battle Rural District Council by Mr. W.O. Humphrey, Acting Planning Officer. This gives a well researched historical background to Winchelsea's urban development and, for the first time within the documents known to me, reveals the names, residences and occupations of those on the waiting list. These include Mrs. Heels, a cook employed at Keith Cottage, V.G. Setterfield, a mechanic at Strand Garage, G. Jones, a farm labourer at Ferry Farm, three drivers employed by Walter Alford including two of his sons and no fewer than nine men employed in various trades by local building firms, these workers including L.P. Polhill, E.G. Streeton, L.W. Turner, G.T. Turner and C.H.V. Barden. Mr. Humphrey thought Rye a better centre than Winchelsea for those whose place of work was always changing, but conceded that Winchelsea's needs were clearly established at a maximum of twenty properties.[6]

Unfortunately, despite acknowledging extensive help from W.M. Homan on the historical background, the planning officer again opted for the Mill Farm site which Homan had earlier so vehemently opposed. Thus the whole row was rekindled, centred on the suitability of various sites.

By 1950 the Mill Farm site had been dropped as a possibility, no doubt much to Mr. Homan's relief, but the site then favoured by both district and parish councils was what would appear to Mr. Homan an equally controversial one in the Greyfriars orchard where the replacement St. Thomas's School was eventually rebuilt sixteen years later. The opposition case was stated by the town clerk:

> 'As far as the suggested orchard site is concerned, building on it is viewed with apprehension by my corporation and by many inhabitants and it is a matter of concern that the beautiful open space containing the orchard and beyond it the old Abbey ruins which are amongst the finest of their period should have a clump of council houses erected in their vicinity.'[7]

At a stormy 1950 Annual Parish Meeting the case in favour was argued by Alex Finch, chairman of the parish council, who vacated the chair in order to press the argument. The need, he said, was proved. The problem of acquiring a site of adequate size was so great that even for the one now favoured the district council had had to threaten the use of compulsory purchase powers against the county council. A wide cross-section of speakers argued for and against including Mr. Charles Potter whose remarks were thus reported:

> 'In 1922 the laying out of council houses in Winchelsea was begun but this had not come to anything, principally because of objections by the Mayor and Corporation. The Battle council had been listening to them all along and they should stop doing so.'

A resolution was eventually proposed by the Rev. R.A. Cochrane and seconded by Miss Edith Holmes welcoming the choice of site and supporting the use of compulsory powers to obtain it. 'The resolution was carried by an overwhelming majority'. Despite this the project went no further.[8]

However, progress had already been made in a small way towards the resolution of this apparently insoluble problem. A site at Spring Steps, formerly let as allotments by Miss Peel, had been developed by Battle Rural District Council with four houses and four flats. Here, between 5 December 1949 and 9 January 1950 tenancies had been taken up by eight families. Although the Housing Committee minutes do not give any details about the occupations of the applicants, there

(60) The Trojan's Plat houses.

is no doubt that they were men working locally for whom accommodation at a reasonable rent was so vital to keep the community alive. The first tenants, in the order of the numbers of the properties they occupied, were C. Barden, W.N. Walker, H.P. Jones, E.G. Streeton (who still lives at No 4), G.W. Lewis, L.H. Whiting, F.J. Ward and G. Badman.[9] Much satisfaction derived from this provision although Messrs. Barden and Walker did complain at the 1952 Annual Parish Meeting that the district council's specification had been deficient in providing soundproofing between the flats.[10]

Three years later, following further convoluted debate, came the larger and much applauded development at Trojan's Plat and thus were provided the remainder of the projected need for twenty homes. The name is a corruption of 'Truncheons', part of the area having been earlier known as 'Little Truncheons'. The site had actually belonged to Mariteau House and had contained its tennis court but the general opinion was that to continue the use of the name Mariteau on the opposite side of German Street would be confusing. The construction involved the moving of an old gateway, referred to in the relevant correspondence as Trojan's Gate but elsewhere usually as the former entrance to Jew's Hall. This was to have been at the Greyfriars end, beside No. 8, and is there shown on the plans but following representations from Mr. Anthony Freeman, was sited next to No 1 opposite the churchyard and much more within the normal orbit of visitors walking in the town.[11]

It was in September and October 1953 that the first Trojan's Plat tenants moved in. They were: At No.1 N.J. Turner, No.2 A.L. Hibbert, No.3 F.W. Hickmott, No.4 C.P.J. Barden (transferring from Spring Steps) No.5 R.G. Turner, No.6 J.A. Wheeler, No.7 R.W. Gall, No.8 G.S. Neaves No.9 J.E. Buttonshaw No.10 T. D'Arcy No.11 J.A. Johnson and No.12 W. Walker (also transferring from Spring Steps). Norman Turner, Frank Hickmott and Cecil Barden still live there. One condition of the tenancies was that television aerials could be erected only on poles in the gardens. On 16 November the housing committee was told of a complaint from Norman Turner about a large tree stump which he had not been able to remove from his garden. It had obviously been there a long time and was not part of the felling necessary to clear the land for building. The housing manager was authorised to investigate but by the time he did so the stump had been successfully removed by a tenant who was not prepared to give up.[12]

And so council housing provision in Winchelsea was made. Those working in and near the town were accommodated and a reasonable balance within the community was ensured, at least for the time being.

It was twenty years later that the next development to split opinion in the town was deemed to be needed, the resulting arguments attracting at best leg-pulling and at worst ridicule from observers outside.

The seeds of this new problem can be observed growing as long previously as 19 January 1897 when a suggestion by Mr. A. Eldridge to Icklesham Parish Council that the district council should be asked to provide 'places of public convenience' in Winchelsea 'was met with derision and no support whatsoever'.[13] This provoked a response in the *Sussex Express* from a correspondent using the name 'Common Sense' who castigated the councillors for treating the idea so dismissively. Such facilities were vital for visitors who had to stay hours because of the poor train service or 'tramp on'. 'In England we are lax over such facilities – in France they do much better. There should be provision not only for men, but for women, in all frequented localities.'[14]

For even longer than with the council houses nothing was done. In fact action was not really necessary while landlords of the New Inn were prepared to leave their outside toilets unlocked and available for use even if on a strictly unofficial basis. The situation changed in October 1970 when the parish council was told that the New Inn facilities were to be improved and re-designed so that access was available only from the bars.[15] The Castle Inn later made similar provision on a temporary basis but the need for a permanent site in Winchelsea was established and the cat was really among the pigeons. To continue the analogy, hackles rose even further when the rector, the parish council and the rural district council came out in favour of a site in the churchyard, adjoining St. Thomas's Street, next to the electricity sub-station. The basis of their argument in favour was that this was right at the centre of the town, exactly where the facility was needed, particularly as coaches were at that time parking in Castle Street.

The mayor and corporation were horrified, as were many residents. The original suggested position was actually on the highway verge next to the sub-station[16] but the highway authority objected and planning applications were later submitted for sites within the churchyard both beside the original position and opposite Nelgarde.[17] Douglas Turner, practical and down to earth as always, commented to the parish council on the unsatisfactory temporary arrangements:

> 'All it needs is a coach load of women and there will be a queue a mile long. I am not happy at all with the situation. What we need is a permanent *central* convenience.'[18]

A complication which further inflamed the furore was that a Draft Tourist Appraisal published for the town had foreseen the need for a public car and coach park to meet the requirements of a growing number of visitors. This could not be provided centrally and the construction of the toilets at whatever place might be chosen for this other facility was an obvious possibility which attracted many of those so fiercely opposed to the sites in St. Thomas's Street. Numerous positions for the toilets and the vehicle park were suggested, a popular one for the former being on the old reservoir site in Rectory Lane. Others included a garage site in Back Lane, beside the police house in Friars Road and beside the New Hall. A fifth was at Blackfriars Barn, opposite the reservoir site, with the possibility of the later addition of parking facilities nearby.

Winchelsea Corporation, however, was adamant that the public conveniences should be provided in the Trojan's Plat corner of Greyfriars Park adjoining German Street. They believed that a car and coach park of suitable design, not using asphalt and maintaining the trees, as at many National Trust properties, could be provided alongside when it could be afforded.[19] Eventually, as the battle raged on, the parish council called a public meeting at the New Hall to which were invited as speakers a representative of the county planning officer, the assistant county surveyor, the surveyor and engineer of Battle Rural District Council, Mr. Thomas Bruce, deputy mayor, to put the corporation's view and the rector, Rev. R.M. Ware, to put the case for the churchyard site. The hall was packed. The parish council chairman, Mr. A.C. Hancock from Rye Harbour, presided. The council's clerk, an office I held at the time, was needed only to keep a record of what was said and I can well remember sitting near the back and keeping my head down!

The *Sussex Express and County Herald* admirably picked out the essence and flavour of the discussion:

'... Mr. R.P. Field, Surveyor and Engineer to Battle R.D.C., said the Rector had persuaded the church authorities to allow the conveniences to be built entirely on churchyard land. If that site was chosen the building would be constructed in such a way as to blend with the surroundings.

The reservoir site in Rectory Lane had been considered, he added, but Hastings Corporation were submitting a plan for a house on it and there was also the problem of providing lay-bys.

A representative of the Methodist Church said it would be wrong to put the toilets on the reservoir site [beside] the historic Winchelsea Chapel. Traffic hazards on what was to become the trunk road would also be created. He thought there was no room in Winchelsea for public toilets and suggested they should be put outside the town near [either] the Sandrock [or] Strand garages.

Another resident said toilets were not necessary in Winchelsea. "People should be able to control their bodily functions until they reach Hastings or Rye," she said. The provision of toilets would not stop "warped and evil people" from using the churchyard [which was what they had been doing in the absence of other facilities].

But the landlord of the Castle Inn said that he knew from the number of people using the toilets at the inn of the need for the amenity.

The rector said Winchelsea had a responsibility as a community to provide toilets for the many visitors to the town. Nearly 100,000 people visited the church each year and, in donations, paid most of the money for the upkeep of the churchyard – the centre point of the town. "It is a moral obligation and a desperate need," he added.

Then came the corporation's idea... Mr. Bruce said the corporation thought it necessary to link the new toilets with a coach and car park. They considered the site in German Street could be used without detriment to the town's character. The county surveyor had been informed of their suggestion and had said he would strongly recommend it to the planning committee.

A member of the corporation, Capt. Herbert Lovegrove, said he had reservations about the plan. It would be all right as long as the car park was used by cars and coaches. He was supported by another member, Mr. Harry Wenban.

But Mr. Field said he thought there was a lot of sense in the proposal and he would be prepared to put it before the rural council.'[20]

And so a further step was taken in seeking a solution. Winchelsea was becoming something of a laughing-stock over the matter. This was made clear in the mayor's letter apologising for his absence because of a long-standing business meeting. He referred to a television broadcast 'to the whole of South-East England' of which he had been told. Had he known in advance, 'I would have done my utmost to stop such unnecessary, unwanted and undignified publicity. The matter was, and is, of no concern to anyone other than those represented here. It is a private matter between the people of Winchelsea and the civil authorities.'[21] Some hope then, no hope now!

The idea of building in the churchyard was further pursued after the corporation's apparent victory. In December 1972 the planning applications mentioned above were submitted. On 6 January 1973 Mrs. Clare Tanburn reported to the honorary secretary of the parochial church council that 237 residents, nearly all living in the town area, had so far signed a petition headed 'We, the undersigned, being parishioners of Winchelsea with Winchelsea Beach, petition that a Faculty BE NOT GRANTED for the building of public toilets in the churchyard, as we consider it would be desecrating ground consecrated for 600 years and still in use as a graveyard.'[22]

However, things were running in favour of Mrs. Tanburn, her supporters, and Winchelsea Corporation, despite allegations from their opponents that all they were trying to do was to get the toilets placed as far outside the town as possible. On 14 September 1973 a *Sussex Express* article was headed 'GERMAN STREET CHOSEN TO END THAT BATTLE OVER WINCHELSEA LOOS'. The final agonised debate on the subject took place in the county planning committee where a lady member, succinctly if inelegantly, declared to laughter: 'This has been going on for three years and we have just sat on our backsides and done nothing.' Doubts were still rife. Dr. Michael Klust, vice-chairman of the committee, said, 'I went to Winchelsea on my own and there are a great number of people there who do not agree with this site. I am not sure whether this is being pushed through by local councils with the non-agreement of the local people who merely live there, or not. It seems to be a complete Clochemerle situation.' However, strong assertions that it was indeed the local people who had suggested and supported the site carried the day and permission was granted despite a statement that the social services department, as owners, would not agree.[23]

The protests of the residents of Trojan's Plat fell on deaf ears. One of them wrote, 'I am sure that many tourists who have admired the park when driving into the town would share our objection.'[24] A highly valid point at the time although in the later years of East Sussex County Council's ownership the park was so shamefully neglected that the same objection could not have been made.

One interesting side product of the rather unexpected granting and implementation of this permission was that the archaeological exploration of the site was undertaken before major building commenced although some damage had already been caused by the stripping of the turf. A detailed article about the outcome entitled *A Medieval Town House in German Street, Winchelsea* was later published by Anthony King B.A. This records the discovery of the remains and layout of two houses, set slightly differently upon the site, the first probably dating from the foundation of New Winchelsea, and the second having been abandoned between the mid-fifteenth and mid-sixteenth centuries. Those interested in archaeology and in the fact that the vast majority of Winchelsea's original layout remains available for excavation beneath the fields, will find this account rewarding and informative.[25]

After the excavation the toilets were built. Controversy between the corporation and others has been reported elsewhere. In this chapter the score might well be one all. It is not the purpose of this book to be controversial, to comment on whose observations reported above were prophetic, or to re-open old wounds. Those readers who know the town must decide for themselves whether, in the context of current needs, the conveniences are in fact convenient.

(61) The Winchelsea public conveniences.

29. ST. THOMAS'S SCHOOL

As we saw in the previous chapter, one of the controversial sites proposed for council housing in Winchelsea, that in Greyfriars' orchard, was later used for the replacement of the old St. Thomas's School which had been in St. Thomas's Street, where the rectory now stands, since 1873. The new premises were first occupied in 1966 but the official opening was not carried out until 5 July, the eve of St. Thomas's Day, in 1968. A visit today will reveal the school, nestling purposefully and unobtrusively into the site where, even though a large number of its pupils come from outside the town, it provides a heartbeat for a largely elderly community and plays a vital part in giving the town balance, as do the council houses eventually sited elsewhere.

The pre-nineteenth century history of education in Winchelsea is, as far as is yet known to me, a matter of conjecture. Best qualified to undertake any such conjecture was Captain Herbert Lovegrove who was not only a leading Winchelsea resident and historian but also, for a considerable time, Deputy Secretary of the National Society for Promoting Religious Education in Accordance with the Principles of the Church of England, generally known for brevity and convenience as the National Society. In a paper entitled *Education in Winchelsea* he suggested that at the foundation of the new town the Knights of St. John, the gable end of whose training place for squires survives in Chapel Field, and, rather later, the Blackfriars, established under the patronage of Queen Eleanor, first wife of King Edward I, would both have assumed responsibility for the education of the young, as, doubtless would the six priests attached to the Church of St. Thomas the Martyr, and the Franciscans (Greyfriars), part of whose site is now occupied by the school.[1]

For definite evidence we have to move ahead almost four hundred and fifty years when the overseers of St. Thomas's paid a Mr. Hogsflesh one pound ten shillings on 30 May 1766 for a year's education of three boys. This information is included in John Caffyn's forthcoming book *Sussex Schools in the Eighteenth Century* and during his detailed and painstaking research Mr. Caffyn discovered similar payments made in the following two years. He presumes that Hogsflesh was keeping a private school to which the three boys were sent.[2]

On 4 May 1815 a public meeting was held at the Court Hall with Richard Stileman in the chair. The purpose of this well attended gathering was to seek to found a school in succession to Hogsflesh's, specifically for the children of the poor of the parishes of Winchelsea and Icklesham. This establishment was to give extensive religious instruction with the children attending divine service in their respective churches every Sunday. It is no surprise to find that Rev. Drake Hollingberry, Rector of Winchelsea and Vicar of Icklesham, was the prime mover and he was elected secretary and treasurer at the head of a committee of no fewer than thirty-two leading citizens. Among the committee members the Winchelsea family names which feature elsewhere in this book were, apart from the two already mentioned, those of Denne, Browne, Wright, Tilden, Gybbon and Fuller. The committee was empowered to limit the pupils' ages to between six and fourteen, to accept annual subscriptions of ten shillings, each conferring a right to send one child to the school, to make all the necessary rules and regulations for its management and to find suitable premises. Those found were in a thatched building situated beside the present site of Saffron Gardens and were the origin of the name School Hill. It later became a cottage, one time home of Charles Potter, and was not pulled down until the 1950s.

At a subsequent meeting it was decided that subscribers might pay for the education of more than one child, that any pupil 'incorrigibly ill-behaved' could be expelled after appearing before the committee's monthly meeting in the Vestry Room, and that a schoolmaster and mistress 'regularly instructed in the plan of the National Society' should be appointed.[3]

The project was not successful in the longer term. Although in 1818 it was stated to be educating forty boys and forty-two girls as originally planned, by 1835 it had slipped from notice and Winchelsea's only day school, established by the then rector, Rev. James John West, was educating 38 children at the expense of their parents while West himself paid the master's salary.[4] Pigot and Company's *Directory of Sussex* for 1839 lists a National School, which nevertheless is not included among the records of the National Society, with Samuel Cloud as master and as mistress Caroline Easton. This must be Mr. West's establishment for Samuel Cloud was one of the rector's strongest supporters in the disputes which bedevilled his incumbency. Also listed by Pigot in the same publication are Winchelsea schools run by Charles Jones (day), Mrs. Kennett (boarding and day) and Kitty Maplesden (day) but we have no other details about them.

Information about a school which existed in the town a little earlier was discovered by William Maclean Homan and included in his unpublished *History of Winchelsea,* even though its date is well after the period it was his intention to cover. His account is best quoted verbatim:

'For a number of years from 1822 onwards the educational needs of Winchelsea were attended to by Mr. W. Needham, familiarly known to his scholars as "Cocky" Needham. He does not appear to have succeeded in keeping order among the boys and these therefore were often sent to Rye School. A card by Mr. Needham, announcing his venture, is of interest and reads as follows: "W. Needham respectfully acquaints his Friends and the Inhabitants of Winchelsea that he has taken a House in (that) town for the purpose of establishing a Day and Evening School for a limited number of pupils and that by a strict attention to their Education and Morals to merit the honour of their support. Terms include books. Reading three shillings and sixpence per quarter; Reading and Writing eight shillings per quarter; Reading, Writing and Arithmetic twelve shillings and sixpence. Drawing fifteen shillings per quarter. Books, Pens, Ink and Paper sold." We do not know where the worthy Dominie's school was situated or when it ceased to function but the parents of persons still living acquired knowledge and no doubt had their minds improved by the worthy gentleman's tuition.' [Written in about 1939][5]

By the 1850s when John Carey attended the School Hill establishment the mistress was Mrs. George Hearnden, wife of the postmaster later to be chamberlain.[6] Carey made no complaint about the instruction he received there despite the fact that in 1849 it was noted as being in an extremely unsatisfactory state and by 1873, as pressure grew to establish a new school, evidence about its predecessor was given as follows:

'There is a school, held in a cottage of two rooms, belonging to and supported by a residential landowner [Major Robert Stileman], undenominational; taught by a dame [Mrs. Hearnden]. This will be superseded. This school is "scarce worthy the name". There is no Sunday school nor, till these schools (sic) are built, any place in which to hold one. With the exception of the residential landowner [mentioned] above the population is almost exclusively poor.'[7]

Principal instigator on this occasion was Rev. Edward Whitehead who had very recently succeeded James John West on his precipitate departure. Whitehead wanted to build a mixed and infants' school of three rooms with accommodation for 70 boys and girls and 45 infants. For each family fees of twopence a week would be chargeable for the first child and one penny for each younger brother or sister. The site in St. Thomas's Street was in fact sold by the rector, who held the glebe property, to himself and the churchwardens for the sum of £46. 19s. 0d.[8] The certificate of completion lists the income and expenditure account as follows: [9]

Receipts	£	Costs	£
Subscriptions	402	School	533
County	115	Fittings	25
Diocese	30	Legal	20
National Society	30		
	577		578

A loss of £1! The design of the building, beautifully drawn by the architect, shows the school so well known to all of us who were residents attending meetings there or were pupils during almost one hundred years of its use.[10]

The introduction of the 1870 Education Act under which the children's attendance became compulsory was a major preoccupation for the school's managers in the following years. In 1879 a special vestry meeting of ratepayers was convened to consider school attendance. It was decided to apply to the School Attendance Committee of the Rye Union for the introduction of by-laws implementing the acts. Parents of children between the ages of four and twelve were required to ensure their offspring's attendance unless they were ill, 'under efficient instruction in some other manner', or unless there was no school within three miles of their home. A child over the age of ten need not attend if he or she was certificated as having reached Standard V, or, if gainfully employed, for more than 75 school days between 11 October and 6 April annually. Sixteen leading citizens, under the guidance of Dr. Robert Vaile Skinner, worked their way through many intricacies of the legislation and concluded by passing a vote of thanks to their chairman 'for his services at this meeting'.[11]

A further result of the legislation was that the school became overcrowded within less than twenty years of its construction. In 1892 Mr. Marshall Ames was contracted by the managers, on whose behalf signed Rev. Henry Patch, rector, Robert Stileman and Frederic Inderwick, to build an additional classroom with 'Gallery to hold 47' at the north side of the building, extending towards St. Thomas's Street.[12] The school log books of the period show numbers ranging between 80 and 100 so this would have been a most necessary relief of the pressure on space.

These log books, kept meticulously if somewhat unimaginatively by the school's long serving and conscientious head, Miss Susannah Passey, provide us with many insights into the school life of the times. Those who visit the school are noted, usually without comment. Most frequent were the rector, Rev. Mr. Patch and his successors who were ex-officio chairmen of the managers. Major and Miss Stileman were regular callers in the early days as was Mrs. Annie Freeman later. Assistance was also given by residents from time to time, notably by Mrs. Patch with needlework. Such help was normally warmly welcomed but there seems a certain guarded lack of enthusiasm in the entry written by Louisa Fagg on 16 February 1917. 'Miss Beddington has kindly been to school each day this week to try and give some help with Standard II'. Miss Fagg, formerly headmistress of West Wratting School, Cambridge, took up her post in 1915 to succeed Miss Passey 'whose certificate had expired', presumably on grounds of age.

The illness of both staff and pupils features frequently in these records. In 1903 the examination of Standards I and II had to be postponed from August to November 'as nearly all the children were absent with whooping cough'. It was the same disease which later earned Douglas

Turner a special entry which noted that he had 'come back to school after six weeks' absence on account of whooping cough.' An epidemic of 'flu, which was also caught by the head, caused complete closure of the school in 1905. In 1910 ringworm was the current scourge, 'Dr. Finch came and excluded some children'. Much later an outbreak of measles caused a further complete closure.

The weather, too, had a great impact on attendance particularly as those living at a distance, notably the coastguards' children, had to walk every day. In October 1896 those pupils were prevented from attending and there must have been a severe winter to follow for in January and February 1897 the school failed to meet for a considerable time. An entry for 9 December 1929 reflects, in this connection, an incident to which I have already referred: '34 children are absent today owing to the violent storm and flooding of marshland.' (see pp.103-104)

Occasionally the log books provide us with glimpses of the curriculum. A hundred years ago educational practice revered the object lesson as a purposeful way of imparting knowledge. On 29 April 1895 the head recorded a list of such lessons which had been given during the previous two terms. They were:

> 1.Tea 2.Sugar 3.Coal 4.The Camel 5.Timber 6.Salt 7.Rice 8.Chalk 9.Cork 10.The Silkworm 11.A Lead Pencil 12.Cotton 13.Needles 14.Pins 15.Slate 16.Silver 17.Coffee 18.Chocolate 19.Candles 20.Gold 21.A Lighthouse 22.The Elephant 23.The Horse 24.The Ostrich 25.The Bear 26.The Whale 27.The Cuckoo 28.Matches 29.Potatoes 30.Bees[13]

No doubt the children, under a firm hand, and with the encouragement they seem to have had, eagerly took in and sought information about this strange assortment. Miss Passey's commitment to the school was beyond question and when problems appeared she set about solving them with whatever means were available, including her own. In 1910 His Majesty's Inspectors reported of her:

> 'The mistress has taken special pains in which she is well supported by her assistant to introduce organised games, even procuring material at her own expense. Unfortunately the school yard, [always a bone of contention, particularly as regards its surface], the only space available, is somewhat limited. It is to be hoped that the occasional use of a field may be secured'.[14]

It was during the headship of Miss Marson, thirteen years later, that this was eventually achieved, although without the equal consideration of the sexes which would be expected today. Mr. Piper of Fairview, Hawkhurst wrote:

> 'Dear Madam,
>
>   I have given permission for your boys to play in the 10 acre, hoping they will keep the gate shut and conduct themselves in a proper way. I have told my shepherd, Cooke, about it.
>
> Yours faithfully,
>
> Edward Piper[15]

Occasionally the availability of such facilities and the practice they provided was spectacularly successful. The log-book entry for 4 December 1929 records: Guestling School football team visited for a friendly match today. The result was Winchelsea 10 goals, Guestling 0.'

The facilities on the school site were pretty primitive. In 1903 the managers resolved that 'lavatories be not provided'. 'Closets' were already available but there was to be no additional paving

(62) The old school in St. Thomas's Street.

between them and the school. H.M. Inspectors later complained that there was no proper supply of water for drinking purposes. 'Resolved that the correspondent... arrange for the supply and fixing of a tap by the wall near the old well.' Complaints 'of a bad smell in the infants' room' were received and the managers 'being unable to detect any smell and considering it impossible that the smell could arise from any drain decided to take no steps at present.' Toilets were again under debate in 1929 when no extra lavatory would be provided because numbers were about to fall 'and then it would not be necessary', and in 1930 when 'a special teachers' W.C. will not be provided.' The open fires recalled by Margaret Muggridge and Ted Streeton's stove (see below) appear to have lasted until 1936 when a replacement stove was fitted and the guard placed further away in case coals fell out. Electricity was eventually installed in 1935 to replace the oil-lamps.

In the early days the main school holiday was between late August and early October to allow the children to work at harvest time and hop-picking. An attempt to change this in 1918 was singularly unsuccessful. After opening on 9 September the school had to be shut again because so many were away on agricultural employment. Even when term re-commenced on 23 September there were still twenty absentees. Other distractions occasionally intervened: '24 August 1920: Only 52 children present this afternoon on account of a circus in Rye.'[16]

Maybe the leading students were not among them for under Miss Fagg's stern guidance the school was approaching one of its more notable academic achievements. The log-book for 14 July 1921 records:

'We have heard today that all the five children who entered for the Rye Grammar School scholarship have been successful and obtained free places. Their names are as follows – Dorothy Cooke, Margaret Boley, Arthur Penney, Douglas Turner and Kenneth Jeffery.'[17]

Later the head discovered that her pupils had obtained the first four and the seventh places on a list of fifty competitors. Douglas Turner was never told which of those places was his but it was an achievement, both personal and collective, in which he took great pride throughout his life. Douglas's recollections of St. Thomas's School were enthusiastic:

'In my days there the schoolroom was in two sections and a glass partition came through. The bit nearest Nelgarde was the upper school and the bit this side was the junior and the infants'. There was a piece built out on this end next to Haskards for a separate room [the 1892 extension] You moved through the classes. Ted Streeton was at school with me – he still lives in Winchelsea… I think the others have all gone… Miss Fagg was the head and we had various second teachers, Miss Walker was there for some time. A Miss Passey was the infant teacher. Her older sister was originally the head – she retired soon after I went there. Miss Fagg was a very good disciplinarian and, to give you an idea, there were ten free places to the grammar school in our year and this school took five of them – that's the sort of teacher she was. She was also organist and choirmistress and if you'd got any kind of voice you were in the choir whether you liked it or not.'[18]

Margaret Muggridge was not so convinced that Miss Fagg's passion for church music was good for the school's academic record. She recalled, of her move from Rye to Winchelsea:

(63) Miss Fagg with her pupils, 1918.

'It was a church school and the parson had quite a lot of say in the running of it. Two maiden sisters ran the school named Miss Passey and Miss Annie Passey who took the infants which Lester [Margaret's brother] was in. I don't think Miss Passey liked us new arrivals but we had not been there long when they retired and a new teacher arrived named Miss Fagg. Most of the war we were a teacher short and the older children had the privilege of taking the younger ones which we loved.

The school was heated by big open fires with a guard round and if you sat at the back it was perishing cold. During our teaching duties we started baking potatoes. One day Arthur Wheeler was seen in front of the class eating an enormous potato. As the classroom was divided by a glass partition he was in full view of Miss Fagg – that put an end to Arthur's teaching.

I liked Miss Fagg very much but I don't think we learned as much as at Rye. She became the organist of the parish church and took the choir so we spent quite a lot of time practising church hymns etc.'[19]

Ted Streeton, who describes himself as one of the school's worst pupils, vividly remembers the stove which succeeded these fires. When it was really cold, which it frequently was, he would, when unobserved, quietly open a window, slip out and make his way home.

Whether Douglas Turner or Margaret Muggridge made the better assessment of Miss Fagg, she certainly provided a stability which the school sorely lacked during the 1920s and early 1930s which saw as head teacher successively Eleanor Johnson, Eunice Marson (who unfortunately left under a cloud following a critical H.M.I. report), Katherine Brown, Eva Peulevé (of whom mention has been made elsewhere), Violet Prentice, Mary Coates and Gladys Walker. Whatever the individual qualities of these various ladies, the school struggled in the face of such numerous changes and despite much accompanying encouragement this is reflected in reports which were made.

The principal reason for the instability was that Winchelsea had no school house. Miss Fagg left, immediately after the great success of her grammar school scholarship winners, for this very reason and the problem made appointing successors increasingly difficult. Madame Peulevé made strong representations about the rent she was having to pay but when she suggested that the school authorities should purchase a bungalow at the bottom of Strand Hill, they declined on grounds of cost and she departed to take charge at Fairlight. Numerous solutions were suggested and negotiations undertaken. One principal potential site was on land adjoining the school but its legal status and ownership rights created a long wrangle; eventually it became part of Miss Forbes-Dunlop's garden when she was living at Glebe. Anthony Freeman offered a plot beside the New Hall in exchange for the land beside Glebe but this came to nothing. No help was forthcoming from the county council and the managers eventually surrendered to the inevitable for, even if they acquired a suitable site, they would not be able to afford to build a house on it.[20]

Saviour of the school amidst all this uncertainty was Miss Lilah Christine Smith. Her headship from April 1934 until July 1962 provided rock-solid stability through frequently troubled times. She was unfailingly supported by Mrs. Florence Brakefield who had earlier served the school as Miss Harman from 1918 until 1928 when she left to get married. On her appointment Miss Smith inherited seventy-six pupils and one assistant. Her request for a third teacher was turned down by the local education authority. When the numbers increased to 86 a further request was similarly dismissed but on 11 September 1935 it was finally agreed to appoint a monitress, Miss

Eileen McDonald, at a salary of five shillings a week.

Lilah Smith had to cope with further uncertainty not of her own making during her early days at the school. Within a month of her arrival the rector and chairman of the managers was complaining to the National Society that the local attendance officer was telling parents of the advantages to children of eleven years and over of attending a senior school, one of which had been opened in Rye, and thus seducing pupils away from St. Thomas's. The Society was sympathetic but opined that it was not 'practicable within limits of reasonable

(64) Mrs Brakefield and Miss Smith (right) welcome their pupils c.1960.

expenditure to give as great educational opportunities to the elder charges as can be provided for them at a larger senior school.' The rector responded sharply that religious instruction was far more important for the children than any secular instruction. The trickle of older pupils moving to Rye did not become a flood but the inevitable consequence was that, despite Winchelsea's insistence on retaining an all-age school, Miss Smith lost her third teacher, so recently hard won. Further pressure followed in which East Sussex County Council declined to help financially with the essential reinstatement of the playground unless the managers expressed a willingness to co-operate in reorganisation which would involve the promotion to Rye of all senior children when they reached the age of eleven. This rather spiteful piece of blackmail was sustained even when the chairman of the county council took Winchelsea's side.[21]

All such problems paled quickly into insignificance beside the confusion with which Lilah Smith had to deal following the outbreak of the Second World War. Only seventeen days after war was declared the children of Crawford Street School, Camberwell were evacuated to Winchelsea, thus effectively doubling the town's school population in one day. Apart from the addition of this complete school community, another 34 children entered the area as evacuees not under the government scheme and these were added to the St. Thomas's register. Education in the town was prevented from bursting at the seams by a double shift system with the pupils of St. Thomas's meeting between 9 a.m. and 1 p.m. during which times one of the Crawford Street teachers came to assist with the extra numbers.[22] On 21 June 1940, by which time invasion rather than the bombing of London had become the threat, Crawford Street School was re-evacuated to Wales. Numbers returned to normal but were soon to be reduced by the complete evacuation of Winchelsea Beach which became a military area. An increasing number of the school's pupils came from there and Miss Smith was urged by the authorities to try to persuade the parents of these pupils to allow them to accompany the Rye school party due to leave on 21 July.[23]

Arrangements had, of course, to be made for the children's safety during air raids. An official from the County Architect's department inspected and approved the church crypt which was being used for that purpose. If it was not possible to get them there they were to be assembled in the infants' classroom. Whole mornings and afternoons were spent in the crypt but fortunately during that time numbers were low, average attendances being only in the twenties. It was not until August 1943 that eight Morrison table-shelters were delivered to the school for the children's use. Only seventeen pupils were present on 16 June 1944 and they spent almost all the time in these shelters for 'pilotless planes were passing overhead.'

With the school mercifully escaping serious damage during the war, as did its parent church, the tenure of Lilah Smith and Florence Brakefield settled to post-war normality. Their long and distinguished service ended when they retired together in July 1962. The attitude of the mayor and corporation was in contrast to their reaction to Alex Finch's leaving as postmaster. Both ladies were sent a cheque for £10 and a letter from the mayor, Anthony Freeman, deeply appreciating their services to the community. Both responded gratefully and graciously. Miss Smith, emphasising her great enjoyment of her work in the town, suggested that as they were planning a holiday in Italy together, she might well purchase a camera and colour film to use there.[24] Lilah Smith spent her twenty-one years of retirement in Winchelsea. On her death in 1983 the *Sussex Express* published a short appreciation in which her brother was quoted as saying that she took much pleasure in having taught the grandchildren of pupils who were there when she first became head.[25] Although this might have been possible for Mrs. Brakefield who started at the school in 1918, it seems less than likely for someone with just over twenty-eight years' service. Nevertheless it emphasises the value to a school and a community of such continuity when it is accompanied by kindly but very firm leadership.

Before these retirements there were already plans for the replacement of the 1873 school buildings in St. Thomas's Street which were becoming both unsatisfactory and unsafe. The situation deteriorated rapidly, provoking visits by the Chief Education Officer to view cracks in ceilings and walls, the arrival of Southern Television cameras after an anonymous tip-off about the dangerous state of the school's roof, an urgent call to Turner Bros. asking them to come and repair collapsing pillars on the wall bordering St. Thomas's Street and, in December 1965, a note by the head, Arthur Webb, 'The builder advised me to move my class from the southern classroom because the widening cracks may lead to falling plaster.'[26]

The school in Greyfriars orchard first came into use twelve months later in December 1966 under a new head, Enid Harper. The move was not without its traumas. Mrs. Harper returned from the previous half-term holiday to find that her telephone had been transferred to the as yet unopened building. She had an awful job getting it back![27] The former site was sold for a new rectory following which the land and house in Rectory Lane where Rev. J.J. West had built in the mid-nineteenth century were sold, the land subsequently being developed as St. Giles' Close.

As already mentioned, the official opening of the new school took place on 5 July 1968. The guest of honour was Lady Winifred Paget, widow of General Sir Bernard Paget G.C.B.,

(65) The present school at Greyfriars.

Commander-in-Chief Home Forces during the Second World War and a former Governor of the Royal Hospital, Chelsea. Their family had long and distinguished connections with the Church of England. Lady Paget was accompanied by the Bishop of Lewes, Rt. Rev. J.H.L. Morrell who dedicated and blessed the building. The school was packed with 250 people including more than sixty pupils. Chairman of the Managers was the rector, Rev. R.M. Ware, who was described by the head teacher, Mrs. Harper, as 'a tower of strength and a very real focal point in our community.' The *Sussex Express*'s account of the speeches and their content suggests that there may have been some glassy-eyed guests and some wriggly children but the proceedings burst into life when the pupils 'expressed their thanks to Lady Paget and the bishop in song', guests viewed an exhibition of the children's work and tea included a celebration cake.[28]

In the school log-book the headmistress wrote:' The children behaved beautifully, sang well and tried to be very good hosts and hostesses. They served tea and showed their exhibition of work.' They received their due reward, Lady Paget asked for a full day's school holiday and this was granted.[29]

The financing of the new school had caused considerable problems, particularly for the managers of whose share £1843 6s 4d remained unpaid on completion of the project which had cost a total of £30,353. The managers put out an appeal to parents which met with limited response and an attempt to claw back diocesan funds which had earlier been raised for education in Winchelsea was unsuccessful. The financial uncertainty was supplemented by doubts over St. Thomas's status as a Voluntary Aided School which was the responsibility of the parish and whether, in view of the shortage of money and the fact that its pupils were being drawn increasingly from outside the parish, Voluntary Controlled status should be sought.[30]

Such doubts had no effect upon the school's great educational success and rapidly increasing numbers were attracted by the success of Mrs. Harper and her staff and that of her successor, Mr. Haydn Davies. Indeed, the situation improved so much that the managers had to consider what were their rights to refuse pupils above their standard number of 75 rather than how on earth to attract more.

Mr. Davies produced a booklet entitled *Coming to School* which was considerably ahead of its time in providing advice for parents about preparing their children for the school environment, information about the school's day to day procedures, its curriculum, its sports and even its menu. Under his leadership a uniform was adopted and he neatly pointed up a problem which has escalated in education generally over the thirty years that St. Thomas's has been in its new buildings:

> 'School does not exist to save parents from teaching their own children; it is merely a society between the intimate life of the home and the wild life of the world. Teachers cannot do their job properly unless there is mutual co-operation.'

He also took an intense interest in local history and, with the support and help of his family, produced a study guide for the use not only of his own pupils but also of other schools. Haydn Davies and his wife Margaret who had been school secretary retired in 1981 after ten years' service.[31]

Since that time the work of the school has continued to thrive. Additional classroom space has been added and in 1995 a further extension providing a resources room, staffroom and headteacher's office was opened by the Bishop of Lewes. Such developments succour and support a vital part of any small community. I am sure that under the present head, Mrs. Hilary Moore, and her successors, Winchelsea's school will sustain its progress and prosper in the future.

30. KEEPING THE LOOKOUT

For many years in the middle of the twentieth century, during the time that the old school was reaching the end of its life and the new was being constructed, the one piece of information known to very large numbers of people with no other knowledge of Winchelsea was that there was still an official appointed annually to keep a watch lest the marauding and invading French should once again appear in numbers over the horizon with the intention of ransacking the town as their predecessors had done six centuries previously. Sadly such a watch was never officially kept but the story of how this myth became current is well worth telling.

Until the Municipal Corporations Act of 1883 came into force Winchelsea Corporation appointed annually at the Easter Monday mayoring a pound driver whose duty it was to take charge of cattle and sheep found wandering in the streets and to keep them in the pound until they were identified and claimed, presumably on payment of a charge or fine. Winchelsea's pound was, in the early years of the nineteenth century, next to part of the Mariteau House garden but the Denne family, then resident, felt it a somewhat degrading neighbour and exchanged the site with the corporation for a piece of garden land between Yew Tree House and Rectory Lane.[1] The mayor and jurats decided to let their new property to the owner of Yew Tree House as part of his garden and to find an alternative place for the pound which they eventually did, in School Hill. Its occasional use for detaining animals was eventually discontinued and the land is now largely occupied by Pound Cottage although a small section remains the property of the corporation and is leased to Seeboard for an electricity sub-station.

With no cattle to arrest the pound driver became a caretaker and at the mayoring in 1887 his duties on appointment were described in the official record as 'To see after The Lookout and The Pound'.[2] By 1894 reference to the pound had been deleted and the maintenance of Spring Steps, referred to as 'paths to the Tanyard' substituted. During these changes the office holder was James Wheeler who was paid one pound a year as caretaker of these two properties. The occasional reference to 'keeping' The Lookout rather than looking after it left much opportunity for different interpretation later!

It was Frederick Barden who first set about generating publicity by re-interpreting the phrase 'Keeping the Lookout'. An undated newspaper cutting held in the Court Hall Museum features a picture of a gentleman wearing a top hat and wellington boots. The caption reads 'No Norman Conquest again while Mr. "Chummy" Barden, aged seventy-seven, continues to perform the duties of look-out that he has undertaken at Winchelsea, Sussex for fifty years. He gets paid £1. 12s. 6d. a year for his job of watching the English Channel for invading ships.' Since Mr. Barden held the position only from 1929 until 1943 the newspaper's estimate of his length of service seems somewhat exaggerated but he certainly made the best use of potential interest in his presumed duties. One of his great-nephews, Graham Bevis, wrote of him:

> '"Chummie" Barden lived in the town all his life until he was bombed out in January 1943 [he is listed among the casualties of that incident as having been seriously injured[3]] when he moved to live with my mother in Hastings until his death in 1945 at the age of 85. He was Keeper of the Lookout for many years until the 1939/45 war. He could often be seen at The Lookout where he was a popular figure with visitors and children as he always had a good tale to tell. He could be persuaded to have his photograph taken in his "official" uniform.

If he was not at The Lookout he could usually be found at his "local", the New Inn. Another of his titles was Shove-Penny Champion of all England and there was never any shortage of visitors during the summer to challenge him on the shove-penny board. I never knew how good he was but I do not think he bought a lot of beer!'[4]

Chummy Barden could neither read nor write, although in his later years he learnt to sign his name. Those who knew him remember, however, almost with awe, his skill at mental calculations. He was the last manager of the quarry in Greyfriars Park and when the road through the Hiham estate was to be laid Chummy worked out the amount of materials required accurate to one wheelbarrow full.

During Chummy Barden's term of office a letter to the *Sussex County Magazine* from a reader in Northampton sought information about Winchelsea's Lookout and a similar one at the end of Watchbell Street, Rye. The writer added, 'I have been informed that the one at Winchelsea is still used as a sort of coastguard, a payment being made to the official in charge. Is this correct?' There was only one authority in the town at the time who would readily respond to such an inquiry, W.M. Homan. This he duly did in the February 1938 edition when he wrote forcefully pointing out that this belief was nonsense and that if a watch had been kept from any point, the adjoining towers of Strand Gate would have been much more convenient. Mr. Homan added that The Lookout, in its present form with the lean-to shelter was constructed during Samuel Griffiths' mayoralty in 1866/67, a contemporary newspaper giving the reason as 'because it has a prospect of great beauty and is a resort of visitors and the poor.'[5]

(66) Chummy Barden

Its use as a local gathering place was evocatively described by Ford Madox Ford:

'Here, on a rainy day, one may sit and enjoy life at leisure. The marsh stretches out below one's feet; beyond that a narrow strip of sea and the narrower strip of pebble-land on which stands Dungeness Lighthouse; beyond that again more sea and the cliffs near Folkestone. The whole expanse of Romney Marsh is visible on the left and, on the right, the full sweep of the Channel. One may sit there and lazily read, glancing occasionally at the small figures of the people wandering along the road towards the sea. One may, if one cares, speculate on who they are, where they are going, why they are none of them a whit better than they should be, and, if it is a soaking day, on how wet they will get. For the patron of the nook is, without doubt, Dame Gossip.'[6]

But it was as a place of watch-keeping that the general public insisted in viewing it. Writing soon after the Second World War, undeterred by W.M. Homan's denials, Ronald and Frank Jessup solemnly reported that a daily watch was still kept 'between seven and eight in the morning by the Keeper of the Lookout… A frock coat, top hat and large telescope seem to be the accepted uniform for this officer, who still watches for the ships from France'.[7]

They may have been so informed pre-war by Mr. Barden for it was he who wore the top hat, but from the time of his appointment in 1944 it was Fred Curd who further embellished the story and attracted much attention. Inquiries to the town clerk, Edwin Dawes, from journalists in Wimbledon and Liverpool in 1950 elicited somewhat vague replies as though he was reluctant to deny the story.[8] By 1958 Michael Frayn, writing for *The Guardian*, again despite such denials as Homan's, invested the watch-keeping with factual certainty:

> 'Every now and then they find some forgotten island in the Pacific inhabited by
> Japanese soldiers who have still not heard that the Second World War has ended. This,
> I now discover, is nothing. I have just found a place in Sussex where they are still
> paying a man to look out for the coming of the French invasion fleet.'[9]

This man was, of course, Fred Curd, one of the corporation's macebearers, also appointed to 'Keep the Lookout'. Mr. Curd was wounded in the First World War and later became blind in one eye. After he suffered a fractured skull while fire-watching during the Second World War he was told he would never work again but his corporation responsibilities provided considerable opportunity to keep himself occupied and sometimes to earn himself tips from tourists for whom he would dress up in his sergeant-at-mace's costume and pose as keeping the lookout. Charles Croggon well remembered him doing this and even wearing a black patch over his bad eye to heighten the effect.[10]

All this enterprising acting was entirely unauthorised and it provoked considerable consternation in the corporation, particularly to the mayor, David Homan, son of William, when in November 1964 Fred Curd told a *Daily Express* reporter that he had asked for a telescope to assist him in his duties. He complained to his eager listener that the sea was two miles away and his eyesight was not getting any better although he could occasionally pick out a French fishing boat, a few tankers and the outline of Dungeness Nuclear Power Station. He had once seen a barge on fire and spotted 'the doodlebugs' during the last war. Pressed as to what he would do if the French fleet came into view Fred said that he would 'run straight to the local for a large whisky to get over the shock'. The reporter managed to track down the mayor who responded testily: 'No, Mr. Curd can't have a telescope. He needn't worry looking out for a French invasion.'[11]

The news spread rapidly round the world.

A few days later the German newspaper *Die Welt* published a picture of Fred Curd standing on the sea wall at Winchelsea Beach dressed in a cap and donkey jacket rather than robes, staring out to sea through a telescope. This in turn provoked an inquiry from John P. Wynn who was compiling for the B.B.C. a programme entitled *What Do You Know?* 'in which we regularly use interesting old facts.' From Toledo, Ohio came a stern warning that Winchelsea stopped looking out for the French at its peril. 'Would you leave your house, with all your possessions, unlocked and unguarded? Would you leave the children of your town without the protection of local police? Likewise will you leave your coast unguarded?' From Pukekshi, New Zealand came a similar anguished plea. The provision of a telescope 'would preserve tradition and heritage, provide a human touch in a frequently inhuman world, and "cock a snook" at those who would have everyone living in drab uniformity in a life devoid of small pleasures… and the sparkle of a slightly daft touch

(67) Fred Curd 'on duty' with an admiring crowd.

of eccentricity.' *The People* quoted Fred Curd as saying, 'Bain't no local folk take a happorth of notice of me doing me duty. But if some of them there Americans were to see me aspying away in me uniform, well, I'd make a few bob for beer money wouldn't I?' The paper commented, 'Crafty old Fred!' Southern Television prepared a programme about Winchelsea based on Fred's activities. The magazine *She* published the story with graphic illustrations, Hagar Visual Communications wrote from St. Louis, Missouri to say they would soon be in England and would like to shoot some footage of Mr. Curd together with general shots of Winchelsea to be added to their 'colour travelogue' of southern England which had already been seen by 20,000 people and would soon be seen by 35,000 more.

But the approach which really caused the mayor's patience to snap was one from Tasco Optics of Toronto. 'We should like you to present Mr. Curd with one of our TASCO telescopes which will be mailed to you this day.' The offer was declined by return and the sergeant-at-mace received the following:

> 'Dear Curd,
>
> I have suffered considerable inconvenience from foolish stories about you and a telescope.
>
> As you well know you are *not* employed as a lookout, and in fact the Corporation has never employed anyone to look out for anything and I must ask you to cease spreading such ridiculous tales.
>
> David Homan
>
> Mayor[12]

Within a few weeks the corporation suggested that the time had come for Fred Curd to retire and this he did at the Easter Monday mayoring in 1966 to be succeeded by Barry Stocks who received strict instructions not to perpetuate the lookout legend.

Fred Curd died in 1968 but fame and reputation lived on for him beyond the grave. In 1971 Lady Longford wrote to say she had found it stated in a book on Walmer Castle that a man was paid £5 a year to this day to watch for the French fleet. Was this at Winchelsea and could she safely include it in her forthcoming biography of the first Duke of Wellington?[13]

On Christmas Eve 1978 the *New York Times* returned to the story, telling it accurately and in full and quoting 'John Clark, a member of the town governing body [who] reflected on the old disputes between Winchelsea and the French as he and friends hung Christmas decorations in the 700 year old church built by Thomas a' Becket (sic). He shook his head and said "I don't know which were the bigger scoundrels." The article regretted Fred Curd's passing and said some Winchelsea people were not sure he was wrong in his suspicions of the French. 'Several residents assured a visitor – mistakenly as it turned out – that the town still kept a lookout on the payroll. An elderly habitue of the pubs added that it was not a bad idea either.'

This entertaining article prompted an even more entertaining response dated Christmas Day 1978:

> 'His Worship the Mayor,
>
> Town Hall,
>
> Winchelsea,
>
> Sussex,
>
> England.
>
> Your Worship,
>
> I have just read, gravely, the report in yesterday's *New York Times* that the lookout to France is no longer on guard at the port of Winchelsea.
>
> What if the French mobilize? My information is that their training and equipment have greatly improved since 1337. I also hear, less reliably, that they have built vessels with wheels which traverse the land once the crossing is made.
>
> It is alarming. What arms might they have we know nothing about. Guns? Guns? Have you heard of those things they call guns?

The thought troubles the night as well as foggy mornings. I left my native England 28 years ago, but have been returning frequently to check the fortifications, noting flaws here and there in the fletching, yet never doubting that England was safe with Winchelsea on guard.

Let me repair the breach. If you can enlist the man (or the woman nowadays) to keep watch o'er the beach from a high enough tree. I will commit myself to his (or, of course, her) keep at the time honoured (and still reasonable) rate of one pound 12½ pence per annum. Please do not thank me. Let me be Winchelsea's Fidus Achates [guarantor]. However, I will not approve any increase in remuneration above five per cent in any one year.

Faithfully for Winchelsea and England,

John Hutchinson,

Professor of Industrial Relations,

University of California, Los Angeles.

cc: Giscard d'Estaing, as a warning.'[14]

So ends this cautionary tale. Whatever may be its rights or wrongs, Chummy Barden and Fred Curd were the finest publicists that Winchelsea ever had.

(68) The Lookout – nineteenth century.

31. CLUBS AND SOCIETIES

In 1991, during the mayoralty of Anthony Tremeer, the corporation published a list which it entitled *The Societies, Clubs and Associations of the Antient Town of Winchelsea*. In an introductory message the mayor said it had been felt for some time that it would be of great benefit to new residents 'and for some who are not so new' to have brief particulars of organisations operating 'in and about our town'. The list includes some which are now defunct such as The League of Friends of Greyfriars and the Friary Gardeners, the social service to the community of Greyfriars and its park having been ended by the county council's sale to a private owner. It also includes specialist support organisations like the Rye and Winchelsea Centre of the National Trust, Rye and Winchelsea Care Group for the Blind, Friends of Rye Harbour Nature Reserve, Friends of Winchelsea Church and the Friends of the Ancient Monuments and Museum of Winchelsea.[1] All do excellent work and some have been referred to elsewhere in these pages. To illustrate the opportunities and activities offered by such clubs and societies over the years I have chosen two which are no longer in existence and five of those included in Mayor Tremeer's list which, while the excellence of their provision attracted many members from a wider area, are named for and eminently representative of the town.

The first of these and, as it is now constituted, one of the youngest, is the Winchelsea Singers, formed by the gathering together of members of numerous local choral groups in 1971 under the leadership of Hilda Clark, mayoress in 1973 and 1974, and meeting at her home, Haskards in St. Thomas's Street. Winchelsea had had a choral society for many years previously, the earliest mention of it I have so far found being in 1939 when the *Sussex Express* reported that the society had enjoyed a successful season. Its honorary secretary and treasurer at the time was Mrs. Cochrane, wife of the rector, who reported a credit balance of £5. 16s. 7d; their conductor was a Miss Deane. The day following Mrs. Cochrane's report the choir entered the Hastings Music Festival and was awarded the De La Warr Cup, a certificate and £1 in prize money. Perhaps the edge was taken slightly from this success by the fact that theirs was the only entry in the class but nevertheless 'they obtained higher marks than last year and were greatly encouraged by the adjudicator's remarks'. The cup was proudly displayed at The Little Shop, then under the proprietorship of Herbie Shepherd.[2]

The society reformed after the war with Pat Turner, nee Kirkman, as a leading soloist and Dorothy Merry as conductor. When it joined with others at Haskards to become the Winchelsea Singers it was officially as an evening class and had to follow further education rules including disbandment should the attendance fall below a certain level. Rumour has it that names such as B. Britten and E. Elgar occasionally appeared on the list to circumvent these regulations. Early performances included extracts from Faure's *Requiem* with Pat Turner as soloist and Leo Halle conducting as he was to do for many years until quite recently. Vivienne Bridges was rehearsal pianist at the time but expressing a wish to retire. This coincided with the arrival in Winchelsea of Mary Densem whose piano was spotted being moved into The Retreat, an observation which provoked instant recruitment by Hilda Clark. Mary, now Mary Chetwood, has since become the driving force behind the Singers and has encouraged them from strength to strength.

Turning through just a small section of the pile of posters which was kindly lent when I was researching this chapter, I came across performances of Rossini's *Petite Messe Solenelle*, Verdi's *Ave Maria*, Brahms' *Requiem*, Bach's *St. Luke's Passion*, Britten's *St. Nicolas*, Beethoven's *Choral Fantasia*, Mendelssohn's *The Hymn of Praise*, Haydn's *The Creation*, Faure's *Requiem*, Schubert's *Mass in G* and

Dvorak's *Stabat Mater* at venues including the church of St. Saviour and St. Peter in Eastbourne, the parish churches of Rye, Icklesham and Fairlight, Christchurch, Ore, and, most frequently, of course, St. Thomas's Church, Winchelsea. A varied, challenging and impressive list.

It was in 1981, before many of the above performances, that the further education connection was broken by cutbacks and the Winchelsea Singers went independent. Fund raising then became an urgent matter and 'fun evenings' began. The first, devised by Kay Streatfeild and produced by Mary Densem with Judy Plummer, was at the New Hall on 9 January 1982. Details of what took place are sparse but the tone was set by a rendering of 'We're the Winchelsea Singers' to the tune of Burlington Bertie. Among the large number of supporting items Leo Halle entered as Superman-on-a-Bicycle and, with Ann Whiteman, had a good deal of trouble with a hole in his bucket.[3] From this beginning highly successful and enjoyable pantomimes have developed, most recently *Alice Through the Wine Glass, Cinderella in Winchelhagen* and *A Lad in Winchelsea* from the pen of Henry Dormer.

Leo Halle handed over the baton to Jean Taverner in 1995 after many years of devoted leadership. The strength and musical skill which he has imparted over the years with his always unflappable approach have led to a current membership of fifty five and an enviable reputation for choral excellence, all growing from a small group singing entirely for the pleasure of its choristers. No doubt under their new conductor the Winchelsea Singers will develop these skills still further.

The fore-runners of the Winchelsea Gardeners' and Allotment Holders' Society could probably be found active at least a century before the Singers first gathered at Haskards. Any reference to the earliest flower shows has so far eluded me but the *Sussex Express* of 27 August 1895 reports in glowing terms the Winchelsea and District Annual Flower Show, describing it as 'second of the revived series'. The event was held in the Wall Field, then part of the grounds of Mariteau House, by kind permission of F. A. Inderwick and it was a good deal more than just a flower show. The villages of Icklesham and Udimore combined with the ancient town to make it all a resounding success. G.M. Freeman Q.C., mayor, was the president with Mr. Inderwick and Major Stileman as his vice-presidents. The organisation was under the guidance of the joint honorary secretaries, Messrs. J. Kenward and R. Chandler, but the real driving force behind the whole thing was Robert Voller, gardener at Mariteau, whom we have already met through his controversial election to Icklesham Parish Council (see p.81). He is described in the press report as 'not only the manager, practically, of the show but the chief workman also.' Voller's own produce was displayed on Mr. Inderwick's behalf in the 'Not for Competition' tent along with that of the wealthier residents and, judging by the lists, leading tradesmen who employed gardeners. He had arranged 'a grand display of plants including a fine collection of the adiantum family of ferns for which the Mariteau nurseries have been noted for years.' Of others whom we have met elsewhere, G.M. Freeman's gardener at the time was Mr. T. Watson who also staged ferns with a wide selection of pot plants, cut flowers and vegetables. Rev. Mr. Patch's gardener, W. Stevenson, had taken space as had the employees of Miss Ellen Terry and Major Stileman. Thomas Turner, Charles Carey and Henry Streeton also displayed in the 'Not for Competition' tent. Class distinction, of course, reigned and while the gentry and tradesman eschewed competition the 'cottagers' certainly did not. Their entries, in a separate tent, were both numerous and praiseworthy, 'indeed the professional gardeners were fain to admit that the competitive exhibition was unusually good, there being a splendid lot of fruit, while the potatoes, considering the season, were simply lovely.'

Among other forms of competition, Robert Voller's wife carried off first prize for table decorations with Mrs. Skinner as runner-up. Each of the three communities had its own events within the show and the lists of Winchelsea prizewinners record, among the surnames we shall recognise, Bessie Homard first for her collection of flowers, W. Barden first for carrots, runner beans and onions and Mrs. Buttonshaw frequently mentioned in the flower classes. Blanche Patch was second in the cake section. In fact the Patch family were enthusiastic competitors all round and even won every available prize in the buttonhole section. The art tent was a non-competitive attraction and featured 'snap-shots' by Miss Ellen Terry, an oil painting by William Padgett, roses on satin painted by Mrs. William Martindale and pencil drawings by Rev. Henry Patch.

A series of sports were also held during the afternoon including 'an amusing obstacle race' and a tug-of-war between teams from the three parishes, joined by Rye Harbour. The band of the Rye (E) Company 1st Cinque Port Volunteers under Bandmaster Stutely played a much appreciated programme of selections 'in capital style'.[4]

Reports of succeeding shows in 'the revived series' reveal an expanding list of vice-presidents, among them Sir Henry Irving. By 1897 the sports section, too, had been considerably expanded and included both adults and children. In the high jump 'H. Pilbrow (boy) and G. Winchester (man) tied at a height of 4' 4" and divided first and second prizes.' Incredibly they tied at the same height the following year. The same Winchester won the throwing the cricket ball event, not too surprising as he was Winchelsea Cricket Club's leading player at the time. Rye Harbour beat Winchelsea in the tug-of-war with Icklesham and Udimore not entering. There was a dead heat in the egg-and-spoon race for girls under 21 and the 50 yards threadneedle race for boys and girls between 14 and 20 was won by S. Streeton and Alice Barling.[5] It is delightful to note that in 1898 the nursery race for those under the age of eight was won by Anthony Freeman.[6]

The flower shows continued for many years and their accompanying sports later included an ambitious development, the Winchelsea 'marathon'. The course for this event began in the Wall Field where the shows were still being held, continued down Pannel Lane to the New Gate, thence to Icklesham village and back via the main road. The cup which was presented for the marathon records that in 1928 and 1929, the first two years listed, the winner was Douglas Turner who later became the organiser. Robert Hickman was victorious in the next three years when the trophy records that he reduced his time considerably from 30 minutes 17 seconds in 1930 to 27 minutes 57 seconds in 1931 and then marginally to 27 minutes 48 seconds in 1932. The race was discontinued in 1937 but revived in 1950 and 1951 with prizes of one pound, fifteen shillings and ten shillings to tempt more competitors. Whether this ploy was successful we do not know but the revival was short-lived because of the danger to the runners, particularly as traffic volume increased on the main road. The trophy, however, survived to provide much of this information many years later. Since 1980 it has been presented as the Challenge Cup for Floral Art, won, often on more than one occasion, by Elsie Turner, Audrey Hills, Evelyn Whiting, Tessa Potts, Barbara Murray, Jackie Stevens and currently held by Sheila Horobin.

The post-war revival of the 'Horticultural Show and Sports' in 1949, later including the last two runnings of the marathon was encouraged by the New Hall Entertainments Committee. Douglas Turner took a strong lead in pressing for a new allotment site, eventually established on land near the cricket field, the controversy over which led to the show committee establishing itself as the Gardeners' and Allotment Holders' Society, affiliated to the National Allotments Society. Douglas was secretary of the newly constituted body and continued to serve it for the rest of his life. The society has generally flourished over the years, although he must have been greatly saddened when he was in the chair for the Annual General Meeting in November 1969. The minutes record the names of eight committee members present but no other members of the society or of the general public. In view of the fact that the committee was growing smaller and the public response less the meeting was adjourned until the following March but this never took place and there were no further shows for eight years. Even when a further revival attempt was made in March 1978 with Douglas again in the chair there was another poor attendance but letters were distributed after the meeting to every house in the town and the following month thirty-four people attended to ensure the society's successful revival.

The 1996 show, apart from the usual competitions and sideshows – the sports section has long been dropped – was further enlivened by the Rye Harbour based firm CMR bringing its fire engine and a celebrity, James Hazeldine who plays Bayleaf in television's *London's Burning*. Its success and the society's present flourishing state can be measured from the attendance figures; no fewer than eight hundred people paid admission at the gate.

At the time that the 'second revised series' of flower shows was becoming established, the Winchelsea Quoits Club, long since defunct, was flourishing. This pastime was clearly considered suitable for, and much enjoyed by, the town's artisans, the gentry remaining aloof. The club's existence is best characterised for us by a photograph taken on the present cricket field at the turn of the century. This shows the quoits team in assorted agricultural and labouring dress, proudly holding their quoits and with one member even demonstrating the throw. The strength of the Quoits Club and the enthusiasm of its members are also captured for us by a *Sussex Express* report of October 1898. On the Tuesday of the week of the publication there had been an individual challenge match 'on the ground of the Winchelsea Quoits Club' between 'Messrs. Pellett and S. Drawbridge' with Drawbridge receiving a ten point handicap of which he took no advantage for he won 31 – 28 anyway. Where Pellett came from we do not know but he must have been a good player to be ranked ten points above Drawbridge who later in the week won a knockout competition for Winchelsea members only, beating E. Freeman convincingly by 21 – 14 in the final.

That competition was followed the same day by a dinner held at the New Inn which thirty-four of the club's forty-five members, some from outside the town, attended. It was clearly a lively evening for the paper reports:

> '"Very old inhabitants" with lengthy experience of festive functions fail to remember a merrier evening than that spent by the members of the Winchelsea Quoits Club assembled at dinner on Thursday evening. Much was due to the friendly feeling engendered by the fine old sport. The club is singularly successful... the large company was thoroughly representative of the population of the ancient "City".'

Toasts and speeches abounded. 'The Queen' of course, and 'The Army, Navy and Reserve Forces' were patriotically included among the former. During the latter Mr. C. Barling, Vice-Chairman, spoke of how the club had developed, providing good exercise and amusement in which almost every member had taken part, and most interesting matches. Mr. J. Kenward, a much acclaimed honorary secretary, reported that £4. 7s. 6d. had been collected in subscriptions with £3. 8s. 0d. of it spent on the dinner, 17s. 6d. on a new set of quoits and five shillings on a new clay bed onto which the quoits were pitched. As the rent of the field, ten shillings, had been paid from the previous year's balance in hand, the club remained seven shillings and sixpence in credit. Honours were accorded to Mr. Thomas Wicks, a local carrier and resident of the house now known as The Oast House, opposite the cricket field, who had skilfully and successfully laid the new clay bed. The chairman, too, was warmly thanked for his keenness 'always to promote the interests of the inhabitants'. This was H. J. Elliott so here we find him involved in yet another aspect of the life of

(69) Winchelsea Quoits Club.

the town.[7] No doubt a good deal of ale was consumed on this festive occasion but we do not know whether it was drunk at Winchelsea during the actual playing of the game. 'Quoits was also played among fishermen in Rye where a four gallon jar of beer was "deemed essential for keeping the players' eye in"'.[8]

It seems logical to conclude that Winchelsea Bowls Club was the natural successor to the Quoits Club and that as the one became less popular the other began to flourish. The first indication we have of bowls being played in the town since medieval times is that a club was formed in 1922 using first a rink in the garden of Yew Tree House at the invitation of Robert Nichols and later one at The Mount, home of Col. and Mrs. Goldschmidt. This use continued until the colonel's death when his widow wished to move to a smaller home. Prior to this move she gave the club which had been so close to her husband's heart every possible help and consideration. The *Sussex Express* reported:

'Mrs. Goldschmidt who is proving such a great friend of Winchelsea Bowls Club – she is allowing them to play matches at her home 'The Mount' pending completion of a new rink adjoining the cricket field – recently presented them with a handsome challenge cup. The final of a series of games to decide who should hold it took place on Saturday and resulted in Mr. T. Griffin, hon. secretary of the club, beating the mayor, Mr. J.C. Rogers, 10 – 6. They played eleven ends... Work on the new rink is progressing satisfactorily and has now reached the seeding stage. The club has received generous support but would welcome further donations.'[9]

(70) Winchelsea Bowls Club at The Mount, 1930s
(back left to right) H. Barling, E. Barling, F. Trill (front) G. Barling, B. Barden, J. Rogers

Tom Griffin's and Jo Rogers' successors still compete for the Goldschmidt Cup. In recent years it has been won five times each by two corporation members and former mayors, Guy Hughes and Ken Chetwood. The rink which was constructed near the cricket field is in a delightfully peaceful spot with extensive views across the Brede Valley, views made even more dramatic recently by the removal of a hedge to allow the rink to be enlarged. The little pavilion, tucked into one corner of the site was constructed, partly at least, with materials from the former Winchelsea Tennis Club pavilion which stood beside the club's courts when they were opposite Mariteau House. This tennis pavilion had stilts so that nets and other equipment could be stored underneath and contained a kerosene stove which made it very cosy. When former tennis club member Mrs. Petronilla Barclay joined the bowls club many years later she instantly recognised the timbers of the central section of the pavilion back wall!

Mrs. Barclay's memories of the tennis club which flourished in the 1930s particularly include the underarm service of Effie Briggs which she describes as 'coming viciously over the net at 90 miles an hour!' Miss Briggs, who later married Col. Wildeblood, mayor in 1940, was one of the last underarm servers, other club members such as Edith Holmes, Malcolm Ritchie and Petronilla Barclay herself adopting the now normal method of beginning a rally.

Winchelsea Bowls Club has over the years undertaken a considerable programme of competitions and matches. Apart from the Goldschmidt Cup two other well known Winchelsea names are commemorated by the Knox Trophy, a mixed pairs event, and the Barling Cup, ladies' and gentlemen's handicap singles, which are competed for annually. John Knox was mayor in 1949, 1950 and 1955; the Barlings, apart from holding various public offices, were grocers serving the town over three generations. Of the matches perhaps the most notable is the annual Cinque Ports Bowls Tournament in which teams from all fourteen member towns compete. When asked whether Winchelsea has ever won this tournament, one leading member replied: 'Oh, no – we can't compete with the county players available to the other teams and it takes us a long time to get used to the quality of their rinks which are so much better than ours. We've done well if we're not last.' Perhaps with its larger green Winchelsea might one day host the event and see how the opposition fares in those circumstances.

It was during the First World War, not all that long before the Bowls Club was started, that the women of the town felt the need for an organisation which would bring them together in fellowship and mutual support as they suffered the long absence of their menfolk on active service. Thus began the Winchelsea Women's Institute which was meeting regularly in 1939 when the *Sussex Express* reported a gathering at which Mrs. Burke presided over a talk on 'Period Costumes in the Eighteenth Century', a competition for the best fancy dress in crepe paper and notification that a whist drive in aid of the People's Dispensary for Sick Animals was to be held. The report notes, 'The monthly letter was read.'[10] It was many years later that the Institute began to view such requirements and other formalities as an imposition. Feeling far removed from headquarters at Lewes and with financial contributions coming from fewer and fewer pockets leaving less and less for expenses such as the engagement of speakers, the members eventually decided with great reluctance that they would break away and form their own independent organisation which it was decided after some debate to call the Second Wednesday Club. This has since flourished, holding an annual meeting, appointing officers and submitting accounts for audit as its constitution requires. The monthly meetings to which are invited speakers on topics of local and general interest, are relaxed and sociable with numbers now greatly increased, aided by the freedom to admit gentlemen.

During the time of its normal membership of the Federation of Women's Institutes the group had a distinguished record which included compiling in 1952 a collection of photographs of every house in the town with the names of the residents. Sadly the whereabouts of this most valuable document is currently unknown but active investigations are taking place in the hope of its recovery.

The most popular of the W.I. activities, both within the town and outside was their weekly market, held during the summer months in the 1970s and 1980s on Friday mornings. The venue was initially a garage in Castle Street owned by Mrs. Miller of Periteau House; later Mrs. Elkington allowed the similar use of her garage nearby. The produce sold included jams, cakes, fruit, bantam eggs and much, much more. Numerous residents would save a considerable amount of their shopping until the W.I. market was open. With Lilah Smith, Winifred Foster, Doris Carter, Margaret Bowen and Jack Foster among the leading participants the market attracted such attention that the *A.A. Book of British Towns,* published in 1979 recorded as part of Winchelsea's entry 'Market Day: Friday – Summer only.'!

While the Women's Institute's demise was the result of the pre-meditated if reluctant actions of its own members, that of Winchelsea Football Club was due in large measure to external influences and it was never to rise Phoenix-like from the ashes in the same way. Of the early history of the club I have so far come across a 1929 press report of a 3-0 defeat by Hastings Rangers in the first round of the Rye Charity Cup. The match was played on 'the Rectory Field' where very bad weather caused its curtailment to thirty minutes each way. The reporter observed that Charlie Trill led several good attacks for Winchelsea and 'ought to have scored at least twice'. Significantly the account ends by telling us that Rangers did not field their strongest team.[11] Undated, but presumably in the 1930s are a series of cuttings in a scrapbook lent to me by Phil Barling. This was compiled by his father and includes not only matches played by Winchelsea Football Club but also Winchelsea and Rye Cricket Clubs. Ominously there are two references to misbehaviour by Winchelsea F. C. spectators who indulged in prolonged barracking and directed abusive remarks at players and officials during a home match against top of the league Bexhill St. Barnabas, thus provoking a critical referee's report.[12]

Following the Second World War Winchelsea were quite a strong side, included a considerable number of local players and competed in Division II of the Hastings League. Of those still living in the town, Cecil Barden was the captain, Bob Collins the secretary and John Dunk a young player who always turned up in the hope that somebody else would not. The club had its headquarters at the Castle Inn where the players changed in the stable block which has recently been so beautifully restored by Reg and Frances Packard who now own the Castle as a private house. Matches were played in the Wall Field which was at the time the subject of negotiations with its owner, Anthony Freeman, with a view to its formal establishment as a recreation and football ground.

The team had an extremely keen and competent, if somewhat volatile and eccentric, goalkeeper in Charlie Osborne. Charlie would change early and enjoy a few drinks at the bar in his goalkeeper's jersey before setting off for the ground. No respecter of authority, if he became bored with a game he could sometimes be seen, as the end drew near, folding up the netting from his goal and setting off for the Castle with it as soon as, or even before, the final whistle blew.

The cloud on Winchelsea F. C.'s horizon came in the form of a team called Ukranian Rangers who began to play friendly matches during the 1947/48 season. They were the only team in Sussex of displaced persons who worked on local farms and lived at Oakside, a hostel run by the Agricultural Executive Committee at Bodiam. Mr. W.T. Hammersley, warden of the hostel, told the *Sussex Express:*

> 'They came to this country last February after years of hardship and suffering on the continent. Most of them had been under either German or Russian rule. Some bore wounds received when fighting to defend their country and others showed signs of suffering in concentration camps in Siberia. But they don't like talking about these things. They are here to forget the past and one way in which to do that is to play football. They asked me to get a team together.'[13]

All this would engender much sympathy but unfortunately, despite their footballing prowess, the teams's disciplinary record was poor. Their only season in Hastings League Division II, during which they met Winchelsea home and away, produced some remarkable wins. They beat Crowhurst 12-1, Old Hastonians II 18-0, Ore United II 11-0, Brede 10-0 and Bodiam 14-0, finishing the season with a remarkable 137 goals to their credit. Far be it from me to suggest that intimidation might have been involved. Their first brush with authority came as early as November when they were severely cautioned and censured by Hastings Football Association following the abandonment of their away game with Peasmarsh because Rangers refused to allow a penalty to be taken against them. They were ordered to pay the expenses of the inquiry and thirty shillings towards Peasmarsh's costs in travelling to replay the fixture.[14]

The following month, playing at Bodiam, Winchelsea, unlike many of Rangers' opponents, more than held their own and achieved a 2-2 draw. There was no reported misdemeanour on the field but what was happening unreported and presumably unnoticed by the referee caused trouble among the spectators and enraged Barry Stocks, honorary treasurer, a playing member and son of

(71) Winchelsea Football Club, 1932
(back left to right) C. Field, H. Wainwright, F. Fowle, F. Stocks, J. Hickman, A. Cooke
(front) C. Barling, A. Wainwright, B. Stocks, F. Smith, E. Trill

the Castle's licensee, to such an extent that he declared publicly later that this game was the reason for his decision not to go on the field again while Ukranian Rangers remained in the league.

This festering sore, coupled with Charlie Osborne's volatile personality, did not bode well for the return match at Winchelsea and sure enough the explosion came. Whatever may have gone before it was the award of a penalty to Rangers which provided the spark. As it was about to be taken the goalkeeper was seen leaning against a post. When asked by the referee why he was not defending the penalty he retorted, 'That was never a penalty, if he wants to kick it in let him kick it in.' Osborne was then involved in a fracas and when his name was about to be taken he snatched the referee's notebook and tore it up.

The whole force of authority was brought to bear by a Hastings Football Association commission which met to consider the referee's report which also complained of insulting behaviour towards him by spectators and abuse by unspecified members of the team. Winchelsea F.C. had its ground closed for the first three months of the following season was banned from playing within five miles of the town, was severely censured for failing to maintain order, cautioned as to its future conduct, fined two guineas and ordered to put up warning notices when the ground reopened.[15] Osborne was given a two year suspension. Unfortunately as he left the hearing with his captain, Cecil Barden, and the secretary, Bob Collins, one of the commission's members said, 'Think yourself lucky you didn't get a life ban, young man.' Charlie Osborne's response ensured that the sentence was changed and he did get a life ban.

The matter was splashed all over the local press but made the national press as well where it was blown up out of all proportion, not so common then as it is now. One result of this was that a professional goalkeeper from as far away as Lincolnshire wrote to Cecil Barden giving details of his wide experience, saying that as the club was short of players he could play in any other position as well and offering to pay his own fare to attend a trial. Somewhat bemused, Cecil said, 'I shall have to tell him what we are like. I think he must have got the impression we are a bigger club.'[16]

It was certainly true that Winchelsea were short of players. Gloomily viewing the future, Bob Collins observed that with only about thirteen on the club's books, some of whom tended to lose interest if their duties prevented them playing, the outlook was bleak. He did not think there would be a team the following season.

Bob turned out, despite his own efforts, to be absolutely correct. Following the expiry of the ground closure he announced in the local press that it was hoped to start friendly fixtures on 17 December so that 'we can have a game or two and see how things go,' with a view to applying for readmission to the Hastings League in 1951/52. Practices would be at the Wall Field on Sunday mornings.[17] Sadly it did not work out. Although Osborne's life ban was later lifted at the request of East Guldeford F.C. who wanted him to play for them, Winchelsea Football Club was no more.

Fortunately no such disaster has threatened Winchelsea Cricket Club whose known history has lasted longer than any of the other organisations whose activities are included here, the nature of its bi-centenary celebrations fully justifying pride of place at the end of this chapter. The club's history is taken to date from 1795 for the *Southern Weekly Advertiser* of 5 October in that year reported:

> 'A few days since the officers of the Winchelsea Volunteers regaled their company with an excellent dinner. In the afternoon the men amused themselves with Cricket and other diversions; in the evening they returned to the bottle, and after drinking loyal and constitutional toasts till near 12 o'clock, retired to their respective homes in a manner which did great credit to themselves and their entertainers.'[18]

To provide a full history of the club is a task far beyond the scope of this book. Of years gone by I can only record here occasional items which have come to my notice from various sources. For example, a collection of press cuttings made by Thomas Parkin of Hastings, mostly referring to events in which he had some personal involvement, shows that in 1879, at least in its clashes with H.S. Marriott's XI, Winchelsea was suffering some pretty disastrous defeats. On 5 August at Ore the home side scored 221 with Parkin contributing 51 and Marriott himself top scoring with 62. The Winchelsea team contained three members of the Skinner family including Ernest William and two Padgetts. These five and their colleagues were dismissed for 76 in their first innings and, following on, suffered even more disastrously, capitulating for a meagre 22 runs all out. E.W. Skinner, of whom among the players we have learnt most in these pages, contributed 3 and 0. G.H. Gladstone top scored with 21 not out in the first innings; that distinction in the second went to R. Padgett with just 5. Parkin's interest in the cutting was no doubt enhanced by his five wickets in Winchelsea's second innings.

The two teams played again at Winchelsea three days later. Once more Marriott's XI batted first and this time Winchelsea had much more success with the ball, E.S. Chapman taking five wickets and Rev. W.W. Richards four to dismiss the opposition for 50 runs. Here was the chance for revenge but it was not taken. In their first innings Winchelsea were bowled out for just 17 with seven ducks and a 0 not out and, batting again, they managed just 21 with E.W. Skinner highest scorer on 3 not out.[19] To suffer an innings defeat at the hands of a team which has itself been bowled out for 50 might well qualify for the *Guinness Book of Records*!

The club suffered another heavy defeat a quarter of a century later, this time at the hands of their local rivals from Rye who scored 206 for 5 declared and then dismissed Winchelsea for 84. This match is notable for us because Anthony Freeman, aged 13 and involved in all aspects of the town's life as always, took the wicket of one of Rye's opening batsmen, W.G. Clark, who got his own back on the boy by having him stumped for two in Winchelsea's innings.[20] By 1911, aged only 19 and still using the initial P for Philip, the name which he so disliked and later dropped, he had become the club's vice-captain.

The fixture card for 1930 shows Lord Blanesburgh, Lord Ritchie of Dundee, G.M. Freeman K.C., Lt. Col. Goldschmidt, Major Burke and Dr. J.R. Skinner among the vice-presidents, the colonel also serving on the committee, and Douglas Turner was honorary secretary. The cricket field rent of £7 per annum for the ground and pavilion was at that time being paid to Albert Fuller, descendant of Walter. The club had its headquarters at the New Inn and opponents included Peasmarsh, Crowhurst Park, Brede, Beckley, Hastings and St. Leonards, Rye, Westfield and Iden. Four years later the headquarters had been transferred to the Castle Inn, no doubt through the involvement of the Stocks family for Barry was honorary secretary and his father a committee member. Leslie Whiting and Dr. Knowles were captain and vice-captain respectively.

By the time of the immediate post-war years Anthony Freeman had become the club's landlord. In a list of suggestions for a lease, undated but surely written at that time, he proposed a rent of one shilling per annum, much more generous than that of his predecessors, but retained the grazing rights. Another clause required that the field should not be used for football or hockey while he was 'willing to offer the Wall Field, Winchelsea for such games for public use with nominal charge only,' We have seen that this use, for football at least, was current if not for long. The lease as then proposed was to be for his lifetime only so Mr. Freeman provided that £500 be allocated from his estate in recompense for expenditure incurred should his heirs and successors not continue the arrangement.[21] In fact the National Trust most generously allowed it to carry on until the club was eventually able to acquire the ground's freehold.

A *Sussex Express* report of this same post-war period shows the club enjoying far greater success than we observed earlier, but appeared under a rather odd headline:

THEY DO NOT RELY ON THE UMPIRE AS TWELFTH MAN

> Winchelsea's cricketers are faring much better than they did a year ago. By putting in a lot of work they have made a big improvement to their ground, particularly the wicket, and this is having a marked effect on their play. Of their eleven matches so far this season they have won five and lost six. They have taken 103 wickets, 51 bowled, 43 caught and only five l.b.w., three run out and two stumped which shows that they do not rely on the umpire as 12th man,' [22]

Perish the thought that some clubs might! At that time F. Jowett and G. Hickman appear to have been Winchelsea's leading players.

A year later the success was apparently continuing for the *Sussex Express* reported an exciting victory over Hastings Wanderers 'on an uncertain wicket at Bulverhythe'. Those of us who have played there know that it has always been thus! Don McKenzie, landlord of the New Inn to which the club's headquarters had returned, took 7 for 38 as Wanderers were dismissed for 78. Winchelsea seemed to be cruising to victory on 76 for 6 when Glazier of Wanderers did the hat-trick, leaving Cecil Barden and R.J. Thompson as last pair to knock off the three runs needed for victory. This they did amid some excitement but the game did not then stop as is the custom now – Barden and

Thompson went on to carry the score to 131 for 9 scoring 37 not out and 22 not out respectively.[23] One wonders how they decided to call a halt at that point.

Now we must move to the memorable occasion which most notably marked Winchelsea C.C.'s bicentenary in 1995. The club was honoured with an invitation to play a match at Lord's against the Cross Arrows on 30 September. This was indeed a high point for Winchelsea cricket and those of us lucky enough to have been there will long remember it. I travelled up by car, leaving very early, and managed to talk my way into the car park a considerable time before the ground was supposed to be open. It was then politely suggested that I should pass the time by going for a cup of coffee in St. John's High Road. This I did, only to be joined a few minutes later by members of the coach party who had left Winchelsea at 6.30 a.m. and arrived similarly early. The reminiscences of Winchelsea cricket began there and then, hardly stopping all day. We greatly enjoyed a guided tour of the Lord's pavilion, taking particular note of the portrait of George, Ninth Earl of Winchilsea, who financed Thomas Lord's building of the ground, and of the extensive work in progress on the main square after the recently ended season. By the time we reached the Nursery End, home ground of the Cross Arrows for their September fixtures, play was already in progress. For an account of the game I could not possibly improve on the one written by Richard Merricks who has kindly given me permission to quote it in full:

'On a pleasant autumn day, brighter than had been forecast, the Cross Arrows batted first against the medium pace attack of Charlie Reid and David Glazebrook. The first few overs were accurate and both batsmen were watchful but soon 'Budgie' Burridge, 58 years of age, ex Durham and Herts, started to plunder any short-pitched balls of which there were rather too many. Stephen Crisford replaced David Glazebrook but this only increased the quantity of short balls and accelerated the run rate – anything remotely off length was soon summarily despatched to, and often over the short leg side boundary by such a quality player. On more than one occasion he cleared not only the boundary but also the main ground stands. Charlie, however, was bowling a good spell from the northern end and from time to time beat the other opener who was playing a very second-fiddle role. Budgie raced to his hundred before holing out to a well judged catch on the square leg boundary by David Wheeler. The number three batsman, Stewart Brown, could have fallen to a chip shot landing just wide of mid-on. The bowler was Richard Flood who had settled into a good length at the Indoor School end.

This was virtually his only mistake, however, and with the other opener, Dare, playing more confidently and cover driving especially fluently, the scoreboard began to race along again after a quieter period either side of lunch. Bowlers were brought back, switched round, and generally bowled better than earlier but it was all too late. Stewart holed out to John Crisford after making an elegant fifty and the declaration came at 279-2 once Dare had completed his hundred, made in two and three quarter hours.

John Crisford and David Simmons were also watchful in the early overs, especially against Fay, ex-Middlesex staff, who was bowling sharply off a short run and regularly beating the bat. He produced a good ball to bowl David and made one lift to have Stephen Crisford caught in the gully for a duck but John, using his feet well, launched an attack on the off-spinner Sketchley who had been on Hampshire's books. Having got into the forties, however, he became too ambitious and fell to a good catch at extra cover and when Richard Flood was unluckily bowled off his pads hopes of making a reasonable challenge began to dwindle. David Wheeler, starting confidently with a four off his first ball, then fell to a juggled caught and bowled and Stephen Turner succumbed to the last ball before tea.

Frank Cooke, however, recalled after a dubious bat-pad catch, used the long handle in his own inimitable style and rattled up a quick 36, taking 20 in one over from Wyse. Once he had left the tail did not prolong the agony too much longer, though Graham Tree played a composed and mature little innings and the main interest centred on whether 'Raj', the left arm spinner bowling tidily from the top end could take enough wickets to create a Cross Arrows record. He managed it by cleaning up the tail and the game finished just inside the 20 over period and before the rain began to fall.

It had been a wonderful and memorable day. Winchelsea felt, with some justification, that they had not really done themselves justice on the field, but they were up against an eleven of high class cricketers and the Arrows were suitably impressed with the visitors' positive approach and cheerful attitude. They were well supported from the stands and the bar and all who were present will treasure the memory of an unforgettable day and the privilege of being allowed to play at all in such hallowed surroundings.'

(72) Winchelsea Cricket Club at Lord's, 30 September 1995
(back left to right) Jim Bilsby (12th man), David Glazebrook, David Symonds, Alan Crouch, David Wheeler, Frank Cooke
(front) Stephen Turner, Charlie Reid, Richard Flood, Stephen Crisford (Captain), Graham Tree, John Crisford

Full scorecard:

Cross Arrows C. C.

1.	A.J.Burridge	c Wheeler b Glazebrook	108
2.	C.R.S.Dare	not out	100
3.	M.S.Brown	c J.Crisford b Tree	52
4.	A.N.Crockert	not out	8
	Extras		11
	Total (for two wickets)		279

Did not bat: M.G.Pether* P.Kearns Dr.R.K.H.Wyse M.M.Rajabali C.E.Sketchley R.A.Fay A.C.Reeves[+]

Winchelsea C. C.

1.	D.Simmons	b Faye	5
2.	J.M.Crisford	c Reeves b Wyse	45
3.	S.D.Crisford[+]	c Dare b Fay	0
4.	R.J.L.Flood	b Sketchley	1
5.	D.J.Wheeler	c & b Wyse	19
6.	F.A.Cooke*	b Reeves	35
7.	S.J.Turner	c Pether b Rajabali	6
8.	C.A.M.Reid	c Wyse b Rajabali	0
9.	G.L.Tree	not out	4
10.	A.D.Crouch	c Brown b Rajabali	0
11.	D.M.G.Glazebrook	b Rajabali	4
	Extras		7
	Total		126

[+] Captain * Wicket Keeper
UMPIRES: T.Duckett and A.J.Dunk
SCORERS: E.Soloman and P.L.Stone[24]

A memorable occasion indeed. May the club continue to prosper as, led by its president, Peter Stevens, it ambitiously seeks to support the management committee in restoring the New Hall and bringing it back into use as a dual purpose pavilion and community hall.

32. ROYAL VISITS

Winchelsea's royal connections have their roots in its royal foundation. We have already seen how the present town owes its site to King Edward I, how King Edward III fought a major battle off its shores and how Queen Elizabeth I officially recognised the corporation's land-holdings.

Of other earlier monarchs, King John arrived in Old Winchelsea on 27 April 1213 with his massive retinue and stayed three days[1] during which time he received ambassadors from the French king, made proper religious observance and arranged for the distribution of alms and the feeding of a hundred poor citizens.[2] King Henry III stayed a little longer, between 4 and 8 May 1264, but his visit was disastrous by comparison. Accompanied by his entire army he was preparing to combat the de Montfort threat. The soldiers' eager consumption of Winchelsea's wine stocks led to 'depredation and rapine' throughout the area.[3] King Edward II, in whose time New Winchelsea stood well established by his father, visited with Queen Isabella in 1315. It is something of a surprise to find that they made many purchases in the town, far too great an amount to be for current use because it included: 'Bread to the value of £5. 19s. 0d., six tuns of wine costing £16. 10s. 0d., wax, presumably for candles... at a total cost of £4. 13s 1d. and various supplies for the kitchen costing £15. 5s. 5d.' Payments were made to Richard Battaill and Gilbert de Wynston in respect of accommodation provided for the royal couple and their party.[4] Edward III made a further visit twelve years after the Battle of Winchelsea for his edict adjourning parliament until 3 November 1362 was signed in Winchelsea. Brigid Chapman comments:

> 'This was the last occasion on which a Plantaganet set foot on Sussex soil and for the county it was the end of years of battles and sea skirmishes, royal feuds and family quarrels and all the rough stuff of British history in the making.'[5]

That may be generally true but the Plantaganets' association with Sussex had its advantages as well. Without them Winchelsea might well have ceased to exist!

Passing by Queen Elizabeth I whose involvement has already been noted and in the process moving forward 320 years, we find included in a scrapbook made by Anna Wray and dated 1807, an unusual account of another royal visit:

> 'During the reign of James the 2nd when the people were much oppressed with taxes, in the course of a tour thro' England, having stopped at Winchelsea, the Corporation resolved to address His Majesty, but as the mayor could neither read nor write, it was agreed that the Recorder should prompt him on this occasion. Being introduced, the Recorder whispered to the trembling Mayor, "Hold up your head and look like a man." The Mayor, mistaking this for the beginning of his speech, addressed the King, "Hold up your head and look like a man." The Recorder in amazement whispered to the Mayor, "What the devil do you mean?" The Mayor in the same manner instantly repeated [it]... The Recorder, alarmed, whispered more earnestly, "By God, sir, you will ruin us all." The poor Mayor, still imagining this his speech, repeated it aloud to the King.'[6]

Mayors whose terms of office occurred during King James II's reign were Thomas Hovenden (1685), William Alderton (1686) and John Richardson (1687, 1688). Which of them thus accidentally stumbled upon the town's message to its monarch we shall never know, if we can believe it of any of them.

We move forward a further 250 years to find the much more recent royal family visiting Winchelsea in 1935. On 11 March in that year Her Majesty Queen Mary visited St. Thomas's Church and spent an hour there with Rev. R.A. Cochrane who explained the church's history and showed her Lord Blanesburgh's munificent gift of the stained glass windows. Her majesty later had tea with his lordship at Cleveland House.[7] During the afternoon the children of the school were taken by Miss Smith into the churchyard to see the queen.[8]

Maybe news got round the royal family that Winchelsea is a very interesting place to visit for later in the same year the Duke and Duchess of York, the future King George VI and Queen Elizabeth, also visited the church. This was Winchelsea's first glimpse of the royal lady who through her more recent position as Lord Warden of the Confederation of the Cinque Ports and two more official visits has so firmly earned herself a place in the residents'

(73) At St Thomas's Church, 1935.
Princess Elizabeth, our present queen, H.R.H. the Duke of York, later King George VI, and the Duchess of York, now H.M. Queen Elizabeth the Queen Mother.

affections as she has in those of the nation. On that first visit Princess Elizabeth, our present queen, accompanied her parents[9] and in 1938 her uncle, H.R.H. the Duke of Gloucester came to the town with the children once again having time out of school to greet him.[10]

The first local announcement of Her Majesty Queen Elizabeth II's tour of the area in connection with the nine hundredth anniversary of the Battle of Hastings appeared in the *Sussex Express and County Herald* on 15 July 1966. The proposed programme for 28 October said that she would travel from Battle to Rye where she was expected at about 11.30, driving thence to Hastings for lunch. Here was an opportunity not to be missed. Within a few days Charles Croggon, on the corporation's instructions, had written to her private secretary saying that since it appeared she would pass through Winchelsea, it was hoped that:

'… Her Majesty will be graciously pleased to break her journey for a few minutes to receive a Loyal Address from the Ancient Town and Member of the Confederation of the Cinque Ports. In so doing she would be repeating a favour conferred on the Town by her Illustrious Predecessor, Queen Elizabeth I, and would earn the gratitude of the smallest in size, but by no means in loyalty, of the Ancient Guardians of the Narrow Seas.'[11]

Even this magnificent eloquence drew, initially, only a tepid response. Sir Edward Ford replied that the programme for the day appeared very crowded and that it was no longer customary for loyal addresses to be presented to the queen on all but very special occasions. She would, of course, drive very slowly through the town. Captain Lovegrove was inclined to accept this decision and wrote from his London office suggesting elaborate plans for the corporation and townsfolk to line the High Street and to invite residents of nearby villages not on her majesty's route to join them. On the same day Charles Croggon, less willing to agree without further efforts, wrote a brief reply to Sir Edward saying he fully understood the crowded nature of the queen's programme but it would still be very much appreciated if she would stop a few minutes in Winchelsea. This letter was passed to the Lord Lieutenant, the Duke of Norfolk, who wrote reinforcing the point that her majesty could not possibly satisfy the wishes of everybody, but later asked to be allowed to call on the mayor to discuss the matter. The meeting took place on 19 September at the Court Hall. David Homan must have been very persuasive for the next day his grace wrote to say that the queen would be accompanied by the Duke of Edinburgh and they would get out of the car at Winchelsea.

Frantic preparations were immediately put in hand. Barriers were to be provided in German Street with temporary flagpoles and an awning. Letters were exchanged with the chief constable about security and road closures, invitations issued to 84 official guests and a vin d'honneur arranged to take place in the Court Hall afterwards. The corporation's request to borrow a royal standard to fly at the Court Hall was politely turned down by Sir Martin Charteris, writing from Balmoral, on the grounds that the standard was flown only on buildings where the queen stayed for 'some appreciable time'.

In fact she was to stay only five minutes but that in no way dampened the enthusiasm of those concerned. The instructions issued by the mayor were in painstaking detail and of military precision. The mayor and mayoress would greet the queen when the car stopped (he anxiously asked on which side she would be). His worship would then present the members of the corporation who would be lined up in the road. Behind them the wives of corporation members, Mr. Bryant Godman Irvine M.P., the rector and Mrs. Ware, corporation widows and other distinguished guests would have places beneath the awning. On their right were to be the members of the parish council and their clerk, with their wives/husbands and led by chairman Mr. Alf Hancock of Rye Harbour. Beyond them members of the Over 60 Club with their leader Mrs. Stella Chappel and residents of Greyfriars Old People's Home for whom chairs were brought from the Court Hall. To the left of the awning were local authority and town organisation representatives and the children of the school who had the bus shelter reserved if it was wet. Since the school numbers were about 60 at the time it would have been quite a crush!

It was not only Winchelsea which planned in detail. It perhaps gives a tiny insight into what goes on behind the scenes on such occasions to point out that the Chief Constable's *Operational Order 1/66 Royal Visit* for the complete day's programme ran to 24 large pages of tiny type.[12]

In the general press coverage Winchelsea's five minutes find little space among accounts of visits to Battle Abbey and parish church, to Cadborough Farm and the parish church at Rye, to

(74) Members of Winchelsea Corporation are presented to Her Majesty and H.R.H. Prince Philip.
(left to right) David Homan, mayor, Lord Ritchie of Dundee, Anthony Freeman, Capt. Herbert Lovegrove,
A. Vernon Owen, Anthony Thomas, Thomas Bruce, Lt. Col. P. Vivian Gray, Charles Croggon, town clerk.

Winkle Island in Hastings where the Duke of Edinburgh was made a member of the Winkle Club, to the Hastings Embroidery and Hastings College of Further Education, to the de la Warr Pavilion and the Sutherland Avenue Children's Home in Bexhill and to Chelsea College of Physical Education in Eastbourne. Nevertheless the Winchelsea stop was a memorable and impressive occasion for those of us who were present.

The day was still, dull and grey as the royal party was enthusiastically cheered to a halt but while the presentations took place, a complete silence fell among the crowd, allowing the voices of those involved to be clearly heard. A bouquet was presented by Frances Davies of Winchelsea Beach and, a neat touch which has not found its way into the corporation's files but was reported by the *Sussex Express,* her majesty was presented with a photograph of herself and her parents during the 1935 visit. The cheers were doubly renewed as the party left for Hastings, after which the corporation's official guests walked to the Court Hall for the vin d'honneur.

Understandably among headlines such as 'A Right Royal Day as Conqueror's Coast Welcomes the Queen', 'Royal Couple Greeted by Happy Crowds', and 'Royal Smiles at Battle and Rye', there was little mention of the shock and sadness enveloping the country at the time following the disaster to the schoolchildren of Aberfan.[13] The queen and Prince Philip in fact fulfilled this long-planned tour on their way to visit the stricken village whither they were to travel from Sussex the following day. In view of this sombre note it is perhaps not inappropriate to mention Winchelsea's own sadnesses which are recalled when examining the list of those present. Walter Alford, among the parish council party, was attending his last public function after a life of service to the town and Mrs.

Margie Merricks, present as a county councillor, whose enthusiasm and energy did so much for the area, was later to lose her life in a tragic accident while fruit-picking in the orchard at her home.

The personal interest shown by the queen on her visit certainly added an extra dimension to Winchelsea's recognition of her silver jubilee eleven years later. We have remarked before and we shall find again that Winchelsea is very good at celebrating. This was no exception. The parish council most worthily and appropriately established, after long negotiations with the county council as owners, a children's playground in the Greyfriars Park just opposite the school. This facility has remained for the children of the town and its visitors to this day. Less permanent but extremely enjoyable was a day of special events held on 7 June 1977. This had been meticulously planned by a committee led by the mayor, Lt. Col. Peter Gray. The earlier part of the day was devoted largely to the children for whom were provided a fancy dress parade and prizegiving, numerous sideshows which no doubt the adults joined in enthusiastically as well, a sports including sack race, egg and spoon race, three-legged race, obstacle race and a '30 yard dash' for those aged '0-5 years'. Highlight of the afternoon was the children's free tea party and at this stage the 'Over 60 year olds' were given tea in the New Hall followed by all the other adults who were charged 10p. The evening saw a whist drive, barbecue of chops, sausages and rolls costing 50p and a social evening/dance at the New Hall during which 'All drinks [were] to be paid for at pub prices'. The quite exceptionally reasonable prices charged with Winchelsea residents free for almost everything were the result of an appeal for funds by the mayor which raised no less than £728.32 plus additional later donations. This left a surplus which was used to make a substantial donation to Her Majesty the Queen's Silver Jubilee Appeal Fund, to provide an additional seat in St. Thomas's Street, and to add a climbing frame to the equipment installed by the parish council in the silver jubilee playground.

The spirit in which the arrangements were so enthusiastically and successfully made was epitomised by Police Constable Hodgson who offered to give up his free day to be on duty at the cricket field gate. In those days when an officer was truly attached to a community he was confident that he would easily be able to 'sort out those who should pay for admission and those who should not', quite apart from controlling traffic and erecting warning signs.

No such opportunity for voluntary duty would have been available for him on Saturday 4 September in the same year when the formal and ceremonial side of the celebrations took place. In fact, as Winchelsea's mayor held the speakership, the occasion was the tribute of the Confederation of the Cinque Ports as well as of the town. Mayors of all the confederation ports with their consorts and a macebearer were invited to a service of thanksgiving at St. Thomas's Church. Charles Croggon, town clerk, at the centre of things as always, made the most detailed plans for this event and put them into effect so that the intricate timing and movement looked effortless. Civic dignitaries robed at the school and proceeded to the church followed by the members of Winchelsea Corporation. The deeply impressive service included the anthem *Rejoice, O land, in God thy might* composed for the occasion by Charles Proctor, a Winchelsea resident, St. Thomas's organist and conductor of the Alexandra Choir whose members joined him for the service.

In his address the Rt. Rev. Eric Kemp D.D., Bishop of Chichester, spoke of the ideal of service represented by many distinguished Lords Warden of the Cinque Ports but most of all by Her Majesty the Queen. The bishop had, the previous July, visited Walmer Castle and seen 'the room with its simple furnishings' in which the Duke of Wellington, as Lord Warden, had lived and died. After quoting lines from Tennyson's *Ode on the Death of the Duke of Wellington* Dr. Kemp concluded, 'Our Queen too has manifested that sublime simplicity and that self-sacrificing devotion to duty. It is perhaps these two of her virtues that we, her subjects, most need at this time.'

After a stirring rendering of *O God, our help in ages past* and two verses of the national anthem the procession emerged into the sunshine and made its way back to the school where the mayors disrobed before attending a reception at the Court Hall. It is apparent from the many letters of congratulation and thanks which Col. Gray received that this was an occasion more than worthy of the ancient confederation's tribute to its monarch. In due course the mayor, as speaker, sent a full report of the day's events, with photographs to the then Lord Warden, Sir Robert Menzies, former prime minister of Australia, at the same time expressing the confederation's regret that Sir Robert had not been well enough to accompany his wife on her visit to England that summer.[14]

Sir Robert's death the following year led indirectly to Winchelsea's next royal visit which followed the installation of Her Majesty Queen Elizabeth the Queen Mother as his successor in a historic and deeply impressive ceremony at Dover on 1 August 1979. Winchelsea's representatives, for whom preparations were made with a precision worthy of David Homan's earlier example, were listed in the traditional and elaborate official return of the delegation as:

Hugh Stanley Hargreaves Esquire
A Jurat and the present Mayor of the said Town
William Kenneth Whitehead Esquire
Jurat and Deputy Mayor
Captain Herbert Lovegrove
Companion of the Most Excellent Order of the British Empire,
Royal Navy, Jurat
Charles Clayton Croggon Esquire
Jurat and our Town Clerk
John Benjamin Leslie Clark Esquire
Companion of the Most Excellent Order of the British Empire,
Jurat
and
Noel Allenby Eccles Esquire
Jurat

They were accompanied by Rev. C. Geoffrey Scott, Mayor's Chaplain, and attended as macebearers by John Herbert Creasey, Chamberlain and John Roy Bullock, Sergeant-at-Mace.[15]

There is no room here to give an account of the proceedings but the inspired appointment of her majesty as the first lady Lord Warden in succession to the distinguished terms of office of Sir Winston Churchill and Sir Robert Menzies served to revitalise interest in the confederation and the traditions that its present members cherish and preserve. It has been aptly suggested that previous appointments to the position of Lord Warden had been an honour to the appointees, whereas this one was an honour to the confederation.

It did not take long for the Queen Mother to keep the promise made at the ceremony that she would as soon as possible visit all fourteen ports. Winchelsea's turn came during a Cinque Ports tour the following year. The first indication of her intentions came from her comptroller, Sir Alastair Aird, who wrote explaining that after leaving Hastings at approximately 3.45 on 9 July she proposed to drive via the ancient towns of Winchelsea and Rye to New Romney:

'It would naturally give Queen Elizabeth the greatest possible pleasure if the Mayor and senior citizens were able to greet Her Majesty for a moment that afternoon. I fear that due to the timetable it will not be feasible for the Queen Mother to stay in Winchelsea more than ten to fifteen minutes.'[16]

Well, it was at least double the time of her daughter's visit and the mayor and corporation earnestly set about making the arrangements. They assumed that the 'senior citizens' mentioned in the letter were those holding public office rather than those of more advanced years but invited the latter category as well, once again as represented by the residents of Greyfriars.

The records kept by the town clerk, Charles Croggon, show that the visit took place rather later than originally intended and probably lasted a little longer as well. It was raining when her majesty's car stopped in German Street where she was greeted by the mayor, Kenneth Whitehead, who presented the corporation members. She was scheduled to pass other guests such as the chairman of the parish council, Harold Tansley, but characteristically she stopped to shake hands with them all. Moving on under a see-through umbrella she met the schoolchildren in the churchyard and was presented with a bouquet by Louise Skinner. It was a neat and kindly touch that the head, Haydn Davies, invited his predecessor, Miss Lilah Smith, to join the school for the occasion. The children, and Miss Smith, happily put up with getting wet but the Greyfriars residents who should have been with them were escorted into the shelter of the church. The rector, Geoffrey Scott, greeted her majesty at St. Thomas's and showed her round, drawing particular attention to the Rye Lifeboat Disaster memorial window and the tomb of Gervase Alard. Sir Ralph and Lady Millais were also presented. They offered as gifts a copy of the book *Millais* by their son, Geoffroy Millais, and a print of *The Random Shot,* set in St. Thomas's Church and painted by their famous ancestor Sir John Everett Millais.

Led by the macebearers the royal party walked to the churchyard gates opposite The Little Shop where the gathered crowd sent the Queen Mother on her way with three cheers led by the mayor. The next day her private secretary, Sir Martin Gilliat, wrote from *H.M.Y. Britannia* at Dover to say how much the Lord Warden had been touched by the warmth of her reception by the people of Winchelsea.[17]

Her Majesty Queen Elizabeth the Queen Mother was to make a further visit to Winchelsea eight years later in connection with the celebration of the seven hundredth anniversary of the founding of New Winchelsea, other aspects of which will be covered in the next chapter. Despite security considerations precluding her majesty attending the Anniversary Service, her visit a week earlier was readily agreed and at last, on Friday 8 July 1988, Winchelsea was to have its royal visitor to itself for a complete afternoon rather than for a snatched interval while passing by.

The many detailed preparations included a reconnaissance visit by the helicopter of the Queen's Flight which would bring her majesty to Winchelsea. Mayor Guy Hughes and town clerk Charles Croggon, who had not been given any warning about this preliminary visit, by chance witnessed its arrival and introduced themselves. After a most interesting tour of the inside of the machine they were somewhat startled when the pilot remarked, 'Now, let's see, we're in Kent aren't we?'

On the day of the visit the helicopter landed dramatically in the field beside the cricket field. As her majesty alighted the Lord Lieutenant presented, in accordance with protocol, various dignitaries from outside the town. From that moment on Winchelsea took over with Guy Hughes controlling events with a sure and well prepared touch. Proceedings began with the by then well rehearsed procedure of a car-borne arrival in German Street to be greeted by the mayor who in turn would present the corporation members and the town clerk. In the preliminary discussions it had been pointed out that the royal lady was almost 88 and the Court Hall Museum could be reached only by a rather steep flight of outside steps. Her household saw this as no obstacle at all and the museum was accordingly included in the arrangements. Col. Noel Reeves, whose supervision of the building's public opening provided such a vital contribution to the museum's success at the time, was presented, following which Charles Croggon gave her majesty a guided tour of the displays and she signed the distinguished visitors' book with a firm and steady hand despite using an unfamiliar pen. She also accepted from the mayor a plate made at Rye Pottery in commemoration of the occasion.

(75) Her Majesty signs the corporation visitors' book, watched by Mayor Guy Hughes.

Thence to the churchyard where her majesty planted a horse chestnut tree as a replacement for the three hundred year old specimen so dramatically destroyed in the great storm of the previous October. Pausing to talk to Mr. John Wheatley of Winchelsea Beach who was on duty as a guardsman on the occasion of her wedding and who carried her personal standard at her first public engagement, the Lord Warden again visited the church. At St. Thomas's School the head teacher, Mr. John Read, was presented and there was time for her to make an extended tour, speaking to almost half the pupils and actively encouraging Lucy Cook who was painting Her Majesty's picture to put the appropriate white flowers on the royal dress. She also talked for a considerable time to residents of Greyfriars, some present remarking that the royal visitor was probably considerably older than most of them.

The Queen Mother, after bidding the mayor farewell at the school, returned by car to the helicopter and made a dramatic departure to match her arrival with the machine sweeping away to the east and north to fly over the Cinque Ports on its way to her official residence at Walmer Castle.[18]

Winchelsea was able, in a small way, to repay the compliment it received through these visits when the then mayor, Anthony Tremeer, took part with his colleagues of the confederation in the parade which was part of the 90th birthday tribute held on Horse Guards on 27 June 1990.[19]

This chapter's last royal visit was, in keeping with the character of the visitor, quiet, unassuming and caring. Her Royal Highness the Duchess of Kent came to Winchelsea in 1992, with a particular interest in the Friary Gardeners, a scheme which existed in the grounds of the Greyfriars for several years with the purpose of providing opportunities in horticulture for workers with mental handicaps. The project was undertaken on a commercial basis, successfully and purposefully employing those for whom it was designed. The duchess's obvious interest and concern must have given both the leaders and the participants great encouragement. Arrangements within the town were made by Antony Sandeman, at that time mayor and speaker, and included, as well as the Friary Gardeners, an inspection of the ruins of the Greyfriars Chapel, a tour of St. Thomas's Church and tea at the Court Hall with members of the corporation and of the parish council.[20] It was unfortunately an extremely cold day and those of us who watched the royal party make its way across the churchyard in a biting wind felt that we were fortunate to be well sheltered. The cold, however, could not reduce the warmth of the greeting offered to Her Royal Highness or that of her interest and friendliness. Her departure by helicopter brought to an end the last royal visit which this book can record but hopefully Winchelsea will see many more such occasions in the future.

It is perhaps not inappropriate to mention here two visits which were most definitely not royal but occurred during this period and created considerable interest in the town. The first was by Ian Botham who made Winchelsea one of his overnight stopping points on the 1992 South Coast Walk in aid of the Leukaemia Research Fund. His wife had written giving almost eight months' notice of this event and Winchelsea entered into the spirit of it with a will. It was even suggested that the mayor, Ken Chetwood, and corporation, fully robed, might lead the walk down the High Street at the beginning of the day's stage. This was tactfully declined on the grounds that when Ian starts walking there is no stopping him and he walks fast, an observation readily confirmed on the day by those who went at a sedate pace to The Lookout to wave the party on their way and found they were already half way to Rye!

Scaffolded banners announcing the walk and the amount raised so far were erected in German Street for the arrival the previous evening and a large crowd gathered to cheer Ian and his fellow walkers with their support party when they left on the morning of 14 October. Fund-raising being the principal object of this demanding exercise, a number of cheques were handed over by local organisations and individuals before the walkers left with buckets rattling on the next stage of their 535 mile progress from Land's End to Margate, completed in 22 days.[21]

Winchelsea's next non-royal but nonetheless distinguished visitor was not so energetic, his fund-raising was done by taxi! Advance notice in this case was highly unexpected. I answered the telephone one afternoon to be told, 'It's the Earl of Winchilsea speaking.' Bearing in mind that I often get my leg pulled about my obsession with Winchelsea and its history, it was fortunate that I did not respond with, 'Now pull the other one!' His lordship was planning another long-distance journey entitled 'Cab Around Britain' in aid of the Saharawan Aid Trust, a registered charity which he has established to provide humanitarian aid for some 200,000 refugees from the Western Sahara who were forced into exile from that country when in 1975 it was invaded by both Morocco and Mauretania. Fund raising was augmented by a sweepstake on what the fare on the clock would be at the end of the twenty six day trip which included a three-night stop to attend the Liberal Democrat conference in Glasgow.

Despite the variation in spelling, Winchelsea is the town from which his title is taken for his ancestor was ennobled by Charles I in recognition of services rendered to the crown in connection with the Cinque Ports. Since that time many of those who have held the title have made a mark upon the history of this country, one being an Augustan poet, another accepting the surrender of Dover Castle on behalf of Charles II and later being made Lord Warden of the Cinque Ports, a third financing the founding by Thomas Lord of Lord's and the M.C.C., a fourth fighting a duel with the Duke of Wellington, and a fifth driving a wagonette in the first London to Brighton car run in 1896. The present holder is Liberal Democrat spokesman in the House of Lords on the police service, Britain's licensed taxi drivers, and on the Saharawi refugees. In this project he used the first two to support the third, borrowing a London cab painted in many colours and being accompanied by an off duty police officer.

In the circumstances he thought it inappropriate to drive through Winchelsea without stopping, a feeling strongly endorsed by the corporation and he was given a warm welcome at the Court Hall where, with the gaudily painted taxi parked outside, light refreshments were served and collection boxes were again rattling. Lord Winchilsea was sent on his way with the hope that he would keep in touch with the town of his title's origin and a good donation to his cause including, in a neat touch, a gift from the mayor and mayoress, Henry and Sue Dormer of the equivalent of one year's corporation income from the queen's dues.[22]

(76) The Earl of Winchilsea bids farewell to the mayor, Lt. Col. Henry Dormer.

33. SEVEN HUNDREDTH ANNIVERSARIES

It was Charles Croggon who, in plenty of time, reminded the corporation members that 1988 would be the seven hundredth anniversary of the handing over to the men of Winchelsea of the land on the hill of Iham on which their new town was being built. Clearly this was an event needing recognition on a scale compatible with the pleasure and gratitude shown when, on 25 July 1288, Sir John de Kirkeby, Bishop of Ely and representative of the king, in the presence of 'the Sheriff of Sussex and other nobles and knights' granted 'absolute and quiet possession rent free for seven years' and confirmed all the citizens' ancient rights and privileges as a head port of the Confederation of the Cinque Ports.[1]

The mayor in 1988, Guy Hughes, eagerly grasping this opportunity, gathered together a committee representative of the corporation and town organisations to consider what form the celebrations should take. There was much enthusiasm. Suggestions made on the evening of the first meeting included a film show, a barbecue, an art exhibition, a theatrical performance, a pageant, a sports day, a best kept garden competition, a band concert, fireworks and a service of commemoration. It took only a few minutes to realise that many such suggestions could be incorporated and even at the first meeting these various ideas were distilled into a provisional programme which looks remarkably like the eventual one. Originally it was planned to begin with the service on 15 July and end with a grand fireworks display on the actual anniversary date ten days later. During the meeting it was suggested that the fireworks might perhaps be in the Mill Field with the windmill floodlit as a backdrop to the display.[2]

Little could the committee members have known as they sat considering this possibility that within forty eight hours of the end of their meeting a two hundred year old landmark would have disappeared for ever and there would no longer be a Winchelsea Mill. The first seven hundredth anniversary event which Winchelsea witnessed burst upon the town on the night of 15/16 October 1987 with a violence similar to that of the great storm of 1287 which had finally brought about the destruction of Old Winchelsea. The sights which next morning greeted Sussex and south-east England were such as are statistically unlikely to be seen again for centuries to come.

I could not for some time visit Winchelsea to see the damage for the storm, some called it a hurricane but I am told this is meteorologically incorrect, had ripped the roof from the main assembly hall of the William Parker School in Hastings where I was working at the time and had caused extensive damage to the rest of the buildings. My preoccupations and responsibilities lay there. On that dramatic morning I clearly remember the head, Roger Mitchell, saying, 'Someone go and fetch a camera, this is history.'

Fortunately there were Winchelsea residents similarly minded and an album of photographs taken on the morning of 16 October and still on display at the Court Hall shows the trail of devastation which greeted the town as day dawned after that frightful night. St. Thomas's Street, German Street and The Walk were blocked by fallen trees. Two enormous chestnuts and an oak had been lost in Rookery Lane. Hundreds of other trees, particularly on Friars Cliff, had been destroyed as had the roof of the barn beside the surviving gable of St. John's Hospital, together with countless greenhouses and fences. The school had a remarkable escape, and remained largely undamaged but surrounded by fallen trees. The marsh and Royal Military Canal were severely flooded for these enormously powerful winds had been preceded by weeks of rain. It was highly fortunate for Winchelsea Beach and all towns and villages on the coast that as the height of the storm raged the tide was out.

Most dramatic loss of all was of the mill. This outstanding feature of the local landscape, visible not only from the town but also from large areas of the surrounding countryside lay irreparable in shattered pieces, its resistance to the force of the wind probably weakened by the earlier removal of its internal machinery (see p.151). Those of us who knew the mill for many years have, since that sensational night, often felt a pang of loss when confronted by its empty site.

Perhaps the most important tree which fell was the three hundred year old horse chestnut rooted by the ruined north transept of St. Thomas's Church. The mighty trunk had split, leaving part of this enormous specimen lying across the graves and part still standing but in a dangerous condition. Urgent investigations by the parochial church council which included the possibility of saving the remaining part by bracing it up eventually came to nothing for such expense would not guarantee its survival. In the following January a team of five workers with chainsaws completed the work the storm had begun and, apart from its enormous stump, the great tree was no more.[3] Its replacement, judiciously sited further away from the building, was six months later planted by Her Majesty Queen Elizabeth the Queen Mother.

The visit which enabled her to perform this ceremony (see pp.242-243) preceded the week of celebrations whose outline had been drawn up at the committee meeting already referred to and finalised through many debates and much hard work since. In charge of these extensive preparations was mayor Guy Hughes, a wartime naval officer who served on aircraft carriers as secretary to Captain, later Admiral of the Fleet, Caspar John, the son of Augustus John, and who, on leaving the navy, became a director of the pharmaceutical company Goya. His energy, qualities and interest in the town had earlier led to his installation as a freeman after the shortest period of residence in recent times. Here the corporation had found a leader able to draw the community together in a united effort which not only transformed and invigorated the town but also attracted great interest from outside.

On Friday 15 July his worship led the speaker, with the seneschal and registrar of the Confederation of the Cinque Ports, followed in turn by the mayors, each preceded by a macebearer, in solemn procession from the school, along Friars Road, St. Thomas's Street and part of the High Street to a packed church. The procession passed a considerable gathering of residents and visitors in a town bedecked with bunting, much of it put up with considerable effort, some personal hazard and not a little leg-pulling by the corporation's newest jurats, Maurice Humphreys and Peter Hoskins.

We have noted many impressive services on occasions both joyous and sombre which have been acted out within the incomparable surroundings of St. Thomas's. This was one of the most memorable. Among the congregation were the High Sheriff of East Sussex, the Deputy Constable of Dover Castle, the Chairmen of East Sussex County Council, Rother District Council and Icklesham Parish Council, together with many other dignitaries, notably Dr. Errol Pickering, Director General of the International Federation, officially representing the Shire of Winchelsea, Victoria, Australia. The service began with the national anthem, all three verses, and included part of *The Gloria* by Vivaldi sung by the Winchelsea Singers directed by Leo Halle and accompanied at the organ by Charles Proctor. Most appropriately for a Cinque Ports occasion the address was given by the Right Reverend Richard Third, Bishop of Dover and Chaplain to the Lord Warden. The congregation joined in three hymns, rousingly sung and including *O God our help in ages past* and as the service drew to a close the prayer of St. Richard was sung by the St. Thomas's School choir.[4]

Nevertheless, no aspect of the service, however memorable, could overshadow the stunning impact of the flower arrangements by the ladies of the parish led by Mrs. Gwendoline Sandeman and I well remember, despite our having admired the general effect at the service, returning later with my wife to have time to study and take in more of the detail of this remarkable display.

Even larger crowds were attracted the following day for a magnificent pageant which was the culmination of much research into the history of the town, particularly by John Read, head of St. Thomas's School, his pupils and staff, supported by other local groups. With martial music providing a stirring lead, large numbers of young people, appropriately costumed, represented historical events across New Winchelsea's seven centuries, with proceedings much enlivened by touches of humour such as those created by Cliff Dean of the school staff, by the chairman of the managers, Rev. Geoffrey Scott, being spotted playing his violin among a group of minstrels and by such striking moments as those provided by the poise and dignity of Queen Elizabeth I, as played by a red-haired young lady from Rye Harbour.

The conclusion of the pageant permitted no let-up in the activities. A stoolball tournament and a barn dance later the same day were followed by a crowded patronal service at St. Thomas's on the Sunday, an organ recital by Charles Proctor O.B.E. and a bowls match between the ladies and the gentlemen on the Monday and school sports day on the Tuesday. The mayor and his leading colleagues must have wondered when they were to be allowed a few minutes off. Certainly not on the Tuesday evening when the New Hall was packed to capacity for an event which commenced with a talk in costume by Kenneth Clark of Rye on 'Winchelsea, Rye and the Armada Challenge' which was followed by 'Reminiscences of Winchelsea', billed as 'a programme of talks and memories by some of the older inhabitants'. Miss Katharina Forbes-Dunlop, Messrs. Douglas Turner and Anthony Thomas, together with many of the stories they told, have featured elsewhere in this book. The force of the first named's personality dominated the evening. Her energy, enthusiasm, clarity and audibility at the age of 96 were the admiration of all present. Eventually the charming and tactful lady from Radio Sussex who was in the chair took Miss Forbes-Dunlop gently by the arm and wondered whether she might like to have a rest, a suggestion with which she concurred, thus allowing the others to play their full part but no doubt was left by the audience's reactions as to who was the star of the show!

Wednesday 20 July saw, at St. Thomas's Church, a much praised 'Celebration in poetry and song of 700 years of historic Winchelsea' by Molly Townson, Mary Densem, Richard Firmager, Clifford Foster and Duncan Brown, followed the next day by a 'Military Band Concert and Beating Retreat at the cricket field by the Queen's Regimental Band (TA) and Corps of Drums of the 5th Battalion (V) Queen's Regiment by kind permission of the commanding officer. If wet a modified programme in the New Hall.' It was wet. The highly enjoyable 'modified programme' took place inside and some think that the drumming and playing were so forcefully rousing that they led to the final destabilisation of the New Hall roof! The concert was so greatly appreciated that the cheers and applause of the audience could certainly be more conventionally described as bringing the roof down.

As the week built towards its climax a street party in Castle Street for children under 13 on the Friday led to a Saturday so packed with events that residents wishing to attend them all must have been left somewhat bemused. An exhibition 'The Life and Art of John Everett Millais (1829-1896)' including original drawings, prints and other memorabilia (see also p.99) was mounted in St. Thomas's Church throughout the day. Winchelsea Cricket Club played an eleven raised by its president 'including former Sussex players' in the afternoon and in the evening there was a barbecue/disco at the New Hall and Cricket Field. Perhaps the greatest transformation of the week was achieved through the medieval market, morris dancing and arms display which transported

(77) The medieval fayre in full swing.

Castle Street back in costume, appearance and atmosphere to the times of seven hundred years before when King Edward I was establishing the town.

To sustain a celebration of this kind was a remarkable achievement for a small community, made even more remarkable by the fact that it made a profit! When all the excitement was over and Winchelsea had resumed its normal tranquil state the mayor produced for the information of all concerned a detailed balance sheet showing as major items of expenditure the purchase and hire of bunting, the hire of 'Portaloos', transport and refreshments for the band, materials, props and entertainers for the medieval market, illumination of the town gates, together with the kind of expenses one would expect to be involved in staging the children's pageant, the barn dance, the children's party and the numerous other events. The enthusiasm and persuasiveness of the mayor and his committee shines through this section of the accounts which notes that the band's appearance fee was paid in full by NatWest Bank, refreshments for the medieval market were donated by Phoenix Brewery, the principal programme was paid for by J. Alsford Ltd., and those for individual events by South-East Computers, with posters financed by National Girobank. To these were added a long list of additional donations and grants. Perhaps the level of participation by the public is best shown by the total takings from the sale of tickets for the barn dance, historical evening, concert, barbecue and disco. Although modestly priced these tickets raised no less than £1765.90 and the takings, including the bar, at the medieval market £710.41. The surplus was allocated partly to the corporation for its work in preserving the town's architectural heritage and partly to St. Thomas's Church.[5]

The second of the major commemorative festivals took place four years later in recognition of the seven hundredth anniversary of the original rent roll for the new town. Several years previously it had been suggested that 1992 should be the principal year of celebration on the grounds that it represented the anniversary of the completion of the town and as 1942, despite the forced absence of any jollifications, had been taken to be the 650th. Fortunately other counsels prevailed and the official handing over of the site to the people was rightly accepted as the key event.

Although quite properly on a reduced scale by comparison the 1992 events, this time under mayor Ken Chetwood's leadership, were thoroughly appropriate to the occasion and made a considerable impact in the town. The circumstances of the rent roll's compilation, the celebratory residential roll and the mayor and mayoress's Cinque Ports luncheon have already been described. (see p.95). Writing to all the residences in the 'citadel' area and the Strand to collect information for the residential roll was a big undertaking, as was the actual delivery and collection where David Bourne, jurat and postmaster, provided enthusiastic leadership. There was a most gratifying response which typified the interest shown by large numbers of residents in matters related to the town's history.

A further three years elapsed before the third celebratory event came to fruition to complete the sequence. The records summarised on the Court Hall boards show 1295 as the year when, on Easter Monday, Gervase Alard junior was installed as Mayor of Winchelsea. There is no certainty that he was the first mayor, although he can hardly have been preceded by more than a few others of whom no record has survived. In view of this doubt the title of the celebration had to be carefully worded: 'The Seven Hundredth Anniversary of Winchelsea's First Recorded Mayoralty'. One might expect that a man taking office seven centuries earlier would be a shadowy figure of whom only his name is known. In this case, not so. Gervase Alard, whose surname derived from the Saxon Aethelwald, was one of a family of successful goldsmiths, vintners and traders who had been leading Winchelsea residents for centuries. Their powerful influence and maritime skill climaxed with Gervase's royal appointment as admiral of the Cinque Ports fleet, later including the fleet of all the ports as far as Cornwall. That he should also serve as mayor of his home town on at least two occasions, in 1295 and 1308, provides us with evidence not only of his family's leading part in Winchelsea life but also of the importance attached to the mayoralty in those days.

It was, however, Gervase Alard's national significance which led to the construction of the tomb normally assumed to be his, positioned in the south aisle of St. Thomas's Church and adorned with carvings of the heads of his monarch, King Edward I and of Queen Margaret. St. Thomas's has, over the centuries, been the focal point of the vast majority of Winchelsea's major events, the presence of his tomb made it essential that these particular celebrations should be, initially at least, within its doors.

The planning and preparations became very largely the responsibility of the man honoured to be the seven hundredth mayor since Alard, Lt. Col. Henry Dormer, a retired Royal Artillery officer. He arranged a civic commemoration concert to take place at St. Thomas's on the evening of 27 May 1995, featuring the Winchelsea Singers under their conductor, Leo Halle, with Charles Proctor O.B.E. at the organ, Mary Chetwood at the piano and with soloists Janice Reeve and Roy Bicknell. Henry Dormer is himself a leading bass with the Winchelsea Singers but on this occasion, attending with the corporation in mayoral robes, he had a rare opportunity to enjoy their performance as a member of the audience. The entry of the civic procession was accompanied by the playing of *The Lord Warden's Rondo*, a piece composed by Charles Proctor for the visit of Her Majesty Queen Elizabeth the Queen Mother to Rye Church in 1980. The mayor gave a warm and witty welcome to all present and particularly to the corporation's official guests who included the Deputy Constable of

Dover Castle, Brigadier Vere Hayes, the M.P. for Hastings and Rye, Mrs. Jacqui Lait, local mayors and council chairmen. He also made mention of another anniversary by drawing attention to a plaque in his garden at Waterstone Cottage, built on the site of the old reservoir, which reads:

> 'Water was brought from Newgate Spring into Winchelsea, November 1895. Kingsnorth Reeve Esq., Chairman of Committee. George Burnham, Contractor. Charles Smith, Surveyor.' (see also pp.62-63)

The mayor's welcome was followed by a rousing and accomplished performance by the Winchelsea Singers of *Through the Mists of Time* by Elgar, epilogue of his *Banner of St. George,* a piece popular with choral societies and intensely relevant to the occasion with its exhortation, 'Ne'er forget the glorious deeds of old'.

I had the privilege of being asked to follow this with a talk entitled *The Mayoralty Established* in introducing which I could not but point out that many of the deeds of the men of Winchelsea of old included violence, piracy and wrecking and were far from glorious. However it remains true that the heritage accumulated over those centuries is glorious indeed and must be warmly cherished. I also gave a warning which, as we approach the end of this story, it is perhaps relevant to repeat for it certainly applies to the earlier years of that heritage and such accounts as I have given of them:

> 'The times of which I shall speak this evening, viewed across the divide of seven centuries, are misty indeed. As all students of medieval history are aware, very little information about those days can be confirmed as fact – documents are untrustworthy, accounts were written many years later from hearsay, sources conflict and, most frequently of all, no information survives on points which it would be vitally helpful to know. It is not much fun, though, to have to qualify every statement with ifs, buts, possiblies and perhapses. You must therefore accept that what I have to tell, while it will be stated as fact, is largely reasonable supposition based on the available evidence.' [6]

The musical evening resumed with a performance of *Sea Pictures* by Elgar, sung by Janice Reeve, accompanied by Mary Chetwood. Like all the pieces chosen for the occasion, this moving work, beautifully performed, fully reflected Winchelsea's maritime past. The Winchelsea Singers were then joined by soloist Roy Bicknell for a spirited performance of *Songs of the Fleet,* settings of the poems of Henry Newbolt by Sir Charles Villiers Stanford. The programme notes pointed out that Stanford 'revitalised the oratorio which had been the province of the privileged. There has not been an acknowledged English genius such as his since the days of Purcell whose 300 year anniversary is being celebrated this year,' thus allowing Charles Proctor to squeeze yet another anniversary into the evening's proceedings, the organ voluntaries and recessional music being exclusively by Purcell.

It was therefore to his *Trumpet Tune and Peal* that the mayor, corporation and official guests emerged into a fine spring evening to make their way to St. Thomas's Street where the Cinque Ports Corps of Drums, resplendent in their scarlet ceremonial uniforms, were called to attention by bandmaster Lt. Paul Casson, ready to lead the official party at a tactfully gentle pace to Castle Street. When the guests were settled in an enclosure on the grass verge outside The Armoury the Beating of Retreat began. The skill of the pipes and drums of the Corps, most of whom are young people made this a truly memorable occasion witnessed not only by the civic party but also by other members of the concert audience and a large gathering of local people. The weather was kind, the applause generous and appreciative, and the choice of music, more military than naval, added extra relevance by recalling Winchelsea's past as a garrison town.[7] The members of the Corps were clearly delighted to perform before an audience including the Deputy Constable and he made a particular point of congratulating them on their smartness and musicianship.

And so, with Castle Street ringing to martial music, and a large crowd of residents and visitors gathered together, we leave this story of a community which, while assimilating and largely enjoying the changes brought by the nineteenth and twentieth centuries as it moved from abject poverty to comparative prosperity, jealously guards the traditions which have survived those changes.

(78) The Cinque Ports Corps of Drums beating retreat in Castle Street.

EPILOGUE

A final word brings us, as we began, to the annual Easter Monday mayoring ceremony, proud symbol of Winchelsea's civic longevity. As the guests assemble and rise for the entry of the current mayor, jurats and officers, we should do well to bear in mind the words of Ford Madox Ford:

> 'There is only one Winchelsea and there is no place like it, no place that so effectually and so pleasantly teaches us the lesson that we most need in these days of hurry and forgetfulness. Where else can one so well realise that there were strong men before Agamemnon; so well learn that the Agamemnons of today are but strong men that will fall and be forgotten at the rise of the Agamemnons of tomorrow,' [1]

Winchelsea's Agamemnons of the nineteenth and twentieth centuries, Richard and Robert Stileman, George Mallows and Anthony Freeman, Frederic Inderwick, Ernest Goldschmidt, Harriett McIlwraith, Maud Peel, William Maclean Homan, Douglas Turner, Alex Finch, Herbert Lovegrove and Charles Croggon have all frequently taken part in or witnessed this ceremony. Strong and enthusiastic successors will be needed to carry the traditions forward, to add to the list of mayors until it outgrows its Court Hall wall, to lead the community, whether or not as members of the corporation, in such a way as to retain the town's unique individuality so that some successor of mine as yet long unborn might one day find it of interest to write the story of Winchelsea in the twenty-first century and beyond.

APPENDIX I

(see pp.94-96)

In compiling this list from the forms submitted I have tried wherever possible to use the single christian name and surname which were used in the 1292 Rent Roll. Titles have been added where only initials have been given in the returns.

THE WINCHELSEA RESIDENTIAL ROLL 1992

ABOVE THE PENDENTS OF THE HILL

Lord Ritchie of Dundee
Lady Ritchie of Dundee
Roy Horobin
Sheila Horobin

THE FIRST QUARTER

(Mrs.) A. Gladwish
Jessie Carter[1]
Bernard Dibble
Bridget Dibble
George Carman
Edward Streeton
Peter Fielder
Patricia-Anne Fielder
Daphne Robertson
Evelyn Whiting
Dominic Leahy
Margot Leahy
Daphne Lovegrove
(Mr.) G.M. Hayward
Marcia Bruce

THE SECOND QUARTER

Francis Holland
Hilda Holland
John Dunk
Brenda Dunk
Ian Forbes-Watson
Evelyn Forbes-Watson
Helen Wynne-Thomas
Mary Hodgson
Alan Woodburn
Eileen Woodburn
Esther Simpson
Norman Cooper
Pauline Cooper
Vivienne Bridges
(Mr.) J.D. Spencer
(Mrs.) M.E. Spencer

(Miss) K.J. Spencer
(Miss) C.E. Spencer
Malcolm Bridges
Jayne Bridges
Robert Beecroft
Charlotte Beecroft
Barbara Murrell
Josian Andrew
Vera Atkins

THE THIRD QUARTER

Babette, Lady Millais
Sir Ralph Millais (died 14/5/1992)
Carol Prior
Oliver Prior
Catherine Prior
Natasha Prior
Sophie Prior
Margot Bruce
Lady Wendy Batsford[2]
Janet Plummer
Michael Plummer
Matthew Plummer
Emily Plummer
Jack Evans
Marie Evans
John Chilton
Peggy Chilton
Robin Hazelton
Brenda Hazelton
Terence Gauntlett
Anita Gauntlett
Neil Thompson
Ruth Thompson
John Evans
Janet Evans

THE FOURTH QUARTER

Jan van Heuven
Dorothy van Heuven

THE FIFTH QUARTER

Ian Whittall
Yolé Coaks

THE SIXTH QUARTER

Andrew Bradshaw
Maureen Bradshaw
Sharon Bradshaw
Christopher Wenban
(Mrs.) Christopher Wenban
Alan Cox
Adam Cox
Dr. H.B.J. Chishick
(Mrs.) J.R. Chishick
Paul Chishick
Toby Chishick
Mary Chetwood
David Doe (d. 3/3/1992)
Delyth Doe

THE SEVENTH QUARTER

Muriel Crowhurst
Walter Slade
Stella Chappel
Jacqueline Stevens
Peter Stevens
Bernard Doherty
Barbara McFadyean
Michael McFadyean
Anthony Moore
Susan Moore
John Bevis
Hazel Bevis
Wynne Champion
John Gooders
Roberta Gooders
Stuart Chapman
Nancie Lyle
Barbara Lyle

THE EIGHTH QUARTER

Antony Sandeman
Gwendoline Sandeman
Douglas Turner
Hugues van Stratum
Wilma van Stratum
Reginald Packard
Frances Packard
Maureen Satow
Trevor Kirby (to August)
Peter Wheatcroft (from August)
(Mr.) F.W. Packham
Patricia Dawes
Heather Flowerdew
(Mrs.) H.S. Tanburn
Mary Cullwick
Charles Proctor O.B.E.
Rosemary Proctor
Gordon Goodrich
Elisabeth Goodrich
Bernard Ross
Mark Hitchings
Ian Marven
Ann Sparks
Knightley Chetwood
Peter Baker
Sara Baker
Simon Baker
Lucy Baker
David Bowen (d. April)
Margaret Bowen
Patricia Norman

THE NINTH QUARTER

Owen Prideaux
Marie Prideaux
Michael Shaw[3]
Marguerite Fuller
Marjorie Williams
Morag Simpson
Walter Simpson
Sarah Simpson
Yvette Allen
Michael Allen
Michael Roud
Jack Dunk
Robert Collins
Philip Fernau
Barbara Fernau
Gertrude Finch
David Lee
Jane Lee
Joanna Lee
Victoria Lee
Vincent Kevins

Marjorie Kevins
Jack Foster
Winifred Foster
Sheila Priestley
John Priestley
Iris Rudd
Ada Smith
Anthony Tremeer
Renée Tremeer
Royston Coxon
Ann Coxon
Christopher Coxon
Daisy Rengert
Margaret Skeggs

THE TENTH QUARTER

Doris Mason

THE TWELFTH QUARTER

James Lindars
Bethia Lindars

THE THIRTEENTH QUARTER

Peter Mason
Muriel Mason
Ronald Winter
Eileen Winter
Douglas Allison
Joyce Allison
Rev. Geoffrey Scott
Heather Scott
Dr. Colin Alexander
Gillian Alexander
Ben Alexander
Katy Alexander
Petronilla Barclay
Pamela Ridler
David Bourne
Anne Bourne

THE FOURTEENTH QUARTER

Richard Joyce
Eileen Joyce
Graham Joyce
Andrew Joyce
John King
Jennifer King
Paul Johnson
Paula Johnson
(Mrs.) R. Paton
Maurice Humphreys
Jacqueline Humphreys
Martin Esslin
Renata Esslin

Guy Hughes
Eve Hughes
Amy Goddard (d. 1/3/1992)
Rosemary Andrew
Guy Fitzmaurice
Lt. Col. Henry Dormer
Susan Dormer
John Reeves
Susi Harries

THE EIGHTEENTH QUARTER

Audrey Hills
Andrew Williams
Peter Bligh
Beryl Bligh
Ashley Bligh
Nathan Bligh
Jonathan Jempson
Sarah Jempson
Katherine Jempson
Amy Jempson

THE NINETEENTH QUARTER

Terence Cuthbert
Anne Cuthbert
Tobias Cuthbert
Helen Goldie
Rev. Harry Potts
Tessa Potts
Richard Handley
Ellenor Handley
Reginald West
Brenda Milton
Christopher Cook
Sam Milton-Cook
Tom Milton-Cook
(Mrs.) Margaret Gall
Jean Gall
(Miss) Margaret Gall
Norman Turner
Patricia Turner
Dianna Tennant
Derek Tennant
Gareth Tennant
Gayle Tennant

THE TWENTIETH QUARTER

Charles Meek C.M.G.
Nona Meek
Barbara Murray
Hilary Baker
Jack Baker
John Melford Stevenson[4]
Demy Stevenson

William Everett
Jean Everett
Gervase Moore
Leila Moore
Betty Bevan
Sheila Lockhart-Mure
Michael Stickland
Stella Stickland

THE TWENTY-FIRST QUARTER

Cyril Sanders C.B.
Kate Sanders
Peter Hoskins
Patricia Hoskins
Terence Farrell
Doreen Farrell
June Hyson
Denis Hyson
Katharin Page
Mary Wright
Paul Praeger
Charlotte Praeger
Catherine Praeger
Thomas Praeger
Edmund Praeger

THE TWENTY-FIFTH QUARTER

Mary Elms
Antony Mackenzie Smith
Isobel Mackenzie Smith
Katherine Woolf
William Cleveland-Stevens

THE TWENTY-SIXTH QUARTER

Cecily Skinner

THE TWENTY-SEVENTH QUARTER

Phyllis Bullard
Rhoda Burnett
Katie Burt
Dorothy Bradbury
Modhitt Carter
Madge Colgate
William Etherington
Frances Elgood
Whaley Glover
Helen Hedgler
Elizabeth Lay
Martha Molyneaux
Margaret Ord-Hume
Jack Payne
Joan Petfield
Edith Saunders
William Penfold
James Webb
Herbert Wells

BELOW THE PENDENTS OF THE HILL

Roger Pownall
Ann Pownall
Joanne Pownall
Donald Cameron-Clarke
Peta Cameron-Clarke
Grant Cameron-Clarke
Sidney Smith
Joan Smith
Rod Gould
Julie Gould
Joanne Gould
Christopher Gould
Andrew Pettitt
Judith Pettitt
Matthew Pettitt
Barbara Slater
Stephen Moore
Tricia Moore
Megan Moore
Kenna Moore
Geoffrey Hatton
Anita Blair
Allan Pope
Diane Pope

Notes:

1 Mrs Carter's late husband, Norman, served the Greyfriars Estate for well over thirty years from Lord Blanesburgh's time until his retirement in 1977.

2. Lady Wendy Batsford's husband, Sir Brian, the distinguished publisher, artist, and politician died in 1991. They were for many years residents of Rye, for part of that time as tenants of the National Trust's Lamb House, former home of Henry James. Sir Brian took a great interest in preserving the atmosphere of the house as it was in James's time, collecting memorabilia with this purpose in mind. They both enjoyed tending the garden which their predecessor had loved so much. All matters of environmental concern were close to Sir Brian's heart and as chairman of the Rye Preservation Society he exerted considerable influence. Sir Brian and Lady Batsford, both painters, moved to Winchelsea in 1988.

3. Michael Shaw's parents, Sir John Shaw K.C.M.G., a former Governor of Trinidad and Tobago, and Lady Josephine Shaw lived for many years at 2, White Close, German Street. Both were greatly respected residents who took a close interest in the town and its activities. Sir John arranged the testimonial to Alex Finch (see p.160).

4. In 1992 when the residential roll was compiled John Melford Stevenson was living at Truncheons, Rectory Lane, formerly the home of his parents, Sir Melford and Lady Stevenson. It is sometimes assumed that the name of the house is associated with Sir Melford's reputation as a forthright and distinguished barrister and later high court judge who took part in many famous trials, most notably sentencing the Kray twins. In fact the land on which the house stands was, partly at least, known as Truncheons as early as the mid-eighteenth century. Trojan's Plat is a corruption of the same name.

APPENDIX II

FREEMEN OF WINCHELSEA (1800 - 1998)

ALCE Robert 1834-1847 [1]
ANDERSON John Coussmaker 1908-1914, Mayor 1910
    Deputy Mayor 1909
BALFOUR Arthur 1795-1803
BARWELL Richard 1794-1804
BARWELL Richard 1800-1803
BEAUMONT John 1834-1841, M 1837 DM 1835 1841
BEECROFT Robert George 1996-Present, M 1997 1998
BENNETT William 1854-1864
BLACKMAN George 1834-1866
BOURNE David Richard 1900-Present, DM 1995 1996
BRAY William 1834-1873, DM 1846-1849
BROWNE Barwell 1793-1828, M 1796 1800 1802 1805
    1807 1809 1811 1813 1815 1817 1819 1821 1823
    1825
BROWNE Fielding 1827-1835, DM 1830
BROWNE William Barrington 1912-1919, M 1913
    DM 1914-1918
BRUCE Thomas Alan Nicholson 1950-1976, M 1960
    1961 1972 DM 1959 1965 1971
BURKE John Addison 1922-1945, M 1926 1927 1933
    1936-1938 1943 DM 1925 1929-1932 1935 1939-
    1942 1944 1945
BUTLER Henry Pearch 1807-1829
BUTLER Richard 1769-1808
CAMERON-CLARKE Donald 1996-Present
CAMPION Charles Walter 1907-1925, M 1909
CHETWOOD Knightley Wilfred 1987-Present, M 1992
    1993 DM 1990 1991
CLARK John Benjamin Leslie 1970-1983, M 1973 1974
    DM 1972
COFFIN Jonathan 1794-1800
COLE Donovan Dennett Wilding 1972-Present, M 1975
    1976 DM 1973 1974
COOKSON John Wyndham 1946-1958, M 1951 1954
    DM 1949 1950
COOPER Edgar 1872-1875
COWIN Matthew 1873-1875
CROGGON Charles Clayton 1965-1995, M 1967 1968
    1984 1985 DM 1975 1976
DAVIES Robert Coker Nash 1850-1852, M 1852
DAVIS Spencer 1866-1888
DAVISON George 1804
DAWES Thomas 1834-1844, M 1834 1840 1842
DORMER Henry George 1990-Present, M 1995 1996
    DM 1994
DOWSE John 1806-1807
DUNK Arthur John 1996-Present
DYER William 1882-1885

ECCLES Noel Allenby 1978-Present, M 1981 1986
    DM 1983
FRASER James Elder 1882-1887
FREEMAN George Mallows 1894-1932, M 1895 1897
    1904 1905 1907 1911 1915-1919 1928 DM 1912
    1922 1926 1927
FREEMAN Phillip Anthony Mallows 1918-1970,
    M 1929 1930 1944-1946 1952 1953 1957 1962
    DM 1934 1943 1956 1958 1960
FULLER Walter 1834-1870
FULLER Walter 1866-1907
GARROD Ralph Eddowes 1960-1964, M 1964
    DM 1963
GOLDSCHMIDT Ernest Zven 1927-1947 M 1941
    1942 DM 1938
GRAY Patrick Vivian 1965-1982, M 1971 1977
    DM 1968 1978
GRIFFITHS Samuel 1866-1876, M 1866 1867
HARGREAVES Hugh Stanley 1976-1990, M 1978 1979
HARRISON Edward Lake 1904-1907
HARROD George 1834-1837
HEMMINGS James 1867-1873
HENNAH Joseph 1821-1858, M 1836 1844-1849
    DM 1828 1853
HILL Charles 1836-1859
HILL George 1814-1848, DM 1843-1845
HOLMES Basil 1914-1936, M 1925
HOLT Jacob 1834-1864
HOSKINS Peter Leonard 1988-Present, M 1994
    DM 1993
HUGHES Guy Alexander 1983-Present, M 1987 1988
    DM 1985 1986
HUMPHREYS Henry Maurice 1988-1993, DM 1992
INDERWICK Frederic Andrew 1878-1904, M 1882
    1885 1891 1892 1896 1902 DM 1883 1884
INDERWICK Walter Andrew 1898-1911, M 1906
JONES Charles 1836-1848
JONES Henry Robert 1866-1870
JONES John 1808-1815
KNIGHT George 1796-1803
KNOX John 1946-1962, M 1949 1950 1955 DM 1947
    1948 1952 1953
LAMB Richard 1781-1811, M 1790 1792
LAURENCE David 1834-1848
LAURENCE George 1867-1894
LEGG Rowland Thomas George 1860-1889, M 1871
LIPSCOMB William 1827-1834, M 1832 DM 1831
LLOYD Thomas 1804-1813, M 1804-1806
LONGLEY Thomas 1872-1876

LONGLEY William 1835-1862, M 1853-1855
    DM 1852 1856 1857
LOVEGROVE Herbert 1948-1988, M 1958 1959 1963
    1970 DM 1951 1954 1955 1966 1969 1980
MALLOCK John (1919) [2]
MANSER David 1837-1844, DM 1838 1839
MARTEN Thomas 1769-1807, M 1772 1774 1776
    1778 1780 1781 1783 1785 1787 1789 1791 1793
    1795 DM 1800-1807
MARTEN Thomas 1793-1804
MARTINDALE William 1889-1901, M 1893
MARTINDALE William Harrison 1905-1932, M 1923
MCDONNELL Edward Thomas 1927-1929
MCGOWAN Brian McIlwraith 1936-1965, M 1939
    DM 1936
MCGOWAN James 1916-1938, M 1921 1922 1935
MERYON Charles Pix 1878-1879
MITCHELL William 1872-1897
MOORE Anthony Richard 1992-Present
MORANT George 1832-1834, M 1832 1833
MOSLEY Thomas 1806
NEAVES Roger David 1996-Present
NEWBERY George Rolls 1914-1919
NICHOLS Robert Malise Bowyer 1934
OSBORNE Richard 1834-1856
OSMAN Alfred 1912-1928, M 1920
OWEN Arthur Vernon 1929-1981, M 1932 DM 1933
PADGETT James Dearle 1883-1890, M 1889
POWELL Henry 1816-1828, DM 1823-1826
RADDISH Thomas 1795-1817, M 1801 1803 1808
    1810 1812 1814 1816
RITCHIE OF DUNDEE Lord 1913-1947, M 1924
    1931
RITCHIE Hon. John Kenneth (later Lord Ritchie of
    Dundee) 1923-1975, M 1934
ROBINS Charles 1854-1875, M 1856 1857 1861 1865
    DM 1854 1866 1867
ROBINSON Arthur (1901) [2]
ROGERS Joseph Corbin 1944-1960, M 1947 1948 1956
    DM 1945
SANDEMAN Antony Gerald Faraday 1983-Present,
    M 1989 1991 DM 1987 1988
SCARTH Thomas 1804
SERGEANT William 1834-1857, M 1850 1851
    DM 1855
SHAKESPEARE John 1795-1803, M 1799
SHEPPARD Samuel P. 1818-1831, M 1827 1829 1831
SHORTER Lewis Richard 1906-1911
SIMPKINSON John 1795-1802
SKINNER Arthur David 1901

SKINNER David 1875-1877
SKINNER Ernest William 1889-1930, M 1890 1898
    DM 1889 1894 1899
SKINNER Ian William Sylvester 1928-1935
SKINNER John Rutherford 1899-1936, M 1900 1908
    1912 DM 1901 1903 1910 1911 1913 1919-1921
    1923 1924
SKINNER Robert Vaile 1858-1890, M 1860 1868 1869
    1872 1875 1878 1881 1886 1888 DM 1858 1859
    1862-1864 1870 1871 1873 1874 1876 1877 1879
    1880 1887
SMITH John 1882-1886
SMITH John 1889
SOUTHEY William 1850-1852, DM 1850 1851
STACE George 1782-1816, M 1794 DM 1809 1811
    1813 1815
STACE George 1807-1826 DM 1818 1820 1821
STACE William 1867-1876
STEVENS Alan Peter 1993-Present, DM 1997 1998
STILEMAN Richard 1837-1844, M 1838 1839 1841
    1843 1844 DM 1837 1840 1842
STILEMAN Robert Curteis 1858-1908 M 1858 1859
    1862-1864 1870 1873 1874 1876 1877 1879 1880
    1883 1884 1887 1894 1899 1901 1903 DM 1860
    1861 1865 1868 1869 1872 1875 1878 1881 1882
    1885 1886 1888 1890-1893 1900 1902 1904-1908
STONE James Ambrose 1957-1965, DM 1957
STREATFEILD Victor Charles Frederick 1980-1983,
    DM 1982
TERRY Charles 1807-1817
THOMAS Anthony Hugh 1939-Present, DM 1962
TILDEN George 1807-1819, DM 1808 1810 1812 1814
    1816 1817 1819
TILDEN John 1823-1837, M 1835 DM 1827 1829
    1834 1836
TREMEER John Anthony Fodenelle 1983-Present,
    M 1990 DM 1989
TULLOCK Alexander 1795-1831, M 1818 1820 1822
    1824 1826 1828 1830
TURNER Douglas Haydn 1980-1993, M 1982 1983
    DM 1981 1984
WENBAN Harry James 1967-1979, M 1969 DM 1970
WHITEHEAD William Kenneth 1974-1985, M 1980
    DM 1977 1979
WILDEBLOOD John Peake 1938-1946, M 1940
WILSON Richard 1834-1855
WINSTONE John 1818-1835
WITHALL William 1916-1919
WOOLLETT Charles 1867-1871
WRIGHT John Edward 1807-1834

NOTES:
1. The dates given are the first and last years in which a freeman attended the mayoring in that capacity, was
    appointed a jurat in his absence, or sent apologies as a freeman unable to attend.
2. During the period covered by this list only two men were sworn as freemen at a separate assembly and never
    attended the mayoring ceremony in that capacity. The date of their appointment is bracketed.

HONORARY FREEMEN

DR. EDWIN FRESHFIELD F.S.A. Installed 1890
MALCOLM NORMAN PRATT   Installed 1994

BARONS OF THE CONFEDERATION OF THE CINQUE PORTS
(Coronation Barons)

1821	George IV	Henry Peter Brougham M.P.
		Lucius Concannon M.P.
1830	William IV	Honours at Court not granted
1837	Victoria	ditto
1902	Edward VII	Frederic Andrew Inderwick K.C.
1911	George V	George Mallows Freeman K.C.
1937	George VI	Major John Addison Burke J.P.
1953	Elizabeth II	Phillip Anthony Mallows Freeman M.B.E.

SPEAKERS OF THE CONFEDERATION OF THE CINQUE PORTS

1802 - 1803	Barwell Browne	1900 - 1901	Dr. John Rutherford Skinner
1803	Rev. Thomas Raddish	1901	R.C. Stileman
1809 - 1810	Barwell Browne	1907 - 1908	G.M. Freeman K.C.
1810	Rev. Thomas Raddish	1908	Dr. J.R. Skinner
1816 - 1817	Rev. Thomas Raddish	1914 - 1915	G.M. Freeman K.C.
1817	Barwell Browne	1921 - 1922	James McGowan
1823 - 1824	Barwell Browne	1928 - 1929	G.M. Freeman K.C.
1824	Alexander Tullock	1929	Anthony Mallows Freeman
1830 - 1831	Alexander Tullock	1935 - 1936	James McGowan O.B.E.
1831	Rev. Samuel Philip Sheppard	1936	Major J.A. Burke
1837 - 1838	John Beaumont	1942 - 1943	Lt. Col. Goldschmidt
1838	Richard Stileman	1943	Major J.A. Burke
1844	Richard Stileman	1949 - 1950	John Knox
1844 - 1845	Joseph Hennah	1956 - 1957	Joseph Corbin Rogers
1851 - 1852	William Sergeant	1957	Anthony Mallows Freeman
1852	Dr. Robert Coker Nash Davies	1963 - 1964	Captain H. Lovegrove C.B.E., R.N.
1858 - 1859	Robert Curteis Stileman	1964	Ralph Eddowes Garrod
1865 - 1866	Charles Robins	1970 - 1971	Captain H. Lovegrove C.B.E., R.N.
1866	Samuel Griffiths	1971	Lt. Col. P.V. Gray M.B.E.
1872 - 1873	Dr. R.V. Skinner	1977 - 1978	Lt. Col. P.V. Gray M.B.E.
1873	R.C. Stileman	1978	H. Stanley Hargreaves
1879 - 1880	R.C. Stileman	1984 - 1985	C.C. Croggon
1886 - 1887	Dr. R.V. Skinner	1991 - 1992	A.G.F. Sandeman
1887	R.C. Stileman	1992	K.W. Chetwood
1893 - 1894	William Martindale	1998	R.G. Beecroft
1894	R.C. Stileman		

APPENDIX III

OFFICERS OF THE CORPORATION

TOWN CLERK

John WOOLLETT	1798 - 1819
Weedon DAWES	1819 - 1823
Henry BUTLER	1823 - 1826
John Haddock LARDNER	1826 - 1848
Edwin Nathaniel DAWES	1848 - 1876
Walter DAWES	1876 - 1930
Edwin Plomley DAWES	1930 - 1961
Charles Clayton CROGGON	1961 - 1967
Thomas Alan Nicholson BRUCE	1967 - 1969
Charles Clayton CROGGON	1969 - 1984
Malcolm Norman PRATT	1984 -

CHAMBERLAIN

Isaac COFFIN	1796 - 1806
Thomas LLOYD	1806 - 1810
John Edward WRIGHT	1810 - 1834
Walter FULLER	1834 - 1845
Richard WILSON	1845 - 1856
George BLACKMAN	1856 - 1867
George HEARNDEN	1867 - 1895
John CAREY	1895 - 1921
William BENNETT	1922 - 1925
Frank NASH	1926 - 1935
Alexander Henry Thomas FINCH	1935 - 1943
Charles TURNER	1943 - 1958
Leslie WHITING	1958 - 1973
John Herbert CRESEY	1973 - 1988
John Joseph PAY	1988 - 1989
Bernard Llewellyn DIBBLE	1989 -

SERGEANT-AT-MACE

Josiah BOOTS	1799 - 1812
Thomas Sylvester KEENE	1812 - 1828
Charles HILL	1828 - 1860
Stephen LAURENCE	1860 - 1869
Edwin LAURENCE	1869 - 1887
John CAREY	1887 - 1921
William BENNETT	1922 - 1925
Ernest FREEMAN	1926 - 1936
Archibald John BRITTAIN	1936 - 1938
Charles TURNER	1938 - 1943
John TILTMAN	1945 - 1951
Frederick CURD	1951 - 1965
Albert Barry STOCKS	1966 - 1967
John Herbert CRESEY	1968 - 1973
John Roy BULLOCK	1977 - 1979
John Joseph PAY	1979 - 1988
Bernard Llewellyn DIBBLE	1988 - 1989
Christopher BEATTIE	1989
Ian Douglas SHEARER	1989 - 1995
Neil CLEPHANE-CAMERON	1995 -

The above lists are only for those whose offices remain in existence. During the nineteenth and twentieth centuries the corporation has also appointed annually at the mayoring ceremony:

> COMMON SERGEANT (until 1885)
> ATTORNIES OF THE COURT OF RECORD (until 1885)
> CONSTABLES (until 1885)
> POUND DRIVER (until 1887)
> KEEPER OF THE LOOKOUT AND THE POUND (1887 - 1965)
> WATER BAILIFF'S SERGEANT (until 1885)
> TREASURER (until 1885)

NOTE: The post of Treasurer was revived in 1992 as an honorary position and is currently held by
Jurat Antony Gerald Faraday SANDEMAN.

DUTIES OF THOSE OFFICERS MENTIONED ABOVE

COMMON SERGEANT – also known as TOWN SERGEANT. His work overlapped with that of the SERGEANT-AT-MACE which in those days included serving notices of meetings, proclaiming them as TOWN CRIER and serving as gaoler.

ATTORNIES OF THE COURT OF RECORD. This is an obscure office. The holders were not legally qualified. One source states that the SERGEANT-AT-MACE was one of the ATTORNIES 'and the person to whom the process was directed'. They seem to have been a cross between a court usher and a prisoner's friend.

CONSTABLES. They had policing duties within the town and liberty. They were said in 1833 to have been seldom called upon. Before the establishment of a county police force they were the only representatives of the law acting under the direction of the magistrates. After that time we would know them as special constables.

POUND DRIVER. This task was also usually carried out by the COMMON or TOWN SERGEANT. Animals found loose in the town were impounded by him and a charge made for return to their owners.

KEEPER OF THE LOOKOUT AND THE POUND. The holder of this office was responsible for caretaking duties at these two sites.

WATER BAILIFF'S SERGEANT. He was authorised to execute warrants to make arrests at sea. The extent of this jurisdiction is said to have been three miles but the holder in 1833 reported that he had never operated more than a quarter of a mile from the shore.

TREASURER. He was a paid local official who took over the corporation's finances from the CHAMBERLAIN for a large part of the nineteenth century. The duties were returned to the CHAMBERLAIN when the Municipal Corporations Act of 1883 came into force. The job then involved only collecting the queen's dues and making small payments from them.

APPENDIX IV

WINCHELSEA CENSUS RETURNS[1]

		1841		1891	
		Male	Female	Male	Female
Residents	80+	5	2	10	5
aged	60 - 79	23	21	23	35
	40 - 59	54	58	47	71
	20 - 39	52	73	49	92
	15 - 19	18	29	29	33
	10 - 14	42	34	20	29
	5 - 9	45	44	30	30
	0 - 4	48	33	31	36
	not known	1	0	0	0
		288	294	239	331
	Total population		582		570

		1841	1891
Numbers of	9	1	1
children in	8	1	0
families	7	3	2
	6	8	5
	5	5	5
	4	12	9
	3	17	10
	2	18	16
	1	6	12
	0	4	3

	1841	1891
Households	107	136
Average persons per household	5.44	4.19
Uninhabited dwellings	22	12
Children of school age[2]	119	80
Born in Sussex	517	420
Born in Winchelsea[3]		238
Declared occupations	167	261

OCCUPATIONS

	1841	1891		1841	1891
Married Woman[4]	71	61	Carrier/Carrier's boy	3	5
Agricultural Labourer	59	29	Charwoman	3	6
Servant (female)[5]	28	37	Dressmaker	3	4
Of independent means	24	25	Schoolteacher	3	4
Tailor	7	0	Apprentice[6]	2	2
Carpenter	6	3	Blacksmith	2	1
Shoemaker/Bootmaker	5	2	Gardener/Jobbing gardener	2	6
Bricklayer	4	1	Grocer/Grocer's shopman/porter	2	4
Cordwainer	4	0	Innkeeper/Hotel keeper/		
Farmer	4	3	Licensed victualler	2	4
Baker/Baker's boy	3	2	Miller/Miller's loader	2	3
Butcher/Butcher's assistant/boy	3	6	Servant (male)[7]	2	16

Occupations (continued)

	1841	1891		1841	1891
Bonnet maker	1	0	Dairyman	0	2
Cattle salesman	1	0	Fisherman/Eel spearer	0	2
Coal merchant	1	0	Grazier	0	2
Draper/Draper's assistant/			Lodging-house keeper	0	2
errand boy	1	4	Student/Law student	0	2
Governess	1	1	Barrister	0	1
Hairdresser	1	0	Barmaid	0	1
Housekeeper	1	4	Boots (inn)	0	1
Jeweller/Jeweller's traveller	1	1	Builder	0	1
Labourer[8]	1	14	Chemist's porter	0	1
Laundress	1	14	Clergyman (Rector of Winchelsea)	0	1
Painter	1	1	Companion	0	1
Plumber	1	1	Eating-house keeper	0	1
Postmaster/Postmaster's assistant	1	2	Fly proprietor	0	1
Pot boy	1	0	General dealer (shop)	0	1
Retailer of beer	1	0	Insurance agent	0	1
Sawyer	1	0	Market gardener	0	1
Surgeon/General practitioner	1	2	Merchant seaman	0	1
Veterinary surgeon	1	0	Parish clerk and sexton	0	1
Washerwoman	1	1	Proprietress of lunatic asylum	0	1
Wheelwright	1	0	Railway porter	0	1
Wine merchant	1	0	Road surveyor and assistant overseer	0	1
Yeast dealer	1	0	Ship's steward	0	1
Retired[9]	0	11	Tea dealer	0	1
Attendant to lunatics	0	5	Telegraph messenger	0	1
Inmate of lunatic asylum/lunatic	0	5	Waggoner	0	1
Artist (painter)	0	2	No declaration	10	5

NOTES:

1. The residential area covered by this survey includes only those parts of Winchelsea on the hill of Iham, at Tanyard Lane/The Strand and at Station Road/The Ferry.
2. School age is that which applies in the latter part of the twentieth century for infants/juniors. i.e. 5 - 11.
3. This information is not available for 1841 when the census questions asked only for the county of birth.
4. The category 'married woman', created for this survey and not included in the returns, indicates women living with husbands and/or children and declaring no other occupation.
5. The 1891 figure for female servants includes: housemaid (7), cook (6), nursemaid (4), kitchenmaid (2), lady's help (1), sick nurse (1), under housemaid (1), parlourmaid (1).
6. The apprentices were: 1841 – one carpenter, one butcher, 1891 – one draper, one dressmaker.
7. The 1891 male servants were: domestic gardener (9), groom (2), coachman (2), footman (2), butler (1).
8. The 1891 figure for labourers includes: general labourer (9), bricklayer's labourer (2), quarry labourer (1), sewer labourer (1), stone breaker (1).
9. Those listed in 1891 as retired were one each of army, bailiff, blacksmith, cab driver, farmer, gardener, grazier, innkeeper, navy, police constable and tea dealer.

APPENDIX V

PROPERTIES LIABLE TO PAY THE QUEEN'S DUES AND TOWN RENTS
(As listed in the Chamberlain's account book 1995)

MILL ROAD

Three Kings
Sharon
1/2/3 Salutation Cottages
Hill Farm
Mill Farm House
The Mill House
Pipewell
Mulberry Cottage
Manna Plat

CASTLE STREET

Chelsea Cottage
King's Leap
Amerique
The Armoury
The Well House
The Garage

HIGH STREET

The Retreat
Tower Cottage
Winchelsea Cottage
Periteau House
Firebrand
Nesbit House

FRIARS ROAD

1, Friars Road
2/3, Friars Road
Cleveland Place
White Cottage
Greyfriars

COOKS GREEN

The Mount
Alards

NORTH STREET

Cordwainers
Broad View

GERMAN STREET

New Inn
1, White Close
2, White Close
Ballader's Plat
Little Plat
South Mariteau
2, Mariteau
3, Mariteau
4, Mariteau
5, Mariteau

BACK LANE

Mariteau Court

RECTORY LANE

The Old Rectory
1, Backfields (Trees Bank)
2, Backfields
3, Backfields
Backfields End
Wesley Chapel

PETT LANE

Chapel Field
Newgate Field
Quarry Field

THE STRAND

Bridge Inn
Strand House (Hillside)
Strand Cottage (Apple Tree Wick)

TOWN RENTS

Greyfriars Park (part)
Becket (part of garden)

NOTES ON SOURCES

The prefix ESRO is used for all documents kept at East Sussex Record Office. References marked D are in my collection of Winchelsea papers, notes and cuttings, eventually, I hope, to be transferred to the Court Hall or the Record Office; those marked F are in Winchelsea Corporation's current files. When these are moved to the Record Office it may be possible to include the original file numbers in the listings. H/A refers to the corporation's Hundred and Assembly Book (1883-1996) which includes minutes of the town's courts and formal occasions; MM refers to the Mayoral Minute Book, 1952-1989 which records corporation business meetings. At present, I am afraid, D, F, H/A and MM references can only be examined by arrangement with me. Where author's names are used, more details of their books will be found in the bibliography.

PROLOGUE

1 Moore p.80
2 ESRO WIN 63 f.71

1. DEVELOPMENT AND CONFEDERATION

1 Floyd
2 D34/12
3 Jeake p.103
4 Cooper[HW] p.3 inter alia
5 V.C.H. ix p.62

2. A CENTURY OF STORMS

1 Inderwick p.18
2 Quoted Brentnall p.272 inter alia
3 Ibid
4 Cooper[HW] p.18
5 Ibid p.19
6 Prestwich p.10
7 Ford [CP] p.7
8 V.C.H. ii p.137
9 Bagley[RM] p.59
10 Cooper[HW] p.30
11 Ibid p.21
12 Floyd p.42

3. PROSPERITY

1 Cooper[HW] p.53
2 Ibid pp.44-53
3 Homan[HW] p.8
4 Cooper[HW] p.55 inter alia
5 Burrows p.131
6 Cooper[HW] pp.57-58 inter alia
7 Prestwich p.111
8 Inderwick p.100
9 Beresford pp.3-5

4. DECLINE

1 Homan[HW] p.83
2 Ibid p.77

3 Cooper[HW] p.69
4 Homan[HW] p.119
5 S.C.M. 9 pp.476-479, 551-555
6 Homan[HW] pp.119-120
7 V.C.H. ix pp.66-67
8 Cooper[HW] pp.89-91
9 Baines p.142
10 D34/18
11 Homan[HW] pp.152-153
12 Meynell p.183
13 Homan[HW] p.159
14 S.A.C. 9 p.296

5. FOUR CENTURIES OF IMPOVERISHMENT

1 See Collard pp.36-42
2 H/A ff.154-164
3 S.A.C. 8 pp.202-206
4 Cooper[HW] pp.98-100
5 Mais p.86
6 Cooper[HW] p.99
7 D29/5
8 Cooper[HW] p.107
9 Guide to Winchelsea (1915) p.10 [D6]
10 Sx. Hist. 24 pp.16-17
11 ESRO AMS 2381
12 Goodsall pp.138-9; Inderwick p.131
13 S.A.C. 81 p.28
14 Homan[CW] pp.30-31; S.A.C. 4 p.280
15 Fiennes p.129
16 Defoe Vol i p.130
17 S.C.M. 22 p.10
18 ESRO PAR 511/1/1/2
19 S.C.M 7 pp.193-197
20 S.N.Q. 16 pp.7-8;D38/10
21 ESRO NMA 4/1/1
22 D38/10
23 ESRO NMA 4/1/2

6. THE NAPOLEONIC WARS

1 Williamson pp.304-305
2 Ford[CP] p.370
3 Collard p.46
4 See Hutchinson [MC] inter alia
5 See Hutchinson [MT] and Sutcliffe
6 The Defences of Sussex Against Napoleon by Frank Kitchen. Sussex Hist. 22 pp.17-20
7 ESRO WIN 2019/2021/2022
8 ESRO WIN 1689
9 ESRO WIN 1690
10 ESRO WIN 1741
11 ESRO WIN 1720
12 ESRO WIN 1722
13 ESRO WIN 1942
14 ESRO WIN 1965
15 ESRO WIN 1762-1764
16 ESRO WIN 1770-1772
17 ESRO WIN 1835
18 ESRO WIN 1692
19 Clark[W] pp.23-24
20 ESRO WIN 1701
21 Bagley[BR] pp.52-53
22 ESRO WIN 1696
23 ESRO WIN 2017
24 Baines p.220
25 Williamson p.305
26 ESRO WIN 618 1804-1805 et. seq.
27 ESRO AMS 2396 p.112
28 ESRO PAR 511/1/1
29 ESRO WIN 203
30 ESRO WIN 204
31 ESRO WIN 207
32 ESRO PAR 511/12/1 1 August 1813
33 Clark[W] p.24

7. POVERTY AND THE WORKHOUSE

1 Barty pp.11-12
2 *The Sussex Almanac 95* pub. Observer Newspaper Group (1994) 3 November 1830 (D38/2)
3 Baines p.129
4 *Abraham Graham Thorpe (of Pett): A brave venture in middle age* by Joyce Wheatley (D26/13)
5 ESRO PAR 511/12/2 20 February 1829
6 D30/14
7 ESRO PAR 511/37/1/1
8 ESRO PAR 511/37/1/2
9 ESRO PAR 511/12/1 9 November 1800 et. seq.
10 These paragraphs are based on information extracted from ESRO PAR 511/12/1, PAR 511/31/1/1, and PAR 511 31/2/120-121. It is my intention when the study is completed to present two copies to Winchelsea Corporation, one to be available, by prior arrangement only, at The Court Hall Museum and one for inclusion with the Winchelsea Archives at East Sussex Record Office, almost certainly in the seqence WIN 2362.
11 ESRO PAR 511/12/2 20 February 1829
12 ESRO PAR 511/13/6
13 ESRO PAR 511/12/2 4 September1823
14 ESRO PAR 511/35/1/1-361
15 ESRO PAR 511/29/1
16 ESRO PAR 511/35/1/302
17 ESRO PAR 511/35/1/307
18 ESRO PAR 511/35/1/313
19 ESRO PAR 511/35/1/321
20 ESRO PAR 511/35/1/322
21 Old Bailey Sessions Papers 1826-1827 pp.205-207 (D42/1)
22 ESRO PAR 511/12/1 4 May 1800
23 ESRO PAR 511/12/2 22 April 1825
24 ESRO AMS 2330 ff.45-46
25 ESRO PAR 511/31/1/2-10
26 ESRO PAR 511/37/7/28
27 ESRO PAR 511/37/7/32
28 ESRO PAR 511/38/5/1
29 Dickinson p.146 also quoting Holloway
30 Ford[CP] p.234
31 Muggridge pp.10-11
32 ESRO PAR 511/13/9

8. SMUGGLING

1 Stileman p.3
2 ESRO AMS 2404
3 Skinner p.9
4 Ford[CP] p.174
5 ESRO WIN 283
6 ESRO WIN 284
7 ESRO WIN 61AA 8 April 1822
8 ESRO WIN 2030
9 ESRO WIN 2029
10 ESRO WIN 2151
11 Ford[CP] p.107
12 Clark[SRD] p.30
13 Ibid p.32
14 ESRO WIN 616 Part 1
15 Cooper[SS] p.41
16 Sx.Exp. 7 April 1838
17 ESRO WIN 547
18 Skinner p.10
19 ESRO WIN 2151
20 Thomas p.11

9. PARLIAMENTARY REPRESENTATION

1 Winchelsea Court Hall list of mayors/Cooper pp.244-246
2 ESRO WIN 54 f.168r
3 Horsfield ii Appendices p.72
4 Inderwick p.134
5 Horsfield ii Appendices pp.72-73
6 *The Diary of Samuel Pepys* 21 October 1666
7 Horsfield ii Appendices p.73
8 S.C.M. 17 p.117
9 Redman pp.88, 90, 97
10 But see Cooper pp.215-217 and *Arnold Nesbitt and the Borough of Winchelsea* by Janet Stevenson S.A.C. 129 pp.183-193
11 Bessborough p.60
12 See *The Bastards of Westbourne* by Peter Ellacott (Westbourne Local History Group, 1996)
13 D.N.B. 20 pp.130-131
14 ESRO WIN 2127
15 Horsfield ii Appendices p74
16 D.N.B. 4 pp.1157-1158

17 Ehrman i p.71
18 D21/15
19 Baines pp.51-52
20 *Hastings & St. Leonards Observer* 30 July 1898
21 Horsfield ii Appendices p74
22 ESRO AMS 3713
23 D.N.B. 12 pp.291-293
24 Ibid 2 pp 1356-1366
25 ESRO WIN 61B f.17
26 Churchill iv p.38; Trevelyan pp. 337-349

10. THE CORPORATION THREATENED

1 ESRO WIN 618 1800-1801 et. seq.
2 ESRO WIN 2361/2/1 ff.3,11
3 ESRO WIN 61 f.138r
4 ESRO WIN 294
5 ESRO WIN 2049
6 Research by Christopher Whittick, see his introduction to ESRO WIN 2359 – Town Clerk
7 ESRO WIN 89/ESRO WIN 124
8 ESRO WIN 1561
9 ESRO WIN 1558 inter alia
10 ESRO WIN 1561
11 ESRO WIN 1564
12 ESRO WIN 61B f.48
13 Ibid f.49
14 Ibid f.50
15 But see Appendix III for duties of officers.
16 Report of Commissioner, Municipal Corporations Act 1835, included in ESRO WIN 616 Part 1

11. THE STILEMAN STORY

1 D32/9
2 ESRO WIN 62
3 Stileman pp.1-3
4 S.C.M. 29 pp.226-228
5 S.A.C. 8 p.234
6 D28/12 p.1
7 ESRO A6077/29/26-30
8 ESRO AMS 6192/1/2
9 Ibid f.32
10 Ibid f.146
11 Ibid f.79
12 Ibid f.130
13 Ibid f.180
14 Ibid f.109
15 ESRO PAR 511/35/1/335

16 ESRO PAR 511/35/1/203
17 ESRO PAR 511/35/1/190
18 ESRO WIN 2035
19 D19/5

12. WELLS AND WATER

1 Cooper p.38
2 F50 21 May 1964
3 D34/19
4 ESRO WIN 61D f392
5 Jessup p.114
6 Ford[CP] p.83
7 Ford[RY] p.17
8 ESRO WIN 61B ff.97, 100-104
9 ESRO WIN 1035
10 ESRO 2361/3/1
11 ESRO RRY/A1/1 f.87
12 ESRO A6192/4/2
13 D33/4
14 Dickinson p.83
15 ESRO G8/71/1 f.320
16 Ibid f.316
17 Sx. Exp 3 April 1891
18 ESRO RRY/A1/1 ff.307-309
   inter alia
19 In *The Benefactor* by Ford Madox
   Hueffer (1905)
20 Sx. Exp. 10 October 1896
21 Ibid 12 September 1896
22 Ibid 14 August 1897
23 Ibid 24 April 1897
24 Ibid 23 April 1898
25 Ibid 30 April 1915
26 Ibid 17 March 1939
27 MM f.81
28 F31 22 August 1961
29 ESRO WIN 2359/4/2
   30 December 1887
30 ESRO WIN 2359/4/5
31 D35/5
32 D23/13

13. CAREY, COURTS AND CORONERS

1 ESRO WIN 2350
2 Carey pp.1-4
3 ESRO WIN 2151
4 Carey pp.3-4
5 Rossetti Vol 1 p.610
6 ESRO WIN 614 Part 1
7 ESRO WIN 61D ff.57-58
8 Ibid ff.330-332
9 Sx. Exp. 18 January 1868
10 ESRO WIN 614 Parts 2 & 3
11 Ibid Part 3

12 ESRO WIN 524
13 ESRO WIN 605
14 H/A f.3
15 ESRO WIN 604
16 Carey p.9
17 Patch p.165
18 ESRO WIN 2359/4/6

14. THE CORPORATION THREATENED AGAIN

1 D27/18
2 D.N.B. 1901-1911 Vol II
   pp.338-339
3 ESRO A6192/4/2
4 D.N.B. 1901-1911 Vol II
   pp.338-339
5 ESRO A6192/4/2
6 ESRO WIN 616 Part 2
7 Ibid
8 Municipal Corporations Act
   1883 Sect. 14
9 Bagley[BR] p.20
10 ESRO WIN 61E ff.29-31
11 ESRO WIN 2151
12 H/A f.11
13 V.C.H. ix p.184
14 W.T. Pike's *District Blue Book
   1885* (D26/23)
15 ESRO WIN 2360/2/10
16 Capt. H. Lovegrove gives a
   different account of the effect of
   this legislation. See S.N.Q. 16
   p.103
17 Sx. Exp. 22 December 1894
18 Ibid 28 March 1896
19 Ibid 22 December 1894
20 Ibid 2 March 1895
21 Ibid 5 January 1895

15. THE COURT HALL

1 ESRO AMS 2391 p.13
2 Inderwick p.35
3 D29/7
4 ESRO WIN 2362/1/63
5 ESRO AMS 2391 p.10
6 Inderwick pp.35-36
7 Pevsner p.636
8 Ford[CP] p.78
9 ESRO AMS 2391 pp.8-9
10 ESRO WIN 64 f.100
11 ESRO WIN 2151, 2151A
12 ESRO WIN 1228
13 ESRO WIN 61D ff.29, 130
14 ESRO WIN 1661; 2151A
15 It was F.A. Inderwick's belief

(*The Story of King Edward and
New Winchelsea* pp.36-37) that
the Court Hall was always the
property of the bailiff. I have
preferred considerable
documentary evidence discovered
by W.M. Homan since
Inderwick's time.
16 ESRO WIN 981
17 ESRO WIN 1350
18 Sx. Exp. 16 August 1873
19 ESRO WIN 615 Part 3
20 ESRO WIN 2360/2/3
   7 December 1869
21 *The Times* 2 September 1918
   (D19/1)
22 ESRO A6192/4/2
23 Inderwick pp.59-60, 137-139
24 Sx. Exp. 3 April 1891
25 ESRO WIN 2359/4/3
   24 October 1891
26 ESRO WIN 1330
27 Patch p.167
28 *Guide to Winchelsea* 1915 p.12
   (D6)
29 D39/2
30 D32/5
31 D32/6
32 D28/11

16. CENSUSES AND ROLLS

1 Clark[W] pp.24-25
2 V.C.H. ii p.228
3 ESRO PAR 511/1/1/4
4 ESRO WIN 61D f.87
5 Pike, Winchelsea (also
   transcribed as D26/23)
6 ESRO XA 19/3. PRO H.O.
   107/1109
7 ESRO RG12/0759 f.107
8 Homan[HW] p.258
9 S.A.C. 113 p.36
10 PRO SP 12/38 Folio 28
11 Inderwick pp.64-66, 71-74
12 Homan[HW] p.100
13 Cooper[HW] p.42

17. ARTISTS AND AUTHORS

1 Ford[RY] p.3
2 Judd p.25
3 Shanes pp.20-21, 31-32
4 Ford[PRB]
5 Lindsay p.75
6 Hemming pp.67-68
7 Dunlop p.21

8 S.N.Q. 7 p.126
9 Swinfen p.90
10 *Thackeray in Sussex* by John Wright S.C.M. 21 p.211
11 Hillier p.261
12 Ford[CP] p.84
13 Dunlop p.11
14 Judd p.109
15 Finlayson pp.111-112
16 Ford[CP] p.76
17 Ford[RY] p.18
18 Finlayson p.69
19 Dunlop p.13
20 Finlayson pp.93-94
21 Dunlop p.11
22 from *English Hours* by Henry James, included in *Winchelsea, Rye and Denis Duval* (1905)
23 *The Third Person* by Henry James, included in *Selected Stories* O.U.P. World Classics (1957)
24 Ford [RY] pp.8-9
25 Ibid pp.390-394, 404
26 *Victorian Painters* by Christopher Wood (1995) *British Artists 1880-1940* by J. Johnson & A. Greutzner (1976)
27 Finlayson pp.138-139
28 H/A 154-164
29 Finch p.6
30 *Some Soldier Poets* by T.S. Moore (1919)
31 *Books and their Writers* by S.P.B. Mais (1920)
32 *Sussex Life* September 1979 (D33/8)
33 D25/25
34 D23/10
35 D32/2

18. THE STILEMAN STORY CONTINUED

1 Skinner p.7; D19/24
2 ESRO WIN 841; Sx. Exp. 26 March 1859
3 ESRO WIN 617
4 Carey p.2
5 Sx. Exp. 16 August 1873
6 Skinner p.7
7 Ibid p.10
8 Finch p.3
9 ESRO PAR 511/12/6 14 December 1866
10 These letters are the property of Mrs. Linda Steward of

Beckenham who has kindly provided me with transcripts and photocopies. (D45/2) Copies are also at ESRO AMS 6412/1-4
11 ESRO AMS 6192/1; 6192/2
12 ESRO AMS 6192/1 ff.130-131
13 ESRO PAR 511/37/5/1
14 ESRO PAR 511/31/1/16
15 ESRO PAR 511/37/5/28
16 PAR 511/38/8/1
17 Carey pp.4-5
18 ESRO AMS 2403
19 Skinner pp.6-7
20 *The Sea Chaplains* by Gordon Taylor (1978) p.287; *The Royal Navy Day by Day* Ed. Shrubb and Sainsbury (1979) pp.24, 25, 253
21 Skinner p.10
22 Ibid p.6
23 Ibid
24 ESRO PAR 511/12/6 4 April 1872
25 Sx. Exp. 19 April 1873
26 ESRO AMS 6412/6
27 Sx. Exp. 15 February 1898
28 ESRO AMS 2396 p.114
29 ESRO WIN 2359/4/5 13 March 1902

19. THE FREEMAN SUCCESSION

1 F54
2 Muggridge p.2
3 Finch p.9
4 ESRO Acc 7519 (D32/10)
5 Ibid
6 Sx. Exp. 16 April 1914
7 F35 18 July 1914 p.21
8 D34/22
9 D40/12
10 D44/2
11 D22/3
12 D28/6
13 F31 15 February 1961

20. TOWER COTTAGE

1 Skinner p.7
2 Patch p.103
3 Ibid p.104
4 Carey pp.5-6
5 Dunlop pp.15-17
6 Terry p.269
7 S.C.M. 21 p.40
8 Judd p.110
9 D29/1

10 F28 12 January 1915

21. THE FIRST WORLD WAR

1 Dunlop p.9
2 ESRO AMS 2396 p.76
3 *East Sussex News* 26 May 1983 (D21/10)
4 Muggridge p.11
5 D38/24
6 *East Sussex News* 9 June 1983 (D21/14)
7 H/A f.106
8 Ibid f.107
9 Arscott pp.17-19
10 Muggridge p.16
11 Arscott pp.20-21
12 ESRO WIN 2362/1/7
13 D23/7
14 D21/25; F28 10 August 1975

22. WINCHELSEA, VICTORIA, AUSTRALIA

1 Koenig p.13
2 Ibid p.14
3 Ibid
4 ESRO ESC 267/1/2 f.61
5 Koenig p.15
6 Ibid pp.78-79
7 D33/12
8 Koening p.79
9 H/A f.228
10 MM f.355
11 Ibid ff.447-448
12 Gross p.138
13 D43/11
14 Ibid

23. RESIDENTS AND RIVALRY

1 D40/10
2 ESRO AMS 2395 (Foreword)
3 Ibid
4 D30/2/3
5 D29/6
6 ESRO AMS 2395-2398
7 D29/7
8 ESRO AMS 2395
9 F30 16 November 1935
10 Muggridge p.14
11 Ibid p17
12 D44/13
13 H/A f.345
14 Muggridge p.17
15 D44/9/2
16 ESRO P401/1/1 6 March 1950
17 D35/12

18 D23/31/7
19 MM ff.172-173

24. ST. THOMAS'S CHURCH

1 Homan[CW] p.3
2 ESRO PAR 511/1/1/2
3 Saville p.5. This booklet
   (available at St. Thomas's
   Church) provides an excellent
   account to which the interested
   reader should turn for much
   which it is not possible to include
   here.
4 Lucas p.362
5 Saville p.10
6 Brentnall p.158
7 Cooper p.122
8 ESRO PAR 511/12/2 13 January
   1826
9 Cooper pp.125-128
10 Patch p.183
11 ESRO AMS 2396 p.114
12 ESRO WIN 2362/1/1
13 S.N.Q. 5 p.252
14 Sx. Hist. 11 p.9
15 Patch p.104
16 Sx. Hist. 11 p.9
17 Homan[CW] p.23
18 Patch pp.104-105
19 D26/26
20 ESRO WIN 2362/1/8
21 S.C.M. 6 p.272
22 ESRO WIN 2362/1/1-75
23 D38/3
24 Hutchinson[MS] p.15
25 D38/5
26 Sx. Exp. 28 January 1873
27 *Shipwreck Index of the British Isles*
   by Richard and Bridget Larn.
   Vol. II 1995 – 22 January 1873
28 D30/16
29 Ibid
30 Sx. Exp. 27 October 1933
31 D30/16 quoting the *Aberdeen*
   University Review
32 D34/2
33 MM ff.81-82

25. THE SECOND WORLD WAR

1 ESRO AMS 2379 6 January 1940
2 Collard p.97
3 Murray p.130
4 D23/31 pp.6-7
5 D40/8

6 D47/14
7 D40/9
8 D40/14
9 D40/6
10. D34/5
11 Sx. Exp. 16 March 1973
12 Sx. Exp. 23 March 1973
13 D44/7 p.4
14 D34/6
15 D34/25
16 D34/21
17 D34/24
18 D26/2
19 D23/31; D47/14
20 D33/6; D34/23
21 ESRO ESC 267/1/3 f.47
22 ESRO AMS 2407
23 D34/4
24 Court Hall Museum display
   folder p.8
25 Collard p.100
26 D23/31 p.6
27 Collard p.100
28 D23/31 p.6
29 ESRO SPA 2/21/42
30 F50
31 D46/23

26. ARCHIVES AND REGALIA

1 *Sussex Daily News* 20 April 1954
2 F43 27 August 1953
3 Ibid 31 August 1953
4 Ibid 1 September 1953
5 Ibid 7 November 1955
6 Ibid 28 August 1954/30 August
   1954
7 MM f.1
8 F43 5 October 1956
9 Ibid 30 January 1959
10 Ibid 9 August 1962
11 F31 November 1960
12 D44/8
13 H/A ff. 79-80
14 D6 p.13
15 F43 13 January 1966 et. seq.
16 H/A f.71
17 Ibid f.182
18 Thomas p.7

27. BASTIONS AND BYPASS

1 Cooper p.37
2 Calendar of Patent Rolls 1413-
   1416 p224; Calendar of
   Miscelleneous Inquisitions Vol
   VII 1399-1422 No 503.

(D44/24) I am extremely grateful
to Dr. Roy Hunnisett for drawing
these documents to my attention.
3 F8 7 September 1924; 27 May
   1925
4 H/A ff.137-138
5 F25 10 May 1950 et. seq.
6 Cooper p.37
7 F24 3 December 1955
8 Goodsall p.139
9 ESRO WIN 2359/4/5
10 F24 30 April 1962
11 D34/1
12 Vaisey p.201
13 Defoe Vol i pp.128-129
14 ESRO A5709
15 D35/9
16 *Evening Argus* 2 April 1907
   (D26/24/9)
17 Finch p.2
18 H/A ff.118-119
19 ESRO WIN 2359/4/5 5 July
   1919
20 H/A f.144
21 Sx. Exp. 28 April 1939
22 D34/1
23 F40 15 August 1962
24 F19 29 September 1969 et. seq.
25 Ibid 6 August 1970
26 Sx. Exp. 26 February 1971
27 F40 14 February 1973 et. seq.
28 Ibid August 1974 et. seq.
29 Ibid 1978
30 Ibid 2 November 1983
31 Ibid 19 December 1983
32 Ibid January 1990
33 Ibid November 1994 et. seq.
34 D40/19

28. COUNCIL HOUSING AND CLOCHEMERLE

1 D23/31; D29/1
2 ESRO AMS 2398
3 D44/9/4
4 D35/4
5 ESRO AMS 2392
6 ESRO Search Room – Parishes:
   Winchelsea
7 F48 14 January 1950
8 ESRO P401/1/1 ff.68-75
9 ESRO RBA/A2/2 19 December
   1949 p.6, 16 January 1950 pp.4-5
10 ESRO P401/1/1 f.157
11 D35/2
12 ESRO DR/B14/1 19 October

1953 pp.2-3, 16 November 1953
p.2, 21 December 1953 p.1
13 Sx. Exp. 23 January 1897
14 Ibid 2 February 1897
15 F10 24 October 1970
16 Ibid 8 November 1971
17 Ibid 13 December 1972
18 Sx. Exp. 23 April 1971
19 MM f.233
20 Sx. Exp. 11 February 1972
21 F10 2 February 1972
22 Ibid 6 January 1973
23 Sx. Exp. 14 September 1973
24 Ibid 28 September 1973
25 S.A.C. 113 124-145

29. ST. THOMAS'S SCHOOL

1 ESRO ACC 6759; D43/10
2 ESRO PAR 511/31/1/1 30 May
   1766
3 ESRO ACC 6759; D43/10
4 D43/10
5 Homan[HW] pp.270-271
6 Carey p.1
7 ESRO ACC6759; D43/10
8 Guilmant p.137
9 D43/10
10 ESRO BGP 61/1, 61/2
11 ESRO PAR 511/12/4 18 January
   1879
12 ESRO ACC 6759
13 ESRO ESC 267/1/1 f.19
14 Ibid f.293
15 ESRO ESC 267/1/2
16 ESRO EMA 254/1/1
17 ESRO ESC 267/1/2 f.94
18 D23/31
19 Muggridge p.12
20 ESRO EMA 254/1/1
21 ESRO ACC 6759
22 ESRO ESC 267/1/2 ff.486-487
23 ESRO ESC 267/1/2 f.502
24 D33/19
25 Sx. Exp. 9 July 1983
26 ESRO ESC 267/1/3 f.244
27 Ibid f.251
28 Sx. Exp. 12 July 1968
29 ESRO ESC 267/1/3 f.285
30 ESRO ACC 6759
31 Ibid

30. KEEPING THE LOOKOUT

1 ESRO WIN 129
2 H/A f.16
3 D34/23
4 D45/24
5 S.C.M. 11 p.746; 12 pp.140-141
6 Ford[CP] pp.83-84
7 Jessup p.113
8 D28/16 31 January 1950 et. seq.
9 Ibid
10 F22 8 December 1972
11 Daily Express 3 November 1964
   (D28/16)
12 D28/16 7 November 1964 –
   27 November 1964
13 F22 24 November 1971
14 D28/16

31. CLUBS AND SOCIETIES

1 D32/11
2 Sx. Exp. 17 March 1939
   (D21/12)
3 An amble through 21 years of the
   Winchelsea Singers by Jim Austin
   and notes made for further
   development of this account.
4 Sx. Exp. 24 August 1895
5 Ibid 24 August 1897
6 Ibid 23 August 1898
7 Ibid 22 October 1898
8 Dickinson p.139
9 Sx. Exp. 24 September 1948
10 Ibid 17 March 1939
11 Ibid 27 December 1929
12 D47/23
13 Sx. Exp. 12 March 1948
14 Ibid 5 November 1948
15 Ibid 20 May 1949
16 Ibid 27 May 1949
17 Ibid 9 December 1949
18 D26/11
19 The book containing these
   cuttings is the property of Mrs.
   Marcia Bruce whose kindness in
   allowing me to borrow it I greatly
   appreciate.
20 Sx. Exp. 9 September 1905
21 D36/6
22 Sx.Exp. 25 June 1948
23 Ibid 29 July 1949
24 D44/1

32. ROYAL VISITS

1 Chapman p.28
2 V.C.H. i pp.492-493
3 Chapman pp.31-32
4 Homan[HW] pp.58-59
5 Chapman p.50
6 D23/15
7 D38/4
8 ESRO ESC 267/1/2 f.409
9 Guilmant 149
10 ESRO ESC 267/1/2 f.466
11 F16 22 July 1966
12 Ibid 25 July 1966 – 28 October
   1966
13 Evening Argus 29 October 1966;
   Sx. Exp. 4 November 1966 (F16)
14 F15
15 F21 30 July 1979
16 Ibid 20 March 1980
17 H/A ff.281-282; F21 20 March
   1980-10 July 1980
18 Evening Argus 9 July 1988; Rye,
   Battle and District News 13 July
   1988; (F6)
19 F6 27 June 1990
20 D22/4
21 Rye and Battle Observer 16
   October 1992 (D22/10); F36
   14 February 1992 et. seq.
22 D43/12

33. SEVEN HUNDREDTH ANNIVERSARIES

1 Cooper pp.53-54
2 F6 14 October 1987
3 Sx. Exp. 22 January 1988
4 H/A ff.311-312
5 F6 26 October 1988
6 D41/10
7 F15

EPILOGUE

1 Ford [CP] viii

BIBLIOGRAPHY

Works to which direct reference is made in the text

Arscott	*Tales from the Parish Pump* by David Arscott (1994)
Bagley[BR]	*The Book of Rye* by Geoffrey Spink Bagley (1982)
Bagley[RM]	*A Pictorial Guide to Romney Marsh* by Geoffrey Spink Bagley (1986)
Baines	*Historic Hastings* by J. Manwaring Baines (Revised 1986)
Barty	*Sussex in 1839* by Hugh Barty-King (1974)
Beresford	*New Towns of the Middle Ages* by Maurice Beresford (1967)
Bessbor'gh	*The Enchanted Forest – The Story of Stansted in Sussex* by Lord Bessborough and Clive Aslet (1984)
Brentnall	*The Cinque Ports and Romney Marsh* by Margaret Brentnall (1972)
Burrows	*Historic Towns – Cinque Ports* by Montagu Burrows (1892)
Carey	*Some Reminiscences* by John Carey (1923) [D7]
Chapman	*Royal Visitors to Sussex* by Brigid Chapman (1991)
Churchill	*A History of the English Speaking Peoples* (4 Vols) by W. S. Churchill (Paperback edition 1974)
Clark[W]	*Winchelsea – The Story of an Historic Town* by Kenneth Clark (1988)
Clark[SRD]	*Smuggling in Rye and District* by Kenneth M. Clark (1988)
Collard	*A Maritime History of Rye* by John Collard (1985)
Cooper[HW]	*The History of Winchelsea* by W.D.Cooper (1850)
Cooper[SS]	*Smuggling in Sussex* by William Cooper (1858)
Defoe	*A Tour thro' the whole Island of Great Britain* by Daniel Defoe (Everyman edition)
D.N.B.	*The Dictionary of National Biography* Ed. Sir Leslie Stephen (1901 et seq.)
Dickinson	*Around Rye in Old Photographs* by Alan Dickinson (1989)
Dunlop	*Winchelsea Memories* by Katharina Forbes-Dunlop (1988)
Ehrman	*The Younger Pitt* (3 vols) by John Ehrman (1969 - 1995)
Finlayson	*Writers in Romney Marsh* by Iain Finlayson (1986)
Fiennes	*The Journeys of Celia Fiennes* (Illustrated edition pub. Macdonald 1982)
Finch	*Seventy Years in Winchelsea* by Alex Finch. [Unpublished – D48/4]
Floyd	*Wynchelse: A Geographical and Historical Study of an Ancient Town* by Professor B.N.Floyd (1962) [unpublished – available by prior arrangement only at Winchelsea Court Hall Museum]
Ford[CP]	*The Cinque Ports* by Ford Madox Ford (1900)
Ford[PRB]	*The Pre-Raphaelite Brotherhood* by Ford Madox Ford (1907)
Ford[RY]	*Return to Yesterday* by Ford Madox Ford (1931)
Goodsall	*The Eastern Rother* by Robert H. Goodsall (1961)
Gross	*Charles Joseph La Trobe* by Alan Gross (1956)
Guilmant	*Bygone Rye and Winchelsea* by Aylwin Guilmant (1984)
Hemming	*British Painters of the Coast and Sea* by Charles Hemming (1988)
Hillier	*The Bulwark Shore: Exploring Thanet and the Cinque Ports* by Caroline Hillier (1982)
Holloway	*History and Antiquities of the Ancient Town and Port of Rye* by William Holloway (1847)
Homan[CW]	*The Churches of Winchelsea* by W. Maclean Homan (1939) [Unpublished – available East Sussex Record Office Search Room]
Homan[HW]	*History of Winchelsea 1292 – 1800* by W. Maclean Homan (1942) [Unpublished – available East Sussex Record Office Search Room]
Homan[NW]	*The Founding of New Winchelsea* by W. Maclean Homan, reprinted from S.A.C. 88
Horsfield	*The County of Sussex* (2 vols) by T. W. Horsfield (1835)
Hunt	*My Grandmothers and I* by Diana Holman-Hunt (1960)
Hutchinson[MT]	*Martello Towers – A Brief History* by Geoff Hutchinson (1994)
Hutchinson[MS]	*The Mary Stanford Disaster* by Geoff Hutchinson (1984)

Hutchinson[MC]	*The Royal Military Canal – A Brief History* by Geoff Hutchinson (1995)
Inderwick	*The Story of King Edward and New Winchelsea* by F.A. Inderwick Q.C. (1892)
Jeake	*Charters of the Cinque Ports* by Samual Jeake (1728)
Jessup	*The Cinque Ports* by R.F. and F.W. Jessup (1952)
Judd	*Ford Madox Ford* by Alan Judd (1990)
Koenig	*The History of the Winchelsea Shire* by W.L. Koenig (1964 edition)
Lindsay	*William Morris: His Life and Work* by Jack Lindsay (1975)
Lucas	*Highways and Byways in Sussex* by E.V. Lucas (1907)
Mais	*The Land of the Cinque Ports* by S.P.B. Mais (1949)
Meynell	*Sussex* by Esther Meynell (1947)
Moore	*Henry James and his World* by Harry T. Moore.
Muggridge	*Childhood Memories of Rye and Winchelsea 1910-1918* by Margaret Palmer nee Muggridge (1987)
Murray	*Romney Marsh* by Walter J.C. Murray (3rd Ed. 1982)
Patch	*Thirty Years with G.B.S.* by Blanche Patch (1951)
Pevsner	*The Buildings of England: Sussex* by Iain Nairn & Nicolaus Pevsner (1965)
Pike	W.T. Pike's *District Blue Book 1885*
Prestwich	*Edward I* by Michael Prestwich (1988)
Redman	*The House of Hanover* by Alvin Redman (1960)
Rossetti	*Letters of Dante Gabriel Rossetti* Ed. Doughty & Wahl (1967)
S.A.C.	*Sussex Archaeological Collections* (1848-Present)
Saville	*The Story of Winchelsea Church* Retold and Revised by Malcolm Saville
S.C.M.	*Sussex County Magazine* (1926-1956)
Shanes	*Turner's Picturesque Views in England and Wales 1825-1838* by Eric Shanes (1979)
Skinner	*Reminiscences of Dr. Ernest Skinner of Mountfield, Rye* (1926) [Unpublished – included in ESRO AMS 6412 and D28/13]
S.N.Q.	*Sussex Notes and Queries* (1926-1971)
Stileman	*Memoranda and Reminiscences of his Early Life* by Richard Stileman (1829-1831) [Unpublished – D19/12]
Sutcliffe	*Martello Towers* by Sheila Sutcliffe (1972)
Swinfen	*People of Hidden Sussex* by Warden Swinfen and David Arscott (1985)
Sx.Exp.	*Sussex Express* (1837-Present) [combined at times with various other newspaper titles]
Sx.Hist.	*Sussex History* (1976-1990)
Terry	*Ellen Terry's Memoirs* with Preface, Notes and Additional Biographical Chapters by Edith Craig and Christopher St. John (1933)
Thomas	*Recollections of Winchelsea, 1911-1915* by Anthony Thomas [unpublished – D49/20]
Trevelyan	*Lord Grey of the Reform Bill* by G.M. Trevelyan (1920)
Vaisey	*The Diary of Thomas Turner 1754-1765* Ed. David Vaisey (1984)
V.C.H.	*The Victoria County History of Sussex* (Vol i 1905, Vol ii 1907, Vol ix 1937)
Williamson	*The English Channel* by James A. Williamson (1959)

Other works of interest

Hitler Confronts England by Walter Ansel (1960)

The Sussex Story by David Arscott (1992)

The Ingoldsby Legends by R.H. Barham (Everyman's Library 1960)

The Sound of Maroons – The Story of Life-Saving Services on the Kent and Sussex Coast by Howard Biggs (1977)

Kent Shipwrecks by Alan Bignell (1991)

South-East Britain Eternal Battleground by Gregory Blaxland (1981)

An Old Gate of England by A. G. Bradley (1917)

The English Channel by Nigel Calder (1986)

Romney Marsh Yesteryears by Edward Carpenter (1983)

Kent by Richard Church (1948)

Smuggling in Rye and District by Kenneth M. Clark (1988)

The Forging of the Modern State 1783-1870 (Second Edition 1996) by Eric J. Evans

The Fifth Continent: The Story of Romney Marsh and its Surroundings by Duncan Forbes (1984)

Romney Marsh and the Royal Military Canal by Fay Godwin and Richard Ingrams (1980)

The Book of the Cinque Ports by Ivan Green (1984)

The Channel Coasts of England by John Grimson (1978)

Castles in Sussex by John Guy (1984)

Ward Lock's Red Guide – The East Sussex Coast Ed. Reginald J.W. Hammond (1967)

The Rye and Camber Tramway by Peter A. Harding (1985)

A Short Account of the History and Antiquities of Winchelsea by W. Maclean Homan (1936) [Edited and republished by
             H.McL. Goldie, 1960]

History, People and Places in the Cinque Ports by Edward Hinings (1975)

Scarecrows Legion – Smuggling in Kent and Sussex by Geoffrey Hufton and Elaine Baird (1983)

A Calendar of the White and Black Books of the Cinque Ports 1432-1955 Ed. Felix Hull (1966)

Pitt the Younger: An Introduction by Geoff Hutchinson (1996)

Sussex Money by Peter R. Jenkins (1987)

The Story of the Nine Windows by Gertrude Leigh [Available from St. Thomas's Church, Winchelsea]

Franciscan Architecture in England by A.R. Martin (1937)

South-East England: The Channel Coastland by Roy Millward and Adrian Robertson (1973)

South Coast Railways – Hastings to Ashford by Vic Mitchell and Keith Smith (1987)

Henry VIII and the Development of Coastal Defence by B.M. Morley (1976)

Constutional History of the Cinque Ports by K.M.E. Murray (1935)

An Historical and Descriptive Account of the Coast of Sussex by J.D. Parry (1833)

Fishermen of Hastings by Steve Peak (1985)

Kent and the Cinque Ports by H.R. Pratt Boorman (1957)

The Gift of the Sea – Romney Marsh by Anne Roper (1984)

An Index to William Holloway's 'History and Antiquities of the Ancient Town and Port of Rye' Rye Local History Group (1994)

Sussex by Desmond Seward (1995)

The Saxon Shore Way by Alan Sillitoe and Fay Godwin (1983)

A Concise Historical and Topographical Sketch of Hastings Winchelsea and Rye by Fred W.L. Stockdale (1817)

Wealden Iron by Ernest Straker (1931)

Sussex Shipwrecks by Nicholas Thornton (1988)

The Royal Military Canal by P.A.L. Vine (1972)

Smuggling in Kent and Sussex 1700-1840 by Mary Waugh (1985)

Discovering the Cinque Ports by C.E. Whitney (1978 but since revised)

The Heraldry of the Cinque Ports by Geoffrey Williams(1971)

Portrait of Sussex by Cecile Woodford (1972)

Companion into Sussex by Norman Wymer (1972)

INDEX

excluding lists of names in Appendices

INDEX